Praise for *The Book of Absolutes: A Cri*
and a Defence of Universals

M000290192

"A brilliant analysis of the chief intellectual pathology of the modern age ... Writing with wit and erudition, William Gairdner goes to the heart of the defining spiritual malaise of our time, showing (among much else) that relativism and tyranny, far from being opposing forces, actually collude to undermine genuine freedom. *The Book of Absolutes* is sure to emerge as a modern classic of political and moral maturity."
Roger Kimball, editor and publisher, *The New Criterion*

"Strikingly original and important."
Tom Flanagan, Department of Political Science, University of Calgary

"Gairdner's intellectual range and control of his material is breathtaking ... almost no one writing today has the command of the literature in as many disciplines as this author has."
Ian Gentles, Department of History, York University

"The Appendices and the Index alone would be worth the price of admission. (I had to force *The Book* from my hand in order to get lesser things done!)"
Sherwood J.B. Sugden, managing editor,
The Monist: an International Journal of General Philosophical Inquiry

"Today, it would seem, absolute truth doesn't exist and as a result William Gairdner's latest, *The Book of Absolutes*, will appear as a bolt out of the blue. In it, the author and public intellectual gives relativism a run for its money through factual, thorough research. And though you may not believe it, he actually demonstrates the reality of universal truth in our world today."
Institute for Marriage and the Family

"Fifty years ago William F. Buckley wrote that the purpose of his brand new *National Review* magazine was to 'stand athwart history, yelling Stop!' History had to be stopped, he opined, because western culture had embraced relativism as a guiding philosophy and was rushing headlong toward destruction ... Canadian author William D. Gairdner has taken the torch from Buckley's failing hands and lifted it high with his new work, *The Book of Absolutes* ... [and by the end] an objective reader is left wondering how relativism ever got a toehold in the popular imagination in the first place."
Shafer Parker, *The Calgary Herald*

The Book of Absolutes

A Critique of Relativism
and a Defence of Universals

WILLIAM D. GAIRDNER

McGill-Queen's University Press

Montreal & Kingston · London · Ithaca

© William D. Gairdner 2008
ISBN 978-0-7735-3413-1 (cloth)
ISBN 978-0-7735-3619-7 (paper)

Legal deposit third quarter 2008
Bibliothèque nationale du Québec

Printed in Canada on acid-free paper that is 100% ancient forest free
(100% post-consumer recycled), processed chlorine free.
First paperback edition 2009

McGill-Queen's University Press acknowledges the support of the Canada
Council for the Arts for our publishing program. We also acknowledge the
financial support of the Government of Canada through the Book
Publishing Industry Development Program (BPIDP) for our publishing
activities.

Library and Archives Canada Cataloguing in Publication

Gairdner, William D. (William Douglas), 1940–
    The book of absolutes: a critique of relativism and a defence
of universals / William Gairdner.

Includes bibliographical references and index.
ISBN 978-0-7735-3413-1 (bnd)
ISBN 978-0-7735-3619-7 (pbk)

1. Cultural relativism.   2. Universals (Philosophy).   I. Title.

BJ1500.R37G33 2008   111'.2   C2008-901842-7

This book was typeset by Interscript in 10.5/13 Baskerville.

Contents

For Jean

Acknowledgments

Throughout the writing of this book I have been the fortunate beneficiary of assistance from many quarters, including research help and critiques from academic colleagues, the encouragement of friends, and the ever reliable insights and support of my wife, Jean. The process of creating a book often seems to take over a writer's whole life at the expense of pursuits that to others appear far more reasonable and compelling. Once the fever is over and normalcy regained, however, the realization hits home that from original conception to finished production there are a lot of people involved in a book besides the author, and the debts of gratitude are keenly felt.

I wish to begin by thanking those many academics and authors I have never met personally but who, whether living in Australia, Germany, the USA, Hong Kong, or other far-flung places, have felt close-by electronically, so to speak, because, without exception, they unhesitatingly took time from their busy lives to respond with generously detailed replies to the email queries of a complete stranger. From the start, I relied especially on Professor Donald E. Brown of the Department of Anthropology at the University of California at Santa Barbara, whose seminal book *Human Universals* first got me thinking about relativism and universals. He has been unfailingly helpful with his new foreign student. Then I met two Canadians, again by email. The first was Professor Richard Beis, now retired from St Mary's University, Nova Scotia, with whom I enjoyed correspondence after reading his important article on anthropology and ethics. Then I made contact with Professor William Ryan, now retired from McGill University and also living in Nova Scotia, who has continued to send many helpful articles and books on a variety of topics surrounding relativism and natural law. Heartfelt thanks are especially due to my close friend Ian Gentles, professor of history at York University and Tyndale College, for having read every chapter and for offering helpful insights along the way, sometimes even when we were coasting down a long hill while cycling together on a beautiful summer's day. And there are also new intellectual compatriots such as Richard Bastien of Ottawa, whom I thank for his close comments on two chapters and also, as things proceeded, for the gift of translating into French and publishing some of my work in the Quebec periodical *Égards*, of which he is an editor.

Finally, special thanks are due to Nelson Doucet, with whom I had the pleasure of publishing seven books while he was at Stoddart Publishing. After the demise of Stoddart, I and many other authors suddenly found ourselves bereft of a publisher and so, when this book was near completion, I went hunting for Nelson again. After looking at a couple of chapters of this book he felt it needed an academic publisher and he kindly introduced me to his friend Philip Cercone, head of McGill-Queen's University Press. So it is fitting to conclude by thanking Philip and all the staff at MQUP for their confidence in this project, and for their friendly support and assistance, from steering me through the referee process, to the close editing with Robert Lewis that has definitely improved the book, to discussions about cover and design, and ongoing planning for publicity and marketing.

Introduction

There is a lovely French short story in which a distraught elderly philosopher laments to his young student that in modern times the word "truth" has lost all meaning. She is amazed by this insight, and in response declares, "How true that is!"

It is easy for us to nod our heads and miss the irony altogether because for more than a century, the citizens of the Western world have been uncritically subjected in the media, the public square, and the classroom to the disturbing idea that there is no permanent truth in human life or in the material world and that the meaning of something can therefore be found only relative to something else. For most of us, this has become the only indisputable truth of modern times, and we announce it from a higher moral ground as a badge of our open-mindedness.

Nothing, it seems, escapes the reach of this relativism. We are told that time and space are relative. Cultures are relative. Moral values are relative. Laws are relative. Even biological distinctions such as gender are said to be relative (or "constructed" at will). For the extremists of relativism, truth and certainty are simply fictions we make up "to get through the day," so to speak. And on it goes. Ironically, relativism has become our only absolute.

But I have always felt that relativism is a confused and false conception of reality that produces a great deal of unnecessary anxiety and uncertainty, both for individuals and for society as a whole.

Hence the motive for this book.

It is a book meant to restore human confidence by presenting the truth about the permanent things of this world and of human existence.

Before starting to gather the facts and arguments, I was anxious about where I would find support. But not for long. It soon became apparent there is a sizable army of important thinkers, moral philosophers, physicists, mathematicians, legal experts, and just plain thoughtful people who are convinced that our world continues to be governed by absolutes, as it always was. Lots of them, as we shall see. In these pages we will hear their comforting voices.

From a certain imprecise and limited point of view, we may indeed claim that everything is relative, for it has always been possible to concentrate only on the ways things differ. But that is only half the truth. It is also possible to concentrate on what they have in common, on the laws and principles (physical, mathematical, moral, legal, and so on) that govern their existence and behaviour. For this reason, it is important to ask why we insist so adamantly on the former rather than the latter, especially when a moment's reflection reveals that it is laws and principles, constants and universals, that dictate and describe the existence of particulars, not vice versa. So why, exactly, have we decided to ignore or dismiss the commanding certainties of human life and nature? Why do we stand by as so much of what we have always shared and believed disappears into the vertiginous whirlpool of relativism? What, exactly, has seduced us so easily into an unquestioning acceptance of such a patently corrosive human attitude?

At least one important reason for wanting to know the answer is that it is plainly impossible for human beings to form a community of any kind whatsoever when all their judgments are relative. For taken to its natural conclusion, the relativist position on any subject will always result in a collision of private viewpoints and in human disconnection.

It is curious that in all former periods of history such an attitude would have been immediately ridiculed as preposterous. The ancient Greeks actually used the word *idiotes* (one we now apply to crazy people) to describe anyone who insisted on seeing the world in a purely personal and private way. And what seems to distinguish all prior civilizations from our own is their insistence on a physical, mythological, philosophical, religious, or moral unity. What they all reveal is the fervent and often beautiful struggle of the human mind to understand the circumambient universe as a cosmic home, as something that makes sense and is governed by laws, constants, and absolutes.

We moderns have by now departed so far from such a confidence, however, that belief in relativism has become a mainstream banality. The most common bit of cocktail-party philosophy that we are likely to hear in reaction to anyone who dares utter a truth, especially a moral truth, is: "That may be true for you, but it's not for me!" And this is generally spoken with deepest gravity, combined with a relieved tone of escape from judgment.

Very few spy the two self-defeating paradoxes at work here. The first is that although a statement may be either true or not true, it is not possible to have two contradictory truths about the same thing or state of affairs at the same time and in the same way. One of the two must be true and the other false. The second, of course, is that the very declaration that all truths are relative must surely mean that this statement is itself relative – which is to say, not true.

But the unfortunate practical consequence when such a widespread habit of (un)thinking takes hold of an entire culture is that it becomes acceptable, even expected, that you will curl up with your warm little truths and I with mine, and we will simply agree to disagree on most of the important things in life and leave each other alone. Today it is considered a kind of impropriety, or even a moral trespass, to challenge another person's beliefs. We are subjected everywhere to public reminders to respect without question the beliefs of others, *regardless of the merit of those beliefs!* The result is that what the Germans call *denkverboten*, or "the forbidding of thought," is now pervasive in the liberal democracies of the West, the former bastions of free speech.

Such an attitude is in the sharpest possible contrast to former times, when people of maturity were expected to present their strongly held beliefs to public scrutiny and to debate if challenged. It was either that or confess with embarrassment that they had not yet formed any beliefs! Certainly, no young person in the past would have expected to impress a teacher by arguing that all truths are relative. That would have been to confess a conclusive moral and intellectual cowardice. But now the story is reversed. A student who insists on truth, standards, and absolutes that were likely learned at home is just as likely to get a first lecture on relativism from a teacher.

The conviction that two contrary beliefs cannot both be true has always been a standard governing intelligent debate in the West and is still called the *principle of non-contradiction*, even though it has all but disappeared from the public mind. We hardly seem to notice or care when people say things that contradict what others around them have said, or even when they contradict themselves. We shrug. Or we chalk it up to "cognitive dissonance," or creative indifference, or some such flattering notion.

And we move on.

But under the sway of relativism, there is no longer any expectation that an individual *ought* to hold consistent, connected beliefs, and this suggests that the core philosophy of modernity rests on a moral and intellectual laxity.

The root meaning of contradiction is "to speak against yourself," and needless to say, while it was once thought very interesting to hear someone speak against the arguments of others, it was considered bizarre, if not pitiable, for them to be caught speaking against themselves. But today this is not always so. If we dare to point out obvious contradictions, we are as likely to trigger a retreat by our opponent into the lofty silence of private opinion. We quickly get the message: this belief is off limits. We are made to feel like moral intruders for pointing out inconsistencies or contradictions.

This general tendency is a natural result of relativism, and it can mean only that we have all, to a distressing degree, consigned ourselves to intellectual and moral loneliness. We have each gone into hiding with our little knapsack of private beliefs, and we'll just keep them there for our personal use, thank you very much. The centuries-long ideal that human beings are expected to form a community of understandings, assumptions, and beliefs about themselves and their world – even about the whole universe – that are tempered by the uncomfortable fires of public debate and scrutiny is pretty much dead, or at least comatose. We all move in separate orbits now.

No absolutes. No universals. No constants, either of nature or of human nature.

Important people say so. The man in the street says so. People of reputation say so. Hollywood and television certainly say so. Most of my professors said so. Most journalists take it for granted. And of course, our archetypal genius, Einstein, said so, didn't he?

We continue to hear about relativism from all sorts of experts.

But none of it is true.

The truth, to be documented in this book, is that all of nature, all human experience, cultures, moral systems, and all sciences, from the softest to the hardest – while they are repositories of sometimes countless differences (for in principle, differences may be tallied forever if we are willing to continue subdividing them) – are characterized by the existence of a very large number of absolutes without which the subjects themselves could not be meaningfully discussed in the first place. Another way to say this is that it's not the differences that constitute a particular field of thought but the constants, or absolutes (usually expressed as laws, formulas, classifications, equations, forces, or universal standards of performance or behaviour), that define and regulate the differences. It is the general concept of "a forest" that enables us to speak of thousands of different trees as one of a type, not each different tree that enables us to understand the term "forest."

This distinction has always been so, and it is true that in different periods of human history we have thought the forest more important than the trees. At other periods, such as the one in which we now live, we have delighted in trying to prove that only individual trees really exist, and because none is exactly like any other, a common perception, or definition of, or dialogue about a forest is considered impossible. It is just a "generalization" or a "stereotype" and therefore something (possibly) false. Suddenly ... there is no forest!

The point I wish to make is that this oscillating tendency to focus either on the forest or on the trees – on what is general, universal, and common or on what is particular, unique, and relative – is not new, although it is true that each time the pendulum swings it does so with a difference. That is because for each swing there is a different underlying human motive, according to the times.

One objective of this book is to uncover the motive behind our modern belief in relativism and, in so doing, to show that we may have swallowed popular misconceptions about nature and human nature a little too easily. In the process, we have created a story for our time that, while clearly not true (it is even self-refuting), seems to be telling us something we need to hear. I am already suspicious that the general motive we will find for denying the crucial place of absolutes in life is, at bottom, simply anti-authoritarian and self-serving.

Elsewhere, I have argued that Western civilization has expressed itself a surprising number of times through revolutionary outbursts against all kinds of religious, political, and moral authority, and in turn, that much of this behaviour has been motivated by a love affair with what has been variously understood, according to the period, as personal freedom, progress, and democracy. The underlying ideal of moral autonomy, freedom of choice, and personal liberation to which all this gives rise is so ingrained by now that modern relativism has found a welcome home in millions upon millions of hearts ready to repudiate all constraint.

Even a smattering of history or political theory will reveal that the three key myths of modernity, the "modern trinity,"[1] so to speak, all have to do with repudiating controls. We accept as dogma the idea that our minds begin as blank slates (have no innate character-determining properties), that we are all inherently good people to start with (and if bad, are made so by poorly engineered societies that can be fixed up), and finally, that we exist as freely choosing selves unencumbered by any constraints of temperament, biology, or pre-existing moral obligations or standards. We accept at face value the modern conceit that our minds, instincts, and societies start off clean and empty, to be filled with whatever meanings we choose.

Absolutes, constants, and universals, by their very nature, challenge this trinity and are correctly associated in the public mind with controls, rules, authority, and restrictions of one kind or another because all absolutes perform as laws. There is a law of gravity (which few are foolish enough to challenge). There are universal cultural taboos (lots of ongoing challenges here). Moral standards (challenged all the time). Biological imperatives (to test this one, try to stop breathing for two minutes).

And so on.

It is true that absolutes confine us and limit our behaviour and our possibilities. Yet even though we know very well that life would be chaotic without the laws and certainties that govern it, our most powerful civilizational fantasy is to live without them. In this respect, relativism is a very handy concept to keep in our knapsack because *it helps us to dismiss all sorts of rules and absolutes for ourselves, without altogether denying the need to apply them to others.* We resort to relativism when it suits our purposes but keep whatever we know of absolutes and standards at hand to win an argument, discipline our children, or protest an abuse. In this way, our modern belief in relativism remains largely pragmatic and is all the more useful if it continues to operate as an unexamined and adaptable, or relative, concept. In the end, we may find that our civilization's eager embrace of relativism reflects not a need for a true understanding of how the world in fact works but a desire to reorganize it as a pleasant and flattering fiction.

It is this fiction that I want to expose by showing readers the facts.

THE BOOK OF ABSOLUTES

1

A Brief History of Relativism

As a rule, only very learned and clever men deny what is obviously true.
Common men have less brains, but more sense.
                        William T. Stace, professor of history, Princeton (1952)

When asked where relativism comes from, most people are likely to shrug and say: "It's just the way things are." Some might add that Einstein started it all, or that anthropology shows how every culture has its own customs and truths, or that psychology has proven all values are "personal," and so on. And everyone has seen movies or read books that play with the idea that reality is not an objective thing but a composite of different "perspectives." Most of this is trotted out as commonly held truth and often dressed up as morally tolerant intellectual sophistication. But in the end, most people are getting at the same strictly modern idea: they think that *reality is subjective,* and thus dependent on your point of view, and that this fact is as close as anyone can get to the truth.

But on closer inspection, we have to ask what people really mean when they say that things are relative. For there is quite a difference between saying that we can understand something best after relating it to something else and saying that because we must relate things, they can never be understood for what they are in themselves. I mean to say, there is a big difference between *relationism* and *relativism.*

RELATIONISM

The idea that we get at the truth by relating things has been around a long time. We contrast night and day, disease and health, oranges and apples, and so on. And there are experiences everyone has had that dramatically illustrate how what we know can be discovered only by its *relation* to something else.

For example, suppose you are sitting minding your own business on a train, in a car, or on an airplane when suddenly, you start to move.

The trip is finally underway! Then, just as suddenly, you are overcome by a queasy sense of unreality. You are absolutely certain you are moving. But is it true? Could it be that you are perfectly motionless and that the vehicle beside you is moving? Which is it? And how can you know?

This familiar situation typically produces a feeling of radical uncertainty, a moment of panic during which we feel a desperate need to know what is *really* happening. We suddenly find ourselves searching furtively for something that *ought* to be stationary. The ground? The platform? A building? Something – anything – to test whether our feeling of motion is real or imaginary. The very instant we find a fixed point of reference, we feel immense relief as the logic of motion falls into place. But what a shock it is to discover that it is we who were at rest, while the vehicle beside us was moving, and how strange to have been so deeply betrayed by our own senses!

This is the feeling most people casually think of as "relativity." But it is a feeling that disappears quickly once they understand the objective *relation* between moving things and stationary things. For in reality, there is nothing *relative* about this situation. It is just that physical movement of any kind makes sense only as measured in relation to something else. Once we have our reference points, it is precisely measurable, predictable to an extraordinary degree of accuracy, and follows the same exacting – and absolute – laws everywhere in the universe.

Time is the same. It is told in relation to where you are on earth or in space, as anyone knows who has experienced jet lag. In the sense that we have figured out how to segment the unbroken flow of time into years, days, seconds, nanoseconds, and so on, it is also extremely precise and predictable. So much so that we can fire rockets into space that travel millions of miles at incredible speeds yet still predict exactly when and where they will be years later. Space and time together are the most typical ways we experience the need to relate things in order, say, to meet someone at a specific address, time, intersection, and so on. And such is the case for all things physical and temporal.[1]

The most common nonphysical forms of relationism, however, are generally conceptual, moral, or cultural. For example, we are commonly told that good and evil, truth and justice, and many other such notions are "relative." However, this is often an illusion, too, just like the train we thought was moving when it wasn't. When we think of two people who vigorously disagree about the truth of what happened at the scene of a crime, for example, we often say their different perceptions are relative to what each saw. *But we never doubt there is a single truth lurking somewhere.* If someone later shows us a video of the actual event, we might conclude that they were both wrong or that one of them was lying, and everyone can now see the same indisputable truth. In the same fashion, as we shall see in the next chapter, people all over the world recognize general concepts of trust, equality, honesty, love, justice, and so on, even if they often differ sharply over specific instances and degrees of these things.

On a philosophical note, it is interesting to learn that the basic concept of "relation" is itself a universal. The philosopher Bertrand Russell (1872–1970) was a model of clear thinking and writing (I believe these go together) for all philosophers, and in his justly admired little book *The Problems of Philosophy,*[2] he used several chapters to describe the world of universals – what they are and how we know they exist. For Russell, most of the concepts of common language are themselves universals. For example, the words "cat" or "run" or "cut" are universal concepts and become particular only when we think of or engage in a particular act or observation (we see or imagine a certain real cat, we run to the store, or we cut a loaf of bread). But more to the point at hand, Russell expands on the fact that the basic concept of relations is itself universal. For example, the proposition "two and two are four" states a relation of quantity between the universal "two" and the universal "four," and just as for the spatial relation involved in saying Toronto is "north of" New York, such relations are true, absolute, and universal. And, he maintains, relations such as "north of" something, or "two and two are four," as well as relations of time, such as "before" and "after," will always be so whether anyone exists to know it or not.

RELATIVISM

Relativism, however, is a far more disorienting concept than relationism, and in the next chapter I will outline some varieties. But for now we need keep in mind only that in its modern radical form, relativism means not only that we must relate things but moreover, that *there is no ultimate truth possible* because there is no fixed, or permanent, or privileged foundation outside our own perceptions or beliefs or culture from which to judge anything as more "true" than anything else. In a later chapter we will see that some clever thinkers proudly style themselves "postmodernists" or "anti-foundationalists" on this basis. They do not say there is no truth. They say there is a multiplicity of truths – perhaps an infinity of them – any one of which is as "true" as any other.

Now, as anyone can see, this statement makes a mockery of the basic idea of truth, which is a concept we use to decide between competing reality claims, especially between true and false ones. And of course, if there is no foundation from which to truly know anything, then the view that there is no truth cannot be known either. At any rate, whenever we choose to ignore the fact that basic distinctions between what is true and false are always possible, relativism quickly turns into an intellectual snake that swallows its own tail. Unfortunately, a lot of modern academics and social scientists have been all too uncritical of the self-devouring tendencies of relativism to notice its corrosive effect on their own disciplines.

Most human beings, however, instinctively understand the need for action based on some kind of logical or moral precision, so they find the suggestion that there can never be certain truth very disturbing, if not obviously wrong. This is especially problematic for parents striving to raise good children. So why, despite this, do so many embrace relativism? One answer is that people live double lives. They are relativists in public but certainly not in private, nor with friends or family. We will speak more of this modern split personality later. Regardless of the motive, however, it is clear that relativism, especially in its moral and cultural form, has swiftly become our public philosophy. But it did not simply materialize from thin air. So we need to ask where it came from.

ANCIENT ROOTS

Some say relativism is very old, quoting the ancient Greek thinker Protagoras. He was a Sophist famous for the line "Man is the measure of all things." But in Plato's critique we find him quoted in more detail: "As each thing appears to me, so it is for me, and as it appears to you, so it is for you."[3] Protagoras went on to insist that for this reason there is no such thing as falsehood or truth, overlooking that such a claim meant his own views were meaningless. His famous quotation is more or less what we hear from the ordinary relativist at a modern cocktail party. However, whether this was something we ought to call relativism in the modern sense remains under debate.[4] But the historical pattern is clear. The ancient world experienced a kind of philosophical relativism that lasted barely a century and then evaporated under the withering criticisms first of Plato and then of his student Aristotle, two of the greatest philosophers who ever lived. It next raised its doubting and disruptive head during the sixteenth-century Renaissance and railed with a vengeance through the so-called Age of Reason, which lasted until roughly the end of the eighteenth century. Still, although it is true a number of ancient thinkers were relativists of a sort, they were never quite like us. For even if certain of them denied the possibility of *knowing* reality absolutely, they did not necessarily deny that an absolute reality might actually exist beyond their ken. And certainly no entire civilization before our own ever publicly conceived of the whole cosmos as an utterly alien and meaningless accident, as do many moderns.[5]

The various logical and moral crises that inevitably arise from a belief in relativism will be exposed fully in the chapters to come. For now, let us look briefly at its more recent origins in the hope of understanding why an entire civilization – our own – has so confidently shifted over the last few centuries from an understanding of the world in which everyone had confidence to one that dismisses the very idea that any such confidence is possible.

THE ROOTS OF MODERN RELATIVISM

The Rise of Science

During the Middle Ages, from about AD 1000 to 1500, social and moral authority were generally rooted in religious belief. During the transition to the modern period, however, we begin to see appeals to the worldly authority of reason and science, both of which were increasingly relied upon to examine reality *objectively*, which is to say, without the filters of inherited social or religious values or personal subjectivity.*

So firmly entrenched is this view by now that modern scientists regard this method as the only route to truth and themselves as defenders of objectivity against superstition and moral oppression (even though the modern idea that reason and science have always been at war with religion is in fact quite recent).[6] While we have accepted the

---

* Some extreme relativists today, such as Paul Feyerabend – see, for example, *Against Method* (London: New Left Books, 1973) – say that this is not possible, that even the most "objective" modern science is in fact a product of underlying assumptions, of the choices we make to observe things in certain ways and not others, of what we include and exclude in even the most "objective" theories and methods of observation. To such extreme relativists, even things such as mathematical certainty and the existence of the neutron are but human inventions. Many postmodernists claim that "the world of things is a creation of the world of words." This, and similar attitudes, will be taken up later in some detail.

objective findings of science as superior and now rely on these for our truth, we have just as wholeheartedly – even, I would say, dogmatically – separated them from any religious or higher meaning. Religious explanations of reality are now everywhere considered matters of private subjective faith that have little to do with the objective world. The typical modern scientist simply assumes that the laws and forces of our extraordinarily complex natural world have arisen spontaneously, due to some inherent, if inexplicable, characteristic of matter. But the modern inquiry stops abruptly there. We generally make no public effort to ask where the laws and forces (the many "constants of nature" governing all matter) have themselves come from. This reminds us of the Hindu who, when asked to explain what holds up the world, explained that it rests on the back of a turtle.

"And the turtle?"

"Well, he rests on another turtle."

"And this turtle?"

"From there," he said with a smile, "it's turtles, all the way down."

Now, any thinking person might well ask: Why have so many modern scientists, many of whom are deeply spiritual people, divorced reason from spirit? The most likely answer is that scientific rationalists felt it was impossible to be objective without first rejecting everything subjective, so to achieve objectivity they had to dismiss all nonmaterial, abstract, spiritual, and conceptual solutions. This further opened the door to radical skepticism and doubt.

Reorganizing the Mind

A very early step in this direction was taken by William of Occam, an English thinker of the late Middle Ages (1300?–1349). He was fed up with the interminable abstract debates between scholars trying to prove how many angels could dance on the head of a pin. In the preceding centuries, the dominant philosophers had been convinced that ideas, forms, and universals were the most real of all things and that matter was but a degraded instance of those ideas and forms. The perfect triangle, for example, is described by an abstract geometric formula that tells us precisely what a triangle is. But only imperfect triangles made of pencil lines, wood, or metal can be found in the physical world. The idea of a perfect triangle is by definition prior to, and more *real* than, any imperfect, physical triangle. Opposing philosophers, however, were gaining ascendancy, and Occam tipped the balance. He argued that only particular physical experiences are real. Generalities, universals – indeed, all abstract ideas – are just *names* that have no real existence. They exist only in our minds. This philosophy was later called "nominalism" (from the Latin *nomen*, for "name"). And names, he argued, are but abstractions, mere fluff. Smoke and mirrors. It was a philosophy that fitted perfectly the growing scientific preference for only measurable, physical, testable results.

Another influential step was taken much later by Descartes (he died in 1650), who famously made radical doubt the cornerstone of his philosophy. He claimed that since our senses, as well as bad arguments, may easily deceive us, the only way to find certain truth is to begin by doubting everything except the existence of our own doubting minds. After thus establishing our own existence, we may then move on by logical steps to establish other certainties. With his famous pronouncement "I think, therefore I am,"[7] Descartes opened wide the doors to the specifically modern belief that (contrary to what the best minds had always been saying) *each of us can individually arrive at the truth, and this capacity is equal in all men*. It was then to be only a matter of time before a claim to know *the* truth became a personal claim to *my* truth.[8]

Now, I do not think that people have anything like an equal capacity to distinguish the true from the false. If anything, social science tells us the opposite. The majority of us are most often dupes of appearances, wishful thinking, inadequate facts, and pseudo arguments.[9] Nevertheless, here was a flattering idea that made Descartes very popular, for even though he was himself a God-fearing man, his new philosophy, by relocating truth within the thinking individual, had the effect of undermining the intellectual and moral prestige and therefore the control available to secular and religious authorities.

Reorganizing the World

As if this emerging recourse to strict mental reasoning were not enough, the newly objective science was quick to give a demonstration of how thoroughly our senses (and the authorities) can deceive us. Galileo dropped the first of many intellectual bombs. He stunned the thinking world by confirming that the sun does not travel around the earth, as ordinary perceptions still suggest, but rather the reverse: the earth is just one of many planets circling the sun. Here was *relationism* with a vengeance, and it upset a worldview thousands of years old: the venerable Judeo-Christian view that God had created the earth for human beings and set it as a jewel in heaven to be lit with the sun by day and the moon by night. In expressly denying this comforting Genesis account, science now seemed to be attacking God himself! As a devout Catholic, however, Galileo had tried desperately to save the church from denying his findings and thus from its own self-embarrassment. But it was too late, and the Galileo incident is today considered an important early example of science winning the first of many battles in a war against religious prejudice, even though this is not quite the historical truth.*

Isaac Newton was born the year that Galileo died, and at the tender age of twenty-six he dropped his own Big Bertha. His *Principia* (1687) was a work that would change perceptions of the universe forever. It is one of the most astonishing works of scientific thinking ever created, and in the public mind (although certainly not in Newton's own mind) it finished off the Aristotelian and Christian belief that the cosmos is a natural, organic order, a home of which we are the centre and purpose. The universe Newton described is ours. We think of it as "mechanical in the sense that like a clock it is self-sustaining. There is order everywhere … Physical processes take place within an unchanging vault of absolute space and in accord with the unchanging beat of absolute time. Propelling itself through space, the universal force of gravitation subordinates all material objects to a single modality of attraction. And all this proceeds in accordance with simple mathematical laws."[10]

Ironically, although his extraordinary work seemed to confirm so much of the rationalist rebellion against the idea of a purposeful cosmos, Newton was a religious mystic and alchemist who never once doubted that "this most beautiful system of the sun, planets and comets, could only proceed from the counsel and domination of an intelligent and powerful Being."[11] He has also been charged with reintroducing mysticism to Western

---

* The irony of this misconception bears mention, namely that modern science arose only in the Christian West. It died a whimpering death in the Greek world and also among the Romans and the Chinese. And there is a reason. As Catholic philosopher Stanley J. Jaki has argued – see "Science: Western or What?" in *Patterns or Principles* (Bryn Mawr, PA: Intercollegiate Studies Institute, 1995), 161–78 – modern science would not have been possible without our belief that there is an absolute physical reality separate from ourselves characterized by order and law, the truth of which may be discovered. All scientists today continue to hold this belief, even if they gag a little when they have to acknowledge its theological source. Nevertheless, it is this foundational belief that underlies the secondary belief in "objectivity," and it is this same objectivity that for the past few centuries has been turned against the religious assumptions that spawned it.

science because he so convincingly proved that the reality we know is controlled by universal laws that are invisible and operate "at a distance" (such as the moon pulling the oceans and forming the tides). In a later chapter on physics we will see that quantum physics continues this quasi-mystical bent in the purest of the physical sciences.

Western civilization has followed Newton's physics for more than three hundred years, and despite modifications by later physicists that have more to do with deep space, unimaginable speeds, and the origins of the universe than with what happens here on earth, we will always live under his laws. But we have utterly rejected his theological reasoning for their existence.[12] Newton himself, however, was smart enough to see that figuring out how a law works does not explain its reason for being or its cause. He knew above all that science is silent as to the causes and ultimate purposes of life.

But as mentioned, after centuries of intricate but philosophically barren rationalism, many modern cosmologists and philosophers seeking ultimate causes and purposes are once again leaning toward Newton's view that the universe may be the product of intelligent design. Others deny this, arguing that the universe designs itself. At any rate this *designer vs self-designed* dispute is at the watershed of modern scientific opinion on the origins of the universe and the forms of life. Some highly respected physicists and mathematicians go much further. They are persuaded that *the entire cosmos came into existence so that human consciousness would eventually arise to observe it!* We may have gotten bumped from the centre of our own solar system over recent centuries, but such new and fascinating modern views argue that we belong right back at the centre again. But this time, they mean … at the centre of the entire universe! We will return to this intriguing idea.

For the moment, we need only see that despite deep convictions about cosmic purpose felt by many modern scientists, the general direction of today's scientific community and, therefore, of the public mind – and certainly of public education, which we must assume to reflect that mind – has run strongly against this idea. We increasingly describe ourselves in defiantly *materialist, atheistic,* and therefore, *relativistic* terms, and these three concepts form the underpinning of our thoroughly modern orthodoxy. The bleakness of this view could hardly be better expressed than by Harvard astronomer Margaret Geller, who asks: "Why should the universe have a point? What point? It's just a physical system, what point is there?"[13] Let us not miss the connection between this view of physics and our topic: when there is no point to anything, relativism rules.

Science and the Relativity of Morals

For a stark example of how this newly *objective* thinking led at once to the first detailed *subjective* theory of moral relativism, we could do no better than to turn to the work of Thomas Hobbes (1588–1679).[14] His discovery of the mechanical work of Galileo so filled him with intellectual energy that he immediately set about building a new theory of politics around the idea of individuals and their societies as *machines in motion.* Every human life can be explained as the action of a mechanical apparatus comprised of sense organs, nerves, muscles, bones, and so on, kept in motion by its own natural impulse to satisfy appetites and avoid pain – the greatest pain of all being death. In defiance of all religious opinion to the effect that morality is rooted in a higher moral law, Hobbes simply declared that whatever is the object of any man's appetite or desire he calls "Good," and whatever is the object of his hate and aversion he calls "Evill." And what was the warrant for the use of these words? There is none, he declared, "For these words of Good, and Evill ... are ever used with relation to the person that useth them: there being nothing simply and absolutely so; nor any common rule of Good and Evil."[15]

Mechanical solutions to the problem of morality have been proposed repeatedly ever since, perhaps with greatest effect in the nineteenth century by Jeremy Bentham and the young John Stuart Mill. Once joined with the rising popularity of democracy, their utilitarian formula for how to make "moral" decisions without any reference to God or any other universal or absolute became "the greatest good of the greatest number." Mill surrendered this relativism once he saw that majorities may happily choose very evil things. Nevertheless, the simplistic idea that truth may be decided simply by voting democratically was by then firmly established.

The Run-Up to Modern Relativism

Public confidence that clear reasoning would always somehow point the way to freedom and truth had begun to weaken long before this period – at least by the end of the eighteenth century. There were many reasons for this, perhaps chief among them the shocking disaster of the "democratic" French Revolution, whose effects we are still feeling.[16] That was the modern world's first political attempt to organize millions of people with the tools of rationalism, namely the secular concepts of mass administration and control, order, logic, mass conscription, equality, democracy, uniformity, obedience, and political correctness. At the high pitch of enthusiasm for all this, the Goddess of Reason had been erected in Notre Dame Cathedral in place of Jesus Christ and was worshipped by wine-imbibing, chanting devotees in white robes during special pagan ceremonies. In the same period a proposal was floated to remove all ancient names from French villages – because these carried historical nostalgia – and replace them with numbers. Quaint thousand-year-old villages such as Saint André de Roquepertuis would now be called "village 67724." Fortunately, this idea died with Robespierre. But the practical results of the world's first social upheaval in the name of reason were nevertheless cataclysmic for the Western world. For after a brief honeymoon with the dream of a rationally designed secular utopia, the Revolution began devouring its own revolutionaries on the way to the slaughters of the Terror. This horrendous bloodbath – the French prophets of democracy hacking, chopping, guillotining, stabbing, and drowning thousands upon thousands of their own law-abiding citizens in a rationalist frenzy for equality – created, at least in Europe, what at first seemed a terminal loss of faith in the fruits of reason.

This made it easier for people to turn to darker levels of experience, and eventually to forms of extreme irrationality, for answers to what seemed the intractably depressing realities of human life. In the arts, things moved quickly from the prior rationalist art forms of the eighteenth century (sober, morally instructive poetry composed in measured rhyming couplets and the like) to the wilder, more emotionally spontaneous romantic forms of the next century (Wordsworth, Keats, Shelley, and Herder in poetry, Beethoven in music, etc.). With this came more violent revolution, social and industrial upheaval, a lot of spiritual materialistic philosophies, communist class-warfare, existential angst, the depthless netherworld of psychoanalysis, and … the foundations for world war. By the end of the nineteenth century, the end of modernity, with its unquestioned faith in reason, was upon us – and we soon entered the long, badly named "postmodern" period. This meant a sudden end to the longstanding hope of discovering a universal human nature and a rational ethical foundation and the beginning of an even more energetic search – indeed, of a new hope that the truth might lie in things relative.

The Gentleman Relativists

We moderns were set up for this new embrace of relativism by influential gentleman philosophers such as John Locke (1632–1704) and David

Hume (1711–1776). In striking contrast to his predecessors, so confident of our common sinful human nature, Locke argued that there are no innate or inherent (universal, absolute, constant) characteristics of our minds. A mind is like a school blackboard, a blank slate (*tabula rasa*) on which experience makes impressions.[17] Accordingly, as they have no prior meaning in themselves, to know things means to understand the *relations* and *associations* between them.

The radical skeptic Hume went much further and argued that while knowledge indeed comes from sense experiences, as Locke had described, the relations between things, such as cause and effect, are based only on habit and other unwarranted assumptions. The sun comes up every day, so we are certain it will do the same tomorrow. But we have no proof it will. In both men we see the classical focus on the *essences* of things (Plato) or on the organic *substance* of things (Aristotle) replaced by a focus on the *relations* between them. Much contemporary thinking, even of the serious (as distinct from the stylish postmodern) type, whether in mathematics, philosophy or physics, is wholly submerged in this last mode of understanding reality and is expressed in such areas as chaos theory, spontaneous organization, emergentism, and field theory.[18]

Perhaps the most coolly influential modern philosopher to have pushed us toward all sorts of relativist conclusions, however, was the German Immanuel Kant (1724–1804). He opposed Locke's notion that the mind is a blank slate on the ground that the human mind has an innate (we would say a hardwired) capacity to generalize and categorize sense perceptions and form them into consistent, communicable ideas. The mind is not a blank slate, he argued, but rather more like an active agent, a kind of mental cookie cutter that of necessity shapes its own reality, and because of this, *there is no way to know what things in themselves, outside the mind, are really like.* Well, here was a serious formula that seemed to pave the way for the relativizing of all human reality, and this conclusion so disturbed Kant himself that he developed even more theories to establish universal and constant categories of thought and morality, without which, he maintained, human life would be unlivable. But the damage was done, and the prevalent modern idea is that we all live in Kant's prison house of personal perceptions.

Not long afterward came what amounted to a powerfully influential attack on the moral absolutism of the whole Judeo-Christian system by England's John Stuart Mill in his influential tract *On Liberty* (1859). Although a somewhat snobbish man, with high taste and firm personal expectations for moral behaviour and social "progress," Mill's work was extremely corrosive of Western moral and religious ideas as guides to public behaviour. After he lost faith in his utilitarian ideal of "the greatest good of the greatest number" as his "moral calculus" (during this period he described himself as "a thinking machine"), he turned to "liberty" as a new moral standard to be limited only by his so-called "harm principle." This basically stated that we are free to do whatever we wish as long as we do not harm others. It was an appealing but confused philosophy that enclosed each individual inside a private moral bubble of personal choices as if the opinions of society were of no real account. This led to confusions in Mill's theory, however, as anyone who bothers to read the whole tract will see, for a careful examination of *On Liberty* surprises us with the number of unresolved contradictory claims. Despite this, his principle remains the most powerful and popular "moral" guideline cited by ordinary people in the West today, and its implicit command to "do your own thing, just don't harm me" *now quietly undergirds the philosophy of Western relativism* and, increasingly, the philosophy of Western courts. Indeed, no sharper indication of Mill's influence could be had than the decision of Canada's Supreme Court on 21 December 2005 in *"Swingers Clubs" R. v. Labaye,* which held that the ancient "community standards" test would henceforth be replaced by the principle of "harm." The court specifically referenced Mill as author of this principle. In this sense, it was Mill who almost single-handedly transformed the idea of liberty. Whereas the standard and brake on one's behaviour in the pursuit of liberty had originally been a regard for the good of all society – that is, for doing no harm to society, to the common good – liberty would now be completely self-regarding, its only brake the notion of harm to other individuals.

The Angry European Relativists

Meanwhile, during the nineteenth century there were many angry European relativists who rejected entirely, or sought to reshape as entirely, the whole Western tradition. Among them was Georg Hegel (1770–1831), who cleverly mixed determinism and things spiritual by speaking of history with a capital "H" as a force of nature that evolves with a mind of its own to ever higher levels. The unfortunate boost he gave to relativism was the idea that "History" is not something created with hard facts but an ever-evolving process that cannot be understood or evaluated at all except through the context of particular historical periods. In the end, he insisted, there is no God's-eye view of anything. Nothing stays the same in a universe that is ever-evolving toward its own perfect self-recognition. Now this may seem to be impenetrable German intellectual blather. But it unsettles anyone looking for a stable reality.

Another passionately defiant relativist was the Prussian thinker and romantic poet Johann Herder (1744–1803). He despised the subjection of European nations to the Enlightenment – mostly French – idea of a single universal human nature that is supposed to progress through a series of stages to an ideal rational state. This "filled him with anger." He believed, on the contrary, that "every tribe and people was unfathomably and indestructibly unique ... Each nation represented a truth of its own, which was compounded of blood, soil, climate, environment, experience ... *there was no universal criterion* by which to judge nations ... Men did not create a nation; a nation brought forth men."[19] In this sense, "he was a precursor of the moral and cultural relativism which was a prominent part of anthropology in the first part of the twentieth century and is still very much with us."[20] Indeed. Farther along in this book we will look at the ideological mischief of the relativism that sprang from Herder's concept of "the comity of nations as a garden of wildflowers," a concept derided by a contemporary anthropologist as "the most childish notion ever to have imposed itself on the credulity of an influential mind. Whatever he [Herder] may have imagined, the garden of human cultures contains just as many stink-lilies as violets, strangling vines as primrose, sick societies as those with rosy cheeks – and too many problems in the modern world come from sentimentally denying this fact."[21]

But it was Friedrich Nietzsche (1844–1900) who surely ranks as the most tormented and explicitly angry relativist. He lambasted Western traditions root and branch, particularly Christianity (although even he had a grudging admiration for Christ). The West, he cried, originally made a huge mistake falling for Plato's theory about absolutes that exist in some world of higher Ideals and perfect Forms. This was a terrible, life-denying concept that ruined Western civilization, mostly by producing Christianity, which he deeply disrespected as "a poor man's Platonism" because it substitutes a perfect dream-world heaven after death for the vale of tears in the here and now. He was adamant that such grotesquely false promises prevent us from ever fulfilling ourselves and concluded that as any religion is obviously a lie, there are no absolutes to guide us to admirable human action, only admirable human "Will." His key idea with respect to relativism was his well-known slogan "there are no facts, only interpretations." Accordingly, he called for leaders with strong charismatic personalities who could move us beyond our current deadening concepts of good and evil to create an entirely new world of original values.

The Practical American Relativists

Meanwhile, in America there were similar attacks on the idea of an absolute reality, especially of a moral reality. The philosopher William James (1842–1910) developed a philosophy called "pragmatism" asserting that ideas and actions regarding the good must be judged only in terms of their practical worldly consequences, for there is no higher external standard. "Man" is at the centre of things and must get along as best he can based on experience alone. His theory of reality was that whatever satisfies us is true, while whatever does not is false.

John Dewey (1859–1952), whose "child-centred" philosophy of education permeated North American schools for most of the twentieth century, felt much the same as James: man alone with his evolving experience is the measure of the evolving universe. There is no other truth. No final picture. Indeed, he fairly beseeched philosophers to stop searching for ultimate meanings, beginnings, final truths, and absolutes, for it makes no difference to human beings trapped inside their own experiences and perceptions whether some higher reality may exist, for this we can never know for certain. But we know enough to make sense of this world, to get along, and even to improve it. That should suffice.

Twentieth-Century Relativism

From this variety of influences the seedbed of modern relativism was well prepared by the start of the twentieth century. But it really picked up a head of steam about ten years after Einstein's Special Theory of Relativity appeared in 1905. Although only specialists to this day are able to understand this theory, the news of it at once produced "a vague source of unease," as British historian Paul Johnson puts it, such that after the physical and moral devastations of World War I, "the belief began to circulate, for the first time at a popular level, that there were no longer any absolutes: of time and space, of good and evil, of knowledge, and above all of value. Mistakenly but perhaps inevitably, relativity *became confused with relativism.*" And, he adds, "no one was more distressed than Einstein by this public misapprehension."[22]

In Johnson's view, "the public response to [Einstein's theory] was one of the principal formative influences on the course of twentieth-century history. It formed a knife, inadvertently wielded by its author, to help cut society adrift from its traditional moorings in the faith and morals of Judeo-Christian culture."[23] Johnson goes on to explain how this relativity-become-relativism worked its poison on the public mind through its various insidious combinations with Darwinism, Marxism, Freudianism, and a host of other "isms." And of course, most parents are by now all too familiar with the effects of relativism on moral behaviour in general and aware of its proliferation through systems of education, literature, and the arts.

Although Einstein's theories concern only the behaviour of matter at incomprehensible cosmic scales, energies, and speeds that have no direct effect on human life, the indirect idea that everything in the universe is relative seemed now to have the deepest scientific imprimatur. And just as society had for three centuries patterned its thinking after Newton's idea that the universe is a machine, it now began to pattern all thinking about science, morality, and culture as one or another form of unpredictable relativism. We were suddenly back at the uncertain and unknowable river of Heraclitus.

Alas, it is by now a certain fact (and Einstein had worried deeply this might come to be the case) that various between-the-wars ideologies such as fascism and communism rested on variations of a politically self-serving moral relativism that contributed to Europe's totalitarian nightmare. And even though the central legal foundation for the Western courts that condemned the Nazi machine at the postwar Nuremberg Trials was a form of moral and legal absolutism still called "natural law," this startling truth was easily lost in the general disillusion and the widespread repudiation of authority by the young. Just so, their attraction to existentialism was fuelled by their justifiable moral disappointment over two horrific world wars that displayed the full panoply of human cruelty and degradation. Existentialists argued that as there is obviously, if unfortunately, no God to create a human nature, or essence, of which we are all a manifestation, our existence must be only a brute fact of life and is basically senseless. It has no God-given meaning. We simply exist (hence, "existentialism") and so are abandoned in this world to carry on as free human agents carving out a moral universe according to our private personal choices, for there is no other arbiter of morality. For this reason, existentialists declared – in contrast to just about all prior philosophical and theological tradition – *our existence precedes our essence.*

By the 1970s, however, the disillusioned were no longer young. They were now wearing suits as professors and policy wonks in governments. And the trend was clear. With a mixture of philosophies drawn mostly from the thinkers reviewed here, they were energetically rejecting the old tenets of "modernism," which had taught that reason could reveal an objective world common to all. This belief was now characterized as a "Eurocentric" assumption, a philosophy invented by controlling intellectuals, by bureaucrats, or by the bourgeois-capitalist class (take your pick). Modern philosophy, we were now told – for that matter, all philosophies (take your pick again) – is just one story, or "narrative," that was invented by those striving for the dominance of their particular worldview and that reflects only their interests. Suddenly, it was fashionable to argue that the story about a stable world of objects and essences is false and part of a *controlling myth*. Here was a generation that preferred the idea that reality is unknowable *except as formed by each individual mind*, and as so much of thinking is expressed in language, this in turn produced the so-called "linguistic turn" in amateur philosophy: the idea that there is no reality except as created and perceived through "the prison house of language." We will go into this more deeply in our later chapters on language. Suffice it to say for now that loosely speaking, the idea that everything is relative, invented, and therefore permeated with a controlling motive led at once to new forms of analytical suspicion directed at every aspect of human activity from poetry to politics. All social phenomena, in particular, would become targeted as explicit or implicit power structures justifying one or another form of moral, social, political, or economic control. So in rapid succession we got schools of structuralism, poststructuralism, deconstructionism, postmodernism, post-postmodernism, anti-foundationalism, and much more. With each phase we got a more and more stringent insistence on the essential sleaziness and political – which is to say, self-serving – nature of all accepted forms of thinking, even the most professedly innocent. That is why we now live in an age of extreme skepticism and the almost total privatization of the idea of truth, which has taken cover within the isolated self.

What all these ideologies share is a reliance on the many variations of relativism – although many practical people have suspected that those professing such beliefs also share a need to maintain job security by creating unfalsifiable theories in otherwise exhausted fields of thought. At any rate, it is hard to say what will be next. But a reaction has been forming for some time because so many serious thinkers have by now

grown very tired of misleading and self-refuting claims that there is
nothing of value to know or to teach because nothing is true, fixed, or
stable. Recently, Renato Rosaldo, a professor of anthropology at Stanford University, went public with the opinion that today, "in academic
debate, calling someone a relativist is a mild form of verbal abuse."[24]
That is certainly new and indicative not only of a philosophical rift in
his field of study but also of the hunger being felt once again for what is
known, what can be known, and above all for what is common, universal, constant, or absolute.

To summarize, we began by outlining a key distinction between relationism and relativism and then proceeded to a brief history of relativism
in Western civilization. After its first appearance in the ancient world,
soon to be demolished by the powerfully persuasive logical force of both
Platonic and Aristotelian philosophy, relativism did not arise again in a
serious way until the Renaissance. At this point, after the philosophical
and theological exhaustions of the Middle Ages, we begin to see the wan-
ing of public faith in religious and moral authority. This was soon combined with the Reformation's insistence on the spark of inner truth as
something available to all, with the powerful effects of rationalism, and
with the objective discoveries of science. The result was that the findings
of reason and science began to embarrass religious authority. The new
concept of the cosmos as a Newtonian machine running according to its
own fixed laws of which the earth was but a lonely part began to replace
the old earth-centred idea that the cosmos has a purpose to which human existence is central. This new objectivism soon led to more skepticism and doubt and therefore to a general subjectivism in morals. It was
not a great step from this subjectivism to the birth of modern relativism.
There were many genteel thinkers who used very sophisticated arguments to hone the relativist view of human knowledge and perception.
By the nineteenth century, however, we begin to see a more angry and
defiant repudiation of the old belief that reason would or could lead us
to the truth. There were also a lot of calm but persistent theories in
America and England about the relativism of human knowledge and
therefore of the difficulty in establishing moral standards. Mill, above all,
reduced the idea of morality to a vague subjective ideal. The result was
that by the early twentieth century, relativism had become our new public orthodoxy, and Einstein's theory of relativity, for all the wrong reasons, as we shall see, seemed to give it a foundation in physical reality.
The ensuing postwar intellectual movements can be said to have only further entrenched the modern relativist revival, each in its own way, such

that relativist orthodoxy in many shapes and forms is more or less pervasive in almost all educational and intellectual departments, disciplines, and spheres of influence.

Against the Grain

This is so despite the existence of a sizable community of thinkers, researchers, and scientists from a wide variety of fields who have refused to follow the relativist trend for the reason that they find it both logically incoherent and falsified by actual experience. They also know that the professional fields in which they work would simply not exist but for the presence of a great number of absolutes, constants, and universals of the kind it will be our pleasure to explore in the rest of this book.

Many of these imposing thinkers, from Plato and Aristotle to modern critics of relativism such as Einstein himself, Sir Roger Penrose, and just about every serious philosopher, have put relativism in the stand and examined it thoroughly to see whether it could stand up to scrutiny, only to conclude it is a seriously flawed worldview.

Despite this, relativism remains a public force. It is a radical philosophical and moral claim that tends toward the indeterminate and the mystical and that gives satisfaction to believers by undermining any absolute truths, universals, and certainties they dislike and find uncomfortable. Due to its current omnipresence, however, it deserves to be taken seriously and examined on its own merits. For in the end, each of us must decide if relativism should be embraced as a satisfying and complete public philosophy or be dropped once again into the dustbin of historical triviality.

What follows next is a brief survey of the main types of relativism, followed by a chapter giving some of the reasons why so many important thinkers in history have concluded that relativism richly deserves the latter fate. In none of this do I bother to defend relativism, for the reason that it needs no defence. It is already almost everywhere believed, defended, and promoted, however unsubtly. What it has needed, rather, is a well-rounded exposé and critique, of which there are very few to be found, and this I hope the reader, after reading what follows, will agree I have supplied.

2

The Main Types of Relativism

Between the propositions "We know only the relations of things" and "We know the related thing only insofar as it is related to us," there is a vast difference.[1]

William Turner, *The History of Philosophy* (1903)

Relationism, as we have seen, merely says that things are often seen and judged from different perspectives, or in the philosophical sense, it describes a formal relationship between two or more entities. It does not say that there is no truth but says that any truth statement is often a composite of relations and for this reason may be difficult, but not impossible, to figure out. This is the most commonly understood sense in which people mistakenly say things are "relative."

Relativism, in contrast, argues that there is no God's-eye view, or truth, or foundation for anything, that no claim, or truth statement, or belief, as the jargon goes, is "privileged." We will spend some time examining this idea later on, to see whether that statement is itself true (for on its own terms, how would we ever know?). With these basic and important distinctions in mind, we can then move on to ask how the term "relativism" is most commonly used.

Alas, there is considerable confusion, disagreement, and overlap in the terminology surrounding relativism, so perhaps it is easier to keep special terms at a minimum and simply ask how we know about the *things* of this world and the possibility of knowing objective truth outside ourselves (the area of "cognitive relativism"); about the views and values of individual *people* (the area of "moral relativism"); and finally, about the views and values of groups of people (the area of "cultural relativism").

THE RELATIVISM OF THINGS

Relativism concerning things has to do with the question: How do we know what we know? For most people, this is easy: We know things because we do, it's natural. During the so-called Enlightenment of the eighteenth century, philosophers argued that with enough time and the proper methods, it is possible to arrive at absolute and certain knowledge of the world through reason alone. We just need to know the basic facts, and then by using the rules of logic, induction, deduction, and non-contradiction, we can always discover the truth. But by the early nineteenth century most thinkers were in deep revolt against such a comfortably smug confidence, for was it not this same glorious veneration of "reason" that had led so many to the darkest forms of political anarchy and the guillotine? Undeniably. All totalitarian schemes are products of someone's reason, and that is the problem with them. So the emerging modern tendency was to take the opposite position. Let us agree it is impossible to know reality except in bits and pieces; we can understand it only in relative terms. Some went further, insisting that we can't know reality at all – that we can each know only our personal perceptions of reality.

In general, modern arguments for the relativity of *things* go in a couple of directions. First, there is the idea that a piano note, for example, has meaning only in relation to other notes that form the octave. Like the octave, all things are defined by relation in some way or other. We know light because it is the opposite of darkness, and vice versa, and know the true only because it is the opposite of the false. Evil is the absence of good. And on it goes.

But a deeper form of relativism holds that even though I may know that one thing is understood only by its relation to another, I still cannot know a thing itself, completely, as it is. If I am looking at a tree, for example, I can see only one side of the tree from my particular vantage point, or "perspective." Someone else looking at the same tree from the other side will not see my side. And although each of us is absolutely certain there is a whole tree in front of us, we cannot *prove* it because the whole tree is not presented to our senses all at once, from all sides. It seems that we each "fill in" with our imaginations the parts of the tree that we do not directly perceive; we simply go about *assuming* that there is always a whole tree/person/house there, even though we perceive only part of it. Logically speaking, we know there *must* be a wholeness to the things we perceive, for we can always go around the other side of the tree to check on that assumption. But our senses do not tell us this *directly*. We infer it by *deduction*. So in a way, it is true that we all live in a partial world of our own perceptions and that things "in themselves" exist only as we mentally "construct" them.

The extension of this idea is that whole and complete things exist only in the perceiving mind, never in direct experience. Therefore, if there is no mind there to perceive things, they do not exist at all. Lots of modern movies, such as Kurosawa's *Rashomon*, and novels, such as Virginia Woolf's *The Waves*, exploit this sort of "relativity" of experience to the full. Woolf's characters are known fully only by the reader, who alone gets to experience all the partial perceptions of all the characters (all sides of the tree). Such artists are making the point that *truth is synthetic*. We get to it by combining separate pieces. Art may thus knit together our separateness. In impressionist paintings the idea is that our eye joins together thousands of separate dabs of colour to make a whole picture. There is no picture there in itself. The mind creates the picture. The extreme version of this perceptual relativism is the claim that objects exist only because of their relations to other things and have no real existence in themselves.

RELATIVITY OF THE MIND AND SENSES

Relativity of the mind and senses refers to the argument (most notably by Immanuel Kant, 1724–1804) that we can never know things in themselves because what we know of them is first signalled and filtered, so to speak, by our senses and then this experience (not the thing sensed itself) is *organized* by our minds. Never mind that we can never know a whole and complete thing such as a tree. Even the part that we do perceive "accurately" cannot be known in itself, *as it really is*. God may know what things are in themselves. But we cannot know what other mortal minds – whether of humans, or dogs, or cats – perceive any more than a dog or cat can know what we perceive. There may be conventional agreement between humans as to tastes, colours, experiences, emotions, and the like. But the idea that any two of us are actually experiencing the exact same thing at any one time is an assumption held together only by common language, experience, and feeling and not much else. In my own case, I have two eyes like most people. But one of them sees things tinted slightly blue and the other slightly brown. Somehow my brain combines them. But I have no idea whether the world itself is "really" bluish or brownish. This is just one example of how knowledge may be subjective and relative to a perceiver trapped inside his or her own sense-organizing world, although my eye doctor says I should stop philosophizing, as the colour difference is due to a natural clouding of the lens that occurs with aging. Nonetheless, I still don't know which colour reality "really" is.

We should not miss the paradoxes implied in these first two forms of relativity, however. The first, the *relativity of things*, says things exist in themselves only as composites of, or by virtue of, the *relations of their own parts* and then are understood for what they are as distinct wholes through *relations to other things*. The second, the *relativity of minds and senses*, claims that all reality is a matter of the quality of our individual perceptions and that "reality" itself (the things we perceive) cannot ever be known.

So the first is saying that things are made up of relations *but with nothing concrete that is related*, while the second is saying that as things are really just the sum of particular perceptions, *we can know nothing objective about the thing from which these perceptions spring*. Both of these views "make the given nothing, and the work of the mind everything."[2] This last remark sums up pretty well the difference between the emphasis of almost all former types of philosophy and that of the modern ones. The older forms tend to stress the *objectivity of external* experience. They hold that with some effort we can know things as they really are. The more recent systems – this is especially true of relativism – stress the *subjectivity of internal* experience. They hold that the only thing we can know is our perceptions and what is in our own minds.

COGNITIVE RELATIVISM

Cognitive relativism can be divided into a couple of subcategories: *historical* relativism and *linguistic* relativism. Historical relativism is the claim that all truth changes over time because it is relative to its moment in history. Truth is a historical concept. This worldview is sometimes called "historicism." As mentioned in the previous chapter, Hegel was the most famous historicist, even though he believed that he himself was describing the final, "Absolute" historical truth. Karl Marx, the father of communist theory, was also a historicist as well as a progressive, who believed that truth is a changing product of a historical process that nevertheless will culminate in one final stage as a classless communist society at the end not of "History," as for Hegel, but of the victory of the workers of the world over those who exploit them.

Linguistic relativism refers to the idea that truth is something that is created by, is reflected by, and according to some, is even a product of language. The most famous twentieth-century philosopher to make a reputation on this sort of claim was Ludwig Wittgenstein (1889–1951), who joined the Vienna circle of "logical positivists" and who spoke famously not of reality or truth but of how moral and philosophical statements are factually meaningless. For example, he argued that a phrase such as "crime is wrong" makes only one verifiable observation: that crime *is*. Its "wrongness" is just a feeling about crime, not a fact we can prove or disprove. (Let us overlook the obvious fact that there is no such thing as a good crime and that to say a crime is wrong is redundant.) What interested his group was the rules and analysis of language, which they were convinced are confused with philosophical statements about reality. Hence, they concluded, all that philosophers are really doing is participating in a kind of verbal "game" that all speakers "play" as they create "forms of life." There may be meaningfulness in terms of verbal games well or poorly played, but he did not believe these games refer to anything real in the external world.

One of the most influential linguistic relativists of a different sort was the American anthropologist Benjamin Lee Whorf, who in *Language, Thought and Reality* (1956) claimed that the way we each see the world is decided by the structure of the particular language we speak. For undergraduates in the 1960s, this was a big hit because it seemed like scientific proof for the hippie view that all truth is relative (that is, relative to the self and to one's culture), making it a timely scientific warrant for escape from moral judgment. Whorf's general case has since been weakened considerably, if not disproved entirely, as detailed in chapter 4, on anthropology and "human universals," which highlights the hundreds of cultural facts and truths common to all people. Nevertheless, his influence continues.

Readers will also find several chapters that supply a critique of what can only be called the most extensive and detailed theory of linguistic relativism ever imagined, which takes pride of place in a fast-fading, if not already over-the-hill, contemporary movement called "postmodernism." The main idea, worked over extensively and with an astonishing creativity by its most influential prophet, Jacques Derrida, was that reality and truth are wholly "constructed" and "deconstructed" by language, having no real existence outside the text.

This near-fanatical form of language relativism is then balanced and opposed by the work of serious linguistics scholars such as Noam Chomsky of MIT who have proposed the idea for decades that all human beings are in natural possession of a "UG," or "universal grammar," that forms the basis of all human linguistic ability, if not of all forms of cognition. Let us now turn to the two most serious forms of value relativism.

ETHICAL AND/OR MORAL RELATIVISM

Moral relativism is the most common form of relativism we encounter in daily life. It asserts *that the ethical and moral points of view and practices of individuals (or groups, cultures, peoples) are all equally valid, good, and true.* This type of relativism says there can be no absolute good-better-best to anything because there is no single privileged viewpoint, or foundation, from which the views and practices of others can be judged. This is clearly a defiantly secular position that assumes there is no transcendent reality or moral viewpoint in the whole universe.

But we may best understand it through a clarification of the difference between "ethical" and "moral," two terms that seem to get used interchangeably. The word "ethics" generally refers to the rules of practical and proper *person-to-person* human conduct from a very broad and openly secular perspective. Modern "ethicists" are people who try to decide what the right course of action is in a given situation. And this is our clue. They generally seek to balance the conflicting pressures of *a situation* and then come up with the best answer by weighing all the pros and cons as they see them. The tools of their trade will be a mixture of street philosophy, common sense, legal insights, and usually some utilitarian standard having to do with ensuring that the greatest number of participants is satisfied with the outcome. But ethicists generally refuse to operate from a religious or ordinary "moral" point of view because although they believe it is possible to arrive at the "best," most fair, and pragmatic solution for all parties in a given situation, they do not draw their standards of conduct from any external, or transcendent, or religious principle. Rather, they tend to operate from within the deeply democratic/egalitarian tradition that is ours, and so above all they do not want to "impose" a personal viewpoint (often arguing, in addition, that morality can be only personal). Thus people sitting in conference rooms who don't believe there are any absolutes will feel free to negotiate detailed "ethical standards" or "guidelines." But they don't feel as free to fiddle with acknowledged moral standards. In this vein, we often find that schools and businesses will cheerfully post their "Code of Ethics," detailing how "fairness" and "equality" are a big deal for them. But they would never dare boast about their "Code of Morals."

That is because morality is different. It implies an absolute and transcendent standard of conduct that is generally considered binding on all human beings, even on ethicists. It generally has more to do with

God-to-person conduct and is assumed to be in force without regard to the happiness of individuals or groups. Its source may be something such as the Ten Commandments or its equivalent in another religion. As we will see in a later chapter, all the world's religions have a handful of almost identical commandments and absolute moral laws they consider God-given, or a result of revelation, or the fruit of divine inspiration.

At any rate, people who take the trouble to let us know they are moral relativists are suggesting they are free-thinking, tolerant, and above all broadminded citizens who have given up believing in repressive moral codes because morals are "relative" to the personal standards of individuals (or cultures). So we can relax now. Above all, we certainly don't have to worry about them judging us "negatively" for anything we have said or done, or might say or do (unless, that is, we profess to believe in binding moral absolutes). For such people, all morality boils down to "what's right for you vs what's right for me" or, more commonly, "it may be true for you, but it's not true for me," by which they really mean: "don't get in my way!" This is the most common idea of moral relativism in use today.

We will examine more fully whether this notion can stand on its own feet in the next chapter. But for now I see a fly in the ointment. For I do not believe the word "moral" can properly be used at all except in the context of a hierarchy of good-better-best and still retain its central meaning. That is because moral systems (as distinct from ethical ones) exist in the first place for only one reason: to arrange moral preferences and behaviour gradations from good to bad, to insist on their observance, and to reward and punish accordingly. However, the moment we try to eliminate this core distinction, this requirement for *moral ranking*, we switch from discussing true *moral* choices to discussing mere *personal preferences*. It is fine with me if that is what people admit they are doing. But I object to the gratuitous confusion of the two motives, to the parading of a preference as something we think is moral just because we have chosen it.

To extend the point, it seems an obvious contradiction to say that "all moral choices are equally valid" because by simply stating such a thing, we remove the concept of morality from the discussion altogether. It is as nonsensical as to say that since $2 + 2 = 4$ and $E = mc^2$ are equally valid because both of them are equations, then the meaning of them is up to each of us. But this evades the intended and precise meaning of a mathematical statement, just as to describe a moral statement this way is to evade the intended and precise meaning of a moral statement.

By this common bending of the language, modernity seems to have opted to neutralize the difficulties of living with sometimes incommensurable moral *practices* by evading or watering down the most fundamental understanding of the underlying moral concepts. Such a strategy may conveniently convert morality to personal choice in our individual imaginations, but it cannot do so in reality without destroying the concept of morality itself.

CULTURAL RELATIVISM

Cultural relativism has been central to modern thinking and political life for the past century. We can think of it as relativism applied to groups of people. It argues that *what is believed or practiced as true, or right, or wrong for any culture is whatever that culture believes or practices as true, or right, or wrong.* Clearly, this is a complete departure from the idea central to Western civilization until very recently that the discovery of permanent universal truths ought to be the aim of everyone. That the beliefs and practices of some people and cultures are primitive, cruel, bizarre, undeveloped, or even sick and therefore, by implication, in need of correction or healing or elimination – perhaps by contact with a superior culture – was simply taken for granted. But in the early decades of the twentieth century, as will be explained at greater length in chapter 4, anthropologists, almost as a group, suddenly did an about-face and abandoned the search for *universals* altogether. In its place they began preaching (that is the right word) about the vast range of *differences* between all peoples and cultures, moral systems, beliefs, and practices, taking the surprising view that *one culture is as good as another,* that there may be such things as good-better-best *within* a culture or civilization but not *between* them. This position would have delighted any number of despots from Caesar to Robespierre because it leads to inventing – and if you are so inclined, to enforcing – your own moral standards as a form of justice.

The modern political manifestation of this switch from cultural universalism to cultural relativism, to the idea that what unifies us is our differences, rather than what is common, is glaringly obvious today in the somewhat fanatical public orthodoxy surrounding such contradictory, if politically soothing, ideals as *pluralism, unlimited toleration, diversity,* and *multiculturalism.* The tension inherent in this transition is visible in petrified national symbols such as we find on American currency. There we read the words *E Pluribus Unum* – "From Many, One" –

which continue to inspire despite the recent cultural stampede to the opposing idea "From One, Many," which is the herald of a euphoric and as yet unfinished egalitarian experiment that has pushed America (and just about every other liberal democracy) from the melting-pot to the salad-bowl concept of "a people."

3

Objections to Relativism

Not so long ago an educated person was someone of deep learning prepared to do ferocious intellectual and moral battle to defend deeply held beliefs. But the equivalent today, while perhaps more broadly learned, is more likely to think of him or herself as proudly distinguished by the *absence* of "rigid" opinions and moral values, to be someone "tolerant" and "open." Such a person will generally profess some variation of relativism, or "you do your thing and I'll do mine," as a personal philosophy. Many in this frame of mind privately consider themselves exemplars of an enlightened modern attitude that civilization has worked hard to attain, and if pushed, they would admit to feeling just a little superior to all those sorry souls of prior generations forced to bend under moral and religious constraints.

But anyone who is serious about upholding relativism as a public philosophy, however inarticulate, should at least be thorough enough to defend its superiority. We would expect such a philosophy to be stoutly rational, certainly not self-contradictory or self-refuting, and for them at least, easy to defend. For if a philosophy runs contrary to the facts it pretends to stand on, if it cannot survive serious attack, if it holds a place in the public mind mostly as a novelty, an intellectual trinket, then all who believe in it become vulnerable to the charge of moral sloppiness or, at the least, of lacking in discernment. So let us put relativism in the stand, survey the many objections to it, and let the reader be the judge.

OBJECTION 1: RELATIVISM IS SELF-REFUTING
If we take seriously the relativist argument that all truth claims are equally valid, then the claim that relativism is false must also be true. Put another way, "the relativist contradicts himself by saying that all

statements are only relatively true and then relying on the absolute truth of some statements in order to prove his point."[1] Plato had effectively argued this point long ago in his famous *Peritropé*, or "turning the tables," reply, when he said of Protagoras's position that it had a "most exquisite feature," namely that "Protagoras admits ... that the contrary opinion about his own opinion (namely, that it is false) must be true," and that "in conceding the truth of the opinion of those who think him wrong," he is really admitting the falseness of his own opinion.[2] That was a pretty good send-up, and I do not see how relativism can escape this most serious of the criticisms. (Modern logicians refer to this as the problem of "self-referential inconsistency.")

But if we ignore this first fatal blow, this clear self-refutation, and accept without cavil the claim that relativism is true, we then need to ask: is it absolutely true or only relatively true? For if it is absolutely true, then not all truth can be relative, and therefore relativism is false. But if it is only relatively true, then it is not true for all peoples or societies who do not believe it. Relativists try to escape this dilemma by taking the lazy way out. They insist a thing is "true for me" or "true for you." But they must mean absolutely true for me or you, and this is the very notion they begin by rejecting. So a little panicked by the idea that all beliefs must be equally doubtful, they seem to land on a compromise, arguing that beliefs may be doubtful but certain at the same time.

OBJECTION 2: RELATIVISM REQUIRES ABSOLUTES

To assert that one thing is relative to another implies two or more things being compared and a framework or standard in terms of which we compare them in order to judge them relative. But we cannot compare two or more things unless we know with absolute certainty what they are in the first place. And once we know that, they still cannot be compared unless the framework or standard or foundation in terms of which we compare them remains constant. This means that if we are to prove relativism, then neither the things related nor the framework for assessing the relativity of things can themselves be relative.

Another way of visualizing the relativist's dilemma is to say that the classical, objective view of truth implies a *correspondence* between a statement and what that statement refers to in the real world. It is a two-term, *word>world* relationship. But relativists end up putting something else between these two terms, a kind of filter they say makes a clear and direct perception of the world impossible. That filter could be a personal opinion, or a moral or cultural belief, or more simply, the worldview of a

person or group. In this way relativists end up with a three-term relationship we can describe as *word>world-view>world*. But then they fall into their
own trap, for they insist that because there is a filter, we can never really
know the final term, only the filter itself, which is different for all world-
viewers, so to speak. In this way they manage to make the filter into an absolute (albeit one relative to each worldviewer). The logical complication
this presents is that if all worldviews are truly absolute in this relative way,
they can never be known by any outside observer, and if that is true, then
how would we ever know what they are in the first place? A further complication is that if relativists are correct that we have no grounds to call
any belief false, then it follows that we have no grounds to call any belief
true either. But it is the very nature of all belief to aim at truth, so the relativist denial of the possibility of falsification (because all things are relative) also does away with the idea of belief – even the belief in relativism.

OBJECTION 3: WHAT ABOUT CONFLICTING "TRUTHS"?
Aristotle devoted three sections of his *Metaphysics* to a masterful demolition job on the relativism of Protagoras.[3]
    One of his many criticisms is a variation of objection 1, above,
namely that "if all opinions held and all appearances are true, then
they must be at the same time both true and false."[4] This is so, Aristotle
maintains, because men often hold opposing opinions, some believing
a thing true and some false, each believing his own version to be true
and the other's false, which means, if the theory of relativism is to be
upheld, *then all things must be true and false at the same time.*
    Now this is simply absurd because it violates the most fundamental law
of non-contradiction, a principle that, in Aristotle's words, states that "*it
is impossible for the same thing at the same time both to be-in and not to be-in the
same thing in the same respect.*" And that is because "an opinion opposite to
an opinion is the negation of it." And no one, he maintains, "can believe
that the same thing both is, and is not," for this "would amount to the si-
multaneous holding of opposite beliefs."[5] He is quick to add, however,
that it is *not* impossible to say one thing and believe another, as so many
do. And, he concludes, if all contradictions are simultaneously true of
the same thing, then anyone who signs up for Protagoras's ideas would
have to agree that "a ship, a wall, and a man will be the same thing," and
to conclude his demolition of Protagoras he adds that if it is true that all
contradictions of the same thing are true, then it suffices merely to *think*
that a man is not a ship to make him not a ship, but in this case, thinking
the opposite also makes him a ship.

Well, I think very few modern relativists would want to go up against Aristotle in a formal debate!

OBJECTION 4: MERE BELIEF IN SOMETHING IS NO PROOF OF IT
That individuals or cultures (groups of people) have varied opinions about something does not prove there is no underlying truth. For one thing, they may all be wrong. At any rate, a belief is simply a faith claim that may or may not be related accurately to something objective in the real world. For example, ordinary people believed the sun went around the earth for centuries until the opposite fact was proven. We should not say that the sun-around-earth and earth-around-sun opinions were both relative until one of them was knocked out by a proof and that then suddenly the "relativity" disappeared. For the fact is one of the beliefs was always wrong, but its believers didn't know it. This paradigm may exist for many things we today believe are relative ... but may not tomorrow.

OBJECTION 5: THE DIFFICULTY IN FINDING TRUTH
Some truths are just hard to find, or take a long time, or require special skills, whether in machinery, knowledge, or wisdom, as in the example of an orbiting earth, above, or, say, the discovery of the law of gravity or of $E = mc^2$. But the *absence* of a truth today does not imply its non-existence nor justify the conclusion that if we do not happen to know the truth of a matter, then all personal opinions are equally "true." We will see later that in almost every field there is a profound division between theorists as to how certain truths actually exist. Modern mathematicians, for example, like the ancient ones, still divide themselves into opposing camps of "Platonists" and "formalists." The former, a group that includes such famous thinkers as Albert Einstein, Bertrand Russell, Kurt Gödel, and Roger Penrose, believe that such things as mathematical formulas, constants, and ratios *exist in themselves*, always have, and are out there somewhere, waiting to be discovered. Formalists, in contrast, believe that human beings have always *invented* symbolic languages such as mathematics or physics for their convenience in describing nature and that there is no external or transcendent reality beyond the symbols or names for concepts. (The "nominalism" of William of Occam, discussed in chapter 1, is still around!)

But if the Platonists are correct in believing that the many universal concepts we now have are not invented, but have always existed behind the veil of human ignorance, and that more are waiting there, so to speak, to be discovered (which seems to be the historical trend), then in principle there may exist many more universal truths in all fields of inquiry. The universality of DNA in all biological life is a recent example.

OBJECTION 6: CULTURAL RELATIVISM IS A WEAK
AND SUSPECT THEORY

The notion that what is right or wrong for a culture is whatever that culture believes to be right or wrong seems an especially weak claim. First of all, the idea is in itself a contradiction, for it begins by assuming there is such a thing as right and wrong and then allows that the standard for judging what that may be is in principle infinitely flexible – which is only to say there is no standard of right and wrong. But if there is no standard, then how can there be an identifiable concept in the first place? The mere use of the phrase suggests a standard exists in the mind, thereby admitting the possibility of telling the difference between the true and the false or between good and evil. But by taking refuge in a self-contradictory assumption, cultural relativists are forced to admit that the things they are prepared to acknowledge as relatively good or bad are made so by people's beliefs. But if this were true, then they would also be forced to admit that obvious evils such as Nazism are good just because people at the time thought they were good – which is an absurdity. For that matter, today's cultural relativists, who are typically anti-imperialists (we think especially of anti-colonialism and anti-US imperialism), are put in the position of being unable to resist any entrenched form of imperialism, cultural cruelty, racism, gender discrimination, or so-called ethnocentricism; indeed, they are committed to endorsing all these things just because they are practised and believed by somebody. We ignore for now that intercultural "neutrality" and "relativism" are both Western liberal ideas that they are imposing on others in the first place. Indeed, we might argue that Western intellectuals have embraced the supposed cultural neutrality of relativism *precisely because it enables them to behave as cultural and moral imperialists,* to download Western relativism (egalitarianism, modern democracy, modern liberalism, moral tolerance, etc.) onto other societies while "thinking of ourselves as humane cosmopolitans who have transcended all their cultural prejudices."[6] And as Ernest Gellner asks: "if truth can only exist internally to a culture and its norms, in what interstellar or intercultural void does our Relativist articulate his position? There is no place for him to be."[7] This certainly gives a different slant to Western moral and scientific neutrality.

Two more examples should suffice to embarrass those who hold this position, one physical and one moral. It is true that we may differ in our opinions about almost everything. Yet in most matters we would never accept the idea that just because opinions conflict, there is no truth to be found. One distinguished critic put it this way. Suppose that someone says:

"We believe that the earth is globular, but there was an age and a culture in which it was believed that the earth is flat. Therefore the earth is globular now in our culture, but it was flat in that age and that culture."

Everyone would recognize that this argument is ridiculous. But the logic of it is exactly the same as that of the argument:

"We believe that head hunting is a moral evil, but there is a culture in the South Seas in which it is believed that it is a very fine thing. Therefore head hunting is bad in our culture and good in that other culture."[8]

And to bring this a little closer to our own moral and cultural history, we can recall that ancient Greeks and Romans, as well as modern Americans and Canadians, once believed that the slavery of human beings was morally right.[9] But we do not believe so today. Yet this does not mean that slavery was right then but wrong now, does it? Most people would say they believe that at least the transatlantic commercial slavery of the past few centuries was absolutely wrong.[10] It is always wrong, and it always was.

A possible objection to making a parallel between such physical and moral examples is that it is easier to prove physical things than moral ones. But is that necessarily so? For example, everyone today believes in the law of gravity because we have been told it is true. We can test its effects, and we feel gravity even lying in bed. But that is gravity we feel, not the law itself. Yet the law is true, everywhere in the universe, as far as we can tell. It is a fundamental constant of nature. But Newton's inverse square law of gravity was not published until 1687. Does that mean gravity did not operate or exist until then? Of course not. It has always operated. But the *law* was not discovered until that date. Still, although it will always be true that the *effects* of gravity are physical and constant, the *concept* itself is as abstract, or as transcendent, as any moral idea – say, as the idea of truth or beauty – which is to say that Newton's law is one thing but that actual gravity is another. We still do not know what gravity *is* nor how it can exert immediate force in a cosmic vacuum over millions of light years of distance. That is still a mystery. But a similar mystery surrounds most types of lawful natural behaviour, and thus comes the refreshment of insight when we learn that many modern physicists and mathematicians believe "the laws of nature by which nature is explained *are not themselves a part of nature*. No physical theory predicts their existence nor explains their power. They exist beyond space and time; they gain purchase by an act of the imagination and not observation, they are the tantalizing traces in nature of an intelligence that has so far hidden itself in symbols."[11]

Here, we have something we thought was hard and scientific called "gravity" that remains a mystery and effects us totally – just, I suggest, as do many "softer" concepts and truths.

OBJECTION 7: WE SHOULD NOT CONFUSE
RELATIVISM WITH VARIATION

It does not follow as a consequence that because there is *variation* in the understanding or application of a practice or principle, there is therefore no underlying principle or that the matter is relative. For example, we may say that all people now and always have believed stealing to be wrong. If an anthropologist comes along and says that he has found a culture that applies the no-stealing principle in ways more lax than another, we should not conclude this means the principle is itself useless or relative. It is simply variable. It may mean that the culture that does not employ it fully is malfunctioning or failing. This would be our natural conclusion with respect to the high value placed on stealing in, say, the various prison cultures of the world or in a worldwide society such as the Mafia. We would say something is wrong with them, and we would be correct.

OBJECTION 8: MORE FATAL FLAWS OF MORAL
AND CULTURAL RELATIVISM

First flaw: to say that all beliefs and practices are acceptable. On this point, relativists who assume that all things are right for those who believe or practice them just because they do so expose themselves to the charge of contradiction. For on this basis there is nothing meaningful that can be said or done as to the goodness or evil or efficacy or truth or falseness of anything said or done by anyone. All people and all cultures when considered this way must be declared maximally functional because we have declared them to be beyond criticism. This means that we can learn nothing from others nor they from us, that they cannot improve our lives nor we theirs, for in such an understanding there is no better or worse way to live or die – an absurd conclusion but one that cannot be avoided once we accept the premise.

Second flaw: we may say that a culture's belief in a practice or custom determines its moral status. But what do we say if a society believes cannibalism is wrong today but changes its opinion tomorrow? Does day-to-day belief in itself alter the objective nature of a practice? Are we to say that morality is a question of numbers or votes? If so, what are we to say of the simple fact that most of the world's societies are not internally united? What percentage of "a people" is needed before we can say that something is right for a people when a huge percentage of the same people may disagree? If we answer 50 per cent plus one, we are then applying a specifically Western majoritarian concept to other societies in order to judge their relativism absolutely. But such a measure is in itself incoherent, for if a society is exactly divided except for one person, that person may walk across the floor, so to speak, and (according to our theory) alter the public "beliefs" of the entire people. He or she may then walk back again and alter them once more. Do we really think our definition of what constitutes a people's beliefs ought to hang on the (perhaps capricious) vote of a single person? At any rate, we may rightly suspect from this objection that many moral relativists have been quietly applying an unspoken and alien Western majoritarian principle in order to determine the cultural and moral beliefs of other peoples. As a measure of morality or truth, however, it is a concept unacceptable to many of those same civilizations and cultures. Muslims, for example, say we can never decide by a vote matters on which God has spoken.

Third flaw: it is simply not believable that all societies are equally good or bad. No one believes that late Roman society with its barbarism and cruelty, or Greek society with its pandemic slavery, or Aztec society with its live human sacrifice, or for that matter, our modern communist or Nazi or fascist states with their oppressive controlling governments, concentration camps, and mind-boggling slaughter of their own innocents were "good" just because at one time a vast majority of their people may have thought so. In this vein, some modern scholars have rejected cultural relativism outright in order to examine the many "sick societies" and political systems of the world, past and present. There are many of them, and we may only hope this form of research continues.[12]

OBJECTION 9: NEITHER BELIEVING NOR DOING
MAKES A THING RIGHT OR WRONG

Try as we might, we cannot convert what we simply like, desire, or believe into a moral right simply by making a claim. First of all, many people, when pushed, will freely admit they may not know whether what
they strongly *believe* is actually true or correct. They often say, "I've
never really thought about it that way." Second, most people know that
they like and do many things that are bad for themselves and for others
and that repeating them as a practice or habit – overeating, fibbing, or
being selfish, for example – does not make these things right. For most
people the world over, a belief or practice remains only an opinion or a
habit until it is expressed in a context of right and wrong. Then it takes
on a moral colouration. No ordinary person believes something to be
right or wrong just because it is done or believed.

OBJECTION 10: RELATIVISM IS ANTILIBERAL

Although modern relativism began as a liberal and at times a radical reaction to oppressive authority, it often ends up as a conservative social
and moral force because through its reliance on the concept of toleration, its tendency is to resist change and to defend the status quo.[13]
This is as true with respect to individuals who use the "true for me" tactic as it is for cultures. For relativists commit themselves to saying that
each person's or culture's beliefs are utterly and wholly true for that
person or group. Obviously, this means there can be little room for the
correction of beliefs or practices that are inefficient, maladjusted, or
evil. Indeed, in the field of anthropology, as we shall see in the next
chapter, this has meant that a great many social scientists have committed themselves to supporting the plainly evil practices of other societies. For once they take the relativist position seriously, they cannot, in
principle, do otherwise. In effect, all relativists commit themselves, by
virtue of their belief, to the moral infallibility of all other people: nothing should draw judgment or need correction. Politically, the result is
that this unexpected antiliberalism of relativists is used to justify the
continuation of cultural cruelties as well as authoritarian and totalitarian forms of governance.

   With respect to the forms of government on which nations such as the
United States and Canada have been based, relativism plainly repudiates
their founding liberal-democratic assumptions. All forms of representative parliamentary or congressional government were founded on the belief that if truth is to be known, it will be discovered through debate and

discussion from alternative points of view in a process of argumentation aimed at eliminating falsehood. We might say that the layered structure of the most successful systems of liberal-democratic government in the history of the world were specifically grounded in this understanding. But a belief in relativism removes all need for such discussion or debate and hence eliminates the hope and possibility of the compromises that are essential for the dilution of authoritarian political practices.

OBJECTION 11: RELATIVISM UNDERMINES FREEDOM
AND DEMOCRACY

In the political realm, relativism has become equated with tolerance, freedom, and democracy – and by many it still is. This is so despite the historical irony that relativism clearly undermines freedom and democracy, and for a simple reason: without absolute principles to defend such things as the dignity of human beings, private property, limits to state power, the rule of law rather than the rule of men, and so on, there is no appeal to a higher law or right and therefore no limit to despotism, whether mild or vicious. For when no culture, belief, or moral system can be said to be preferable, "then freedom also must be a matter of indifference."[14] And everything else, too. For without some accepted public standard as a framework for conduct (irrespective of how inadequately it may be observed from time to time), it is impossible to defend ourselves against moral or political tyranny (or for that matter, against the tyranny of our own selves). So the greater irony is that although relativism closes the door to one kind of absolutism, it immediately opens the door to another.

This is not a political book. Nevertheless, it is important to understand that for many millions of people who have suffered under perverse political systems, relativism is not a parlour game. It always has serious political consequences or, if one is wielding the stick of power, usefulness. More to the point, in the dreadful conflicts of the modern world, relativism has been the ever-present smiling midwife of totalitarianism. Nietzsche laid the modern groundwork with his slogan about there being no facts, only interpretations, and Hitler followed his thinking exuberantly. It was specifically moral relativism that freed Hitler's regime to invent political values that were then happily imposed on others ... absolutely.

Friedrich Engels, Karl Marx's intellectual shadow, was another prominent political thinker whose relativist ideas contaminated the modern world. Both these men declared that moral values are really only class values, invented solely for the purpose of defending the property, status, and privilege of the ruling class. An obvious conclusion – one that Marx and his totalitarian acolytes were not slow to take up – is that if there are no absolute values, then there is nothing to stop you from advancing your own agenda with as much violence as you can get away with. Lenin and Stalin were quick learners.

We see the same connection between relativism and Italian Fascism. Mussolini was an articulate defender of the idea that the state creates the individual. He wrote that "If relativism signifies contempt for fixed categories and [for] men who claim to be bearers of an external objective truth, *then there is nothing more relativistic than fascist attitudes.*"[15]

The softer liberal democracies of the West have flirted with relativism for a very long time, as we have seen, and with some distressing consequences. One of these is the plain fact that wherever the materialist attitude of modern science is combined with relativism, we can predict that moral and political statements will soon emerge about the worthlessness of some forms of human life and how we ought to be eliminating certain classes of unworthy people such as "unwanted" children by abortion, or the very old, or Jews, or the infirm by outright genocide or euthanasia. Perhaps the classic example of the antihumanism to which relativism leads is the infamous utterance from Justice Oliver Wendell Holmes that must surely rank as one of the most callous ever. Here was a famous jurist making life-altering decisions who wrote: "I see no reason for attributing to man a significance different in kind from that which belongs to a baboon or a grain of sand ... I don't believe it is an absolute principle ... that man is always an end in himself – that his dignity must be respected."[16] We must be happy never to have ended up in his courtroom – especially when he made judgments like a baboon.

Now, why does relativism in politics always end this way? First, because it preaches that firm moral convictions are oppressive to individual liberty. Arguably, this first ploy is false because the idea of individual liberty itself rests on a moral conviction. Once publicly believed, however, the oppression assumption alone is sufficient to weaken all communities of shared moral conviction. Soon we get terms like "pluralism," "diversity," and "tolerance" as replacement values. But these are in reality value-dispersing terms that serve as an official warning to accept all behaviours of others without judgment and, most important, to keep all moral opinions private. As such, they are the most obvious sign that society is in the process of losing its common moral centre, at which point, where conditions permit, the strong – always the first to detect public moral flabbiness –

step in either to impose a new regime or, as in the Western democracies, where overt totalitarianism is still unthinkable, to further permeate ordinary life with the state's quietly overbearing, regulating role. Relativism is the natural public philosophy of such regimes because it repudiates all natural moral or social binding power, replacing these with legal decrees and sanctions of the state. As such, it manifestly suits masses of autonomous, merely self-regarding, and above all materially sated individuals, contented in their golden sty.

So it would seem the answer to the question "Why does relativism in politics always leads to hard or soft despotism?" is that it removes all former moral resistance to the state by demonizing citizen morality as an oppressive force and by insisting that merely legal individual rights (the new "good," as defined by the state and its courts) are prior to all former traditional understandings of the moral good. So whereas the common moral good was once considered prior to individual legal right, this latter becomes prior to the moral good.

OBJECTION 12: CULTURAL RELATIVISM
IS ITSELF A FORM OF MORALITY
Cultural relativism began, and is supposed to operate as, a morally neutral methodological principle for the study of other cultures. Ironically, however, it has become an imposed universal moral position to be applied and observed by everyone. To be a relativist is *good*. But to see another person or people through the framework of moral assumptions from outside that person's culture or belief system is *bad*. Relativists say that as all values are specific to a given person or group, then no one has the right to *impose* his or her own values or to do research from within a personal moral framework of one's own.

Anyone who has ever studied anthropology or any other social science knows that this is clearly a myth resting on a number of assumed Western moral principles. In Margaret Mead's now-infamous but extremely influential study *Coming of Age in Samoa* (1928),[17] we find not a morally neutral objective study but a piece of social literature masquerading as science that manufactured and then sang the virtues of a supposedly Romantic and free Samoan way of life and sex, a way contrasted with what she took to be an uptight and repressive Victorian sexuality. With patience, implicit moral biases of this sort can be extracted from far too many social science documents.

Nevertheless, this leads us to ask where cultural relativism comes from, and also, by operating within it, are Western scientists imposing alien values on the traditional societies they study?[18] The answer is that no traditional culture in history except our own has ever had a belief in anything resembling a cultural relativism that denies all foundational truth. Even many ordinary Westerners do not believe it. But it reigns officially because it is part of the anti-traditional value system of far too many Western intellectuals. This suggests the answer to the second part of the question: that *for the study of other societies, Western intellectuals rely on a relativist moral principle they covertly regard as absolute.*

This creates a number of *irresolvable logical and moral dilemmas* for such scientists. First, relativism ends up in the foolish position of endorsing absolutist systems that deny and reject relativism. Islam comes to mind, a belief system that finds our type of relativism utterly false and abhorrent. Second, and following from this: by denying the absolutism of cultures such as Islam, relativists demean the very cultures they claim to respect.[19] To risk a mouthful: their anti-hegemonic philosophy is itself hegemonic.

Finally, as has been pointed out by other critics, cultural relativism contains within its own operating assumptions a kind of metacultural set of covert universal assumptions without which it would simply be impossible to understand anything about other societies. In short, the best refutation of the incommensurability thesis upon which cultural relativism rests is the activity of cultural anthropologists themselves. If they really believed what they are teaching, they would never leave home.

4

The Universals of Human Life and Culture

Universally valid truths about human beings, about their bodies and beliefs, loves and laws, politics and principles – many of them deep and startling insights from poets, scientists, philosophers, and sages – have been piling up since the dawn of history. Despite this well-known fact, in 1982 Sir Edmund Leach, one of Britain's most distinguished anthropologists, saw fit to write that "*during the hundred years of their existence, academic anthropologists have not discovered a single universally valid truth concerning either human culture or human society.*"[1]

How was such a statement possible?

For one reason only: by the time he wrote those words most anthropologists had spent more than half a century actively denying that universal truths of any importance have ever existed. If they happened to stumble on one, they ignored it. Discounted it. Or simply pretended universals were trivial. Some even implied that any universally true fact or idea is potentially dangerous and ought to be stamped out – for the good of humanity! Many still behave this way. But fortunately, not all.

One of the purposes of this chapter is to ask: Why, by the end of the twentieth century, did a young academic discipline devoted to "the study of Man" have nothing very much it wanted to say about "Man"? The silence alone was astonishing. And it grew deeper even as professionals in this field kept filling libraries and computer files with data and opinions on every imaginable aspect of human beings and their cultures. Countless articles have been churned out all over the world about different moccasins, kupi dolls, and social customs. But for what?

If anyone except a standard anthropologist were to drop from outer space onto another planet, the first question on spying a novel organism would surely be: What is it? Is it a species? Is it distinct from other organisms that appear *similar*? Do the ones that appear *different* actually share something in common at a deeper level? What sort of social organization, culture, or philosophy of life do they share? From the start, the discipline of anthropology was expected to answer precisely such questions about human beings – here, on planet earth.

THE VICTORIANS

The Victorian period of cultural investigation from the middle to the late nineteenth century rested on a series of assumptions normal for the time that came under severe attack by the end of the century.[2] These were: that culture is formed by *human reason,* not the other way around; that under the right conditions, all human civilizations can *evolve progressively* into a more advanced state; and as a result, that there is an obvious *hierarchy of cultures* because some (most visibly Victorian industrial culture) are simply technologically better, more productive, morally advanced, and humane than others – we have had Christ, Shakespeare, Newton, and Bach, the soaring glories of this world, whereas the primitive races cannot read, and some of them slaughter and eat each other.[3]

Not surprisingly, the strength of these assumptions came from confidence in the Christian civilization that spawned them, especially from the idea that human existence has a revealed meaning within a grand purpose and design.[4] Because the technical and cultural seeds of this civilization seemed to flourish everywhere they were planted, "progress" in the educated mind had to do with ensuring that as many as possible of the "lower" or "primitive" societies be brought to the blessings of the "higher." Drive out paganism. Educate the ignorant. Make them sensible and virtuous like us.

One of the innocent motives underlying this first type of cultural anthropology was the hope of discovering what principles or universals governed the *common human nature* that was assumed to exist and the laws governing the evolution of all humans from the primitive to the civilized condition. The underlying ethical motive supporting much of this early work was the humanitarian hope of resolving the conflicts, confusions, wars, and other evils that have always plagued clashing human cultures.

But the Victorian confidence in reason, social progress, and moral improvement began to falter, even as the British Commonwealth – or "Empire," as it used to be called – itself began to founder. By the middle of the nineteenth century, industrialism had led to enormous increases in general wealth, and this brought with it an increasingly secular materialism, class strife, new forms of pessimism, and the bitter-sweet fruit of new sciences and academic disciplines. Among these were: the attacks on religious faith and moral values by the nihilistic European and utilitarian English and American philosophers discussed in chapter 1; new discoveries in geology that cast doubt on biblical explanations for the age of the earth; the shock of Darwin's theory that humans were not created but evolved from primordial slime into apes, then into humans as an accident of evolution; the disturbing hints, especially in much Romantic poetry, that human motivations may be darkly irrational and wild; and finally, the growing tendency to explain everything in material, historical, or economic terms of class struggle and oppression. It was pretty dismal. Europe began to seem a moral madhouse, and this mood was generating grave doubts about the existence of any central meaning or purpose in life and therefore about the claimed superiority of any single religious or moral view or civilization. There was a pervasive sense of purposelessness in the air, "of man as a moth beating his wings with suicidal vanity against the flame."5

THE ANTI-RACIST GAMBIT OF FRANZ BOAS AND AMERICAN ANTHROPOLOGY

At this point the twentieth century came crashing through the door bearing revolution, blood, bathos, and ... World War I, the first large-scale international crisis to thoroughly puncture the old Victorian balloon.

But there were many who foresaw the omens even before the turn of the century, and some of them fled to America to find intellectual and political freedom. One of them was a young German Jewish scholar with left-leaning beliefs named Franz Boas. Although trained at Germany's Kiel University as a physicist, he was hired by Columbia University in 1896 for work in "anthropology" and was soon busy redefining this new field. In retrospect – and this ought to seem strange coming from a scientist – he set out to fashion a moral weapon from the raw materials of anthropology for the moral battle against racism and political oppression he sensed was coming. His deftly crafted weapon of choice came to be called *cultural relativism.* Today, we can see that it was but "another manifestation of the general skepticism and pessimism that was growing in America [and Europe]. [For cultural] relativism denies the social, moral, and intellectual pre-eminence of Western society: it asserts *that our own values, beliefs, and institutions cannot be shown to be better, and the principle which underlies our position vis-a-vis other societies is the principle of equality.*"[6] In effect, Boas was hoping to show that although all cultures are *different*, they are nevertheless *equal in stature as civilizations* – and therefore none has the right to oppress another.

By war's end, he was using the young science of anthropology for what amounted to a personal propaganda campaign. This was especially relevant at the time, as he had left Europe mostly due to rising anti-Semitism, and now he could see that the shock and chaos of World War I had produced a whirlwind of frantic social schemers and do-gooder intellectuals marauding over Europe preaching absolutist political and racial ideologies such as communism and National Socialism. He sensed rightly that all of them were utopian programs that would require a scapegoat. This frightened him, for once again, in the 1920s, "race theories were in the air, and were increasingly popular in Germany, and Boas saw an urgent need for some opposing ideas to help stop Nazism in its tracks. Racial theory held that biology was destiny, and that if some cultures were inferior to others then inferior racial biology was the reason. An opposing theory would have to show that cultural factors, not biological, explained the diversity of human social arrangements; that was the advantage of culture theory at the time."[7]

Worse, even America had bought race theory. It was already being used there for US immigration screening practices, for social welfare decisions, and for eugenic schemes for the improvement of the American population. Margaret Sanger, the "Godmother" of Planned Parenthood, which is today the world's largest contraception and abortion provider, was notoriously promoting so-called "birth control" (quote marks here because abortion does not control birth; it ensures there will not be a birth) for feminist freedom. She also advocated human sterilization for racial control and the elimination of what she called "human waste" in the American population. Sanger had a lot of friends in high places and grants from the Carnegie and Rockefeller Foundations to promote the idea that racial manipulation (the elimination of future human waste) was the surest route to social perfection. At the time (this seems quite shocking now) the State of California had a state-wide eugenics program in full operation that was eventually examined as a possible model for Germany by Hitler's Nazi planners.[8] Boas was properly frightened. So along with as many as he could convince, he "took vigorous steps to employ anthropology to combat racism."[9]

To put his plan of moral resistance into effect, Boas immediately set about attracting spirited young bohemians to anthropology to help him spread the new relativist word. Many were young litterateurs in hard times, hoping for a career selling stories or poetry. But they had already embraced the romantic myth of the "noble savage," and in a war-torn, increasingly materialistic world this meant they were more than happy to use their talents in the praise of non-Western and assumedly idyllic cultures. The main tenets of Boas's new cultural theory – itself a new anthropological myth in the making – were *egalitarianism, a supposedly scientific moral neutrality*, and a belief in *the plasticity of human nature*. His eager students swallowed it all at first, although some were later to recant.

It is important to grasp that these were *beliefs* only, which rested on some serious contradictions. The most obvious one is that their theory of moral neutrality, or tolerance, is itself a moral theory – and why exactly, later critics were to ask, should we be tolerant of what is clearly intolerable? At any rate, for Boas and his students, the whole package was shaped into a powerful secular creed. I say "creed" because there is no compelling argument that egalitarianism is a good thing (for it can be implemented only by force and by denying natural differences); or that amorality is fruitful (it tends to undermine the firmly rooted belief systems of natural societies); or that science can truly be neutral (social science in particular is notorious for operating from specific moral assumptions, as in this case of anthropology); or that human nature is "plastic" (modern science tells us the opposite: our minds are not blank slates after all; we are hardwired for a lot of things).

Nevertheless, with this creed in mind, Boas and his followers spread out over the academic commonwealth to prove that *all cultures are equally good and already fully civilized; that none are morally better or worse than others; and that to be scientific, cultural research must be neutral in its values and methodology, never ethnocentric.*[10] He believed that the largely unconscious emotional patterns of culture, not biology, make us what we are and that except for the accidents of history, we might all have been Tibetans or Ojibway. Our genetic makeup would be the same, but we would speak a different language and adhere to a different culture.[11]

Despite this creed, it happened that Boas was also a believer in the existence of many universal human ideas, in our common genetic makeup, and in the "psychic unity" of humankind. He even admitted that heredity plays a significant role in the lives of individuals and families. But he had nevertheless persuaded himself that the differences *within* cultural groups and races were far greater than any differences *between* them. He and his followers had no use for theories of innate psychological or biological traits as explanations for human *group* behaviour because such theories inevitably lead to racist claims of moral and cultural superiority.[12] As an antidote to such racism, he chose to focus on the particulars of how the clay of humanity is moulded by cultural influences. In effect, the Boasians were fighting the old "nature vs nurture" battle, which had played such a prominent role in nineteenth-century Marxism, in psychology, and in evolutionary theory, all over again – but this time with cultural tools. And their message came down firmly on the side of nurture. Culture matters, not biology, was the constant theme. Some of Boas's students, such as Alfred Kroeber, became even more radical in this respect than the teacher, insisting that anthropology should study not humankind but our works. As one observer put it, this meant, astonishingly, that for Kroeber the study of humanity "was largely unconcerned with humanity itself."[13]

Although far from being the world's first multiculturalist (a distinction of sorts that belongs to Alexander the Great), Boas rigorously and defiantly rejected the evolutionary social and moral notions of his predecessors, especially the Western idea he found most politically dangerous: *that other cultures ought to be improved to our own higher level*. It was not that a culture could not improve on *its own* terms. Rather, the offence lay in seeking to improve someone else's culture on *our* terms. All cultures must be left to travel in different directions according to their own values. With this radical notion, Boas almost single-handedly redefined the science of anthropology to make the case – against many of the grand theorists of social evolution of his time – *that human history has no particular direction, meaning, or purpose*. But it is important to understand that he took this position not for scientific, but for ideological, reasons. On this point, Carl N. Degler, a prominent Stanford University social historian, stresses that with respect to

> Boas's conception of culture and his opposition to a racial interpretation of human behaviour, the central point [is] that Boas did not arrive at that position from a disinterested scientific inquiry into a vexed if controversial question. Instead, his idea derived from an ideological commitment ... [and] there is no doubt that he had a deep interest in collecting evidence and designing arguments that would rebut or refute an ideological outlook – racism [and this resulted in] a persistent interest in pressing his social values upon the profession and the public.[14]

In short, for ideological reasons that overwhelmed his science, Boas was striving to equalize cultural and moral differences by any respectably available means so he could disempower future political schemes for racial and cultural domination. If the new science of anthropology was to be a moral force for the neutralization of oppression, then cultural relativism (which ironically rests on a particular standard of moral "tolerance") had to be the operating ideology.

THE BOHEMIAN/HIPPIE CONNECTION

An anthropologist is "a person who respects every culture pattern but his own."[15]

Robert B. Edgerton, *Sick Societies* (1992)

Never doubt that a small group of thoughtful, committed citizens can change the world. Indeed, it is the only thing that ever has.[16]

Margaret Mead, quoted in Carolyn Warner, ed., *The Last Word* (1992)

Those who were part of the moral and intellectual hotbed of the between-the-wars generation, whether drifting through coffeehouses or settled in the halls of academe, soon adopted the new cultural relativism as the enlightened orthodoxy of true progressivism. Its emotional appeal lay in what it opposed. First and foremost, it was against all moral and cultural absolutes and therefore against most kinds of authority, especially Western assumptions of cultural superiority. It was definitely against America. At bottom, it was a radical political and moral creed (although deeply flawed, as we saw in the previous chapter) now brazenly promoted as scientific method. Nevertheless, and despite its moral and logical flaws, this brand of relativism managed to infect many generations of Western students and intellectuals. At the time, however, few were interested or willing to follow relativism all the way through to its disturbing conclusions.

In short, Boas and his many star students were moral crusaders proudly using anthropology as their weapon of choice for social revolution. Among the stars were Ruth Benedict and Margaret Mead, both soon to become very influential in their own right. Boas waived various credit requirements to hurry Benedict through her PhD and exempted Mead from her final doctoral examination. And both students were effective beyond his dreams. By the end of the twentieth century, Benedict's *Patterns of Culture* and Mead's *Coming of Age in Samoa* had sold millions of copies, each preaching a relativist creed about the astonishing natural differences in human cultures.[17] It was a sermon accepted as academic orthodoxy for about three-quarters of a century, and young students such as this writer were in the pews.

But very few, until quite recently, had ever thought to ask: "does an emphasis on differences present a true image of humanity?"[18] And only recently has the vast body of relativist work begun to stagger under the body-blows of its critics. Indeed, the work of both Benedict and Mead has been rather put to shame as so much youthful romantic cultural delusion, if not incompetence and fraud. Benedict's veneration of the peaceful Pueblo, for example, was shaken by firm revelations of their former violence and cannibalism (still hotly denied by modern Pueblos), and Mead's romantic rhapsodies about Samoans have been upended and shown to be a naive hoax.[19]

Cultural relativism, it turns out, was the furthest thing from neutral and scientific. The reason, as Roger Sandall makes clear in *The Culture Cult*, is that the new creed for the study of humankind was openly and abrasively leftist, stridently antibourgeois, and anticapitalist. It floated along on a potpourri of its own moral fabrications, among which were ideas of salvation by innocence (as in Rousseau's myth of the noble savage), of an innate human goodness that would be crushed by high-tech civilization, and of preferences for raw self-expression to Victorian-style self-control; beliefs that all people should live for the enjoyments of the moment and glorify the body and sexuality; and in politics, convictions that all people should embrace egalitarianism, freedom, and feminism, among other such things. At bottom, this creed was deeply anti-American and anti-Christian, but its cornerstone was the acceptance without curiosity or question of the belief that our minds are blank slates moulded by culture alone and that all primitive people are pure, unspoiled, and "possess an inner wisdom civilization has lost."[20]

No one cared to confess what every good anthropologist knew, even at the time: "that 99 percent of the studies made by anthropologists were of a defanged tribalism ... cultures [already] pacified and neutralized by colonial authority."[21] In short, beautiful Polynesian boys and girls now tamed by colonial law (no more slavery, human sacrifice, or cannibalism allowed) and schooled by Christian missionaries had been described by Mead as newly emergent babes of Eden. She was feeding us a precursor to the same sort of romantic veneration of the flower-child, sexual liberation, emotional impulsivity, and loose moral relativism that was to befall Western society again in the 1960s. An example of the anger that arguments daring to question this relativist orthodoxy could elicit at the time is the now-legendary story of one biologist who set out to prove the human mind is not so blank after all. His paper (today admired as conclusive) was rejected by a then blue-ribbon panel of academics who wrote that his findings about some of the universals of human cultures were "no more likely than bird-shit in a cuckoo clock."[22]

The distressing message is that many of the most influential American anthropologists of the early twentieth century and onward were willingly acting as political "change agents" under the cover of moral tolerance and social science. Perhaps that is no surprise. Even Edward B. Tylor, generally considered the first anthropologist, declared as early as 1871 that "The science of culture is essentially a reformer's science."[23] Anthropology and radical politics have always been bedmates.[24] But it is hard to imagine a physicist or chemist, a medical researcher, or a mathematician behaving this way.

FIRST HINTS OF WEAKNESS

What sank their theory in the end was the core belief that the way to defeat any dominating social, moral, or political/cultural system was to deny its superiority to any other. At the time, they failed to notice that this idea immediately destroyed the possibility of a "better" cultural or moral response to clear and obvious evils – including those they deplored. Even liberal European culture – perhaps the most accepting and value-neutral culture in all of human history to that point – was denied any superiority whatsoever over other cultures. The European quantum physicist listening to Mozart and the naked Bantu among the drums shaping tools from the bones of his enemies were said to be involved in equally "civilized" pursuits. All differences, they insisted, are equal, and all generalities and absolutes are morally dangerous and to be avoided. Ruth Benedict, later Mead's lesbian lover in a triangle with Mead's own husband, neatly summed up the creed she was living when she said that "human nature is almost unbelievably malleable."[25] For her, and for American anthropology of that period, every culture is self-contained, autonomous, separate but equal, or as we would say today, incommensurable. They cannot be compared or evaluated because, it was believed, there is no neutral or privileged scale of values with which to do this. This is a belief that continues to permeate many educational and elite institutions.

WHAT NOW?

Here was a purportedly scientific ideology that decided to avoid all moral judgment by studying only trees, never the forest, and it is still powerfully appealing to many anthropologists. Plug the phrase "cultural relativism" into any Internet search engine and there will appear all kinds of boosters. The first one I ran across stated that "Cultural relativism in anthropology is a key methodological concept *which is universally accepted within the discipline.*"[26] Now this is simply not true (and that is not a relative judgment). There has always been internal resistance, as we shall see, and there are a number of distinguished anthropologists who currently and openly repudiate the relativist trend as an embarrassment. Indeed, relativism has been deeply embarrassed from the start. First, it was embarrassed indirectly by obvious moral questions about history: does relativism mean we should accept as "good" the slavery, cannibalism, and tortures of history just because the people who did these things thought they were good? And then it was embarrassed rather directly, as no sooner had it got itself firmly planted than it was "rendered nugatory by the rise of Nazism, Fascism, and Totalitarianism"[27] – that is, by contemporary cultures that believed it was morally a good thing to conquer, enslave, and massacre millions of their own citizens. What an irony! The very spectre that sparked the theory of cultural relativism was to embarrass it in practice.

And so it was ironic – and still is – that totalitarianism (in addition to providing a direct embarrassment of relativism) provoked new and more subtle critics who saw that despite the widespread belief that relativism is naturally rooted in freedom-loving liberal-democratic regimes, actual historical experiences have shown the opposite: that "ethical relativism and totalitarian despotism go very well together."[28] For this reason, many social scientists were drawn into the sharply partisan political activities of free-world governments that were actively seeking to oppose "evil" cultures in the decades following World War II. (And who can forget the power of the recent "Axis of Evil" symbolism directed at the "culture" of modern radical Islam after 9/11?)

The result of this Cold War challenge to reality was a deep division among anthropologists, many of whom had gotten recruited by their own governments for postwar field work. No sooner had they embarked on their ostensibly nonjudgmental, value-neutral cultural investigations than they found themselves surrounded and their work directed, sanitized, repudiated, or even vilified by the very government agents who had funded them, or by local leaders trying to protect their personal interests against their own people, and often by revolutionaries accusing them of politically partisan science. The "neutrality" of cultural relativism began to seem impossible and perhaps itself a cultural myth.[29]

THE RELATIVIST IRONY

Show me a cultural relativist at 30,000 feet and I'll show you a hypocrite.[30]
Richard Dawkins, *River out of Eden* (1995), after wondering why
academics who believe in relativism don't travel to their
conferences on magic carpets, instead of in Boeings.

The best refutation of cultural relativity is the activity of anthropologists themselves, who could not understand or live within other human groups unless
[they shared assumptions with] the inhabitants of those groups.[31]
John Tooby and Leda Cosmides,
"The Psychological Foundations of Culture" (1992)

Despite such moral conundrums and the devastating frontal attacks and
often sadly perverse consequences of the logic, the theory of cultural relativism somehow survives quite strongly to this day and determines the
moral posture of most social sciences. This is true even though, as Robert
B. Edgerton, author of *Sick Societies: Challenging the Myth of Primitive Harmony*, writes: most people "would probably react with disbelief" at the relativist idea that the political systems of such as Iraq, or Nazi Germany
(meaning their practices of genocide and torture) cannot be evaluated
"except as the people in those society's themselves evaluate them."[32] Dis-
gusted by this truth, some famously attacked relativism for its moral flabbiness, like the late professor Allan Bloom in his bestseller *The Closing of the
American Mind*, where he cites examples of his own University of Toronto
students, who were such reflex relativists in attitude they were utterly un-
willing to condemn even the most odious cultural or moral practices of
other people or societies (or their friends), not even such grotesque public spectacles as live and screaming widow-burnings by Hindus. The curious and ironic result of such extreme and ostensibly tolerant relativism is
that it has profoundly conservative results. In the name of tolerance –
which now means not judging anything, whatsoever, negatively – it tends,
ironically, to conserve everything, including practices and beliefs that are
clearly stupid, maladaptive, harmful, oppressive to believers, and to most
people deeply evil. In short, wherever promoted, relativism immediately
risks becoming the most oppressive of all possible moral positions, forced
by its own foundational moral assumption (that there is no moral foundation) to agree that whatever is believed to be good must be so.

How could a philosophy that began with such good intentions end
up so wrong-headed, so vulnerable to accusations of execrable timidity

and immoral collaborations? A likely answer is that the problem of moral cross-purposes arises from its original reluctance to rise above the level of things particular to the level of things general. Ever since Boas, the majority of cultural anthropologists have behaved as might a blind man who wanders from tree to tree, studying each tree in detail without ever realizing – or if he has realized, refusing to acknowledge – that he is in a forest.

DOES THE TRUTH LIE IN THE FOREST OR IN THE TREES?

To say that the trees in the forest are *all different* (because they obviously are) is just as true as to say they are *all the same* (because they are all trees). But how can both statements be true? It depends on what we choose to emphasize. Every tree in the forest has roots, a trunk, branches, leaves or needles, and bark, relies on photosynthesis for energy, has a method of reproduction, and so on. This is a very short list of what is common, or *universal*, about the trees in the forest. It defines the essence of "tree." Arguably, without some sense of these universal features, we would not be able to say that the next tree we happen upon is in fact a tree.

But it is no less true to say that no two trees are the same. Each pine tree, for example, while itself part of a defined class of tree, is still different from every other pine tree in the whole universe in myriad ways: arrangement of branches, height, number of woodpecker holes, root structure, and so on. Every pine tree in the world is *particular* and therefore different, and we could never find two exactly identical pine trees. They do not exist. The same is true of individual human beings and their societies.

It is possible to study only what is different and particular about each individual tree, or person, or society, determined to break down each difference into even smaller differences; or we can resolve differences by discovering what is common to them. We can say that no two human beings in the whole universe, even identical twins, are truly identical, or we can say that all human beings are indeed identical: they all breathe, eat, have brains, a heart, arms, eyes, look alike, understand love, speak, sing, sleep, and have so much in common, as we shall see below. But there can be no science of trees, as there can be no study of humankind, until we rise from the level of particulars to this universal, or general, level.

RECENT RESISTANCE TO RELATIVISM

It is a curious thing. There have always been very smart people interested in human universals. Plato and Aristotle wrote mostly about universals hundreds of years before Christ – who himself articulated so many enduring universal truths. There are more than two thousand years of universalist thinkers in our tradition. The Middle Ages simply assumed a constancy of human nature, at least in the sense formalized by such as Saint Thomas Aquinas that all human beings participate in a single essence, or nature. The Renaissance rediscovered and embraced a more classical, less theological version of human nature. The ensuing Age of Enlightenment coupled its conviction that reason is the root of human nature with the idea of social progress. By the nineteenth century we got other forms of universalism – a Marxist economics, a Freudian psychology, an evolutionary biology – and also anthropologists like Tylor and Adolph Bastian (a teacher of Boas), the former amazed that human culture was "pervaded by uniformity," the latter amazed at the common "elementary ideas" of all humans.

There was also early and stiff resistance to Boas's politicized relativism from within anthropology itself. A group of all-star scholars, subsequently characterized as "anthropology's equivalent of the 1927 New York Yankees,"[33] tried to strike him out. But they failed. Boas and his missionaries managed to win the battle on the ground. Amazingly, they were somehow able to taboo and shut down the ongoing universalist resistance for almost a half-century and in the process infected millions of students with the relativist mindset. This professional repudiation of the most basic facts of human nature will surely one day be exposed (by yet more, and hopefully more honest, anthropologists) as one of the most peculiar and wilfully ideological misadventures of Western intellectual life. It succeeded despite the strenuous efforts of many dissenting social scientists from the 1920s to the 1960s to deplore publicly the effect that relativism was having on the moral philosophy of the Western world,[34] and to correct public misconceptions by revealing a growing number of human universals.*

---

* See especially such works as Donald E. Brown, *Human Universals* (New York: Mcgraw Hill, 1991), chapter 3, for a short history of anti-Boasian discoveries, among which he lists "universal patterns" (Wissler, 1923), "universal conditions" (Radcliffe-Brown, 1935), "universal institutional types" and "innate natural tendencies of the human mind" (Malinowski, 1944), "the common denominators of culture" (Murdoch, 1945), "the universals of civilization" (Herskovitz, 1947), "innate mental structures" (Claude Levi-Strauss, 1949), and "universal categories of culture" (Kluckholn, 1953). The cited texts are listed in Brown's bibliography.

But they were spitting in the wind. Interest in human universals waxed and waned a number of times prior to World War II but mostly waned. After the war, with Nazism defeated, appeals to human nature and natural law (of the kind that were instrumental in convicting and hanging war criminals at Nuremberg) seemed even less important, and the subject waned until the hippie '60s, when relativism – especially moral relativism – and many other forms of shrill anti-authoritarianism really took off. Oh, everyone felt so free!

But there was already reaction to runaway relativism brewing.

THE GREAT DIVISION

By the end of the roaring '60s, relativism was being felt in almost every home and classroom, at every cocktail party. Street relativism proclaimed that subjectivity rules and that moral judgmentalism has come to an end: "You do your thing, and I'll do mine." In the universities, meanwhile, theorists were hard at work developing more, and more-defiant, brands of copy-cat relativism mainly borrowed wholesale from Parisian intellectuals. Yet even as relativism spread so naturally and unchallenged down in Greenwich Village in New York, or at Haight-Ashbury in San Francisco, or in Paris, or in the minds of liberated anthropology professors, a great division was quietly opening among social scientists. They were again falling into camps along the old nature-nurture axis. Some embraced the most radical possible forms of cultural and moral relativism (the nurture wing), while others, tiring of this, looked to the more certain discoveries coming from human and animal biology and evolution theory (the nature wing). Still others were developing a theoretical interest in social, behavioural, and language universals of all kinds (yet another aspect of the nature wing). The study of humankind was by now deeply fragmented.

There were two main trends – a deeper subjectivism and, opposing this, a deeper objectivism – each feeding off the other. New objective findings from the nature camp were revealing innate mental, language, and social structures in both animals and humans. The news of this was received by relativists from the nurture camp as justification for a retreat into more deeply radical forms of subjectivity. In effect, they reacted politically and morally (not scientifically or logically) against powerful and decisive new discoveries in animal and human biology, language, and behaviour that emerged after mid-century and that were being openly publicized as a deeper truth by the 1970s. What frightened them was the dreaded possibility that the old idea of human nature was beginning to look more and more like something real that science was demonstrating and, worst of all, that it might be something innate (as the enemies of relativism had always maintained).

If you can't beat 'em, you run. A lot of relativist-minded intellectuals expressed their deep-seated fear of the latest discoveries in biology and other sciences by running away from hard science altogether and as an alternative embracing something soon to be called "postmodernism." In this they discovered a style of thinking (with lots of European intellectual ammunition gotten from Nietzsche and Heidegger, Sartre, Barthes, Foucault, Derrida, and others, to be explored later in this book) that they were certain would make it impossible to claim that anything whatsoever – especially the dreaded idea of "human nature" – is objectively true!

Let us not be intimidated by a fancy word. Rather, let us ask: What is "modern," and what is "postmodern"? The conventional thinking is that the "modern" period began a couple of centuries ago when Western civilization dropped its tired belief that religion would bring salvation and embraced in its place the previously heretical idea that human reason alone could lead us to objective truth and maybe help us to build a heaven on earth. But the dream soon became a nightmare. What did reason bring but war, chaos and cruelty, colonialism, and capitalism? Indeed, reason had been used to justify these very things!

So the most disappointed radicals fought back by insisting that reason and rationality were themselves like a religion. Just another belief system. Soon the idea was floated that all "facts" are (in fact) theory-laden, and therefore value-laden, and therefore subjective. The new orthodoxy was that reason and objectivity are just words in a philosophical mug's game. So in a much more defiant and radical way than their relativist precursors, they began to claim not only that all things are relative but also that there is no objective, let alone universal, truth available about anything whatsoever. Western notions of "objectivity" are part of a dominating (or "hegemonic") discourse of the controlling classes, a philosophical language developed by oppressors to oppress. "Postmodernism" thus became the fashionable term (although it, too, has lately become rather stale) to express cynicism about the idea that anything, let alone reason, can bring truth.

In a later chapter we will open up the whole Pandora's box of postmodernism because although the edge of novelty is gone, it survives as a kind of confused theory still relied upon to justify a pervasive relativist attitude. Suffice it to say for now, however, that by the 1970s relativists were really under attack, and their reaction was: alright, if you objective types are going to tell us that there are – what do you call them? deep structures of language? unconscious motives in psychology? innate predispositions in biology? gender distinctions in the wiring of the human brain? – then we will answer that no one escapes the prison house of language. Words – even, and especially, scientific words – are explained by other words, ad infinitum. The whole world is a text, and therefore we believe it is true, as Wittgenstein (and later Jacques Derrida) put it, that "there is no external text." Nothing! We are all trapped inside our own minds, cultures, and particular forms of life. There is no privileged viewpoint. All is narrative, or fiction making. All is relative.

This trend really got the intellectual pigeons flapping. Some anthropologists began to boast that because all facts are stories, they would now proudly repudiate *any* "objective" scientific observation of another culture as an impossibility: making stories is all any social scientist can do – or *ought* to do! The most defiantly subjective and hypersensitive researchers soon spun out of orbit and began telling anguished stories of how they were (necessarily inadequately) trying to tell their story but could not escape their own tormenting manner of telling.

This extreme postmodernist form of relativism in anthropology has been justly criticized for making the people it studies "falsely incomprehensible and thus dehumanized"[35] and for creating a form of "cognitive apartheid."[36] Ironically, although as mentioned the postmodern focus on reality-as-fiction was – and is – a pseudo philosophy wholly borrowed from French literary critics (who in turn borrowed it all from Nietzsche and Heidegger, as we will see in later chapters), it came in very handy for anthropologists and other social scientists desperate to resist the new and exciting scientific discoveries and theories quietly coming off the presses that were bolstering the objective existence of universals in fields as diverse as social psychology, genetics, evolution theory, sociobiology, and language studies.

SHOTS ACROSS THE BOW

One of the most influential new universalists was Noam Chomsky, who wrote a devastating 1959 review of B.F. Skinner's *Verbal Behavior*.[37] Skinner's book was an icon of sorts for relativists because it rested on the old blank-slate theory that the human mind begins life empty and therefore that not much of human behaviour is preordained or innate, the implication being that with a little clever social conditioning we can produce or adjust human behaviour – and society – as we wish. Skinner publicly boasted that given a child young enough, he could manufacture any type of adult.

But Chomsky made minced meat of the theory by arguing with devastating effectiveness that human language capacities are universal, innate, and likely hardwired biologically. This is to say that language acquisition is a skill expressed naturally by all human beings everywhere; it is not instilled by the environment. You could hear the brakes squealing the moment this deeply antirelativist notion was published. Indeed, Chomsky's revolutionary work was pointing the way to "deep structure" (a concept that soon caught on in many other fields). Deep structures are underlying processes, relations, and laws to be clearly distinguished from the mere surface particulars that to him had been occupying too many social scientists for too long and for the wrong reasons. Chomsky eventually left even this popular concept behind for better ones. But the seeds of "nativism" were planted once again.

Not long afterward, anthropologists Lionel Tiger and Robin Fox published *The Imperial Animal* (1971), getting at the deep structures of practical human behaviour and of whole societies.[38] And then E.O. Wilson dropped a bombshell with his elegantly written (if sometimes tortuously argued) book *On Human Nature* (1975).[39] That title alone was incendiary to anthropologists who had been trained for so long to dismiss the entire concept in principle. Here was Wilson boldly linking underlying human biology to surface social, sexual, psychological, and – the scandal! – even moral behaviour. In so doing, he added fuel to the fire of "sociobiology" – a fire he had started himself with a previous book by that title.[40] It was a label soon avoided as unsavoury due to its potential for genetic, racial, and gender typing of the sort that had frightened Boas. Nevertheless, all this was the first wave of work in a growing number of new fields, such as evolutionary psychology (and psychiatry) and Darwinian anthropology, pointing to human biology, genetics, adaptation, and the brain as causal co-factors of culture. No one was dismissing learning and culture entirely. Rather, they were arguing that the long focus on culture alone as a force independent of biology was plainly misguided.[41] Nature and nurture work together, they argued, and we will see what they have been saying in more detail in a later chapter. It was enough to unsettle any radical thinker of the progressive, social-engineering, blank-slate sort.

Readers who want to know a little more of what we might term "the anthropology of anthropologists" should go to the notes for this chapter, where they will get exposure to some real academic contortionism.[42] I don't wish to be unduly hard on anthropology as relativism's modern culprit. But some censure is richly deserved because for too long it has been cultural anthropologists operating under the camouflage of personal ideological and political motives, which they have presented as science, who are so plainly dishonest. They have not made it clear to paying parents that when their children choose a course in cultural anthropology on the assumption they will be engaging in an unbiased study of other cultures and of humankind, they may instead be subjected (excuse the jargon) to a sustained ideological and political brainwashing by a pseudo-Marxist, anti-Western, anticapitalist, postmodern interpretive anthropologist, with a radical liberationist agenda, who has no intention of teaching them anything universal about human beings or human nature. Indeed, they may attract an "F" for using such a phrase.

THE NEW UNIVERSALISM

In addition to the biological and language scientists exploring the nature side of this debate, there is another group that has been trying to swim away from the relativist whirlpool, energetically resisting the latest forays of anthropology into the conceptual casuistry of postmodernism. They have sought instead to discover all *objectively verifiable human universals*. Their work produces a great sense of relief that at last anthropology may be escaping from politics to reveal an identifiable and common human world. This would give the study of humankind some meaning. So let us now turn to their discoveries, which ought to astonish any relativist.

The questions they seek to answer are: Do human universals exist? And if so, what are they? How many are there? And if they exist, how can they be explained? What is their significance and importance? Do they form a foundation for a conception of human nature in the sense of a common human world of culture and experience shared by all human beings on earth?

One of the first and most important scholars to give impetus to this field of study in recent times was Donald E. Brown, a professor of anthropology (now retired) at the University of California, Santa Barbara. He injected a new air of scientific seriousness into the tenuous – and still somewhat tabooed – scholarship surrounding this entire topic with the 1991 publication of his book, *Human Universals*. Brown tells us he was trained in the usual way as a Boasian cultural relativist. He had swallowed it whole. But one day he bet a colleague who had insisted on the existence of certain human sexual universals that he could find cultures that were exempt. Brown was absolutely certain of the relativist dogma. But to his astonishment and chagrin, he lost the bet. After another similar losing bet, he began to get really curious and wanted to know if there were more human universals. His eventual answer was affirmative, and a whole new world opened up. He began to wonder whether there could be hundreds of behaviours, beliefs, and customs linking all of humankind? And if so, what could this mean? So he set out on a mission of discovery. Eventually, he launched a university course on human universals and then published his groundbreaking book, in which he explains the skimpy history of research into human universals, their context in anthropology, and their meaning, definition, and significance. In performing these labours, he single-handedly reopened the formerly tabooed study of human universals, arming the antirelativist movement with heavy intellectual artillery for the first time.

Brown's book must be read to be appreciated. But suffice it to say he has compiled confirmable data and has categorized the existence of some 311 human universals (and counting).*

Human Universals are observable cultural features, practices, behaviours, or beliefs that appear in all human societies in history. Brown stresses he is presenting only verifiable surface universals, leaving the next step for future researchers, namely the elucidation of innate universals and other kinds that are not so apparent at the surface, the relations between them, their patterns, and the possible laws governing them. That will come. But in doing as much as he has, Brown has definitively established the importance of human universals in social science. And this means the study of humankind can now proceed from collecting facts, artefacts, and tales of exotic practices (or merely idiosyncratic personal cultural narratives, or fictions) about the world's cultures to the more challenging work of deciphering the universal laws and principles connecting their common features.

Whereas Boas and his relativist followers were understandably attempting to morally disable various forms of political absolutism and all

---

* In chapter 2 of *Human Universals*, entitled "Conceptualizing, Defining, and Demonstrating Universals," Brown discusses the many varieties, ranging from universals, to near-universals, to statistical universals, to surface vs formal universals, to implicational universals (if A is found, then B will also be found), to pattern universals, and so on.

potential future racist theories by emphasizing the incommensurable but equally valid cultural and moral differences between the world's peoples, Brown's work is a more sophisticated return to earlier efforts. His universalism diminishes divisions and tension between peoples and cultures not by arguing that their differences make them *theoretically* the same but by demonstrating their *factual common humanity*. In other words, his work is in a sense driven by the same moral imperative that Boas invoked for relativism, but unlike the latter it does not hang itself with relativist rope. In Boas's relativist world all people are the same in abstract theory (he did believe there is a deep psychic unity of all humankind), but all are different in their cultural expressions. In Brown's world of human universals, however, all people are the same in theory as well as in concrete fact because they share so many commonalities and hence the same human nature.

Whereas the earliest universalist efforts lacked sufficient hard evidence for any theory of a universal human nature, by the 1980s the world's museums and libraries were overflowing with mute physical and documentary evidence. Those interested may today examine universals (or any other aspect) of over 400 of the world's cultures (just over 10 per cent of the cultures thought ever to have existed) catalogued in something called the *Human Relations Area File* (*HRAF*), managed by Yale University.[43] This massive cultural inventory was a project begun in the 1970s by anthropologist George Murdock, who, like so many others, began as a relativist but later recanted,[44] eventually declaring that the social sciences as a whole might have to be "started over" due to their erroneous founding assumptions.

The humanitarian ethic driving the new universalist work is multifaceted and driven by the desire to do more honest research uncompromised by "ethnographic liberalism." The hope is to demonstrate once and for all that *a common human nature exists and is expressed everywhere through a large number of universal human habits, practices, and common principle and beliefs* and thus to contribute profoundly to human harmony. In a sense, these universalists have been accomplishing Boas's dream by different means.

WHAT THEY HAVE DISCOVERED?

For most people raised on the so-called "Standard Social Science Model" – the old idea that everything is relative, in flux, unpredictable, and plastic and that nothing is permanent, constant, or universal –

what follows is a bracing shock. I will give just a taste here, in a mix of Brown's words and my paraphrasing of what he calls "the Universal People," a general culture he describes from his inventory of human universals. Every word applies to all human societies, past and present. It is a picture of "Everyman" as he or she exists in every culture in history:

> All humans use language as their principal medium of communication, and all human languages have the same underlying architecture, built of the same basic units and arranged according to implicit rules of grammar and other common features. All people classify themselves in terms of status, class, roles, and kinship, and all practise division of labour by age and gender. Many human facial expressions are universal and elicit the same emotional responses everywhere. All have poetry, figurative speech, symbolic speech, ceremonial speech, metaphor, and the like. All use logic, reckon time, distinguish past, present, and future, think in causal terms, recognize the concept and possibility of cheating and lying, and strive to protect themselves from the same. They distinguish inner from outer body, emotions, sensations, and thoughts, distinguish flora and fauna, motion, speed, location, dimension, and other physical properties of the world, and also have concepts of dualism, polar extremes, parts and wholes, opposites, and equivalents, have the ability to count, to see self as subject or object, to distinguish normal from abnormal mental states, experience empathy, make tools, have patterns of socialization and sexual regulation, have incest avoidance, use reciprocity, distinguish public from private, have government, leaders, law, rules of conduct, sanctions, punishment, distinguish right from wrong and responsibility and intention, have religion, etiquette, hospitality, standards of sexual modesty, a worldview, rituals, rules of inheritance, and so forth.45

The story goes on. A selection from the list of human universals sent to me by Professor Brown is included in the appendix "Some Universals and Constants of Nature and Human Nature" at the end of this book. It reads as a straightforward list of the items all cultures share and display, such as: aesthetic standards, affection expressed and felt, age grades, age terms, age statuses, anthropomorphization, antonyms, belief in supernatural/religion, beliefs (false), beliefs about disease, beliefs about fortune and misfortune, beliefs about death, binary cognitive distinctions, body adornment, childbirth customs, childhood fears (loud noises, strangers), classification of tools, classification of space, classification of body parts, figurative speech, folklore, food sharing, future (attempts to predict), generosity admired, gestures, gift giving, government, grammar, and so on.

Each of these items may seem "normal" because each applies to us all, so we take them for granted. Thus ... what's the story here? Well, the story lies in the bald fact that their existence as universals has been denied and buried for almost a century for the ideological reasons explained, and this news has only recently gotten out of the closet. We have been told again and again, rather dogmatically – and quite falsely – that nothing unites us, that we do not share a common human nature. But now, at long last, we can see the shape of humankind as a true subject of anthropology.

From now on, for an anthropologist to discover any group of human beings – a new tribe in some remote jungle, say – that does *not* have, express, share, or practice all of these features would be just as astonishing to a universalist as the former claim that they are common to all humanity once seemed to the relativist. These universal features and the existence of human nature they signal can no longer be denied, and there are certainly more, and more deeply hidden ones, to be discovered when more is learned.

WHAT DOES THE EXISTENCE OF HUMAN UNIVERSALS MEAN, AND WHAT IS THEIR IMPORTANCE?

Brown is justifiably tough on anthropologists, stating that although "they were sent into the field with the charge of getting the whole picture ... [and to] *tell the world what people are really like*, anthropologists have failed to give a true report of their findings. They have dwelt on the differences between peoples while saying too little about the similarities ... [and have] exaggerated the importance of social and cultural conditioning."[46] These distortions, he feels, inevitably affect the way we look at and treat the rest of the world's peoples and also how we see ourselves and conduct our own affairs.

And he is not alone in fearing that some rather craven, self-serving motives underlie the preference for relativism among social scientists because it is obvious that the more that "differences can be shown to exist, and the more they can be thought to reflect purely social and cultural dynamics," the more social scientists "can justify their role in the world of intellectual and practical affairs and thus get their salaries paid, their lectures attended, their research funded, and their essays read." Nevertheless, his hope is that the many important questions about the nature of human universals – and therefore about human nature – raised by new research in a number of diverse fields will lead to a truer picture of what humanity is and who we are, for "it will be irresponsible to continue shunting these questions to the side, fraud to deny that they exist."[47]

This being the case, some new questions emerge, such as: Given the inherent tendency for different people to develop different cultures, *how can some things be the same everywhere?*[48] Brown delves deeply into possible reasons for the existence of so many human universals, ranging from evolution theory, to innate sex differences, to brain asymmetry, to conservation of energy, to the influence of genes, and more. And the more curious reader will want to read his work in detail.

But it is time to conclude with some reflections on the importance of human universals, their significance, and their implications for our world.

First, we may now legitimately conclude that the undeniable existence of so many universals is a final and firm refutation of the cultural relativism so confidently and misleadingly preached to millions of students for the past century. The news of their existence suggests, at the least, that much of modern anthropology as the study of humankind has been based on wishful thinking, if not a hopeful lie. "Lying for justice" may be a favourite tactic of polemicists and political agitators. But it is unacceptable in scientists.

The encouragement provided by the existence of hundreds of human universals, whereas before we doubted there were any, opens up the possibility that the study of humankind may now proceed from the collection of an endless variety of detail and cultural description to the status of universal science. This goal will be approached through attempts to discover even deeper layers of human universality, much as Chomsky has attempted to do for human languages and as Claude Levi-Strauss did for human myths in the 1960s. For it is surely human universals and the relations between them that are the highest proper object of anthropology, just as the laws of gravity, of inertia, of conservation of energy, and other such laws – not the detailed differences between the particular things affected by those laws – are the proper object of all sciences.

Second, the original political motive for the embrace of moral and cultural relativism that began with Boas, and that continues still to an embarrassing extent with the current linguistic and cultural confusions of postmodernism, was the attempt to diffuse all political power resting on theories of cultural or racial superiority. Fair enough. There is always a danger lurking there. But we have discussed the way this ostensibly humanitarian motive led relativists themselves from problems of logical self-refutation to the moral embarrassment of accepting as normal plainly cruel or evil cultural practices.

Accordingly, the political importance of recognizing these human universals is that political oppression (which is not always well distinguished from the essentials of ordinary authority) may be diffused in a better way – that is, not through a phoney trivialization of universals and a correspondingly false equalization of human differences but through demonstration of what is objectively common to all human beings at all times. In other words, because human universals have now been brought together in one place and laid before us, a firm worldwide knowledge of them ought to make it impossible for any single people or political ideology ever again to succeed with the ruse of its own inherent superiority by denying or trampling on the expression by others of these same universals. It is much harder to convert human beings psychologically or legally into subhuman objects or nonpersons when everyone knows in advance what we most certainly share as expressed through the universals described above, and in this strong sense, the acknowledged existence of human universals ought to give all human rights and obligations a more solid foundation.

Third, the idea that human differences are produced by culture alone and are relative in value has meant to many relativists that other people and their cultures ought to be left alone. They cannot be improved because they are "already civilized." But as we have seen, this frozen-in-history attitude has gotten lots of well-intended anthropologists in trouble with the very people they study. Many of them accuse idealistic Western anthropologists who want to preserve their cultures from contamination by modernity of quarantining them from its benefits – of "putting them in zoos," as the phrase goes. This is understandably seen as a new form of Western intellectual imperialism that too often converts natives into museum pieces for anthropologists. That is the passive side of the coin.

The other is the activist side. Ever since the blank-slate theory of mind became orthodoxy during the Enlightenment, starry-eyed revolutionaries for reason and progress have been disturbing the world with political schemes of forced human improvement. The intellectual force of their arguments has always been that human nature is plastic, so all human differences are created by culture, and that any people can be culturally moulded for "progress." Needless to say, the twentieth century was almost entirely consumed by totalitarian ideologies of progress that rested on this exact formula. The result was unspeakable terror, unspeakable crime, and the most grotesque collectivist systems of human improvement ever invented. But a wider knowledge of universals will eventually give the term "humanity" a stronger sense and hopefully make such abuses of human dignity more difficult.

What deeper meaning do human universals have for human life? Foremost, they are a general guide to human nature. Not all human universals clearly signal a fixed and universal human nature, of course. But most do. That all people use fire, for example, is just a universal human practice. And it does tell us something about a common human biology, the need for warmth, the appetite for tasty and bacteria-free food, even about a profound and universal symbolism of fire, and so on. It is a powerful, but indirect, pointer to human nature. That all people recognize and use the same basic logical concepts, however, is qualitatively different. Such universals point directly to a common mental structure. The same is true for the universal human recognition of basic moral concepts such as right and wrong, true and false, belief in the inherent evil of murder (as distinct from killing enemies), and so on. That peoples so widely separated in time and space who have never had knowledge of or contact with each other in all of history nevertheless share a very large common behavioural and cultural inheritance is simply astonishing. And also very comforting. Human universals so considered must henceforth be seen as the outward lineament of our innate and common human inheritance. We are one people not because we share incommensurable differences – which of course will always be fascinating – but because we are united by real, concrete, and immutable universals.

An eventual worldwide recognition of the existence of so many universals must surely help to bring an end to over three centuries of disastrous assumptions about a supposed human plasticity that has bid fair to ruin us. For in general terms – which is all that need concern us here – we can finally see the shape of human nature. The human species. The human forest. If this new scientific realization (the techniques of science have themselves become a universal mode of knowledge) is to have a meaning beyond science, it should be in serving as an acknowledged – and universal – brake on all future social and political schemes of human perfection that strive to succeed by denying these common and permanent bonds of humanity.

5

The Constants of Nature

Curious people have always wanted to know how the world works. What is the nature of the universe? How did we get here? Why does nature work this way instead of some other way? Whether we look deeply into science, politics, art, or philosophy, we find an amazing range of answers. And although when it comes to the ultimate questions a scientist is no smarter than a poet or a carpenter, it is generally true that throughout history the public view concerning the meaning of existence and the universe tends to follow what philosophers and scientists have told us about the workings of the physical world.[1]

A scientist may say that the material world is strictly determined by cause and effect through the laws of nature. That is why we can fly a spaceship to the moon with pin-point accuracy. Hence there's a lot of determinism in the air. But a philosopher may also say that reality is something made up by our minds, so we cannot know what even the simplest thing is like in itself. We know only our personal human perception of it, which will be different from the perceptions of, say, a fly or a lion. Hence there's a lot of relativism in the air. Yet another (and this is a historically popular view) may say that everything is really a manifestation of God. The universe is God thinking, and we are simply an expression of that. Hence there's a lot of mysticism in the air. Shakespeare famously wrote: "we are such stuff as dreams are made on, and our little life is rounded with a sleep." There is a pretty firm claim that we cannot know anything with certainty and that all that precedes and follows us is darkness. Ordinary people often experience this version when they say, "Was I dreaming, or did you call me yesterday?" One of the great problems of philosophy is how we know for certain that reality, all we experience, is not a dream.

WHAT IS NATURE MADE OF?

We are going to take a little trip through some Western conceptions of nature and the universe that will end in a strange place: our own. For we live at a time of extreme and unusual contradiction in which our public understanding of the cosmos is quite the opposite of the scientific orthodoxy. I say this because most of us believe, are quite certain, that we live in a relativistic universe and that it was Einstein who once and for all proved this to be true. But we will soon see that he never believed this in the way we think he did and sorrowed for the rest of his life that the public took an erroneous and socially damaging meaning from his work. But I am getting ahead of myself.

Past or present, human beings have come up with every fascinating possible explanation for how the world works, although sometimes I think we have been busy with our more precise sciences and instruments rediscovering many of the ideas the ancients developed from naked insight alone. The ancient Greek thinker Thales (600 BC) watched liquid water turn to solid ice in winter, then disappear in steam over his fire, and decided that as nothing can live without it, then all things must come from and return to water. This was not bad, considering water (H_2O) includes a lot of hydrogen, the most prevalent building block of the universe, as well as life-giving oxygen, and ... around 96 per cent of all living bodies is water. In many respects, water, which is a universal solvent, is the most mysterious of all earthly substances, and many have wondered why a fluid absolutely required for biological life behaves – in terms of its unique behaviour when frozen, its surface tension, and its solvent properties, among other things – like no other substance on earth.[2] How all this water got here is another mystery.

Other ancient thinkers said no, the universe really began as a single mass called "the infinite," whence it broke up into the various parts we see, and it simply continues to break up and recombine forever. Interesting, that idea, because many modern "cosmologists," as they are called, are today convinced the universe started from an infinitely compressed point called a "singularity" and then exploded in a "Big Bang" into ... the various parts we see, many of which recombine into huge stars, live, die, and explode ... into particles again. They never explain where the singularity or the laws of physics that enable it to exist came from. That question draws a lot of disturbing silence and makes instant enemies at any cosmology conference.

Pythagoras (580–500 BC) also thought all previous thinkers were wrong (this is a characteristic assumption of many great thinkers). He accused them of being too materialistic. The universe, he said, cannot be understood on the basis of substances like earth, water, air, or any other elements but only on the basis of mathematical laws. Reality is made of numbers. He was pretty clever and noticed that most things in nature, whether musical notes, or the circumference of a circle, or the angles of a triangle, obey universal and constant mathematical laws. Even God cannot make a square circle! So for him, the material world is just a kind of illusory surface of reality beyond which are the elegant but invisible numbers and formulas that control everything material. This, too, is intriguing because most modern scientists now agree with him. The language of nature is expressed in pure mathematics; it is not English, Chinese, mysticism, or magic. It is an abstract language that can be used to describe the operation of all fundamental physical realities in the most exacting detail.

But it soon became apparent to the ancients that the biggest problem with understanding reality is that things *change*. If things were permanent, then change would not be possible. But if all things change, then reality cannot be permanent. For change surely means that something *new* arises out of nothing – an impossibility. So change must be an illusion, a surface appearance. This problem really got ancient thinkers scratching their heads (it is still the central problem of metaphysics, the most foundational branch of philosophy), and to solve it they came up with another pretty good idea. Democritus (460–370 BC) developed an atomic theory simply by deduction, without benefit of experimental data, to argue that the only way permanence and change could be possible at the same time would be if the universe is made up of permanent and unchanging little bits that are always combining in new ways. Then the surface, or appearance, of things could change, but the underlying elements need not. He actually called these little bits "atoms" and spoke of the clever ways they hook together and separate.

Probably the most famous explanation for how the world works was put forth by Plato (427?–347 BC), who argued that everything in the world of experience is actually a corrupted manifestation of a perfect Form, or Idea. We are able to recognize a triangle, say, or a car that we have never seen before only by mentally invoking the form of a triangle or a car. The things we experience somehow correspond to our intuition of their abstract, universal forms, and although forms are always perfect, our real-world triangles, chairs, cars, and people are not. For example, we can *imagine* a perfect circle and write a perfect mathematical formula for one. But we can never draw a perfect circle or make a perfectly circular ball. There will always be minute imperfections. At any rate, Plato seemed to believe that we can know someone we have just met is a human being only because the form of a human being already exists, separately from the matter of which it is comprised in actuality. Don't ask me where it exists. Plato didn't really say, although he implied it exists in some "transcendent" realm beyond the physical. For if such forms did not exist, then how, indeed, would we know that each new person, or car, or triangle we perceive *is* one? Plato's idea of pre-existing forms is a pretty good explanation. We can disagree with it, and probably most philosophers today do, but it is impossible to disprove logically, and that is likely why such an eminent modern philosopher and logician as Bertrand Russell thought it was one of the most successful attempts to explain the nature of reality ever made.[3]

What makes Plato's concept especially interesting today is that it is still very much at work in modern physics, in pure mathematics, and in some branches of law and moral philosophy. Indeed, it is somewhat surprising in our deeply materialistic age to discover that a lot of prominent scientists, such as the late Austrian mathematician Kurt Gödel, were strong self-proclaimed "Platonists," as is Oxford University's Emeritus Professor of Mathematics, Sir Roger Penrose. The latter, a winner of the Dirac Medal, the Einstein Prize, and many other honours (Dirac and Einstein were also Platonists), confesses: "I have made no secret of the fact that my sympathies lie strongly with the Platonistic view that mathematical truth is absolute, external, and eternal, and not based on man-made criteria; and that mathematical objects have a timeless existence of their own, not dependent on human society, nor on particular physical objects."[4]

But Aristotle (384–322 BC), Plato's student, rejected his teacher's idea of separable and universal Forms as illogical and mystical, arguing instead that the human mind can generalize without the need of an ideal world of Forms. If you see one orange, you don't know what it is. But when you see another, you naturally make a mental generalization based on what the two oranges have in common. The Form, for Aristotle, is joined with the matter of the oranges themselves in an act of existence that makes the orange what it is, and the two things appear inseparably in the mind of the observer.[5] So where Aristotle differs from Plato "is in denying that form has any existence apart from the matter in which it exhibits itself"; Aristotle's philosophy, in a nutshell, is that "the Absolute is the universal, but the universal does not exist apart from the particular. Plato supplied the thought of the first clause of the sentence. Aristotle added the last clause, and it is the essential of his philosophy."[6] He also argued that there has to be something more than atoms in things, for billions of separate atoms could result only in chaos. There has to be some kind of internal *design* or final purpose in the very natures of things that is the cause of what they are or become, and this is what makes eggs become chickens, not the other way around. Why do chickens never become eggs? Because although in principle the laws of nature are reversible, their *direction* is not. Nature seems to be based on an inherent one-way design that manifests through an "arrow of time" (not Aristotle's phrase) due to the existence of an inherent end and purpose in all things that exist. Aristotle's views became the philosophical centrepiece of Western civilization before they, too, were eventually overturned, with the result that we have slowly come back to … atoms, of which today we know there are ninety-four naturally occurring kinds, and everything in the universe is made of them.

HOW DOES NATURE WORK? MODERN SCIENCE AND THE MECHANICS OF MOTION

Strolling across the park on a sunny day, I am startled to hear the voice of a friend: "Hey Bill – catch!" Turning just in time, I see a football coming toward me, arcing darkly through the blue sky. Without time to think, I quicken a few steps and leap for the catch. It feels good. The perfect catch.

My friend laughs afterward. Actually, he says, "It was the perfect throw!"

Moving on, I ask myself what actually happened back there? How do we explain something as simple as a ball flying through the air? Most of us try to explain this with what little we remember of high school physics. But how was a flying ball seen, interpreted, and explained by people in the past? What makes it go up into the air, travel so smoothly, and fall right into my hands instead of heading off into space, splitting into pieces, dropping straight down, or even heading off into the woods on its own?

An ancient mystic (or a California hippie) might have said the ball is animated by spirits that carry it forward to an expectant soul. The catcher and the ball are connected by emotional intent. Aristotle argued that all physical things are naturally at rest until a force or impetus comes along to make them move, such as the arm of the thrower. He thought there was a measurable *quantity* of impetus imparted to the ball that wears out, as anyone can see, because it eventually slows down, falls to the ground, and stops moving. It is part of the *nature* of a ball – and of any other moving thing – to come to rest. Aristotle's view of motion predominated until the seventeenth century, and if most of us had never heard of modern physical theories, that is probably how we would still explain it. But his thinking was limited in two important ways. First, he saw only *qualities* in things and, second, for some reason he never thought to subject his ideas to experiment. That was to come much later.

THE DISCOVERY OF EARTHLY CONSTANTS OF NATURE

During the Renaissance a daring and outspoken Galileo set out to prove Aristotle wrong not by argument, as so many frustrated scholars had tried before, but by simple physical experiment.[7] He argued that in themselves things have no "nature" and are not naturally at rest. Things have no preferred state, or condition. If they are already at rest, they will tend to stay at rest until something else comes along to move them. And if they are already in motion, they will stay in motion until something (such as air friction, the ground, or hands that catch) stops them. Galileo was revealing the first really modern law, or constant, of earthly physical mechanics, and he did so by substituting his own law of *inertia* for Aristotle's law of *impetus*. He showed that contrary to Aristotle, a thing in motion will continue to move uniformly in a straight line at a constant rate of speed unless impeded by another material object or force. Galileo especially enjoyed proving laws that seem contrary to common sense. He delighted in showing skeptics that a light penny and a heavy cannonball will fall at the very same speed. And more: although a ball and a feather, say, will fall at very different rates due to air resistance, they will fall at exactly the same speed in a vacuum tube. At first, no one could believe this, and Galileo's demonstration was considered astonishing. It still astonishes modern students who see it for the first time. He was revealing yet another abstract law of earthly physics (the constant speed and rate of acceleration in a vacuum of all things toward the centre of the earth), and he had done this *by removing part of everyday nature* (the air). Here was another constant of earthly physics that had previously been hidden from human beings. As one modern writer puts it, suggesting such thoughts required a remarkable intellectual impudence, and understanding them called for an even more audacious act of abstraction.[8] For in the end, Galileo was showing how perceptions and assumptions can deceive us about the way nature actually works. The key step away from the standard ancient view, however, was his argument that the football did what it was impelled to do by reason of physical forces external to it – the throwing arm and gravity – not because of some internal quality.

The implications were astonishing. For if such hidden universal laws can be revealed by simple experiment, then how much else of what we believe to be true is actually false? Behind (above? beyond?) the physical world we see, is there an entire framework of mathematical formulae, of constants of nature, that has always been there, waiting to be revealed by the human mind? And if so, what is their significance and connection to each other? Galileo took us from the ancient more or less magical idea that things have inherent properties peculiar to them to the idea that the physical world is purely mechanical. Things are moved by other things. It would take another genius (some say he was the greatest scientific genius of all time) to take us from the visible world of mechanical forces to the idea of a world of invisible forces controlling – absolutely controlling – all ordinary physical things in the universe, everywhere, instantly, and from inconceivable distances.

NEWTON AND THE FIRST UNIVERSAL CONSTANTS

Newton was born in 1642, the year that Galileo died, and finished his undergraduate work at Cambridge University at age twenty-three. Soon thereafter he retired to his mother's farm at Woolsthorpe to escape a plague that was ravaging England, and there, in the mere space of sixteen months, in a burst of intellectual passion, curiosity, and determination, this last of the great self-taught European geniuses single-handedly invented the calculus in mathematics (just as, unbeknownst to him, the German Leibniz was also doing), discovered the universal law of gravity, and developed a particle theory of light.[9] In the solitude of his study this very young man was busy changing the world of science forever through the solitary power of mind and imagination. These achievements alone would have deeply satisfied the longing for success of most men. But as it turned out, Newton was but laying the rough groundwork for his *Principia* (not published until 1687), in which he outlined a "system of the world" built on a few precisely defined universal physical constants of nature, which, as David Berlinski writes in his engaging biography *Newton's Gift*, continue to "explain virtually every aspect of material behavior that is larger than the atom and smaller than the universe."[10]

In this journey from Aristotle, to Galileo, to Newton, what we see is a progressively more abstract movement of the human mind in its search for universal causes. From Aristotle's certainty that things had their own qualitative natures, or internal laws, we leapt to Galileo's proofs that earthly things behave in lawful and predictable ways according to the visible material forces exerted on them externally by other things, to Newton's astonishing discovery that the physical cause of things is not other things but invisible forces. Still more astonishingly, these forces could be formulated in abstract mathematical laws that govern not just the earth but the whole universe, even though, as Berlinski puts it, "the laws of nature by which nature is explained are not themselves a part of nature. No physical theory predicts their existence nor explains their power. They exist beyond space and time; they gain purchase by an act of the imagination and not observation, they are the tantalizing traces in matter of an intelligence that has so far hidden itself in symbols."[11] And this fact about the transcendent reality of the laws of physics holds true, as we shall see, even for the aspects of nature that Newton could not have studied: such as the so-called wave equations that govern the infinitesimal workings of the subatomic particle world, right up to the field equations that hold true for the unthinkably remote deep space governed by Einstein's theories.

But it all began with the apple, and it is worthwhile to revisit just how Newton became the first human being to realize that the force that governs the fall of an apple to the ground is the same universal force controlling the earth in its orbit around the sun, the moon's orbit around the earth, the tides of the oceans, and indeed the motions of all the planets and their satellites in their law-governed march through the heavens.

At the moment Newton saw the famous apple fall in the orchard (not on his head, as legend has it), he wondered "why should it not go sideways or upwards, but constantly to the earth's centre?" At that very instant he simply dropped the ancient explanation that the earth is the natural resting place for all falling things that naturally come to rest, and due to some amazing flash of insight concluded "their must be a drawing power in matter." By which he meant, an attracting force. And if that is so, he reasoned, then as all things are made of matter, they all must have this force in some degree. The earth must draw, or pull, the apple, just as the apple must pull the earth. A mere apple pulling the earth? What an audacious thought, indeed! And more: "if matter draws matter," he went on to speculate, then "it must be in proportion to its quantity," or to what we now call the mass of each and every thing. At

that very moment Newton took a huge leap forward from a mere observation of what everyone had thought was a natural *quality* in things
(they always fall down) to the idea that there is some abstract law of nature governing the relations between the *quantities* of things. He meant
not just all things on earth – Galileo's province – but all things in the
whole universe, and this without regard to any of their sensual qualities
such as size, smell, colour, or shape. Looking back, we can see that Newton was issuing a new "manifesto of cosmic interconnectedness."[12] By a
pure act of the imagination, he had unveiled *the first universal constant of
nature*, and once he had this general concept, he was able to refine the
law that today enables a precise calculation of the gravitational attraction between all material bodies from planets and stars, to a small peb-
ble hurtling through space, to the largest collections of galaxies.*

In a single stroke of the imagination, Newton left behind the old mechanical view of nature – that things move other things by *contact* – and
replaced it with an idea he knew would be considered absurd. For "it
was precisely the concept of *action at a distance* that first tantalized and
then captivated Newton's imagination ... Gravity was ... not a *contact*
force at all, but an impalpable presence in the universe whose nature
was hidden but whose form was revealed in symbols."[13] And more, the
nature of Newton's gravity – a force that controls and binds all material
in the universe at all times, in all places, directly, at a distance, and at
once – remains a mystery still. An irreducible mystery. It cannot be explained by appeal to any other forces or aspects of nature. If it were to
stop, even for one second, everything in the universe would fly apart,
just as each human being and every elephant, every dog and fish, all

---

* Newton's universal law of gravity states that every material object attracts every
other material object with a force that is proportional to their masses and inversely proportional to the square of the distance between them. Simply put,
this means that the greater the mass of an object, the greater its pulling power,
which rapidly becomes weaker with distance. For example, if we know the force
of gravity for two objects 100 miles apart, this force weakens not to just half at
200 miles but to one-quarter of the original force. Newton's formula is written:
$F = Gm_1m_2/r^2$. The symbol F designates force, m the masses of two objects, r the
distance between them (squared), and G the universal force of gravity, which is
the same everywhere and for everything. Some modifications have been made
to his formula to explain the behaviour of matter around black holes and at
near the speed of light, but the basic formula remains intact for all aspects of
the everyday world.

the water in the oceans, all rocks, toads, and cars would instantly fly off
the earth into space at about 1,000 miles an hour. People in jumbo jets
would suddenly find themselves heading very rapidly into deep space.
As Berlinski sums it up: "We are acquainted with gravity through its effects; we understand gravity by means of its mathematical form. Beyond
this, we understand nothing ... This was true when Newton wrote; it is
true today."[14]

Newton was elated and never doubted he was discovering the veiled
mathematical language of God. So much did he venerate the cosmos as
God's handiwork and gift that he eventually abandoned all physics for
biblical studies, hoping in the millions of words he wrote on this topic to
unlock theological mysteries even more profound and stupendous than
any mere physical mystery. This is often dismissed as a quirk of his nature. But then it comes as a bit of a surprise, in view of the dogmatically
secular training of most modern cosmologists, to see that many of them
are being forced by their own discoveries to admit to something like the
same feelings about final purposes as Newton's – although more often
than not they energetically strive to avoid the dreaded G-word.

In preparation for *Cosmos, Bios, Theos* (1992), a book on this theme,
the editors sent a handful of questions, including one asking for
"thoughts on the concept of God and on the existence of God," to sixty
scientists of international reputation, among whom were two dozen
Nobel Prize winners.[15] The answers were surprising: the physicists were
far more likely to say that nature and the universe are here for a reason and by design (many believe they were created by God) than
those in the biological sciences, whose answers were grounded in the
same sort of bottomless materialism that has served as a creation myth
for secular science since the nineteenth century. This is interesting in
itself, as it is physics that underlies biology, not the other way around,
atoms and all the smaller particles being more fundamental than cells
and genes. One explanation given for this sharp difference in responses is that biology may be reduced as far as the certainty level of
cellular and genetic material and the molecule. But it stops there and,
as yet, can go no further, else it enters the realm of physics. However,
although the certainties of physics were once deemed as determinate
as those of biology, physics has been shaken up over the past century
by the very large and the very small: by the relativity work of Einstein
leading to the current consensus that there was indeed a Big Bang
creation of the universe some 13.7 billion years ago (whereas before
this, everyone thought the universe was in a steady state and had

existed forever); and by discoveries in the particle world of atomic physics, which has come up against what looks like an ultimate barrier to understanding the very smallest bits of nature. Modern physics has thus been squeezed between the inexplicable flash of creation from nothing on one side (an offence to logic, which has always said that "nothing can come from nothing") and the darkness of human ignorance concerning the fundamental behaviour of matter on the other. This comes very close to evoking Shakespeare's line about how "our little lives are rounded with a sleep."

WHAT EINSTEIN DID TO NEWTON

Perhaps no subject is more misunderstood by the public than what Einstein actually did, said, and meant by what he said, and it will be my purpose here to sort that out because in the sense that public philosophies tend ultimately to be shaped by the public's understanding (or misunderstanding) of physical nature, we need to answer a question all-important to the message of this book: does the modern public, still so adamantly certain that *everything is relative* and that Einstein was the genius of physics who proved this to be so, have any idea what he actually meant? It would appear not. Western publics, for some reason yet to be elucidated, have swallowed whole a media-manufactured spin, or myth, about the "relativity" implied by Einstein's discoveries and have then allowed this to shape their view of nature and human nature, and their own behaviour. More's the pity, as we shall see.

Newton's explanation of the workings of nature still explains with high accuracy all physical motion in nature for things larger than the atom up to cosmic things that are large beyond imagination. But to venture beyond the ordinary Newtonian world of everyday life into really *deep space,* or into what is now called the *quantum* world, in order to study the behaviour of tiny particles is to enter two (or more) very strange realms indeed. Nevertheless, each of these worlds is governed by certain well-defined laws and constants of nature, and as we shall see momentarily, neither would be what it is (nor would we be here to observe and talk about all this) if the constants of nature were different – *in any degree* – from what they are.

The modern telescope and the spectroscopic analysis of light have enabled modern scientists to examine deep space more closely and reliably than anyone had ever thought possible. We need to remind ourselves that it wasn't until as recently as the 1920s that Edwin Hubble (after whom the amazing Hubble Space Telescope was named) proved that there was something *more* than our own Milky Way galaxy out there! Some of the faint whitish-blue smudges that I can easily see with my own backyard telescope, and that I know from their spiral shapes are other galaxies so many light years away, were then thought to be nearby stellar gas clouds. Back then – and it is not that far back – everyone assumed the Milky Way was infinite, unmoving, and in a steady state. Newton had said so. So the very thought that there existed other galaxies – more than a hundred billion of them as we now know, each with about a hundred billion stars or more – came as a huge and sobering shock. And to make things even more shocking, this was followed by Hubble's announcement that the whole business was expanding from the original "Big Bang" (a derisive term made instantly popular by the brilliant if maverick British astronomer Fred Hoyle, who didn't believe it was true) at an enormous speed measured by Hubble's Constant.[16] And then came the news, horrible to contemplate, that the universe could one day – well, in billions of years – collapse in a "Big Crunch." Needless to say, when it came to the mathematics and physics of big things moving at enormous speeds, these discoveries threw Newton's laws of space, time, and gravity into disarray.

What about the world of tiny things? In 1900 Max Planck proved that all forms of energy such as heat, light, and electricity, which most people think of as flowing in a steady stream, in fact move about in discrete energy packets he called "quanta." He was the man who discovered the exact relation between a quantum's energy and its radiation frequency, now called Planck's Constant. Of course, we don't perceive energy as parcelled out this way, just as we don't see the individual frames in a moving film. The film moves so fast that the scene seems to flow in time. But that is an illusion of perception. Energy, Planck showed, seems to flow the same way. By then, physicists had already accepted the ancient theory that solid matter is made up of discrete bits called atoms, and just as atomic theory was developed to explain the behaviour of *matter*, quantum theory was developed to explain the behaviour of *energy*. And more – it eventually showed that matter and energy are interchangeable. The combination of new deep space and quantum discoveries that could not be explained by Newtonian principles soon called for a new theory of space, time, and gravity, and Einstein aimed to supply it.

The most famous problem with Newton's numbers was his idea that the universe is infinite and has always existed. For if gravity operates everywhere, as he had shown, then the force of gravity would also be infinite, and ... everything would collapse into the centre, wouldn't it? Not surprisingly, Newton had anticipated this objection, arguing that in an infinite universe, gravity would pull in all directions at once because infinity has no centre. The centre is everywhere. This was a very clever, if wrong, answer. Newton was trying to solve the problem of infinite gravity by spreading it over infinite space. In the light of modern telescopic and radiation observations, however, this did not compute.

And there was a second problem. Newton had talked about the existence of absolute time and absolute space, as though both were separate things. For him, absolute time is something that has a nature of its own and flows equably, as he put it, without relation to anything. What he called absolute space also has its own nature that remains always similar and immovable, without relation to anything external.[17] He assumed absolutes of space and time as fixed reference points because he couldn't tolerate the idea that God would ever create a relativistic, or everything-is-nowhere, universe. Einstein criticized both notions as "shadowy concepts" and set about replacing them.

But he fretted. Black holes could not be explained with Newton's laws, nor the mysterious behaviour of quanta, and far from every thing rushing *toward* every other thing, Hubble had observed the opposite: all things were rushing *away* from each other. Following the trend of a few colleagues and predecessors, Einstein began to wonder whether some of these problems arose because in Newton's theories, time, space, and gravity, as well as matter and energy, were all conceived as separate. Readers may consult books listed in the notes to try to figure out the details of this now-famous dilemma.[18] Suffice it to say here that Einstein wanted to create a more unified theory of the universe that would eliminate these mechanical difficulties. And he mostly succeeded. His Special Theory of Relativity (1905) showed that time and space are not separate, as Newton (and everyone else) had assumed, but closely linked and that the speed of light is a fundamental *constant* of nature and the ultimate speed in the universe. His General Theory of Relativity (1915) further linked gravity, space, and time into a seamless whole. In so doing, he was putting the world back together in a kind of second cosmological revolution, showing that a single physical reality runs from earth to the farthest stars. In a way, as one writer put it, with Einstein's cosmology we became once again "unified with the spirit of the universe."[19] He got rid of Newton's imaginary absolutes of space and time and replaced them with real-world measurable absolutes, such as the speed of light and a number of famous – and universal and absolute – equations relating all aspects of the cosmos. Einstein, with his famous Principle of Covariance (quite contrary to what is believed) *wanted to ensure that different observers of the universe would observe the laws of nature and physics operating in exactly the same way, no matter where they were located and no matter how they were moving.* Modern physics has followed this lead. Its aim is to describe nature and the universe according to various depersonalized constants and laws of nature in a way that transcends all human dimension and according to principles that hold for all observers.[20]

Einstein was aware, of course, that in getting rid of certain questions about Newton's infinite universe, he had replaced them with even deeper questions about why and how the universe came from nothing and about how it will end. Newton's universe was mechanical, but it was also peaceful, static, and eternal. Einstein's is more organic and integrated, but is evolving toward its own eventual death. Of interest, too, is the fact that because Einstein had settled on a finite universe that in theory could now collapse under the pull of its own gravity (but which Hubble had shown was in fact doing the opposite), he had to invent a mysterious "cosmological constant" (which he called by the Greek letter Lambda) to explain that some mysterious repulsing force must exist to counteract all that gravity. He died regretting that he had to "plug" the numbers, as accountants say when they make up a financial entry to balance the books. He had committed Newton's sin of trying to justify his theory with an unprovable idea. But was it? Ironically, his Lambda idea is back again, under the guise of "dark matter" and "dark energy." The story is not over, and mysteries abound.

Nevertheless, Einstein's achievement was to have successfully conceived of a finite and unified holistic universe completely embraced within a single theory, and every real-world experiment set up to test his theories has thus far proved true. We have a far better understanding of deep space in a finite universe. We also understand quantum behaviour – a little too well, some might say. For while Einstein did manage to unite matter and energy with his famous $E = mc^2$ equation,*

---

* The equation basically says that mass and energy are different forms of the same thing. If we think of something like radiaton – say, a small mass of uranium that always gives off energy – this does not seem so strange. Some types of matter give off energy all the time, and this radiation is actually a kind of sprayed mass. Others – a log in a fireplace, for example – hold on to their energy until something such as heat causes it to unleash. Then in a kind of chain reaction there is a continuous conversion of mass into energy. The log becomes ash as the room heats up by the radiated energy of this conversion. In essence, Einstein showed that all forms of ordinary matter are just condensed and cooled stored energy. Theoretically, if we could figure out how to do it, a single kilogram of matter could be converted into 25 billion kilowatt-hours of energy – enough to heat an industrialized nation for several weeks!

the atomic bomb was an awful demonstration that this theory, too, was true. But that is another subject.[21]

"RELATIVITY" — THAT TROUBLESOME AND MISLEADING WORD

Although Einstein eventually surrendered to the public's misunderstanding of the unfortunate word "relativity" in connection with his work, it was with great regret and a sad capitulation to the growing media promotion of a term that he realized had in the end escaped his control. He regretted having used the word for the rest of his life, especially when he saw how it was seized upon to justify all sorts of unprincipled moral and social practices. Perhaps one of the very strangest examples was in 1916 when his friend Friedrich Adler assassinated the Austrian prime minister for purportedly violating Adler's freedoms. At his trial, this pathetic fellow attempted to defend himself by invoking "the principle of relativity." Einstein was shocked and disheartened. He had no sooner put down his pen than his poorly understood "New Physics" was being used as an excuse for radical politics — and murder! He considered it the saddest of ironies that although he was a man who had strived his entire life to reveal the universal constants of nature, his name was so easily joined everywhere to the idea of moral relativism.

WHAT EINSTEIN REALLY SAID ABOUT RELATIVITY

"Special relativity" is probably the greatest misnomer in the history of science.[22]

> Tony Rothman, *Everything's Relative,*
> *and Other Fables from Science and Technology* (2003)

For the record, Einstein had not used the term "theory of relativity" in his original 1905 paper. He had referred only to the "principle of relativity" (a term he may have lifted from a famous 1904 speech given in Louisiana by the French scientist Henri Poincaré, who almost beat Einstein to the theory).[23] By this phrase, Einstein meant that because all motion must be relative to something, there is no absolute standard of rest, so the fundamental laws of nature themselves *must be the same everywhere,* whether you are standing firmly on the ground or on a train moving at 200 kilometres per hour.[24]

As for "relativity theory"? That phrase was first used by Max Planck in 1906 and took immediate hold in the public imagination, even though Einstein by then very much disliked the term. By 1908 Einstein's former teacher Hermann Minkowski, who had initially proposed many of the key features of the final theory to Einstein (who was astonished by the theory and initially dismissed most of it – including many of the ideas for which he later became famous – as "superfluous erudition"), also disliked the misleading term "relativity" and urged that the phrase "invariant postulates" would be more accurate. But still no luck. Another man concerned about the descriptive dishonesty of the term was the mathematician Felix Klein, who proposed that Einstein's theory be called "The Theory of Absolutes."[25] But by now it was far too late. If Klein's version had taken, we would today be discussing "Albert Einstein and his famous Theory of Absolutes," which would at least have been closer to the truth of the theory – and we must surely wonder what effect *that* would have had on the public mind! At any rate, Einstein himself, so wearied eventually by the public misconstrual of his life's highest achievement, had by 1911 given up on trying to defend his meaning of the term, but henceforth whenever he used it he always put it in quotation marks. The historical fact is that despite his egalitarian social and political ideals, for the rest of his life Einstein scorned the idea that his physics was connected with his politics, for as one observer put it, "any suggestion that his theory showed all 'viewpoints' are equally good [ran] directly contrary to the entire ethos of his search for law-like rationality in an objective physical world."[26]

Nevertheless, as late as the 1920s, when nonsensical controversies connecting "relativity" and social and moral behaviour were growing apace in a world tormented by the shock of World War I, many concerned scientists tried once again to propose that Klein's "Theory of Absolutes" replace the misleading relativity phrase.[27] But it was no use. Ruminating on the social and moral damage of his theory, Einstein protested that he should have been a simple watchmaker instead of a physicist and complained by 1929 that "the meaning of relativity has been widely misunderstood ... philosophers play with the word like a child with a doll ... it [relativity] does not mean that everything in life is relative."[28] In a 1934 speech in Amsterdam, he again stipulated that "The four-dimensional space of the special theory of relativity is just as rigid and absolute as Newton's space."[29] Indeed, Einstein's theory in fact absolutized some of the measures that had been left relative in Newton's theory.

One of the reasons for the enthusiastic public and media promotion of these misunderstandings was that the Western world at the turn of the twentieth century was simply hungry for a philosophy justifying relativism – and moral relativism, in particular. In the arts, sciences, and philosophy, a long and superficially staid Victorian tradition had been generating various schools of relativism all along, and this trend was now coming to a head.[30] From Paul Cezanne forward, we begin to see the old solid forms and feelings of humanity dissolving and fracturing, most notably through Impressionist, Symbolist, and Dada movements in painting and literature. Stream of consciousness writing by such as Virginia Woolf and James Joyce (and the millions of undergraduates who swooned to try it themselves) seemed to reveal a deeper truth about a socially and morally fragmented reality. By then, psychology and philosophy had already fled the ancient verities for theories such as associationism and pragmatism, as we saw in chapter 1. Then came the shocking brutalities of World War I to shatter all presumption. Europe was soon rife with ideological fervour and with calls for political absolutism, so, as we saw in the prevous chapter, social activists such as the anthropologist Franz Boas began desperately promoting moral and cultural relativism as an antidote. In the last analysis, people were ready for relief from what they saw as a failed system of rigid moral standards and eager to embrace the first respectable theory of relativism that came along. So whatever Einstein actually said or meant didn't matter. He had created an intellectually attractive vessel misnamed "relativity" that was morally attractive to the public imagination, and people immediately poured into it whatever they wanted to see there. As *Time* magazine, that final repository of so many public misconceptions, put it as recently as 1979 (in an advertisement meant to attract readers to the magazine): "EVERYTHING IS RELATIVE." *Time* declared that "in the cool beautiful language of mathematics, Einstein demonstrated that we live in a world of relative values."[31] That is still all most people want to believe about the subject. They think that if Einstein, the smartest man alive, said so, it must be true! But of course, he didn't say it. He said quite the opposite.

Einstein had always insisted that "belief in an external world independent of the perceiving subject is the basis of all natural science."[32] He knew that the extreme effects he had revealed would never be perceived in the ordinary human world, and as one contemporary physics writer put it, as plainly as possible: "the fact that the theory actually hinges on a few key invariants being preserved ... is quite the *opposite* of how the theory is commonly presented."[33] And another writes that Einstein's deepest ambition was "the elaboration of a cosmic view in which physical reality was a totality of consistently interacting things, an absolute in the sense that its existence was not relative to any observer, and ... the laws in question had to remain as invariant as the universe is invariant."[34]

In the end, Einstein's physics was also his theology. In addition to his theories about the cosmology of deep space, he made fundamental contributions to the quantum theory of tiny particles. (It was he, after all, who first put forward the "photon" particle theory to explain the strange behaviour of light.) But he could never accept – in fact, he vigorously rejected – the probabilistic and relativistic uncertainties of the quantum theory to which his own theory had led. For he was absolutely certain, as he said in a letter of 1926 to Max Born, that the "Old One," as he referred to the God he imagined, "does not play dice."[35] His deity was not the interventionist God of Abraham and Isaac "but something more complex and abstract ... the embodiment of a beautiful and economical set of physical laws"[36] – by which he certainly meant *absolute* physical laws. And for Einstein, the presence of such absolutes has a meaning. For he was convinced, as he explained to a student in 1936, that "everyone who is seriously involved in the pursuit of science becomes convinced that a spirit is manifest in the laws of the universe – a spirit vastly superior to that of man."[37]

So much for the sorry story of "relativity" in physics.*

---

* An interesting book by Emile Meyerson, *La déduction relativiste* (Paris: Payot, 1925), offers lucid insights into the new theory of relativity and its reception by Einstein's contemporaries. (The following quotations are my translations from chapter 5, "Relativism, Theory of the Real," 60–87.) On the matter of the supposed interdependence of phenomena, Arthur Eddington states that "Mr. Einstein succeeded in separating more completely than has ever been done before, the role of nature and the role of the observer in observable phenomena." And P. Langevin writes that "physics, by means of the principle of relativity, has been able to affirm the existence of a reality independent of all systems of reference which are in motion with respect to each other." In a pithy phrasing, Meyerson writes that "the principle of relativity is, truth to say, the principle of the non-relativity of the real." G. Moch then adds that "the whole problem of relativity consisted in maintaining the laws of physics without regard to the fact of the observer's change [of position] ... which comes down to affirming the existence of laws in themselves, which is to say the reality of a world of relations that exists without the support of, and independent of, human consciousness." And finally, Meyerson again: "the reality of the theory of relativity is, with certainty, an ontological absolute, a true being in itself, more absolute and ontological than the ordinary things of common sense and of pre-Einsteinian physics."

WHAT AND WHERE ARE
THE CONSTANTS OF NATURE?

Now that we have, I hope, gotten rid of the idea that everything in physics is relative and, as hopefully, salvaged Einstein's reputation as the mistaken culprit of modern relativism, we can turn to the modern physical understanding of nature. To be blunt, this understanding is all about underlying universals and constants, without which none of the hard sciences, all of which rest on physics, could be performed, even for a minute.

There are a finite number of constants of nature governing everything in the universe from the very great to the very small, from star factories at the farthest reaches of space to the tiniest packets of vanishing energy on earth. Constants may be expressed in "dimensions" using some human yardstick, such as kilometres or miles per second, as we do in measuring the speed of light in a vacuum, or earthly light years, or ERGS for energy. The "pure" constants of nature, however, are "dimensionless" and are most often expressed as ratios between two or more other constants. They are called pure because they express what many physicists consider a mysterious relationship between their constituent parts in abstract mathematical language. The "fine-structure constant" is an example to be explained momentarily.

All of the constants of nature listed here (there are many more in the appendix to this book) are pertinent and standard to the work of physicists internationally. While some of them occasionally become subjects of dispute, this has mostly to do with arguments over accuracy and precision of instruments, not over their real existence. The word "real," as we shall see, is itself a matter of contention and mystery in physics when it comes to constants of nature in particular, for they have no physical reality in themselves but nonetheless function as precise laws of nature.

THE FOUR FORCES OF NATURE

"As far as we know," writes Paul Davies, "all the various natural phenomena are controlled by just four fundamental forces."[38] In other words, underlying all the other constants of nature and all the workings of the entire cosmos are four absolutely fundamental universal forces:

1 Gravity (G): Because most of us have trouble jumping more than a foot or so off the ground, it is hard to believe that gravity, which

controls whole galaxies – indeed, the whole universe – is actually the weakest of these four forces. But it becomes a very great force when the mass is great. That is why a champion long jumper can jump 28 feet on earth but over 100 feet on the moon (that is, if the jumper could get out of a moon suit long enough to accomplish this without freezing or burning to death).

2 Electromagnetism (*e*): We used to think that electricity and magnetism were two separate forces. But they were combined when it was discovered that all magnetism, from the plastic rod we rub with rabbit fur in science class to the Van Allen Belt hundreds of miles above us, is generated by moving electrical charges. *e* is a universal constant that decides, absolutely, the strength of all electromagnetic effects. It is always attached to certain subatomic particles like the electron and the proton. The electrical charge on these particles is always the same (1.60×10^{-19}) and is a universal constant of nature.

3 The weak nuclear force (g_w): This force is responsible for rates of radiation, atomic decay, and the transformation of atomic particles like neutrons into protons. Such transformations play a big role in the production of common elements such as iron, helium, carbon, and uranium in stellar explosions.

4 The strong nuclear force (g_s): This force holds together atomic particles in the atom. Without it, atoms would all blow themselves apart. It operates only inside the atom and is very strong at incredibly short distances (like a trillionth of a metre or less!) but falls to zero after that range. It plays an explosive role in the making of atomic energy – and bombs.

THE FUTURE OF THE FORCES AND THE GRAND UNIFIED THEORY

What is the future of the four forces? Most physicists dream of uniting them into a single Grand Unified Theory (GUT). Underlying this ambition are two beliefs. First, the belief that forces that play together must stay together in some as yet hidden but ultimately simple way, yet to be revealed (the idea of four *independent* theories for forces that are essential to each other is offensive).

So although far from overtly religious, the most famous physicists and cosmologists have always used euphemisms to say that their theories – and the GUT when it is discovered – are already, as Newton was certain, a slice of the language of God. Or "the Old One," as Einstein called him, repeatedly. Even Stephen Hawking, the British physicist and Lucasian Chair of Mathematics at Cambridge University (Newton's former chair!), who has spent his whole life trying to create a theory of the universe that does *not* require a creator, says that when we discover the GUT, we will "know the mind of God." He is not saying that we will one day recognize God strolling by but will actually know His *mind*! This is a version of the Pythagorean idea that the mathematical numbers that explain and control the universe are themselves the mental activity of God. What almost all physicists share is a conviction that the GUT, when it is *revealed* (they are almost all Platonists and consider themselves to be discovering, or revealing, and not inventing, the laws), must be simple, mathematically expressed, and beautiful. Ugly theories are unacceptable.

The second belief is that beauty plays a profound role in the elaboration and final expression of all correct theories. The British physicist and Nobel Prize winner Paul Dirac became famous for making accurate predictions about the nature of the physical world solely according to the beauty of his mathematical theories. In the 1930s he predicted with pure (and beautiful) mathematics alone that anti-electron particles had to exist. And lo and behold, they were shortly thereafter discovered by experiment. This discovery certainly bolstered his belief in the primacy of beauty in one's equations. He believed that if equations are always based on sound insight and beauty, then reality will eventually be found to fit the theory – so much so that he once scolded Werner Heisenberg and dismissed his basic equations because they lacked beauty. By "beauty," physicists mean *harmony, simplicity, and symmetry*. Einstein echoed this belief in all his own work, and recently, physicist John Wheeler exalted that "the beauty in the laws of physics is the fantastic simplicity that they have ... What is the ultimate mathematical machinery behind it all? That's surely the most beautiful of all."[39] Early in the twentieth century Sir James Jeans, in the same vein, concluded that "The Great Architect seems to be a mathematician" and opined that the universe seems more like a great thought than a great machine. And 1965 Nobelist Richard Feynman in *The Character of Physical Law* wrote that "to those who do not know mathematics, it is difficult to get across a real feeling as to the beauty, the deepest beauty, of nature."[40] What all are seeking is the final, ultimate beauty from which physical reality unfolds in a lawful and flawless sequence.

Table 5.1
Four of the fundamental constants of nature

Name	Symbol	Numerical Value (SI units)
Planck's Constant	h	6.63×10^{-34}
Speed of light	c	3.00×10^{8}
Newton's gravitational constant	G	6.67×10^{-11}
Electromagnetic fine-structure constant	Alpha	7.30×10^{-3}

Source: Paul Davies, *The Accidental Universe* (Cambridge, UK: Cambridge University Press, 1982), table 3, 39. See the appendix for the rest of the fundamental constants of nature.

A LOOK AT SOME LARGE AND SMALL CONSTANTS OF NATURE AND THEIR EFFECTS

In a world saturated with misleading relativity talk, it may be fruitful to see just how precise and nonrelative some of these constants of nature are, to ask about their importance to the existence of our specific kind of universe and to organic life, and then to ask a few questions about what seems to be their astonishingly coincidental existence, for the probability of all these constants occurring together by chance in such a finely tuned way is considered by most physicists to be vanishingly remote.

In a remarkably clear exposition in *The Accidental Universe* of what is otherwise a very complicated subject, Paul Davies begins with the astonishing fact (for it did not have to be so; the universe could have been random and chaotic, after all) that "nature displays a hierarchy of structure. From the smallest known constituents of the atom to the large-scale arrangement of the galaxies, we observe systems with characteristic organization and size, each level of structure interlocking with the others in a highly ordered way."[41] Why is this so? It is because the entire universe is controlled by constants of nature such as those listed above. Which is to say that constants of nature produce constant and certain consequences.

And the very scale of nature considered in this way must be appreciated. Bill Bryson, in his engaging popular book *A Short History of Nearly Everything*, writes that a typical atom has a diameter of one ten-millionth of a millimetre! ... and is mostly space![42] He asks us to imagine that the walls of an average living room represent the whole of an atom with its electrons spinning around out by the walls. The nucleus of the atom, which comprises almost all the atom's weight, would be like a speck in the middle of the room, and between it and the electrons ... is only space. Consider that. And then try to understand that such atoms combine to form molecules. Then ask: how many molecules are there in, say, only two grams of hydrogen? The number is equivalent to the number of popcorn kernels required to cover the United States to a depth of 9 miles, or the number of cups full of water in the Pacific Ocean, or of soft drink cans that evenly stacked would cover the earth to a depth of 200 miles. An equivalent number of American pennies would make everyone on earth a trillionaire!

Even more spectacular is to grasp that it is only the charges of atomic particles that constitute the "hardness" of material things. Without the repulsing negatively charged fields of electrons, atoms have so much space that they would just pass through each other. *We* would pass through each other as we walk down the street! When we sit on a chair, we do not actually sit *on* the chair. The charges of our bodies and of the atomic particles of which the chair is made repel each other so strongly that we have the feeling of something hard and solid. And it stops us from passing through it to fall on the floor (which repels our body in the same way). But with an instrument fine enough, we would see that our skin is actually separated from the "surface" of the chair – we levitate above it – by about one angstrom (a hundred-millionth of a centimetre).

G

Newton's inverse square law of gravity controls the falling apple in an orderly and mathematically predictable way, as it controls our annual journey around the sun, the formation of our galaxy and of other galaxies billions of light years away, and beyond that even the gravitational bonding of many galaxies into "superclusters" of galaxies. *G* was modified by Einstein to explain extreme situations such as black holes, but it remains valid in his theory for all other mass phenomena of the universe. Although Newton knew nothing of the atomic world, his inverse square law operates there also and describes the force holding atomic particles together. (If the distance between a proton and an electron is doubled, the attraction between the two falls to a quarter of its strength.) Indeed, *G* is a constant of nature integral to the lawful motion of the largest cosmic bodies billions of light years away and to the nucleus of an atom a thousand-billionth of a centimetre in size. How precise and constant is the inverse square law of gravity? That is, how precisely is mass proportional to the force of gravity as the law specifies? Most recently, the American physicist Robert Dicke measured it to a fineness of 1 part in 10 billion (1/10,000,000,000). In other words, the force is *exactly* proportional to the mass, as the law states. That this law is so exact and is found operating both in the largest and smallest regions of space – gravitationally between very large bodies as well as in the quantum world – is simply astonishing. However, that the force of electricity is so much more powerful than gravity led Feynman to wonder whether perhaps "the inverse square of the distance has some deep significance?"[43] How could the same law operate at such mind-bogglingly different scales? He illustrates this scale differential of the very same law by comparing the ratio of the powerful inverse square electrical *repulsion* between two electrons and the far weaker inverse square force of *attraction* between them. The *ratio* is expressed as a pure number: $1/4.17 \times 10^{42}$.

And that is just a shorthand way to write: 1/4,170,000,000,000, 000,000,000,000,000,000,000,000,000,000.

Now therein, he writes, "lies a very deep mystery. Where could such a tremendous number come from? If you ever had a [single] theory from which both of these things are to come, how could they come in such disproportion? What equation has a solution which has for two kinds of forces an attraction and a repulsion with that fantastic ratio?"[44] "It is not accidental," he goes on, enthralled by the mystery, "like the ratio of the volume of the earth to the volume of a flea. We have considered two natural aspects *of the same thing*, an electron. This fantastic number is a natural constant, so it involves something deep ... some say that we shall one day find the 'universal equation,' and in it, one of the roots will be this number."[45] We will see below that there are good reasons to wonder why this fantastic number, and multiples of it, recurs among the constants of nature.

c

This is the symbol for light, which is another constant of nature. For conversation purposes, its approximate speed, as mentioned above, is 300,000 kilometres per second. Its exact speed, however (with tiny variations depending on who is measuring and with what instruments), is 299,792.458 kilometres per second. This is considered the fastest rate at which information or any material thing can travel from A to B anywhere in the universe. A special feature of this constancy of light is that, unlike anything else, it is perceived by all observers to travel at the same speed no matter how fast or in what direction they are travelling toward or away from the light source. I still cannot understand why this is so, but it has been demonstrated experimentally. Nothing in nature can exceed the speed of light because as a thing approaches that limit, the energy used to accelerate it is increasingly converted to mass. As the speed of light is approached, virtually all the boosting energy becomes mass, and the thing increases in mass to such an extent that at almost the speed of light it would take infinite energy to boost it faster – an impossibility. An atomic particle accelerated in a nuclear cyclotron to 99.999999 (etc.) per cent of the speed of light gains about 430 times its original mass. If a pea, say, were fired around a cyclotron at that speed (and could survive!) it would end up the size of a basketball. It has even been calculated that a baseball thrown at 100 miles an hour will pick up 0.000000000002 grams on the way to the batter![46]

h

One of the central contributions to physics by Max Planck was his discovery that radiation (which we tend to think of as happening in waves) actually occurs in discrete bundles of energy, or quanta. In 1900 he demonstrated that the energy in a quantum (which is a unit of energy) is directly and exactly related to the wavelength frequency of its radiation. This universal constant of nature, which stays the same in all circumstances and in all frames of reference (the formula is 6.63×10^{-34}, and there is nothing relative about it!) is named after him as Planck's Constant. If a particle's frequency (of radiation) increases, so does its energy. If the frequency drops, so does the energy. But Planck's Constant always remains unchanged, everywhere in the universe. This equation (along with three other constants of nature named after him – the Planck Time, the Planck Length, and the Planck Mass) plays a key role in the development of modern physics and quantum theory.

Alpha: A Fine-Structure Constant

This pure, "dimensionless" constant is made up of three others: the electron charge (e), the speed of light (c), and Planck's Constant (h). By dimensionless, we mean that this constant is a pure number ratio, and it doesn't matter what values it is expressed in, whether metric, or English numbers, or some other value. If we suppose all the masses were doubled in some imaginary world, that world would be *indistinguishable* from our own because the ratios of this constant would remain the same. In this sense, "the only thing that counts in the definition of the world are the values of the dimensionless constants of Nature."[47]

HOW CONSTANT ARE THE CONSTANTS?

The stability of the values for the constants of nature and their interrelations, or ratios, is crucial to the successful outcome of physical experiment and prediction, as well as for accurate calculation of the origins and development of the universe. So the question often arises: How constant are the constants? Eminent physicists such as Paul Dirac and George Gamow once attempted to test the assumption that constants such as gravity (G) and electromagnetism (e) may change over time, as the universe expands. But Dirac soon surrendered, for the stronger value of G that he thought might have existed in past eons would have resulted in the boiling and evaporation of all the oceans and no life on earth. Gamow thought a variation in the value of the charge of the electron (e) might explain things better, too. But he soon gave up, stating that "the value of e stands as the Rock of Gibraltar for the last 6×10^9 years." That's 6 billion years!

But surely one of the most interesting testaments to the constancy of the constants was established in the 1970s when a French scientist was testing the radiation losses of uranium 235 samples mined in what turned out to be a "natural reactor" at a place called Oklo in the African Republic of Gabon. All uranium is created in stars, and a deposit 3 kilometres long and 700 metres wide was laid down with the earth's crust at Oklo over 4 billion years ago. Scientists testing the samples sent back to France could not figure out why some of the Oklo uranium always seemed to be missing. But further investigation revealed something astonishing: the Oklo seam, deep in the ground, revealed about thirty atomic by-products of nuclear explosions. Remarkably, it appeared that the Oklo deposit "had produced spontaneous nuclear reactions below the earth's surface two billion years ago."[48] Eventually, fifteen of these fossilized nuclear reactor sites were discovered at Oklo, and precise measurement has since revealed that "the very finely tuned coincidences that appear to exist between the values of the different constants of nature … must have been in place to high accuracy [less than 1 part in 5 billion] over two billion years ago when the natural reactor was running."[49]

COSMIC COINCIDENCES AND THE "LARGE NUMBERS"

Paul Davies stresses that "the nature of the physical world depends delicately on seemingly fortuitous cooperation between distinct branches of physics … [and] many of the familiar systems that populate the universe are the result of exceedingly improbable coincidence." In cosmology, he continues, we encounter "cosmic cooperation of such a wildly improbable nature it becomes hard to resist the impression that some basic principle is at work."[50] For example, he notes that for a long time distinguished cosmologists have noticed that the huge number 10^{40} (and multiples, or squares, or cubes of it) keeps popping up as a numerical relation in seemingly unrelated aspects of the universe.[51] It appears as a determining value for the stability of stars and the elements they produce, for the number of stars in an average galaxy, for the number of galaxies in the universe, for the number (squared) of protons in the universe, and as we saw earlier, for the ratio of attractive to repulsive forces between atomic particles. Why do we repeatedly see this enormous number, of which the slightest variation – say, dropping it to 10^{39} – would result in a vanishing universe, or stars that never produce life-giving elements such as carbon, or that burn up far too soon? We have no answer, except that it is a very strange numerical coincidence begging for explanation.

Another astonishing coincidence (if that is the word for it) is the expansion rate of the universe since the Big Bang. The values for the expansion in relation to the cumulative force of gravity (contraction) are exceedingly narrow, and it is commonly agreed that the expansion speed *just happens to be exactly right* to produce the universe we have. The slightest bit slower, and we would have long since collapsed in a Big Crunch. The slightest bit faster, and all would have long since flown apart. What explains the delicacy of this life-favouring physical ratio such that the universe is "balanced on a knife edge between collapse and endless expansion,"[52] lying *precisely on the boundary* between these two disastrous alternatives?

This suggests to many otherwise sober thinkers that something is "going on" and that what Davies coyly calls "a hidden principle" may be at work.[53] He is not the only one. Paul Dirac was convinced that such large numbers as 10^{40} and its variations "are most unlikely to be independent and unrelated accidents; there must exist some undiscovered mathematical formula linking the quantities." He asked, "might it not be that all present events correspond to properties of this large number?" and then stated that if this is so, "there is thus a possibility that the ancient dream of philosophers to connect all Nature with the properties of whole numbers will some day be realized."[54] He means that a deeper set of cosmic relationships, when it is revealed, will change what we now call accidents, or *coincidences*, into *consequences*. Astronomer Fred Hoyle, of "Big Bang" fame, was equally astonished at a universe with so many physical constants, all so fine-tuned to each other that they have produced what he called "a monstruous set of accidents." He considered the carbon-oxygen synthesis so remarkable that it seemed like a "put-up job" and thought the laws of physics in general look like a "deep-laid scheme."[55]

In a telling image, Davies asks us to play God. Try to imagine yourself, he asks, at the grand machine of the universe, twiddling the many separate knobs that control the constants of nature, with the ability to set the values wherever you wish. You would soon find that knob-settings anything other than what they are now would quickly render the universe uninhabitable, if not extinct. This inevitably invites speculation on the reason for the existence of human beings and the role of consciousness, if any, in the unfolding of the universe. For it does begin to seem that our merely being here at this time to observe a universe that was able to produce life only in the precise way it has is a telling detail in the vast scheme of things. André Gide once warned us to believe all those who seek truth but not to believe those who say they have found it.

On this note, I should say a lot of work in the field of modern cosmology amounts to exciting and deeply interesting speculation on the nature of reality. What else could it be? Whether or not it is true will never be known with any certainty. But the irony is that no human speculation about origins or creation can take place without the hope it *may* be true. That is what gives the excitement. What follows is one of the more philosophically interesting points of view concerning the possible relationship between human beings and the cosmos. But first, a word about how science has changed

THE "OLD STORY" AND THE "NEW STORY"[56]

The "old story" of science was called *scientific materialism*. It is rooted in the belief that only matter and the laws governing matter exist, along with an absolute fixed time and space, and hence that everything is explicable in terms of matter alone. It is a story that began some three hundred years ago in western Europe with the rise of "scientism." This emphasized empirical methodology and a fascination with means as a replacement for the former, mostly Aristotelian concern with ends, or ultimate meanings. The old question of "Why?" was demoted in favour of the new question of "How?" Scientists of this newer type wanted to extend their materialism to everything that exists, even to the extent of arguing (as their modern counterparts still do) that free will and reason – which many of us are convinced distinguish us from other types of beings, such as rocks and trees, plants and animals – can also (someday) be explained solely by matter. For these people, the notion of free will and consciousness, or spirit, or *mind* – of anything that we may think is not governed by the laws that govern matter – is an illusion.

However, the early twentieth-century revolution in physics was the first chapter in the "new story" of science, and it makes the old one look very old (although many modern scientists still believe it). The principal authors of the new story were Einstein, Niels Bohr, and Werner Heisenberg in physics; the Canadian Wilder Penfield, Sir Charles Sherrington, and John Eccles in neuroscience; many others in cosmology involved in the discovery and proof of the Big Bang; and still others involved in speculations about something called the "Anthropic Principle" (more on this below). The new story began the moment it was discovered that at the most basic quantum level of the material world, the behaviour of matter is unpredictable and, furthermore, as Max Born wrote at the time, that "the act of measurement typically produces an unpredictable change in the state of [a quantum particle] ... the choice one makes about what one observes makes an irretrievable difference in what one finds. The observer is elevated from 'observer' to 'participator.'"[57]

This was quite a change from the centuries-long belief, stemming from Newton's theories, that humans are detached spectators of the world to a belief in which the very existence of "mind" becomes an integral or deciding part of what is observed. The precise reasons for this are of interest and have to do with the interference of instruments of measurement with the "objects" measured.*

---

* Heisenberg first presented his Uncertainty Principle in a letter to physicist Wolfgang Pauli in 1927, stating that in subatomic physics it is impossible to know the exact position and the exact momentum of an object at the same time. The reason for this is that to know something about an object-particle, smaller detector-particles must first be bounced off it, and their pattern of bouncing or rebounding from the object-particle is then recorded by the measuring device. This hitting and rebounding is unobserved at macrolevels, so we say it is insignificant. Practically speaking, we could bounce all sorts of different things off an object and discover what it is like as long as we had a device to record the patterns made by the rebounding detector-objects. To observe a subatomic particle, however, we use light, which is itself made of packets of energy, or particles, called "photons." At the real-world, or macroscopic, level, when light bounces off an object the reflection tells us exactly where the object is in space and time. But at a subatomic level the photons that hit the particle cause it to move significantly, just like a billiard ball hitting another billiard ball, such that although its position may be measured accurately, its velocity will have been altered in performing this measurement of position. Hence precise information on its true velocity is lost at the same moment. To know position more accurately is to know momentum less accurately, and vice versa. This truth operates only at the subatomic level and is of no concern or significance for the real world of macro-objects, which always obey Newton's laws. This means that the fashionable modern penchant for describing the real world as one of uncertainty (and relativism) is a distortion of the human truth that the macro-reality that we experience never behaves this way. Its behaviour is certain to an amazing degree of Newtonian absoluteness, and it is a distortion of our worldview to imagine otherwise.

And this is how "physics in the twentieth century has gradually replaced materialism with the affirmation that mind plays an essential role
in the universe."[58] Of course, at the everyday level of material things,
such as the rocks and trees we observe, nothing has changed. Such ag-
gregate things (aggregates of smaller particles) still obey all of Newton's
laws. So there is no new story here. But when we dive down lower and ask
what those things are made of, when we get to the level of particles themselves, it is literally a different and a very new world. It is a world where
particles behave in completely unpredictable ways – outcomes can be
known only in terms of their probability – and where human observers
and their instruments change the outcomes by their very presence as ob-
server-experimenters. The plain conclusion is that we live in a world
where the most fundamental "reality" of nature cannot be known for
what it may (or may not) be in itself (because it is impossible at this mi-
crolevel to be a noninterfering nonobserver) and yet where the larger
cosmos (made entirely of such particles) displays an acute, mysterious,
and inexplicably precise fitness for the appearance of conscious life. The
paradox is that we cannot observe, without altering it, the most basic reality that in itself seems to have arisen from nothingness to accommodate
our specific existence as conscious, observing beings. This last reality
leads us to a discussion of the awkwardly described Anthropic Principle.

THE ANTHROPIC PRINCIPLE

Thus far the primary purpose of this chapter has been to demonstrate
that contrary to the prevalent public view, the whole universe is characterized and controlled not by anything relative but by a finite set of lawful
and precise constants of nature that operate everywhere. For those of us
brought up on the idea that the universe is a random reality that might
have been otherwise or that human life and consciousness are accidents
of nature that have no discernible importance in the cosmic scheme of
things, the mere existence of so many nonrandom, nonchaotic, unchanging constants of nature ought to at least suggest something very
bold, if only in the form of a question, namely *could this have happened by
chance?* For even the most generous calculations of mere probability, allowing for the billions of years available, cannot have produced as a matter of chance the scenario that we live under and that made us possible.
In any other realm of life, when we observe things that are so obviously
beyond the realm of chance, we look for a cause. So although the main
work of this chapter is done, it would seem interesting and worthwhile to

give some sense of the possible *meaning* of the constants of nature and of the rather astonishing coincidences and consequences they produce, as suggested by physicists and cosmologists themselves. So what follows is a brief survey of one aspect of modern physics that interests this writer because it requires a leap from the question of "How?" to questions about the ultimate meaning – the "Why?" – of existence. Ironically, it is the unavoidable new facts of hard science that have pushed scientists beyond science to begin asking the ultimate questions – with which many of them are admittedly uncomfortable. But first, let me set the stage for this irony.

In the nineteenth century, physics was considered a cold and purely materialistic Newtonian science, whereas the so-called "life" sciences were more humanistic because they defended the idea of a privileged role for human life and consciousness in the overall order of nature. But over the past century this has reversed itself. Biology, in a trend that surely reflects the growing influence of Darwinian evolution theory, has come to embrace the purely materialistic and mechanical view characteristic of the earlier physics, while physics itself has been moving away from its earlier mechanical models and is speeding in the other direction, mostly due to hard experimental and observational evidence. In fact, many contemporary physicists, especially cosmologists, have been embracing the view that the human mind plays a determining role in physical events. As mentioned, this was demonstrated at the quantum level by Heisenberg and Bohr, among others, in the 1920s. Bohr and his "Copenhagen" interpretation of physics maintained that quantum particles exist only if, because, and at the moment they are observed. In the absence of human observation there are just fields of energy. It is the method and instruments that we use to "see" particles that makes them visible. They are as much mental or observational phenomena as they are material.

We have also seen that many – perhaps most – modern cosmologists and mathematicians are self-confessed Platonists, convinced that their theoretical discoveries and the formulae that describe the constants of nature exist in a world of pure ideas or laws or equations that are not invented but rather are discovered and revealed. Such distinguished scientists as Feynman, Penrose, Gödel, Dirac, and Einstein have insisted that the pure constants of nature as expressed in the laws of physics are transcendent, not products of human invention. They exist in an ideal world of their own, but due to our unique consciousness and intelligence we have somehow managed to discover some of them. We know them with our minds. We "make contact" with them, as Penrose puts it, which is to say that until human observational consciousness operates, the laws do their work invisibly, so to speak. The truth is hidden until discovered. Hence the revelation talk from people like Stephen Hawking about "knowing the mind of God."

So the current picture suggests that biology and physics have been speeding in opposite directions. The former has become far more experimental and materialistic, and the latter more abstract and metaphysical. In response to this apparent movement in the direction of anti-materialism on the part of modern physics (a possibly threatening reality for other scientists who are aware that their own fields also rely on physics at a deeper level), and in order to defend their own increasingly materialistic views, biologists, neurologists, and others who are determined to "answer" the mystery of things such as consciousness by solely material means resort to what world-famous neurologist and Nobel Laureate (1963) Sir John Eccles called "promissory materialism." This is the strategy of suggesting that given enough time, materialism will eventually answer all such questions. This emaciated dream Eccles declared to be "extravagant and unfulfillable."[59] For the truth appears to be that the discoveries of quantum physics have made this dream of the "old story" unrealizable in principle. An interesting sidebar to this is that the new physics is nevertheless creeping into fields like biology under such labels as "quantum biology," and today research topics like "the quantum brain" are very hot, moving away, as they do, from the idea of the mind as a machine to the idea of the mind as a self-organizing nonmaterial entity.[60] We may safely predict that this trend will eventually make all the life sciences more metaphysical because current notions of strict biological causation will inevitably end up confronting and then absorbing the realities of quantum probability theory and "uncertainty," just as classical physics has done. Eventually, a lot of today's mechanical sciences (which, due to their continued reliance on the old mechanical story of science, are seen as "soft," or behind the times) will become more metaphysical for the same reason. We are such stuff as dreams are made on! Well, actually – we are made of gazillions of atoms. And atoms are pretty much indestructible. The average one has a life of some 10^{35} years, which is I don't know how many billions upon billions of years. All atoms on earth were once parts of stars, where they were made, and some have argued that each of us has atoms in us from the stars and even – a weird thought – from all sorts of famous, now thoroughly decomposed people, such as Shakespeare, Buddha, and Genghis Khan.[61]

Now all this is ironic in the extreme. For it was hardcore scientists like Copernicus and Galileo who inadvertently drove us out of the centre of the universe as it was then conceived, and now, as we shall see, it is hardcore scientists suggesting we belong back at the centre again. But this time they mean the centre not of the solar system but of the entire universe. As one writer puts it, modern "man" (at least in Western, materialist-minded civilizations) has been searching for meaning "in a universe alien to his needs, beliefs and existence. Now the universe as conceived by postmodern science offers mankind his home again."[62] As the properties of matter, both on the smallest scale and on the scale of the whole universe, appear uniquely suited to conscious life, physicist Freeman Dyson concludes that this argues for purpose, not coincidence: "the more I examine the universe and study the details of its architecture, the more evidence I find *that the universe in some sense must have known we were coming.*"[63] But why has such a recent movement toward things metaphysical originated from the most materialistic of all the sciences?

The most plausible reason, as I have suggested, is that no one who knows how to calculate statistical probabilities believes, even for a nanosecond, that either the constants of nature themselves or the strange and extremely sensitive relationships between them are a result of fluke or chance. When you see a repeated complex constant pattern or design in things of exquisite sensitivity and beauty, and when this pattern as a whole has an "irreducible complexity," as it is sometimes called (which means that each constituent part is useless without the others), you look for a reason, a designer. So a theory has been developed to describe the possible meaning of the design of the universe called the Anthropic Principle (from the Greek *anthropos*, for "man"). It seems at first a little grand, even bizarre, but the more it is turned in the mind, the more fascinating are its implications.

The idea that human beings are central to creation has been around a long time, to say the least. Religions have always said so. But no practical person, especially one raised on materialistic Western science, ever expected physicists to say this kind of thing – that physical laws are central to the creation of life! But then, in 1986, Oxford University Press brought out a strange (to the uninitiated) book by John Barrow and Frank Tipler called *The Anthropic Cosmological Principle,* wherein the authors say "the realization that the possibility of biological evolution is strongly dependent on the global structure of the Universe is truly surprising and perhaps provokes us to consider that *the existence of life may be no more, but no less, remarkable than the existence of the Universe itself.*"[64] Indeed, a main argument of their anthropic principle is that the universe is such as to have produced conscious observing beings at a certain point in time, before which this was physically impossible. The laws of physics did not permit it until their inter-action made it happen (ratios of carbon, oxygen, water, and so on). If we accept that *conscious observing beings* are a unique and inevitable *product of this exact universe, and only of such a universe,* then we arrive at the connected realization that, as we are an essential and inescapable *consequence* of just such a universe, then the universe that has produced consciousness is in a sense (hold on) ... observing itself! And more, we realize that the universe cannot be said to "exist" if there is no conscious entity here to observe it and to say so (an argument that leaves God out of the story, likely because no one could make sense of a creator God making a universe only for Himself). This provoked Erwin Schrödinger, a physicist who played such a significant role in the writing of the new story, to say that without human beings, the universe would be a drama played before empty stalls.[65]

In Barrow and Tipler's words:

> One of the most important results of twentieth-century physics has been the gradual realization that there exist invariant properties of the natural world and its elementary components which render the gross size and structure of virtually all its constituents quite inevitable. The sizes of stars and planets, and even people, are neither random, nor the result of any Darwinian selection process from a myriad of possibilities. These, and other gross features of the Universe are the consequences of necessity; they are manifestations of the possible equilibrium states between competing forces of attraction and repulsion. The intrinsic strengths of these controlling forces of nature are determined by a mys-terious collection of pure numbers that we call *the constants of nature.*
>
> The Holy Grail of modern physics is to explain why these numerical constants – quantities like the ratio of the proton and electron masses for example – have the particular numerical values they do.[66]*

---

* In chapter 8 of their text, Barrow and Tipler outline the sequence of ten essen-tial but independent steps leading to life, each of which, they insist, is of the highest order of improbability. Paraphrased here, these are: (1) a DNA-based ge-netic code, (2) aerobic respiration, (3) glucose fermentation, (4) photosynthe-sis, (5) mitochondrial action, (6) biochemical complexity enabling nerve development, (7) evolution of the eye precursor, (8) the bony skeleton, (9) evo-lution of chordates (creatures with backbones and a central nervous system), and (10) *Homo sapiens.*

The sheer wonder of all this is driven home to physicists (if not to bi- ologists any longer) because, as Feynman put it, "there is nothing that living things do that cannot be understood from the point of view that they are made of atoms acting according to the laws of physics."[67] This precision of the constants of nature and the exact consequences that happen to be favourable to our existence is best captured, once again, in the voice of Fred Hoyle, who in 1970 *predicted* that because carbon- based life exists, there must be incredibly precise atomic-resonance en- ergy levels for carbon production at the heart of main-sequence stars. These energy levels were subsequently discovered to be exactly as Hoyle had predicted. Here was a famous case of *a carbon-based human intelligence successfully arguing theoretically from the fact of its own existence to the likely cosmic conditions-precedent for that existence!* The long and short of this is the conclusion that if any of the many constants of nature dif- fered from what they are by as much as even 1 or 2 per cent we would have a universe without hydrogen-burning stars, without oxygen, or carbon, or water, and hence without life.

Today, many more scientists have come to recognize the strangely and powerfully – perhaps we should say unavoidably – suggestive existence of so many fine-tuned constants. And capping these off are two more mind- boggling numbers to contemplate. These have to do with so-called "boundary conditions" within which all this unfolds. The first, men- tioned earlier, has to do with the initial velocity of the Big Bang. Too fast, and matter cannot form into stars and galaxies. Too slow, and we get the Big Crunch. As Francis Collins, head of the Human Genome Project, put it, "if the rate of expansion [of the universe] one second after the Big Bang had been smaller by even one part in 100 thousand million mil- lion, the universe would have recollapsed before it ever reached its pres- ent size."[68] Game over. But we now have widely accepted models telling us that this initial velocity must be specified to a precision of $1/10^{55}$, a number so exact it simply cannot be due to chance. An even more aston- ishingly precise number having to do with the cosmological constant was sharpened to a precision of 10^{123} in the January 1999 issue of *Scientific American*.[69] We can hardly grasp what such a number might mean.

When asked what could possibly explain the existence of such impos- sible-seeming numbers and ratios, what answers do we hear? The reli- gious say it has to be God. The rational but timorous materialists say that such questions are metaphysical and cannot be answered. This means that although they have no scientific answer, they reject all non- scientific ones. But of course, that is itself a metaphysical response. The rational, but perhaps more bold, type of materialist says that the constants and their relationships are clearly not random or chance events and thus that some explanation is required to account for them. In this sense, it is perhaps a final irony that the new story of physics is really a more scientifically precise continuation of the very ancient story of the universe so well told by Aristotle and others who argued for purpose, or *telos*, in nature. From this view, the materialistic scientism that shaped our more recent "old story" was "a 300-year detour from the mainstream of Western thought,"[70] and the "new story" rooted in quantum physics must be understood, as Schrödinger put it, as "the continuation of ancient science."[71] Hoyle summed up the feeling of a lot of today's more informed scientists when he said that at a minimum it seemed to him that "a superintellect has monkeyed with physics, as well as chemistry and biology, and that *there are no blind forces worth speaking about in nature.*"[72]

6

The War Over Biology: Setting the Stage

Ours is a biological planet.

Just ask yourself: How much life-giving blood is pumped by almost 7 billion human hearts pounding at seventy-five beats a minute all over the globe;[1] how much sleeping, birthing, eating, thinking, talking, dying?

Now imagine that every one of the nearly 7 billion people lights up with a different bright colour according to whatever biological function is underway at the moment. Then picture the whole planet from outer space, with everyone flashing intermittent blue for breathing, green for sleeping, yellow for eating, red for lovemaking, orange for thinking, magenta for birthing, and so on. Add the billions of other organisms, from fleas to bees and shrimp to sheep, and the whole surface of the earth and all the oceans would glow with sparkling waves of colour, blinking through the darkness of space like a beautiful Christmas tree.

We seldom stop to consider that from birth until death we are quasi prisoners of our biology. But anyone who has tried to hold his or her breath for more than a minute or so, fast for a few days, or delay a birth in a rushing taxi, will soon get an urgent demonstration that none of this ceaseless activity can be escaped, except by death – yet another biological event.

THE HUMAN MIND-BODY SPLIT

And yet, and yet ... we fancy ourselves to be free.

It is true that to a considerable degree we can command our demanding bodies, control or inflame our passions, direct – or misdirect – the course of our lives. This dualism, or split between mind and body, is itself one of the most important universals of human biology. No

other life form has anything equivalent to our experience of consciousness, awareness of self, of time, of the cosmos, of the inevitability of
death. As a result – and here is perhaps the most fundamental universal
of human biology – all human beings lead a philosophical existence as
the only form of life that is able to ask, "What is my existence for? What
is the universe for?" This is the first of many reasons to believe that the
gap between humans and all other life forms is absolutely unbridgeable, despite the fact that very earnest scholars from Darwin forward
have devoted entire careers to convincing us we are just a specialized
form of ape.

THE MIND-BODY STRUGGLE: THE ANCIENT VIEW

This first mind-body biological universal also happens to be the first universal of biopolitics, as witnessed by the fact that from the beginning of
recorded history, we find poems, legends, songs, and stories about people struggling not only against numerous external enemies but also
against their own biological body conceived as an internal enemy. We humans
see our selves, our minds, our souls as somehow separate from our biology and our passions yet inescapably entangled with them in a lifelong
tension. Any obese person trying (once again!) to diet, a smoker or hard
drinker to stop their "habit," or any of us to quell our propensity for self-
interest, will vouch for this truth. Virtually all ancient philosophers were
quick to judge this human tension as either a healthy or deranged *master-
slave* relationship. Most admired was the free and spiritual mind as master, controlling an obedient body. Moral and physical weakness, sickness,
and even madness were deemed certain to follow whenever the enslaved
body managed to free itself, so to speak, and assert control over the
mind. This has always been considered a pitiable human condition. Self-
control, moral restraint, and moderation learned from parents, school,
and society – that is, from what we now call the "nurture" of others – have
always been considered key weapons in the struggle to govern one's own
biology, or "nature." The key distinction is between the power of the permanent biological nature inside us and the influences upon that nature
from the nurture outside us.

THE MODERN VIEW – AND ITS RESULT

We should not chuckle at this master-slave metaphor as just a mental
trick thought up by unsophisticated ancients. For it still applies. Today,

so-called "self-actualization," the act of freeing the "true self" (usually considered ourselves "as we really are") from the dark clutches of a controlling biology or outdated morality, or even from our own self-deception or "inauthenticity," is all the rage. The life-enhancing advice of the late Joseph Campbell, a popular advocate of this pursuit, was to "follow your bliss." And most political scientists today simply assume that the "self-flourishing" of the individual (as distinct from the flourishing of society as a whole, to which historically individuals were always considered subordinate) is now the proper object of a democratic system. In such a mood, strenuous self-denial and restraint are more likely to be pitied than admired and may even provoke the thought that we are an undeveloped, unfree, uptight, or even "anal" person. Historians of the future will have a great frolic over the meaning of this last strange Freudian term.

It is surely of the deepest irony, however, that the result of this posture of ultimate freedom is a very badly decayed social fabric in which biology – I use the term here as a shorthand for all the compelling workings of the body – has triumphed almost completely. By any account, the ostensibly more free selves of far too many citizens have clearly become ... freely enslaved to biology. Any thoughtful observer would surely agree that the Western democracies in particular are wallowing in a swamp of physical self-indulgence from which they cannot seem to escape.*

AN ATTEMPT AT CONSENSUS

This ancient mind-body dualism continues to work in a variety of subtle ways, no longer as a public philosophy but as a set of scientific assumptions, methods, and debates about ... the ultimate role of nature and nurture. Anyone who has been exposed to basic social studies has certainly already had a dose of this sometimes quite vitriolic debate. It is

---

* The Western world has managed to produce more depersonalized sex, STDs, pregnancies, and abortions among the very young, more drug and alcohol use and addictions of various kinds, more divorce and broken families, and more obesity and "lifestyle" diseases than ever in history. The picture is of an entire civilization out of control, pornographied, wholly abandoned to its own appetites, the modern "self" now a willing slave – "victim" is the modern word – of the body, which is to say, of biology. There is today an enormous "addiction," "co-dependency," and "recovery" industry in the free nations of the world, counting clients in the many millions.

most often presented to students in the form of a veiled moral question of the type: "Was this person [juvenile delinquent, criminal, thief, prostitute, drug addict – whatever] so bad because of heredity or environment?" Everyone wants to know the exact *cause* of the disturbing behaviour. But why does this seem so important?

It has to do with *moral responsibility, restitution, and rehabilitation.* Whenever something is done, we need to know who did it, who is to be compensated or punished, what needs repair, and who needs rehabilitation – to prevent it happening again. This is simply not possible if we cannot locate *what* or *who* caused the behaviour in the first place. Did a man rape and murder because of a psychological obsession? A hormone? A gene he had to obey? Or was it a matter of free will and intent? We need to know the true cause of our behaviours so we can properly assign responsibility for them. Any society that cannot do this is headed for the abyss. After all, someone (a person? a group?) or some agent (evolution? society as a whole? hormones? capitalism?) must have been the cause of the dirty deed. Oh, how scientists would prefer never to have to deal with such a theme! If only causality were straightforward and obvious! Today, many consensus-seeking social scientists opt for a generous middle ground by denying dominance to either nature or nurture, speaking instead of their "interaction" in all human behaviours. Such interactive thinking feels good and makes us appear less dogmatic. But it does not resolve the "whodunit?" problem.

The great majority of teachers and scientists will tend to take the liberal position that the cause of whatever we are or have done is traceable to the environment, or the poor quality of nurture, which comes down to saying that an imperfect society has made us bad. So let's fix it. The hard fix recommended usually begins with a demand for more funding via tax dollars. The soft fix is always a call for "re-education" of the unenlightened (those who do not agree with the predominant view), and radicals seeking this type of engineered alteration of society describe themselves as "change agents."

The conservative will tend to argue the opposite position – that we are more than likely responsible for our own behaviour. This type will call for more self-control, genuine neighbourly compassion, a stricter moral code, and tougher punishment of offenders. But both answers draw a deep line in the intellectual and moral sand, for at bottom, they reveal a position already taken with respect to what used to be called "human nature." Today, however, simply to mention that term, especially in what is almost always a liberal university hallway, is to raise eyebrows and create a few instant enemies. Indeed, the typical academic rejects the concept of human nature very energetically because if human nature can be proven to exist then it must have been planted in us by some agent: either God or natural biology. For the modern liberal* (or socialist, or social engineer), however, one is as bad as the other because both answers mean that neither individuals nor society can be changed, made over, revolutionized. Hence to admit even the possibility of such a thing as "human nature" threatens the mindset (and also often the income and career) of anyone working to change society by altering human behaviour.

THE RELIGIOUS PRECURSORS

I think that whatever we become is obviously a mixture of nature and nurture in some unequal measure. But the debate itself, however narrow or ill-conceived it may be, is very important because it has to do with morality and therefore the ultimate meaning of existence. After all, a civilization unable to decide in its moral code or its laws whether citizens are masters or slaves of their own behaviour could not function for more than a week. That is why the debate can be found prominently featured in ancient philosophy and religious belief. Ancient Stoicism, for example, promoted a dramatic and very popular dualistic worldview that was rather rapidly imported into the upstart Christian religion. Christ's body may have died on the cross, but His pure spirit was already thought to be something separate and heading upward (to be later rejoined, somehow, with His body). The result of this incorporation into Christianity is that a dualistic structure of one kind or another has tended to permeate all Judeo-Christian conceptions of moral struggle (and most Eastern ones, too, whence this tendency first came to the West). Who has not seen paintings of goggle-eyed penitents scourging their flesh with bloody whips while praying for relief from temptation, from the body as the Satan within? The modern secular version of this confessional process is the twelve-step self-help type of group made famous by Alcoholics Anonymous, a process now used for all manner of rehabilitation. What is common to religious and secular versions alike is the elemental unburdening of guilt and self-torment, the revelation of the true Self within, and the commitment to a permanent transformation of behaviour. There are still lots of religious and

---

* A distinction used consistently in this book is between the classical liberal who is devoutly anti-statist and the modern liberal who is as devoutly pro-statist.

secular people who take this dualism very seriously,[2] and it always leads to the same questions: Is my mind or my body in control? Is it nurture or nature? Am I a determined or a free being? Are all people (individuals as well as genders and races) born the same, and are they thus free and equal, or are they different by nature? These are the restless questions that continue to perturb biological speculations. We will see that the so-called Standard Social Science Model that underlies most Western social science, although currently under what appears to be a terminal attack, nevertheless continues to take for granted that all human beings (and both sexes) are born the same everywhere. On this assumption, most human capacities and differences are assumed to have been learned. It is this claim that is disputed by social scientists who believe that most of the basics of human nature and even some of our very specialized attributes are hardwired.

WHERE DID OUR IDEA OF EQUALITY AND FREEDOM COME FROM?

I have never seen anything close to social equality except in a jail (not counting the guards), and I've certainly never seen or heard of an egalitarian society, if by this we mean one where all citizens are the same, are treated exactly the same, and have the same attributes and skills and values or the same material conditions. No such thing has ever existed in history. The reason is that if you want absolute equality you need absolute control. And that has been tried, but never for very long, for the reason that possibly another constant and universal of human nature is ... rebellion against excessive authority.

As for freedom? Most people are hard pressed to define freedom beyond something like: "it is doing what you want to do." But a moment's reflection tells us that except for a hermit lost in the forest (that is, where no society exists), this is an unworkable notion. For in a real society, if any of us got even close to doing what we really wanted to do, all the time, we would be buried in lawsuits, as our unlimited freedom would conflict with everyone else's unlimited freedom. That is why Lord Acton said that freedom is not important only for doing what we *want* but also, and especially, for doing what we *ought*.

If we bother to drill down deeper and ask what it is that drives our modern (and historically unusual) concept of freedom and equality, we will find its roots in a secularization of the Garden of Eden story. Before their sin of disobedience, Adam and Eve – the primordial couple, the seed of all humanity – were pure in spirit, unashamed, free, and equal, and they required *no human government!* Oh, what a dream! Although it is almost impossible even to imagine such a wholly mythical condition, this continues to be what utopians spend much of their lives imagining. So much is this true that it has become an intensely political metaphor for true freedom in the Western world.[3] It is sometimes called a "pre-lapsarian" view of humanity because back then we supposedly had not yet lapsed, or fallen, into evil. We were pure and good by nature (and this is how social scientists still say we are born, even now). It is a compelling story that continues to pester the consciousness of the West.

THE NATURALLY BAD VIEW

But after the Fall (the story continues) we became "post-lapsarian" and suddenly prone to wickedness due to an alteration of our human nature. It was our badness that brought power and pain into this virginal world, along with stern government and the control by some over others. For many people, this founding story presents the West's historical answer to the most important moral (and social, and scientific) question of all time: *are we good or bad by nature?* Historically, the most common answer the world over is that if unrestrained by moral codes and the law, human beings are by nature overwhelmingly selfish, prone to acts of evil, and probably in need of grace and salvation of some kind. It is this view that profoundly shaped human spiritual and institutional life through to the end of the Middle Ages (from about AD 1000 to 1500). We will soon see that today even some very atheistic biologists have come to believe a similar view: that through Darwinian evolution we have become a self-serving, which is to say, a gene-serving, hostile species. They argue that even our "reciprocal altruism" is at bottom self-serving. It may help to strengthen the group, or kin group, but it is not *truly* selfless. Andrew Brown, in his interesting book with the telling title *The Darwin Wars: The Scientific Battle for the Soul of Man*, relates the sad story of the prominent theoretical biologist George Price, a dogmatic atheist who made what are now famous mathematical calculations proving (!) that "the human capacity for altruism must be strictly limited; and our capacity for cruelty, treachery and selfishness impossible to eradicate. Through algebra, *George had found proof of original sin.*" It was not just the discovery that our acts are fundamentally selfish that undid him; it was "the thought that our ideals are selfish, too ... that it is our nature to be intellectually deceived ... that the longing for truth

is the weakest of all human passions."[4] William Hamilton, whose work
Price had pushed to its natural conclusion, once said it was about "the
darker of [our] 'innate aptitudes' ... [our] warlike inclinations, including, perhaps [our] relish in cruelty, that caused me most pain to
write."[5] Price's equations seemed to prove definitively that there is no
way out. No way, so to speak, to be purely pure. That was enough to
drive him into fanatical Christianity and from there into real poverty in
his attempt to live selflessly and do acts of pure charity. That effort
drove him to a squalid suicide in 1974. Brown writes that we now must
simply come to terms with a world in which all human endeavour
seems an illusion, serving the purposes of brute genetic fact.[6]

THE NATURALLY GOOD VIEW: SOME SEEKERS OF THE MODERN GARDEN

But there have always been people who reject this view in favour of the
contrary idea that humans are naturally good, that the Fall is just a religious myth justifying the status quo. The cause of our woes is not internal, or part of our nature. It is external and social. It had a beginning in
time, so it can be reversed in time. We can – and must – be returned to
our original and *natural* condition of freedom and equality through social and moral revolution. Modern revolutionary talk, however, is more
about a change in the material conditions of existence than about a
change in the human spirit. In the social sciences this usually ends up
as a plea for social and economic "justice" (by which is usually meant
material equality), whereas in biology it becomes a plea to understand
our true evolved human nature before we mess around with society.

In the eighteenth century, Rousseau rested his entire revolutionary
case against societal corruption on a variation of the Eden story, declaring: "Man is born free, and everywhere he is in chains." Karl Marx did
much the same in the nineteenth. The latter's idea for a "true democracy" of self-governing people and the consequent longed-for withering-
away of the state was rooted in the ancient yearning to restore us to our
natural pre-lapsarian condition. Not far beneath the surface is the conviction (again) that *we are all born the same* and that it must therefore be
acquired inequities of property, wealth, and social experience that create
individual differences. This egalitarian belief is like a foreordained answer to the question "What is our *true* nature?" – and it continues to dictate and direct the course and findings of most social science. Indeed, we
will see shortly that Marxist biologists such as Richard Lewontin and the

late Stephen Jay Gould, both of Harvard, were bitterly vitriolic in their complete rejection of all suggestions that human nature is innate. However, as religious language is now by and large rejected in the sciences, the modern argument is no longer centred on the struggle between body and soul, but rather it is about the superiority of either biological or cultural explanations for behaviour. The modern dualistic terms are now settled as "nature vs nurture," or "heredity vs environment," and the like, and lifelong academic careers and massive social projects all over the Western world have been sustained by millions of dollars in research grants devoted to proving one side or the other of this equation to be true, once and for all. The disciples of both positions have been known to cause a lot of trouble, and neither side trusts the other.

NATURE AND NURTURE ARGUMENTS CAN BOTH BE VERY BAD FOR YOUR HEALTH

It turns out that both these views, when taken as the whole truth, have led to the darkest atrocities. On the one hand, the view that all human nature is forever fixed has tended to yield to the nation-flattering idea that one race, or type, or class of people is superior to, or chosen above, or fitter than all others. In other words, as soon as the church of human nature is established, the old insider-outsider, or higher-lower, division of humanity (this insider-outsider tendency for grouping others seems also to be a sociobiological constant) swings immediately into view. The West, if not the whole world, has had – continues to have – a terrible experience with this idea. Many Americans took it as a kind of perverted social gospel when defending slavery and suffered a horrible civil war in consequence. And the European racial stew pots have never ceased to simmer. As for much of Africa and the Middle East, they seem to be black holes of racial hatred, sucking to destruction all who approach.

Most germane to this chapter, however, is the story of Charles Darwin and the glaring abuse of the nature argument that came to the fore in the middle of the nineteenth century. Darwin published his disturbing *Origin of Species* in 1859, subtitled *The Preservation of Favored Races in the Struggle for Life,* and the white industrialized Christian societies, already taking a great deal of pleasure in their supposed moral superiority over dark-skinned people and their pagan cultures, took even more from Darwin's idea of (the phrase was actually Herbert Spencer's) the "survival of the fittest." Darwin mostly used the word "fit" to mean best-adapted to the environment, in the sense of *best at reproducing and getting your genes into the next generation.* But powerful societies soon took "fittest" to mean "strongest" and smugly argued that Darwin's scientific arguments had now proven the right – even the duty! – of the strong to dominate the weak. Everyone then was a racist in a sense they thought normal: races obviously differ dramatically in their behaviour, abilities, and success in the struggle for life; therefore, some races are naturally either more or less fit than others. Hence, after so much time, the superior races must have some *natural right* to their superiority. Social scientists and governments responsible for the poor, the disabled, the mentally unfit, and the criminally minded thus thought it quite normal to look for ways to stop them from multiplying. Society could be cleaned up with a little harmless genetic engineering.

By the early 1900s forced sterilization for such inferior groups was considered a socially responsible policy, just as, in recent years, people have stridently lobbied for abortion-on-demand to rid society of "unwanted" children or for a forced policy of no more than two children per family to prevent "overpopulation." They righteously claim to be "concerned about the planet." Between the two world wars, many Western countries had intense eugenics programs in place, and an extensive sterilization of low-IQ poor people, especially of blacks, was well under way.[7]

In Germany, Nietzsche's philosophy of the Superman was combined with the by now socially poisonous Darwinian recipe and used as an intellectual and moral tool of domination. Thus did the long-nourished Western concept of human nature, one originally constrained and refined by centuries of spiritual and moral caveats (the result a beautiful thing when restricted to what is universally noble, good, and beautiful), become a narrow and thoroughly secular instrument of a dispiriting survivalist biology.

For all these reasons, morally concerned people and especially social renovators frowned on *any* biological attempt to prove there are fixed universal qualities of human nature. They decided to focus on the other extreme, so the pendulum began to swing. The North American reaction to biology between the wars was to develop the nurture side of the argument, to the almost fanatical exclusion of all else. In this, biology, for a while at least, followed the lead of anthropology (but never very closely because biology is one step nearer to our physical human nature than culture, which, biologists argued, is its expression). Anthropology said everything is relative and due to culture. Biology lamely tried to follow this lead, arguing for a time – because it was considered, and is still considered, the most politically correct view – that everything is a result of nurture and "learning."

MANUFACTURING PERFECTION

One of the most famous – perhaps I should say infamous – pronounce-ments in this vein by any social scientist, ever, is worth quoting in full. It was trotted out in 1925 by the American inventor of behaviourism, John B. Watson: "Give me a dozen healthy infants, well-formed, and my own specified world to bring them up in, and I'll guarantee to take any one at random and train him to become any type of specialist I might select – doctor, lawyer, artist, merchant-in-chief, and, yes, even beggar-man and thief, regardless of his talents, penchants, tendencies, abili-ties, vocations, and race of his ancestors."[8]

Both his legacy and this statement reveal the unshakable confidence of those early social engineers in the malleability, or "plasticity," of hu-man nature and the extent to which they dreamed of manipulating it to produce a complete social and moral revolution. A generation after Watson, Harvard's renowned behaviourist B.F. Skinner was so en-thralled by the success of his "operant conditioning" methods – by which pigeons learned desired behaviours by pecking food rewards in a closed "Skinner Box" – that he allegedly built such a box to provide complete environmental control for the training of small children and, the story goes ... put his own daughter inside.

But there is no mistaking the motives of such materialists. Because they *believe* everything is material, they conclude everything *must* be material, and the certain way to *make* everything material is to ignore everything that is not. A good example of such thinking is from Sir Francis Crick, co-discoverer with Jim Watson of the double-helix struc-ture of DNA. In the last phase of his life, Crick was on a crusade to dis-cover the material basis of consciousness itself. He began by simply assuming that everything that goes on in our heads can be explained by the behaviour of billions of nerve cells. From the evidence of peo-ple with damaged brains, he deduced that free will in humans is com-prised of "a bundle of cells on the inside top surface at the front of the brain." He did not seem to consider that his own language was trap-ping him, for if the free will he was looking for is truly free, it cannot be purely material, and if it is purely material, it cannot be truly free. Further, if the will is free, it cannot refute its own freedom, and if all he finds is "a bundle of cells," he has not discovered anything free. At any rate, these contradictions did not stop him from crowing that his "discovery" had provided a scientific refutation of the Roman Catholic definition of the soul.[9]

Amazing, really, to think of science and theology still locking horns over ultimate meaning. But they will do so as long as the first insists we have a universe without a cause and the second that there has to be a First Cause of all things. And it can hardly be sufficiently stressed that all such materialist schemes of human perfection are mobilized, if not by the Garden of Eden story, then by some equally fantastical myth or ideal. How could it be otherwise? As there has never been a real-world example of a perfect human society, the source of the human yearning for perfection must be wholly imaginary, a phantom that for historical and theological reasons happened to become the founding creation story of the Western world. At bottom, when all is said and done, we could say that both anthropology and biology are but modern creation stories under continuous elaboration. Despite their devotion to a materialistic methodology disconnected even from the suggestion of design or ultimate purposes, all serious scientists have a thinly disguised desire to answer such questions as "What are we? How did we get here? What is our true nature?" That is why, as we will see in the next chapter, the world-famous biologist E.O. Wilson simply took the bull by the horns. In his book *Sociobiology* he flatly declared he wanted to set up evolutionary biology as *a replacement creation myth* for Western civilization. At least he was forthright about this motive.

THE EUROPEAN EXPERIMENT WITH NURTURE

During the same decades, and coming to a crisis between the two world wars and their aftermath, European social renovators of a national-socialist (Nazi), as well as international-socialist (Communist) type, relying specifically on notions of *human plasticity* and the benefits of correct social and moral nurture, laid waste to Western civilization. All these totalitarian systems relied specifically on forms of *moral relativism* allowing them to build their favourite totalitarian systems on their chosen ends-justifies-the-means basis. Such moral and cultural relativism, in conjunction with the absence of any restraining concept of human nature, justified the most murderous means available for the chosen political ends. "Human nature," they argued, is not fixed by anything innate or enduring. It can always be created anew by the correct "system." Mother Nurture thus reappeared as a modern social engineer trying to create the Kingdom of Heaven on earth.

In this brief description, we get some sense of the dangers of relying too heavily on concepts of either nature or nurture. However, if I had to name the greater danger, it would be the latter. Undoubtedly, all concepts of inherited racial or class superiority justified by biology are repugnant and have caused, and continue to cause, untold damage and grief. The race oppressions and commercial slavery of earlier centuries and the state eugenics systems such as were found in California in the early twentieth century, and later in Germany, are examples of this evil, as are todays ethnic-cleansing reports from African tribal wars, Bosnia, and elsewhere in the world. All these horrors were justified in large part through biology, or "nativist" thinking.

But they were brush fires compared to the conflagrations and massacres engineered by the "nurturing" totalitarian systems of the twentieth century, from Hitler and Stalin to Pol Pot and so many others. Although the Nazi system had a distinct biological basis in Aryan philosophy, it relied, like the Communist one, on social-engineering concepts promoting a total control of nurture: the Germans called it *Gleichschaltung*. This referred to the building of a cradle-to-grave correct environment that would make you whole and free. Wrought in steel, over their labour camps was the phrase "Arbeit Macht Frei" – Work Makes You Free). All totalitarian systems, from the French Revolution forward, have operated this way, and all have used deadly force without regard to how many of their own citizens are murdered on the way to bringing their correct "environment" into existence. The full and disgusting panorama of such killing by the nurturing planners of social perfection can be gotten from Professor Rudi Rummel's book *Death by Government*.[10] Better be sitting down. He gives us the numbers on how there were about five times as many innocent citizens murdered *by their own governments* in the twentieth century (a proven 167 million) as there were soldiers killed by enemies in battle (some 50 million). His conclusion is that *nurturing governments are bad for your health.* That is why the nurture-based idea that the human brain is a blank slate – empty of anything innate, or hardwired – is, as Noam Chomsky put it, "a dictator's dream."

So much for the downsides of both "philosophies." The ire aroused by each camp is easy to source. The nature camp has been guilty of supporting biologically justified racial regimes and race-cleansing eugenics programs based on the idea that human nature is fixed. The nurture camp has been guilty of building killer totalitarian regimes justified by the conviction that human nature is plastic and infinitely malleable. There are no good guys in this ongoing debate. As a result, biology today, like anthropology, is a field of study at war with itself. For that matter, somewhere within all the social sciences today, we can usually find lurking an implied, if not explicit, morality rooted in the nature-nurture debate and therefore a hidden, if not explicit, political theory.

WHERE THE NATURE-NURTURE DEBATE STANDS TODAY

Today, cultural relativism is on the way out, and moral relativism is looking for the door. As Stanford anthropologist Renato Rosaldo puts it, "cultural relativism has a bad reputation in many quarters."[11] However, as it turns out, most social scientists are quite unsophisticated in philosophy and moral theory, so it was not theory but experience that began to change their minds. Typically, the neophyte cultural relativist argues that whatever another culture does or thinks is good and must be good – until he neutrally observes some terrified teenager's clitoris getting shaved off and her vagina sewed up by a leering local witch doctor. Then he starts to wonder if the nonmoral descriptions provided by his pseudo-scientific relativism could be part of the problem.

At any rate (as we saw in chapter 4), serious people are once again gingerly prepared to say that some cultures are bad, backward, or even sick in their customs and beliefs. Very few will now argue that morally speaking, anything goes. So by the 1970s there was a new perception emerging that relativism was itself intellectually and morally sloppy, even politically dangerous, and attention began turning once again to the quest for human nature. This in turn provoked new thinking about the relationship between nature and nurture. A lot of new research was beginning to show that the learning we call nurture cannot occur without the pre-adaptations of nature.

THE REACTION: RETURNING TO BIOLOGICAL TRUTH

The reaction to extreme nurture-thinking began in the animal labs. Scientists began to wonder why those cute monkeys and chimps so arduously taught new behaviours tended to forget them by bedtime, returning, as if newly born, to their old ways. A lot of new studies were also appearing that showed biological species are not as malleable as once thought. There were big-selling books like Konrad Lorenz's *On Aggression*, Robert Ardrey's *The Territorial Imperative*, Desmond Morris's *The Naked Ape*, and Lionel Tiger and Robin Fox's *The Imperial Animal*.[12] All of them argued for a permanent human nature rooted in an earlier hunter-gatherer history and for such taboo ideas as the existence of innate and permanent gender differences. Humans, they gingerly suggested, share a common "human nature," or "program," that is fixed, universal, and predictable in a great many respects, often without regard to material or social conditions. If we insist on engineering society, they said, then at least the positive aspects of this human nature ought to be taken into account as its basis rather than flatly denied. Societies ought to be structured to promote what is biologically natural and good (the family, social bonding, caring, altruism, and the like) and to discourage what is biologically natural but bad (such as excess aggression, hostility, war, social exclusionism, and the like) rather than simply subjecting everything to an egalitarian myth that has never been substantiated as a natural condition for human beings.

In the meantime, the fast-changing science of biology – now probing aggressively into genetics, the structure of DNA, the molecular workings of the cell, neurobiology via PET scans of the brain at work, more sophisticated studies of animal behaviour, and of course, the Human Genome Project – soon found itself arguing for all sorts of hardwired, biologically based human behaviours and innate characteristics. This meant biology was heading for a lot of moral controversy as it moved to the forefront of the natural as well as the social sciences. It had been acceptable for biologists to study hardwired behaviour in animals and for sociologists to study the effects of environment on humans. But woe to any who dared to merge these two fields of study!

In the next chapter we will see what happened to Edward Wilson of Harvard, the first distinguished scientist who had the audacity to publish his theory that many human social attributes are biologically based, hardwired, universal, and absolute. In what follows it will be important to separate the many interesting features and fixtures of human biological life from the intriguing theories relied on to explain their existence. About the facts, there is not much question, but about the theories, quite a bit. However, we should never let a questionable theory ruin a good fact.

7

Hardwired: The Universals
of Human Biology, Sex, and Brain Sex

The war over biology has been waged – is still being waged – between mostly atheistic natural scientists who deeply believe all things have solely a material cause and (as often) atheistic social scientists who believe the same thing. Despite the affection of both camps for a materialism that if followed strictly would eliminate all intellectual and moral freedom, the latter have a career interest in "social progress." Accordingly, they are acutely worried that to admit human behaviour is hardwired in any way is to surrender to fatalism, to admit that nothing whatever can be done to change the course of society. That is why any mention of innate biological tendencies triggers an emotional fire alarm. If true, it would mean things must be exactly what they are, that all social scientists can forget progress (and most of their research, too). So whereas many biologists are very excited about discovering the underlying *truth* about human nature (right down to the actions of cells and neurons) and hope this will once and for all put an end to moral and political confusion by revealing our human nature, social scientists see only despair. Hence the war over biology. It is a modern manifestation of the ancient dualism discussed in the previous chapter, a war that starts with conflicting beliefs about nature and nurture and the extent of human freedom, with convictions raging from no freedom at all to complete freedom.

Natural scientists, like most ordinary people, have always assumed that animals are born with characteristic hardwired instincts and behaviours that are species-specific. Lions are born to roar, birds to sing, and hawks to fly. For most of history, until the twentieth century, humans were considered this way, too: not quite animals and not quite angels but somewhere in between. Then as a well-intended antidote to centuries of racism and nasty class domination, we suddenly got the argument that humans are completely different from other species. Their minds and natures, we were told, are materially undetermined. Unlike other species, humans have the unique capacity to create and transmit culture, and it is human culture that creates human behaviour and all social and moral differences. For many socially conscious people, this rather recent belief – one never before entertained seriously – was very exciting. It meant that all the injustices in this world might one day be corrected by proper manipulation of the sociocultural environment.

This appealing notion was soon accepted by almost all academics without question as a comforting faith, even though at the time, in the absence of modern CAT and PET scanners and today's sophisticated experimental techniques, there was no brain-based evidence, pro or con. The new faith was underpinned by nothing but an attractive model of the human mind that we saw in earlier chapters and that came to be called the Standard Social Science Model. Others simply called it "the blank slate," referring to an old idea floated by the British philosopher John Locke that the mind is empty except for what is put into it by experience. By the first couple of decades of the twentieth century, this model had become orthodoxy, and it dominated Western social science more or less undisturbed until 1975, when a small bomb exploded.

That year, a brilliant and unassuming – some later said, a very naive – world-famous Harvard entomologist, a bug professor named Edward O. Wilson, published a beautifully illustrated, expensive coffee-table book entitled *Sociobiology: The New Synthesis*. It is true that by then the Standard Model had already been weakened by recent work on animals and on human aggression, and this slow shift from earlier biological assumptions about a fixed human nature to the plasticity of the blank-slate model – and back again – is nicely detailed by Stanford professor Carl Degler in his comprehensive prize-winning book *In Search of Human Nature: The Decline and Revival of Darwinism in American Social Thought*.[1] Degler makes it quite clear that much of the blank-slate belief was created from thin air in obedience to ideological, rather than scientific, imperatives by social scientists with leftist political leanings – which is to say, by (and by their own admission) about 80 per cent of ardent social scientists everywhere, who, as it happens, badly need the blank-slate theory to be true so they can devote themselves to purging society of evil in the name of progressive social ideals. This was the hornet's nest into which Wilson wandered clutching his five-pound book.

Here was a man fed-up with what he saw as a dithering intellectual and moral confusion in the social sciences and who thought the solution was *to study human beings as if they were like any other animal.* He defined this new science of "sociobiology" as "the systematic study of the biological basis of all social behaviour."[2] It was a concise definition that drew blood. For what do *human* social behaviours have to do with things *biological?* people asked. Plenty, said Wilson. We are no different from other species. For him and most other biologists, the ultimate underlying motive for all social behaviour … is biological.

Well, if he wanted to see a swift and viciously adaptive reaction from the human species called *Homo academicus,* he could hardly have done better than threaten their intellects and livelihoods in this manner. They turned on him like an outraged tribe of chimps defending a pile of fresh bananas from a brash intruder. The ongoing "debate" is richly detailed in Ullica Segerstråle's fascinating autopsy of the first twenty-five years of the sociobiology controversy, called *Defenders of the Truth,*[3] including the infamous scene – witnessed by the author – where poor Wilson sat quietly in a fine business suit waiting to deliver a keynote speech to five hundred specialists in animal biology.

Suddenly, a rag-tag mob of Marxist professors and students shouting "Racist Wilson, you can't hide, we charge you with genocide!" rushed up to the podium and grabbed the microphone to denounce sociobiology. Wilson sat stunned, but dignified, as two of them poured a whole jug of ice water over his head, soaking him through, and then ran off-stage before anyone could react. The organizers sputtered and apologized as a shocked Wilson got up, soaking wet, to a standing ovation and presented his evidence for the genetic basis of animal and human behaviour. What he got to see first-hand and for the first time in his life was a deeply angry reaction, not from natural scientists who found his work on animal nature scientifically unimpeachable but from social scientists and political radicals whose revolutionary premises about nurture were rooted in beliefs diametrically opposed to Wilson's. They were instinctively aware that if the blank-slate model ever crumbled, so would much of their research, reputations, ideals, and careers. They were scientists who knew they were under attack … but this time from science itself!

To make things worse, Wilson's book announced an audacious attempt to integrate various other social sciences – as well as all the humanities – into biology. He was keen to "biologicize" all the softer social sciences because he was convinced that unless they rested on a modern basis for calculating "adaptive significance" in relation to population genetics, their explanatory and predictive powers were paltry and misdirected, if not useless. So confident was he of the interpretive powers of "neo-Darwin-ian" evolution theory to explain all aspects of animal and human social behaviour that to the dismay of innumerable professionals in what they thought were unrelated fields, he blithely wrote: "it may not be too much to say that sociology and the other social sciences, as well as the humanities, are the last branches of biology waiting to be included in the Modern Synthesis."[4] The humanities were to become a "branch" of biology? If it had not been so outrageous, it would have been humorous. As readers will see from the analysis below, the idea that human consciousness has a strictly material basis is so clearly unsophisticated it would barely merit comment were it not for Wilson's obvious enthusiasm for his subject and charmingly clear expository style. He was merely expressing what the majority of scientists continue to believe.[*]

The fundamental reason for the reaction against Wilson and his new science was that it threatened to redefine human beings as genetic and adaptive material automatons. But the fact that modern scientists are trained to dismiss all but material causes does not prove that all things have only material causes. In chapter 5, on the constants of nature, we saw that a great many illustrious modern physicists reject such a narrow view of human consciousness or, at the least, settle for calling the whole business a mystery. Ironically, although Wilson thinks biology ought to absorb many other sciences, in the end it will likely be physics that will absorb biology.

Wilson claimed that the workings of "the hypothalamic-limbic com-plex" and "natural selection" must be relied upon to explain *even ethics and the very existence of ethical philosophers*, and this led immediately to a kind of moral panic that he was basically saying: humans are not free; they cannot change. So his enemies fairly leapt to one conclusion: Wilson wants us to accept all the injustices of human life just as they are. For in his belief system, everything, *including the moral illusion that human behaviour can be altered at will*, is an illusion, a product of biological forces. Wilson had even dared to say that in the long span of evolution, "the individual organism counts for nothing ... [it] does not live for itself. Its primary function is not even to produce other organisms; it reproduces genes, and it serves as their temporary carrier."[5]

---

* Wilson and his sympathizers fail to see or to admit that in a solely material world noth-ing – that is, no *thing* – can be privileged, which is to say that one thing cannot sit in judgment of another thing. In a strictly material world there can be no degree, no hi-erarchy of values, no true or false, good or bad, no science, no consciousness. Only a nonmaterial entity such as human consciousness can perceive or value or rank a ma-terial thing.

At such a time, when the old idea of a common and universal human nature had been almost entirely extinguished and replaced by a militant moral and cultural relativism in the mind of just about every modern thinker, it was surely refreshing to see Wilson at work. Here was a cat among the pigeons, and any lay reader could access his clear message to the effect that hundreds of human social behaviours are universal (even if they rejected his reasons why). What follows is a short summary of his belief system from the first chapter of *On Human Nature*, where all is laid bare. I say "belief system" because although he presents all his opinions as raw fact, it is not hard to see that while much of the biology is very interesting and likely true, it must be separated from his far-reaching and frankly amateurish moral and philosophical speculation.[6]

My caveat to all this is that while Wilson and many others since (who have undergone a rebranding as "evolutionary psychologists") have indeed laid bare many fascinating – and universal – facts about human social and psychological behaviour, there is quite a difference between accurately determining a fact and explaining its true cause, meaning, and ultimate purpose. For example, we may determine the action of the law of gravity with incredible precision, without having the correct explanation for its existence. As mentioned in my earlier chapter on physics, we still don't understand what gravity is, although we know very precisely how it works. In other words, a fact may be true, while the best workable explanation for it may or may not be true. Wilson's new science has had a great deal of success unveiling new biologically based facts and patterns of behaviour in animals and humans while spawning a number of new fields of study. But what is relied on to explain these facts of human nature? Mainly the neo-Darwinian framework, which at this point does appear to be a fairly simple and elegant explanation for many human and animal adaptations. In science the stage is always given to the theory that explains the most in the simplest and most parsimonious way. And for biology, until a better one comes along, that theory is neo-Darwinism. Deny it and critique it we may. I certainly do. I believe that natural selection is at work in all life to the extent that species do micro-adapt to their environments in many ways. But I and many others who enjoy following this subject do not find the claim that this process explains the creation of new species, nor the claim that humans evolved from apes, very convincing. Even Professor Richard Lewontin, the evolutionist from Harvard mentioned above, has said that "we don't know anything about the ancestors of the human species" and that "all the fossils which have been dug up and are claimed to be ancestors – we haven't the faintest idea whether they are ancestors."7 So for me, evolution theory explains micro-evolution and adaptation pretty well, but it cannot answer the ultimate questions. These remain a mystery. In short, there are many objections to the theory,* and an increasing number of distinguished scientists are now its most eloquent critics. But a theory may stay in crisis a long time and still serve as a powerfully predictive device. So I end up in the position of rather admiring what Wilson and his ilk have revealed about human nature, without buying their explanation for the ultimate causes.

Finally, the main purpose of this book is to reveal universals and absolutes in nature and human nature, not to take issue with the reasons for them or to dispute whole fields of thought like Darwinism – much

---

* Among the objections is the fact that the human brain is vastly overevolved, so to speak. It has capacities far beyond those needed for hunter-gatherer environmental challenges – which is to say, nothing in human experience could have selected by trial and error for a human intellectual capacity to play chess, to discover the law of gravity or $E = mc^2$, to send men to the moon, or to understand the necessary and eternal truth of prime numbers or concepts such as infinity. So "how can one possibly explain that natural selection gave us a program that was vastly more sophisticated than was required for survival?"[8] Missing fossil evidence is also damaging to the theory. Darwin himself saw that if ample fossils of the assumed transitional species were not found, the theory would be disproved. They have not been found. The "Cambrian explosion" is also a mystery: why do most of the species appear in the Cambrian period as fully developed species, most of which have not altered since? Most recently, damage has been done to the theory by arguments from design, claiming "irreducible complexity." In short, organisms can be reduced in complexity only so far, until we reach an irreducible complexity, and then we must explain how it is that complex interacting and interdependent parts of organisms can evolve together in an intricate design without a designer. The mousetrap is an analog. With any of its parts missing, the trap is useless. All had to be designed at once. Logically, this should not be possible without a designer and a controlling final purpose. A most interesting peer-reviewed article on this latter question was published on 4 August 2004 by Stephen C. Meyer in the *Proceedings of the Biological Society of Washington* 117, no. 2: 213–39. This journal is published by the National Museum of Natural History at the Smithsonian Institute, Washington, DC. The importance of this article, titled "The Origin of Biological Information and the Higher Taxonomic Categories," is that it was by a prestigious scientist, was peer-reviewed before publication, and reaches the unambiguous conclusion that intelligent design is "the most causally adequate" explanation for the sudden appearance of so many organisms during the Cambrian period. The article, so far unimpeachable, seems to be the start of a paradigm shift in Darwinian evolution theory. Readers may also enjoy dipping into the books listed in the notes,[9] a number of which are cited in Meyer's article.

as I find the debate fascinating. However, because it is of such great interest, I want to begin by exposing a few of the glaring weaknesses of the crude materialism underlying the sociobiological framework and then get to the meat of this chapter by showing the reader some of the universal, or absolute, facts of human nature that Wilson and other biological scientists have laid bare.

THE MATERIALIST'S DILEMMA

At bottom, Wilson wants to know "how the mind works" and why in this way rather than some other. Most of all (and is this not surprising for a scientist?), he wants an answer to the question: "What is man's ultimate nature?" Straightaway, he departs from the scientific question "How?" and heads for the question "Why?" It was through playing philosopher in this way that he got into trouble in the first place, and his answers are alternately humble and audacious.

He begins by arguing that "if" the brain is a machine made of ten billion nerve cells, and "if" it is the summed activity of chemical and electrical reactions, and "if" humankind evolved by Darwinian natural selection, then "genetic chance and environmental necessity, *not God*, made the species."[10] There you have it. He draws the ancient battle lines up front. This is to be a war between science and theology. In short, he thinks his brand of materialistic science will eliminate the God problem. He is about to propose an alternative, purely material God.

But two things strike me as bizarre about his conclusion. First, he restricts the "if" questions to mundanely materialist possibilities. This is strange given that no one has ever come close to describing the human mind or even the mind of a flea. Brains we know something about. But about minds, almost nothing at all. Ask yourself: where, exactly, is consciousness located? If the brain is fully packed with matter and there is no little theatre screen in there, then where, exactly, *is* all that we see, imagine, wonder, and dream? Everyone has imagined and dreamed in very large stereoscopic fashion! But how, exactly, is that done? We simply have no idea. Large chunks of human and animal brains can even be surgically or accidentally severed without loss of consciousness. We just do not know where or how consciousness is located nor how it can arise from something strictly material. Nor can we dig out bits of a living brain until we find out. But what if the brain is a material object that somehow generates a nonmaterial phenomenon called "mind"? That seems more likely to me than the belief that "if" it is "a machine," then everything it generates is also a machine. After all, a magnet is a thing that generates a nonthing, or force – something nonmaterial. We saw in our chapter on the constants of nature that at the quantum level material reality cannot be determined precisely. Is it so impossible to imagine that the brain, made of atoms and electrical activity, the quantum brain as some are now suggesting, somehow behaves in the same way?

Second, I don't know much about God. Certainly not enough to say what God is and, if He exists, what God can or cannot do. But what if God does exist and Darwinian selection theory, *if* it is true (a doubt Wilson, to his credit, often raises), happens to be His preferred method for creating species? If so, then Darwinism and God could both be true. For that matter, the universe in which we live (if not just one of many possible universes, as some physicists claim) may be a "sacramental" one, as the late and endearing philosopher Etienne Gilson once suggested. When we strike a match, we get a flame. When we jump, we fall to the ground. When we think, we have a thought. Gilson said that logically speaking, there is no way to disprove the possibility that God simply wills these and all other things to be so, thus rendering ... a sacramental universe. Some will say that is a crazy idea. And it may be. But the possibility cannot be refuted logically or disproven practically. What I am getting at is that Wilson has drawn the outlines of his own story – a creation story – that ends by snaring him. It is surely charming that both he and his enemies, materialists all, have a deep concern about the possible ultimate meaning of existence, and this interest sneaks into their science such that most of their speculations, when turned toward human beings, end up having theological implications.

Wilson fairly leaps to such conclusions. He speaks of the "two great spiritual dilemmas" brought to light by his "new naturalism." The first, he declares, is that "no species, ours included, possesses a purpose beyond the imperatives created by its genetic history," which is to say that all species "lack any immanent purpose or guidance from agents beyond their immediate environment" and, more particularly, that "the human mind is constructed in a way that locks it inside this fundamental constraint and forces it to make choices with a purely biological instrument."[11]

Now, here we have a *construction*, locking us inside a *constraint*, that "forces" us to make "choices" with an *instrument*. To make choices? Surely, the very essence of the word "choice" is freedom from constraint, is it not? Wilson attempts to extricate himself from this dilemma by suggesting that even the capacity "to select" certain specific esthetic judgments and religious beliefs, rather than others, "must have arisen from the same mechanistic process." So we end up with a freely choosing machine (the human mind), which is just "a device for survival and reproduction," with reason included as one of the techniques the brain uses to ensure its own end goal, otherwise known as a purpose. Phew! The human intellect, he assures us, was not constructed "even to understand itself, but to promote the survival of human genes."[12] He presents a contradictory model of unconsciously conscious beings.

Wilson betrays a gross naiveté when he tells us that all spiritual belief systems and religions have long since been subjected to "humiliating disproofs" by scientists. He states this without modesty because from his viewpoint all religions are just "enabling mechanisms for survival." But in their place, curiously, he proposes a new religion: Darwinian evolution theory, which he describes as "probably the best myth we will ever have"![13] At least he agrees it is a myth. So let's see now: in the place of a mythical belief in a loving, moral, and all-powerful God whose workings we only dimly glimpse, he wants a mythical belief in a blind mechanical chance process without any purpose whatsoever except blind replication ... the workings of which we only dimly glimpse. For most people, there is no contest as to which is the more desirable myth.

Wilson attempts to salvage his precarious moral expedition by saying that there are "ethical premises inherent in man's biological nature" and that "innate censors and motivators" exist in the brain from which "morality evolved as an instinct." He trusts that scientists studying "the limbic system," where he thinks these moral values hang out, will one day clarify everything, enabling us "to make optimum choices among the competing criteria of progress."[14] Plumping for "optimum choices" in a fractious world sounds to me like an old recipe for majority rule. As for "progress"? This sounds like a dreamlander's recipe for coercive social planning. Perceptive readers will feel the hand of the state (or Wilson) going deeper into their pockets.

What we have here is a biologized philosophy of life in which all human behaviours and social structures are characterized as "organs," or "extensions of the genes that exist because of their superior adaptive value." Wilson is so convinced of his new myth that he imagines a "total knowledge" can be provided by finally getting "right down to the neuron and the gene." Then, astonishingly, he calls for a "genetically accurate and hence completely fair code of ethics."[15] This is weird stuff, for it implies that ethical behaviour may one day proceed materially and automatically *in the absence of all moral standards and deliberation*. No one has ever located such a moral "organ," or neuron, or gene, nor will they. And the idea that true wisdom should one day be a matter of genetic manipulation or Darwinian selection is a sadly dispiriting and woefully inadequate explanation and hope for human existence, by any measure.

In retrospect, Wilson and his followers have simply latched onto a certain incisive interpretive tool and then used it to explain too much. But we have to remember that these are only theories, interpretive *devices*, not real things. Darwinian theory happens to "explain" a lot of animal and human behaviour more neatly than the current alternatives. But the result of using any such intellectual cutting device is similar to what we might expect to find if we gave a clever child a truck full of clay and a specific cookie cutter and ask him to make as many shapes as possible: a fantastic combination of the same cookie-cutter shapes. A different cutter – whether intellectual or physical – will produce different shapes. Darwinian natural selection theory is such a cookie cutter, so the results of the cutting are pretty much predictable in advance. I have no doubt that in the future other cutters will be invented and other intellectual "solutions" to the puzzles of existence arrived at accordingly. For now, it is apparent that these puzzles have tempted biologists out of their field and into confusion. Here is a little example.

GERRYMANDERING EVOLUTION THEORY: ARE WE REBELS OR ROBOTS?

Surely one of the most bizarre positions taken by modern evolutionary theorists such as Richard Dawkins, author of the bestselling book *The Selfish Gene*,[16] is that even as they insist that man is simply an organism serving as a "temporary carrier" of selfish genes that determine everything, they also talk about our "freedom" to alter our social, and hence biological, environment. In imagery that returned to haunt him, Dawkins spoke of the eternal gene thus: "now they swarm in huge colonies, safe inside gigantic lumbering robots, sealed off from the outside world, communicating with it by tortuous indirect routes, manipulating it by remote control. They are in you and in me; they created us, body and mind; and their preservation is the ultimate rationale for our existence." Ignore for the moment the glaring philosophical contradictions involved in believing in a material thing that nevertheless *acts* as a conscious agent, *manipulating, communicating, and creating*, as he puts it. But there is more. After jumping into hot water as the ultimate determinist, Dawkins drew so much objection he tried to jump out again, stating, "My own philosophy of life begins with an explicit rejection of

Darwinism as a normative principle for living, even while I extol it as
the explanatory principle for life."[17] But it seems to me that either we
are utterly determined in our being – robots and carriers – as he first
argued, or we are not. How can we be both free and not free? Once a
little freedom to modify our own biologically dependent behaviour is
admitted, doesn't this precious scientific determinism become a matter
of degree? For either material biology directs the mind utterly or the
mind can affect that direction. Dawkins seems to argue both positions.
This sends us right back to the ancient master-slave dualism, to the
realm of philosophy, and to the problem of free will. When confronted
with questions about contraception, for example, Dawkins has answered that the human brain has grown so large it has enabled us "to
rebel" against our own natures.[18] This is his response to the reality that
since the 1970s all the Western democracies (with the exception of the
United States) have been shrinking in natural population. In other
words, after arguing that the fundamental driving force of all biological
life is genetic self-replication – getting our genes into the next generation – he also argues that we are actually not compelled to do this,
which surely means it cannot be a fundamental driving force of human
behaviour, even though this is what he said it was all along. Certainly,
the history of modern contraception and abortion-on-demand – in this
latter case, the lives of millions of genetic replicas expunged – does not
suggest we are feverish gene replicators. Except in one sense: it is possible to express feverish gene-replicating behaviour we cannot seem to
stop (lifelong sexual desire) and at the same time block its consequences (with contraception and abortion). But this makes a mockery
of the supposed motive of genuine (actual) gene reproduction. It is to
convert real sex and gene replication into purely gestural behaviour.
But this converts the motive into a gesture, too.

Then we come to Wilson's social vision. After stipulating that aggression is a fixed aspect of human nature and how cats and rats become aggressive and cruel when confined to small spaces, he proceeds to his
program for humans. If we wish to reduce our own aggressive behaviour
and "lower our own catecholamine and corticosteroid titers to levels that
make us all happier, we should design our population densities and social systems in such a way as to make aggression inappropriate in most
conceivable daily circumstances and, hence, less adaptive."[19] There is a
lot of confusion in that statement. Notice that his solutions are all materialistic. He doesn't say that the fellow who is feeling too aggressive should
put down his gun and consider jogging, loving, or praying. Rather, he

wants to dial up less aggression through better public housing. This boils down to Wilson and his scientist friends attempting to alter the consequences of human biology through amateur social engineering. In doing so, they are assuming that the mind, or spirit, or soul is free and that by relying upon its good judgments planners can master biology and change the genetic pool through an act of the will. And this brings us back again to the ancient mind-body dualism with which we started. We do have a human nature, but its worst consequences can be controlled by the force of will and the best enjoyed for the benefit of all. That is what Socrates and Christ and Aristotle and so many others down through the ages have always argued.

My main interest, however, is not to dispute Darwinian theory. I have simply wanted to show how weak it is as a philosophy of life but also, as we shall see in what follows, how strong it can be as a predictive device for actual human behaviour. While I am more than ever convinced it is a theory in crisis, it also seems apparent we are stuck with it until a better theory comes along. Such work we can safely entrust to others. For the present, it must be granted that it is very interesting and powerful, just as Ptolemy's theory of the movement of the planets was interesting and powerful, for with the exception of a few particular planetary motions, it predicted things as well as our current theory. But it was too complicated. And above all, it was not true. Just so, Darwinian theories of natural selection (and now, of "inclusive fitness," "kin selection," "reciprocal altruism," and so on) are indisputably powerful and are, as Wilson writes – in rather forthright theological language: "the light and the way."[20] And that language is not that far-fetched, for as Wilson hoped, Darwinian evolution theory is indeed now serving almost the entire scientific and academic priesthood as a kind of new creation myth (although they are very frustrated that the broader public has never even been close to accepting it).

Presently, I am not concerned with the ultimate *why* of the human behaviours detailed by early sociobiologists such as Wilson or by the "evolutionary psychologists" (to be reviewed below) who have largely replaced them. Scholars will always dispute the why. Rather, in a book that critiques relativism, my main interest is to provide evidence that beneath the astonishingly varied surface, certain *universal human biological, psychological, and social behaviours* do in fact exist. So whatever may be the virtues or vices of his explanations for these behaviours, Wilson and his followers have rendered a service to all those in search of *biologically sourced,* if not wholly *biologically dependent,* explanations of human nature. Such people – and I count myself as one – are interested not in denying human freedom in any way but in resisting the modern relativist tendency to discount, ignore, bury, ridicule, deny, impugn, or malign what is *common and universal to human beings everywhere*. In this sense, biology neither limits our freedom nor defends the status quo (especially if, as I believe – contrary to Wilson – a core universal of all human life is the free nature of human consciousness). Rather, it is the opposite: biology provides another natural and universal basis for uniting all humanity, and the knowledge of it must one day serve as a specific repellent to coercive social and moral engineering. In this sense, *whereas culture and ideology divide, biology unites.*

Here, I present a sampling of the biological constants and universals of human nature as gleaned from the field. The rest, including the references for them, are provided in the appendix at the end of this book. There is no attempt to be complete here, and in any case that would be impossible, as nowhere have I been able to find a complete up-to-date inventory of such universals and constants. So what follows is "under construction," so to speak. But I think readers will find these observations of interest. Most of all, I hope that a familiarity with them will generate something like the peace of belonging, the feeling that we are not alone, that we all participate in a human nature that is universal and far from relative. And finally, if we are going to persist in designing societies, then let us do so from a grounding in what is good, natural, and common to all humanity and cease trying to pretend otherwise.

SOME GENERAL BIOLOGICAL LAWS

Here are a few biological "laws" that may be applicable to all organic life. They are not laws in the strict sense of governing something but are rather more like observed patterns that appear to be universal, if not constant. Some call these "ceteris paribus" laws, meaning they hold and are true, making quite accurate predictions possible, "all other things being equal."

- Von Baer's Law, on group characteristics of species
- Wallace's Law, on the relation of species to pre-existing species
- Marsh's Law, on increases in brain size
- Cope's Law, on increases in body size
- Dollo's Law, on irreversibility of evolutionary change
- Hardy-Weinberg Law, on gene frequencies

- Wilson's Law, on number of body parts in a lineage
- Fisher's Theorem, on rate of evolution
- Williston's Law, on number and diversity of body parts
- Universal Scaling Laws,[21] on mathematical descriptions of function and structure

Definitions for these laws are spelled out more thoroughly in the appendix.

Biological Constants, or Standards, Applying to All Organic Life

There is nothing relative about these universal characteristics of all organic life forms:

- All organisms use lipid membranes.
- All organisms use nucleic acid.
- All organisms use an alphabet of exactly four chemical letters to spell out their genetic messages.
- All organisms use DNA for genetic information storage and proteins for metabolically active molecules.
- All organisms construct proteins from an alphabet of twenty amino acids.
- In order to transform genes into living organisms, all organisms use an identical genetic code (the system of rules by which "letters" of every nucleic acid gene are translated into corresponding "letters" of a protein).

Some Biological Features Humans Share with Other Mammals and Primates

The following biological features are shared with other mammals:

- warm-bloodedness
- body hair
- lungs
- four limbs
- an elaborate brain
- ability to learn and communicate
- female mammary-gland milk production

Some biological features are shared only with primates (in varying degrees):

- upright posture
- flexible arms and hands
- separated fingers and opposable thumbs
- prolonged immaturity of offspring
- greater reliance on stereoscopic vision than on smell
- a high order of intelligence
- the ventral premotor area, a cortical site of the brain having to do with visual-motor coordination

I venture to add here that although apes and chimps can be taught an amazing number of clever things, they cannot produce these things themselves. After the teaching and rewarding stops, the tricks stop. Anthropoids cannot approach human intelligence. There is no gap. It is an unbridgeable chasm.

Wilson adds that humans also share with most other primates intimate social groupings that number in general from ten to one hundred adults, never just two, as in some species, or thousands, as with others like fish and insects. Social play is another recurrent and strongly developed activity, featuring role practice, mock aggression, sex practice, and exploration.[22]

John Alcock, in *The Triumph of Sociobiology*, adds another human-chimp trait: "Humans and chimps are ... the only species among the 4,000 species of mammals in which male relatives form groups to raid other groups while living in and defending the area of their birth."[23]

SOME UNIVERSALS AND CONSTANTS OF HUMAN BIOCHEMISTRY AND PHYSIOLOGY

All biological organisms survive due to the existence in them of a relatively constant and universal (across, and particular to, all species) regulating system known as "homeostasis" (meaning "same state").[24] This term refers to the existence of a privately maintained and dynamic steady-state internal environment in which any changes that threaten to destabilize the organism are met by compensatory physiological processes aiming to return the organism to its own particular species-specific homeostatic stability. For human beings, there are seven specific factors that must be maintained in homeostatic balance – that is, which must be *constant* within a very fine range of tolerance for all humans in order to sustain life. These are the body's (1) concentration of nutrient molecules, (2) concentration of salts and electrolytes, (3) ratio of oxygen to carbon dioxide, (4) ratio of

waste-products to nutrients, (5) ratio of acidity to alkalinity, (6) temperature, and (7) blood volume and pressure. For all human beings, these
seven homeostatic factors are coordinated, controlled, and adjusted for
small variances by eleven bodily systems. These are the respiratory, circula-
tory, digestive, urinary, skeletal, muscular, immune, nervous, integumen-
tary, and endocrine systems, to which may be added the reproductive
system, which is not in itself homeostatic but is obviously universal.

Below are given some of the biochemical reference ranges for a few of
the hundreds of substances and values crucial to the survival of human
beings. A more or less complete list of the clinical ranges for these substances and factors may be found at any good clinical biochemistry website. There are differences in some human reference ranges according to
age and gender. But even these are universally observed. All homeostatic
biological systems function in terms of ranges rather than absolute fixed
points, as it is this limited flexibility that enables adjustments of the various internal systems in response to challenges from the internal or external environment. Nevertheless, the ranges themselves are very narrow yet
extraordinarily stable in all healthy human beings.

Reference Ranges for Some Physiological Universals of Human Beings

- temperature: the average human core internal temperature is a remarkably stable 100°F (the average taken by mouth is 98.6°F); convulsions leading to death will occur at about 106°F
- blood pH: the ratio of acidity to alkalinity is 7.35 to 7.45; if the human
body falls below a pH of 6.8 (acidosis) or above a pH of 8.0 (alkalosis),
death follows in a few seconds
- glucose (nonfasting blood sugar): 60-120 mg/dL[*]
- sodium (salt level): 137-47 mmol/L
- oxygen (in arterial blood): 15-23%
- creatinine: male, 0.6-1.3 mg/dL; female, 0.5-1.1 mg/dL
- potassium: 3.4-5.3 mmol/dL
- calcium: 8.7-10.7 mg/dL
- total cholesterol: less than 200 mg/dL

These are just a few of several hundred *standard universal clinical reference
ranges* for human biochemistry and physiology. Others are mentioned in
the appendix.

---

* mg = milligram; L = litre; dL = decilitre; mmol = millimole

*Some Distinctive Human Biological and Physiological Universals**

- A species-specific heritage: we have a human, species-specific genetic heritage, different from that of all other species.
- A complex consciousness: all human beings have a brain-mind consciousness, self-awareness, knowledge of death, interest in the meaning of life, and so on, which manifests at a level of self-reflective depth, complexity, and expressiveness not approached by any other life form.
- A mind-body dualism: humans are the only life form (as far as we know) that experiences a mind-body dualism that in turn produces a brain-mind "freedom" of action in the context of its own biological constraints. Humans can indeed rebel against their own biology, as they do, for example, in using contraception.
- Symbolic calculation: all humans have a brain-mind ability to reason and calculate with pure symbols at a level of difficulty and abstraction not remotely approached by any other life form. As a result, humans alone are able to learn about and solve immensely complicated theoretical questions solely by insight, foresight, imagination, and symbolic manipulation.
- Language and metalanguage: All humans have a brain-mind symbolic language and paralanguage (physical gestures) not approached by any other life form. Human communication even without sound, by way of paralinguistic signals, is the richest known. Other species can communicate in very sophisticated and intricate ways beyond human abilities (sight, hearing, sonar, navigation, etc.). And other animals can use signs. But only humans have the power of rule-based syntactic language constructions and a profound symbol-using capacity *of infinite scope*. Perhaps most distinctive of all, humans have a brain-mind capacity to form and use *metalanguages*. For example, a human grammar is a language about a language, or a metalanguage. The work of such as Noam Chomsky and Joseph Greenberg has after several decades finally persuaded most reluctant blank-slate enthusiasts that the human language capacity is *innate and universal* (see chapter 14).
- Capacity for mathematical abstraction: Humans alone have the brain-mind capacity for mathematical and physical abstraction, as in pure math and physics, and can describe all physical phenomena in the universe in such mathematical terms.

---

* As catalogued by this author, as well as others, as noted.

- All-pervasive cultural systems: Alone among the species, humans have the capacity to create all-pervasive cultures in the form of created and shared symbols and traditions that are learned and passed from generation to generation. Other creatures can be prompted to learn symbols, and even have some "traditions," but none have ever invented true transgenerational inherited cultures on their own. According to Wilson, although it is true that specific human cultures seem independent of each other and infinitely variable, "what has evolved is the [common and universal] *capacity* for culture."[25] However, as discussed in chapter 4, Donald E. Brown has provided a lengthy inventory of human universals expressed by all cultures in history.
- Human infant dependency: Alone among the species, human babies everywhere are unable to feed themselves when weaned, and human children have by far the longest period of dependency. Among mammals, with the exception only of canids (dogs), humans are the only species in which males regularly provision food for females.
- Female lifespan beyond fertility: Alone among the species, human females live for decades after their fertile reproductive years have ended. Evolutionists explain this as an essential adaptation to protect the human newborn during its extended dependency.
- General female lifespan: Female humans everywhere outlive males. Some evolutionists explain this as an adaptation of the caretaker parent – a phenomenon that holds true for all species. Whether male or female, the caretaker parent generally takes fewer life risks, among other things, and hence tends to outlive the noncaretaker parent. The survival advantage in human females in modern times is not due to lesser business stress or lesser aggression. It has deeper biological roots.

MORE UNIVERSALS INFERRED FROM SOCIAL
BEHAVIOUR ACCORDING TO THE MECHANISM
OF DARWINIAN NATURAL SELECTION THEORY

As mentioned, the theory of evolution developed by Darwin, after lingering in the backrooms of social science from the early part of the twentieth century until about the 1970s, has come back strongly as a modified theory (sometimes called "the modern synthesis") including modern genetic discoveries unavailable to Darwin. In this form it has been permeating most of the same social sciences that exerted themselves for almost a century to exclude Darwinism and other biological explanations of human behaviour on the grounds that humans are culture-bound but not biology-bound. That trend has been reversing vigorously.

Wilson sums up the new, or *neo-Darwinian*, theory:

> Let us pursue this matter systematically. The heart of the genetic hypothesis is the proposition, derived in a straight line from neo-darwinian evolutionary theory, that the traits of human nature were adaptive during the time [the five-million-year-long Pleistocene period] that the human species evolved and that genes consequently spread through the population that predisposed their carriers [human beings] to develop those traits. Adaptiveness means simply that if an individual displayed the traits he stood a greater chance of having his genes represented in the next generation than if he did not display the traits. The differential advantage among individuals in this strictest sense is called genetic fitness. There are three basic components of genetic fitness: increased personal survival, increased personal reproduction, and the enhanced survival and reproduction of close relatives who share the same genes by common descent ... [this] process, which Darwin called natural selection, describes a tight circle of causation ... [and] ... if the genetic components of human nature did not originate [in this manner] by natural selection, fundamental evolutionary theory is in trouble.[26]

In even plainer terms, this means that an individual of any species that is born with a genetic variation that turns out to be advantageous is more likely to survive and have more babies than other members of the same species, and if this trait is inherited by these more numerous offspring who will then have the same advantage, the new variation will spread throughout the whole population, eventually displacing the earlier and less advantageous type that had fewer offspring. Presto, a modified species! The simple logic is hard to defeat and, at bottom, is a matter of the advantageous replication of more adaptive genetic variations, the carriers of which replace those with less adaptive genes.

What follows is a culling of Wilson's sociobiological universals drawn from his *Sociobiology* (hereafter, S) and also from his *On Human Nature* (hereafter, OHN). Readers will notice some overlap between these and the cultural universals listed in chapter 4. What distinguishes this set of social behaviours from the former, however, is the consistent reference to the underlying causal mechanism of biological adaptation – that is, to their presumed biological and, ultimately, genetic basis. Brief mention of the adaptation argument in defence of each universal will sometimes be noted in brackets. Readers interested in the full Darwinian story, however, are advised to begin with Wilson's two books and then move to the works on "evolutionary psychology," listed below.

About the existence of these distinctive behaviours there is not much doubt. The controversy lies in debate over exactly why it is that humans everywhere behave in these ways. For the present, whether found to be ultimately true or false (or somewhere in between), the evolutionary myth, as Wilson calls it, is more broadly inclusive, simple, and coherent than other purely materialist explanations, and thus it holds sway among scientists – although not among ordinary people, theologians, or even most serious philosophers. It has serious critics, too, as mentioned, and other than the alternative Darwinian solutions offered by such as Richard Lewontin and the late Stephen Jay Gould, both self-described "Darwinian pluralists" who resist all determinism (and all absolutes), no one has yet come up with a better materialist framework.

Here, I give only a selection of sociobiological universals (readers will find more instances in the appendix):

- Contracts and altruism: Unlike other species, humans engage in long-remembered contracts and acts of reciprocal altruism that may be spaced over generations (S, 180). (Reciprocal altruism is said to be adaptive because it reinforces social bonding and hence mutual protection and survival. It is a selfish altruism, as all altruism may ultimately be from an evolutionary perspective.)
- Complex kinship ties: Humans are preoccupied with kinship ties to a degree inconceivable even in other extremely social species, such as among the bees, ants, apes, and so on (S, 180). (For the same adaptive reason as above.)
- Humans anatomically unique: We are anatomically unique. Our erect posture and wholly bipedal locomotion are not even approached in other primates that occasionally walk on their hind legs.
- Year-round sexual activity: Human beings have a year-round sexual activity not specifically linked to estrus (the female being periodically "in heat" or sexually hungry) or to procreation, as it is for all other mammals (S, 271, 278).
- Massive growth of the human brain: The human brain has grown from 400–500 cubic centimetres to its current range of 900 to 2,000 cc. The growth in the brain and in human intelligence is so great – about a tablespoon of brain matter every thousand years – that no

scale has been invented that can objectively compare man with chimpanzees and other living primates (S, 272). No organ in the history of life on earth, says Wilson, has grown faster (OHN, 87).

- Male domination: Males generally dominate females physically (S, 275). The adaptation is that the better hunters were bigger and faster and more naturally aggressive than their opposites. (This is the sort of obvious statement that drove Wilson's feminist critics crazy. They did not deny the domination. Rather, they were, and many are still, convinced male aggression is a learned behaviour that must be changed through education and social programming. Biologists disagree, and Wilson was blunt enough to say so. Any farmer who has ever owned a stallion or a bull before and after castration does not need a university degree to side with Wilson.)

- The universal family: The family, defined very broadly as "a set of closely related adults with their children," remains one of the universals of human social organization (OHN, 135). In adaptive terms, "it is to the reciprocal advantage of each man to obtain exclusive sexual rights to women and to monopolize their economic productivity ... [this] exchange has resulted in the near-universality of the pair-bond and the prevalence of extended families with men and their wives forming the nucleus" (OHN, 139).

- More kin selection: To this, John Alcock adds that sociobiological research shows it to be universally true. In keeping with neo-Darwinian "kin-selection" theory, he shows that stepfamilies have more conflict than intact families and that stepparents markedly skew their parental investment toward their own biological children. Stepchildren receive much less positive care "and run a vastly higher risk of physical abuse from a step-parent than from their 'biological' mother or father."* He

---

* In this respect, Alcock argues that knowledge of these sociobiological facts of life would inform stepparents that they were "letting themselves be manipulated by an evolved psychological mechanism that exists ... only to propagate segments of DNA, a chemical they cannot even see. Perhaps this realization would help a few stepparents fight against their genes and their evolved emotions instead of fighting with their spouse or stepchildren."[19] This is the sociobiologist's plea for "more evolutionary consciousness." The hope is that by learning more about the previously hidden causes of bad emotions, we will want to suppress them. Well, so much for the naiveté of sociobiologists. I have a hard time imagining a stepparent on the verge of swatting his wife, who suddenly stops because he remembers having read a little Darwin forty years ago. At any rate, an ugly emotion is likely to have ugly consequences whether its cause is believed to be in the genes or in the horoscope.

cites studies showing that for every 10,000 children in biologically intact families, the child-abuse rate is 3 in 10,000, whereas for children in families with a replacement parent, 120 in 10,000 were victims of child abuse. As for fatal child abuse, they calculated "that a child is seventy times more likely to be killed by a step-parent than by a genetic parent."[27]

- Human social bonding: I propose here, Gairdner's Law of human social bonding. I think this process is universal but have no means to test that claim. A Darwinian reason for it can easily be imagined: social bonding has a powerful group-survival value. This is a four-part process, explicit or implicit in the forming of all human groups, that relies on a kind of solemn rite of passage, the markers of which are *sacrifice, subordination, commitment* – and finally, that nasty old thing called *privilege*, with which egalitarians have so much trouble.

Sacrifice refers to the requirement that individuals aspiring to join a social group must voluntarily agree to place the common will of the group above personal needs. That is why the motto of organizations such as Rotary International is "Service above Self."

Subordination refers to the requirement that all members must submit to the authority and discipline of the group. For infidelity, members get expelled, Boy Scouts get demoted, spouses get divorced.

Commitment is the process whereby the prospective member who gets this far is asked formally to make a vow, or a public verbal or written commitment, to uphold shared ideals.

Privilege is the last stage, whereby society (sometimes backed by the law, as in family law) approves the bestowal of specific benefits and protections on each qualified member. That usually means money, status, and legal and group approval. It also usually means exclusion from those same privileges for all those who fail to, or do not wish to, conform to these requirements. Elsewhere, I have argued that this natural human desire for social bonding is inherently anti-egalitarian and that this is an irresolvable tension at the heart of modern liberal (egalitarian) democracies.[28]

FROM MIND TO BRAIN: EVOLUTIONARY PSYCHOLOGY

The central premise of [evolutionary psychology] is that there is a universal human nature ... at the level of evolved psychological mechanisms.[29]

Leda Cosmides, John Tooby, and Jerome H. Barkow,
The Adapted Mind (1992)

As a result of the continuous vitriolic attacks on sociobiology by indignant Marxists (and by other radicals – itself a behaviour that sociobiologists ought to study!), the term is now used with fear and trembling. And this is so despite its fruitfulness and continued predictive success concerning the social behaviour of all sorts of species, including ourselves. Most damaging of all, as mentioned, was the accusation that such research implicitly "supports the status quo" with respect to inequalities in social classes, gender, intelligence, and so on.

So the enemies of sociobiology began clamouring for scientific censorship (something they would deplore if applied to research they happened to favour). Many protest that even if human sociobiological findings are factually true and of scientific interest, they should be off limits to research. I do not see the value in doing research that devalues or debases others, from whatever perspective. The problem is that one person's scientific research becomes another's political weapon. Pretty soon, all research is off limits or at the least subjected to Orwellian approval procedures. In all this, it is important to see that few are resisting research or methodology: they are resisting what the research discovers about human nature.

The campaign against human nature succeeded beyond anyone's dreams and put a lot of reputations in jeopardy. No one wanted to risk being called a racist, as Wilson had unwittingly done. As a result, since 1975 sociobiology has quietly evolved into something now called "evolutionary psychology," which poor Wilson, who took the brunt of the early flack, insists is "the same thing." But evolutionary psychologists say it is different – at least different enough to attract a lot of new research with fewer political risks. Accordingly, there is now much more defiance in defence of the truth. Professor David Buss, an astonishingly productive leader in this field, states bluntly that "we must confront the truth about our human nature, however disturbing it may turn out to be."[30] He does not want pure science bent to ideological demands of any stripe. So let us take a brief look at what evolutionary psychology is and then return again to the main point of this chapter, which is to show that there are a lot of absolute biological, social, and psychological realities common to all human beings that are not in the least relative. Evolutionary psychology claims that because these things are universally true, there can be nothing racist or sexist about them. They are just the facts of life.

Sociobiology stressed that human social behaviour evolved adaptively during the millions of years of our hunter-gatherer period, which ended with the beginning of agriculture about 10,000 years ago, and that all evolution is controlled by, and can be accurately predicted according to, the underlying motive of "fitness," or reproductive success. Underneath all this, of course, are the determining genes that get passed along with each successful generation or eliminated from the gene pool if less successfully reproduced. The reproductive model is used for all evolutionary work and for this reason is sometimes labelled "baby counting" by its detractors.

Evolutionary psychology types all agree that "our modern skulls house a stone-age mind,"[31] but they also object that the simple genetic-fitness model relied upon by their predecessors was too limited. Fitness, they argue, ought to include many other variables such as psychological and environmental ones. Sociobiological thinking, they complain, focuses only on *what* we do, on the *end product of behaviour*, whereas evolutionary psychology focuses more on the *origin of behaviour*, on the *how* and *why* of what we do. We agree humans are social animals, they say, but we want to know why.

Like sociobiologists, they start off by rejecting the Standard Social Science Model, reviewed above, mostly because it claims that we are born with only a few reflexes (eating, sleeping, eliminating, etc.) and a *general* capacity to learn but that otherwise our minds are blank slates. That view, which is increasingly derided as a "romantic fallacy," stated that although our species began as animals, human "reason" and "instinct" got separated a long time ago, from which point on we began to learn everything from culture: the chalk of nurture writes on the blank slate of the mind. But the theory was badly flawed.[32]

In stark contrast, the new psychology claims that reason and instinct have always been inseparable and that the same is true of nature and nurture. Even more boldly, it argues that humans are born with lots of specific brain circuits, or neural "mechanisms," that are prestructured to solve *specific*, rather than vague, *general* problems. In other words, *we can get our nurture only through our nature*. In this view, such things as the human *capacity* to learn a specific culture flow outward from the adapted mind/brain, not inward from the environment. As John Tooby and Leda Cosmides, who co-authored the revolutionary (their enemies would say, "reactionary") manifesto for this new field in 1992, put it: "human minds, human behaviour, human artefacts, and human culture, are all biological phenomena."[33] Just so, we ought to stop opposing "reason" to "instinct" and start speaking instead of our "reasoning instinct" (and perhaps our "natured nurture"). For as Steven Pinker

– one of the most user-friendly explicators of this view – explains, the human brain is not a general tool. It is more like a carpenter's box full of single-purpose tools or like "a Swiss army knife," a multipurpose organ for executing highly specialized adaptive functions. Human instincts were not *erased* by evolution and *replaced* by culture. Rather, they became increasingly specialized psychological mechanisms crafted by evolution. Evolutionary psychology is simply trying to reveal the universal species-typical architecture of the human mind/brain.

Sometimes, these mechanisms, or "mental organs," are imagined as *minicomputers*, or *modules*, or *information-processing* units. However, because it is obvious we have no way of dissecting a living brain to find *actual* physical mechanisms without killing the patient, such language is just a question of the most useful metaphor. A "mechanism" (or whatever) is a handy term for something physical we believe must be going on in the brain because it explains behaviour so well. But we have as yet no way of knowing if anything real corresponds to such words. So the preferred method of study amounts to what Pinker calls "reverse-engineering." Just as we try to figure out the purpose of a strange object found in an antique store by taking it apart mentally (or, if we purchase it, physically) and asking what it was meant to be – an olive pitter? a potato peeler? a carpenter's mould? – we can take human behaviour apart mentally and ask whether it fulfils all the predictions of the best behavioural model we can think up.

The new consensus resulting from this procedure is that human reasoning and learning circuits have five features common to us all: (1) they are mostly designed to solve *specific* adaptive problems rather than general ones; (2) they develop reliably in *all human beings*; (3) they develop automatically and without conscious awareness or effort and in the *absence of any formal or cultural instruction*; (4) they are applied *without our awareness of their underlying purpose or logic*; and finally, (5) they are distinct from the very few general mind/brain abilities we also have (which are also hardwired).[34]

Here are some examples:

• Babies less than ten minutes old will turn their eyes and heads when shown human face-like patterns but not when shown the same facial features scrambled up.
• Newborn girl babies will be attentive to distress cries of other babies, but boys babies will not.
• As early as two and a half months, infants make strong "ontological assumptions" about the world, such as understanding that it is made up

of rigid objects continuous in space and time. When one experimental object is made to pass through another, they express great surprise.

- At less than a year old, they can distinguish causal from noncausal events and distinguish objects that move only when acted upon from those that move by themselves (the animate-inanimate distinction). In other words, they are able to infer internal states such as goals and intentions.
- They also have a well-developed "mind-reading" system that uses eye direction and movement to infer what other people want, know, and believe.

All of these, and more, are described as universal "privileged hypotheses" relied upon by all human beings to understand objects, faces, causality, other minds, words, and meanings. Without them, an infant (or an autistic child) will have difficulty learning anything.[35]

SOME OF OUR PSYCHOLOGICAL MECHANISMS

The human mind must be permeated with content and organization that does not originate in the social world.[36]

Leda Cosmides, John Tooby, and Jerome H. Barkow,
The Adapted Mind (1992)

The appendix at the end of the book gives a listing of some of the main psychological mechanisms and the research authors who put them on the table, as drawn from David Buss and given in his lucid *Evolutionary Psychology: The New Science of the Mind*.[37] Some of these seem so obvious that we say, "Of course. That's the way we are. It's natural." And that is the point. Evolutionary psychology is a field that sets out to demonstrate and explain *why* they are natural. The model relied upon to do this (until a better is discovered) is always Darwinian evolution theory. My purpose in this chapter, as mentioned, is not to dispute what seems to be a rather fruitful model, as it is possible for a model to give a wide range of explanations for things and still be dead wrong about the true cause of those things. Rather, it is simply to show that regardless of the accuracy of the underlying explanation, we now have a new social science that has identified a wide range of absolute psychological universals.

Among them are:

- altruism toward kin (strength of altruism directly related to closeness of kin)

- prestige seeking (status seeking, especially in males)
- preference for present risk to avoid future loss (to preserve resources)
- preferences for sugar, fats, and salts (a now maladaptive adaptation)
- innate fear of snakes, spiders, small animals (for obvious reasons)
- distinct landscape preferences (for shelter, food, water)
- strong female preference for provider males (to protect and provide resources)
- strong male preference for sexual females (to ensure progeny)
- heightened detection of cheating (for survival)
- male desire for sexual variety (for more progeny)

And more.

Again, while there may be some unimportant exceptions to such findings, they do not disprove the general claim that on average these human psychological traits are universal.

THE REAL WORLD:
EVOLUTIONARY PSYCHOLOGY IN ACTION

One of the most interesting and practical places to see psychological traits in action is in the real world of buying and selling. In this sense, the marketing practices of the free world have surely constituted the largest and longest-running social and psychological experiment on adaptive human behaviour in history. Curiously, although sophisticated forms of marketing have been around for more than a century, evolutionary psychology is only a recent development. Accordingly, Professors Stephen Colarelli and Joseph Dettmann decided to examine marketing phenomena in the belief that many consumer products and appeals reflect an accurate view of human nature compatible with the tenets of evolutionary psychology.[38] Their interesting comments, upon which I rely extensively here (although often paraphrased to save space), follow the list of psychological mechanisms they draw from David Buss, cited above. The gist of their findings is that products marketed without sensitivity to the common evolved psychological mechanisms and gender differences of humans will certainly fail.

Their test case was the year 2002, when corporations worldwide spent over \$320 billion on marketing – a figure that did not include the hundreds of billions more spent worldwide by governments marketing their programs to their own citizens. I mean to say, this is not about peanuts. But corporations are distinctive because they market only to get positive financial results, so they badly need to know what "buttons to push," as the saying goes. So let us touch briefly on some of these buttons as marketers see them.

Kin selection. This has to do with Hamilton's Rule (1964), which states that natural selection will favour individuals who make efforts to help others when it is in their genetic self-interest. It will favour them more to be altruistic toward someone who shares 50 per cent of their genes (a sibling or child) than someone like a first cousin who shares only 12.5 per cent or a stranger who shares no genes. And lo and behold, numerous studies have shown that genetic relatedness is very highly correlated with altruistic behaviour according to Hamilton's Rule. For example, parents tend to invest more of their resources in genetic offspring than in step, adopted, or foster children. They also bequeath more of their estates to kin than nonkin. Life insurance behaviour is especially revealing. Insurance selling is strongly directed at the urge to provide for one's family (not for in-laws, cousins, or neighbours). Studies in 1998 revealed that married couples with children were almost twice as likely to own life insurance as unmarried people. Education is also a form of insurance, and sure enough, families with two genetic parents contribute more to their children's education than do families with stepchildren. Stepparents start planning child investment later, set less aside, and spend less per year on child education than do genetic parents. A study done in 1990 showed that genetic children of current mates received on average US$4,293, whereas stepkids of current mates received only US$1,828. To some extent, this may be due to the initially lowered income of divorced people. But the figures are nevertheless striking.

Status and prestige. Both have universal appeal. Status, whether conferred by money, power, or high skill and knowledge, is strongly related to rank in a hierarchy, to greater resource entitlement (money, property, perks), and to greater survival and reproductive advantage. Whereas status is pursued more by males, prestige is pursued by both sexes. Prestige is a type of status associated with a high level of knowledge or a socially useful skill, such as found in a fine artist, musician, or mathematician. It is possible to have high status but low prestige, as might a very wealthy person who happens to be socially unpleasant. Many animals have what biologists call "honest signals" that indicate their reproductive value to potential mates. A female lion, for example, will mate sooner and more often with a lion that has a full and lustrous mane – his honest signal. Accordingly, firms market "status symbols" or prestigious goods energetically as a kind of human honest signal. When I was in college, girls would sometimes say to each other "I'm going out with a Corvette tonight" (or some such fancy car of the year), which is a pretty direct form of this instinct. Men with nice cars and clothes are attractive to women because such things are indicators of their wealth-creating capacity. Clearly, this is also dangerous territory because people with credit can fake honest signals long enough to attract a mate they would not otherwise acquire. A general human reliance on deceit also seems to be hardwired (and is kept at bay by religion, morality, shaming, etc.). At any rate, modern marketing is simply saturated with appeals to prestige (and often to deceit). Books about prestige skills and tastes like gourmet cooking, wine selection, travel, and self-improvement sell in the range of 100 million copies per year in America alone. Marketers always strive to trigger the strongest prestige-seeking psychological mechanism, the most popular method being endorsement of products by beautiful women, successful athletes, billionaires, movie stars, celebrity intellectuals or artists, and so on. The ultimate prestige endorsement is the movie star who endorses his own political campaign! The effort is to create a "prestige aura" around a product even when the product and the skill of the celebrity are unrelated – such as when a famous opera singer flashes a Rolex watch. Price, too, may be marketed as "part of the image." Thorstein Veblen fingered this mechanism a century ago when he spoke of the human tendency for "conspicuous consumption."

Preferences for sweets, fat, and salt. People universally share preferences for foods with these ingredients and spurn those without. The assumption is that during the era of human adaptation, hunter-gatherers needed high calorie foods and salts for high-output physical work. Fatty foods like meats include high amounts of protein, ripe fruits contain sweet complex carbohydrates, and we simply cannot survive without salt. In 1999 American consumers ate about 6 billion pounds of salty snack foods totalling US$19 billion in sales. That's about twenty pounds a year for every man, woman, and child! Potato chips led the field with sales of almost US$5 billion. Needless to say, healthier snack foods with less salt do not sell as well. Almost 22% of the North American food diet is oils, fats, sweet things, and soft drinks (water, flavouring, and sugar). To say nothing of the proliferation of fast-food restaurants! People clearly crave the basic substances that gave them high energy in the past. However, most of this behaviour is as clearly maladaptive today (although only according to the level of personal willpower). In 1999 about 60% of Americans were classified as overweight, and an astonishing 27% as obese! About 25% of American children are overweight, and 10% are obese. The figures for Canada are about the same. No need to emphasize that these are potential killer foods bringing much heart disease, cancer, diabetes, and the like when overconsumed. That's why I always say there is no such thing as junk food. There are only junk diets. As for fitness levels? Modern adults as well as children are bigger and taller than their immediate forebears but nowhere near as fit or strong. Fitness tests show we are much fatter, weaker, and less fit than our parents were, and they less fit than their parents.[39]

Differences between males and females. The story here is that men and women have very different sexual interests and behaviours due to the different natures of their sexual "investment" (see the section below on "brain sex"). Women have one egg a month (leaving aside the rare case of two eggs and fraternal twins) for a limited number of years and pay a huge price in labour, lactation, attachment, and responsibility for each pregnancy. Thus they tend to be sex-averse (to seek sex less for its own sake than men do) and choosy about whom they allow to impregnate them. As Donald Symons puts it, "for men, sex sometimes results in intimacy; for women, intimacy sometimes results in sex."[40] The welfare of each child is dependent more on the mother's survival than on the father's, so adaptation has selected (as they say) less aggressive and risk-averse females over more aggressive and risk-seeking females. Higher female investment also means a higher nurturing capacity for females than for males. Women tend to seek high-status, good-producer, and good-father mates, usually older and wealthier than themselves (a trait called *hypergamy*).

Each man, in contrast – and if it were possible – could potentially fertilize millions of women. The investment in pregnancy for the male is very low (and this is further reduced in modern Western democracies because unmarried males are now told they have no legal or moral claims over their own unborn children). Men tend to seek young nubile women (a lot of them, if possible) displaying all the sexual signs (good skin, good breasts, bouncy gait, lustrous hair, hour-glass shape, full lips, etc.), which are also highly related to reproductive success. To this mix they will add a few more features such as fidelity, kindness, and so on but usually only when they become intent on securing a mother for their children. Women with small waists and big breasts have significantly higher hormone levels, so high that such women – I am citing a recent Polish study published in a journal of England's Royal Society –

are "more than two to three times more likely to get pregnant than women with different body types." The authors concluded that "in Western societies, the cultural icon of Barbie as a symbol of female beauty seems to have some biological grounding."[41]

These sex differences, which, it is argued below, are hardwired, show up in all sorts of ways. In personal ads, for example, males almost always advertise their professional and financial status, while women typically stress their physical beauty. Height, education, resources, and age of male advertisers are positively related to female response rates, while female age, weight, and education are negatively related to male response rates. Marketing closely follows these traits. Women go for safer utility vehicles, romance novels, and wedding products. Harlequin-style romance books, bought mostly by women, account for almost half of the millions of paperback books sold every year! There are lots of lavish wedding books for brides but none for grooms. Gender-specific toys show another interesting pattern. In 1991 the famous Barbie doll accounted for more than US$1 billion of Mattel's US$1.6 billion in toy sales, and its "He-Man – Master of the Universe" muscle-boy toy was one of the most successful ever introduced. Researchers have found that even male monkeys prefer to play with toy cars and female monkeys with dolls. When our sons were born, a feminist friend of my wife's offered to give us the boy's toys she had purchased for her daughters in the hope of gender-equalizing their play. "Why are the toys so new?" my wife asked. "Because the girls never played with them," was the answer. The first night after giving her daughter a brand-new red fire engine to play with, the friend went upstairs to tuck her child in and found the fire engine in her doll bed with the covers pulled up around the cab!

Females also do more same-sex bonding than males, and the success of Tupperware parties – which have been attended by over 72% of American women – reflects this trait. Some 34% have attended over six such parties! This even holds across cultures. The Tupperware company has sales staff in 100 countries, accordingly. Pornography also tells a gender story, especially since the advent of the Internet. About 85% of all porn consumers are male. As of the year 2000, there were 50,000 Internet porn sites around the world, accounting for 70% of worldwide Internet commerce. Pay TV also rakes in 70% of its income from porn (now offered even in most high-class hotels). In contrast, men account for only 7% of the cosmetic and beauty-products market (which focuses on slower aging, lustrous hair, and enhanced body parts). The cosmetic-surgery market – liposuction, resectioning, breast implants, and so on – is dominated by females and is an enormous growth industry. Most cosmetic ads portray women as young and fertile, with "that schoolgirl complexion." In contrast, again, huge bucks are directed at the male market through sports and athletic programs. American universities spend about twice as much on male sports as female sports. The readership of big business magazines such as *Fortune*, *Forbes*, and the like is almost wholly male. Topselling *Sports Illustrated* and *Playboy* (16th and 17th respectively) cater to the combined male interests in sex and sports, while the equivalent sellers to women are *Better Homes and Gardens* and *Family Circle*. *Men's Health*, a hybrid attempting to touch on sensitive male "relationships," ranks only 44th. Meanwhile, *Sports Illustrated for Women* bombed after only two years. *Viva* and *Playgirl* (both now defunct) were attempts to appeal to what feminists assumed was a heretofore buried yearning for gender equality in women. So they both displayed nude males. But by 1976, after only two years on the market, *Viva* had eliminated male nudes, and *Playgirl* had to backpedal on its content vigorously to stay alive because it discovered it was being purchased mostly by gay men who were abandoning it for more explicitly gay material![42] So much for the "mental organs" and their expression.

Is the brain really a reproductive organ, as evolutionists claim? The arguments are persuasive – although I stress once again that there are other possible arguments and that there is no particular connection (except a good argument) between a discovered fact and the theory that explains the fact. I am presenting some of the facts in this chapter and the rest in the appendix. The theory is outlined here because it is persuasive and interesting. It is the best purely materialist account of human sexuality we have to date.

In this respect, however, it cannot approach the inspirational level nor complexity of any number of nonmaterial (or spiritual) explanations. Take, for example, the theory that the entire universe has been created and that our earth is a biocentrically unique planet harbouring humans who are a uniquely intelligent species, the ultimate purpose of which is a slow progression toward perfect cosmic love. Adaptation is not about genes, which are just along for the ride. It is about universal love and the growth of consciousness. Well, like it or not, this is a theory that explains more than any merely materialist theory because it cannot be disproved logically or by evidence, and it includes all other theories. Furthermore, purely materialist theories do not speculate on ultimate purposes. Darwinists, for example, take pride in their belief that there is no transcendent purpose to life or the universe. And they know that a mere thing cannot have intent or a purpose, any more than a finger can lift itself. It must be willed to rise, and no thing can will another thing to do anything. The knee-jerk response is that it is a neuron firing in the brain that sends an electrical signal to the finger and makes it rise. But in the materialist theory, the neuron is itself only a thing, and neurons do not have a will of their own. So pure materialists don't like to ponder the lifted finger because it is an everyday example of something mysterious and nonmaterial (mind) acting upon material (the finger).

SEX AND EVOLUTION THEORY

Social scientists usually try to explain human behaviour in one of two ways. They argue it occurs either because of social learning or because of our evolved biology. This is a brief review of the second way. In 1979 Professor Donald Symons of the University of California at Santa Barbara published a small and by now classic text, *The Evolution of Human Sexuality*, which has spawned many more of its kind.[43]

The story goes like this. Just as natural selection produces differences in stature, sex, and reproductive particulars, it produces biological and hormonal differences in male and female brains because they give reproductive advantages. Accordingly, such differences ought to manifest themselves in specific sex-related attitudes, instincts, emotions, motives, and behaviours that lead to the best chance for gene survival through successful reproduction. Again, in this sociobiological as well as psychological view, we are considered mere carriers (in Dawkins's term, "robots") for our genes. What is the predictive result of such a theory?

If the key aspects of our species indeed developed in the 5 million years of the hunter-gatherer period (when men were hunting and fighting, while their women gathered food and protected children), we would expect to see differences now between men and women everywhere along the lines shown in table 7.1.

And this is what we see. Muscular, fast-running, lean, and strong men (at least until the present age of obesity!) geared to short and fast performance; women with broader hips, more body fat for long-term energy, and a portable supply of breast milk for baby. Men were naturally selected for strength, speed, and offence-aggression and for ruthlessness in battle and hunting, with a high-level spatial and targeting ability specialized for killing man and beast. Women were selected for risk-avoidance,

Table 7.1
Evolutionary differences between males and females

Differences	Males	Females
Physical	Greater size and strength	Lesser size and strength
	Capacity for short-term energy	Capacity for endurance
Mental	Spatial and math skills	Verbal and social skills
	Stress on logic	Stress on empathy
Temperamental	Dominance	Submission
	Rank-related aggression	Defensive aggression
	Independence	Attachment/nurturance
	Psychopathy	Anxiety
	Sensation-seeking	Security-seeking
	Sexual initiation/exploration	Sexual selectivity/relationships

Source: Glenn Wilson, *The Great Sex Divide: A Study of Male-Female Differences* (Washington, DC: Scott-Townsend, 1992), 20.

nurturing, and defence-aggression for protection of home and children, combined with loyalty and communication skills. These are the innate differences we might expect to appear in the human sexes over time. Following from this are the markedly different universal human reproductive strategies of male and female.

To wit: the human female produces some four hundred or so eggs in her brief fertile span, carries each baby internally for nine months, and then lactates, feeds, and protects it for longer than any other mammalian species. She is out of sexual circulation for a long time with each child. So her investment in a pregnancy, as economists (and now evolutionists) say, is enormous compared to the male, who, due to the fact that with the sperm of one ejaculation he could populate half the planet, has more of a "slam, bam, thank you, M'am" attitude due to his paltry investment in the energy and time required to achieve the same result – reproduction of his genes. For him, the best strategy (if it weren't for getting so many upset wives and mothers-in-law along with it!) would be to copulate with and impregnate as many women as possible and let them raise the darned kids themselves. (On this note, the greatest number of children ever born to a single woman is 69, which is pretty astonishing, while the greatest recorded number of children fathered by a single man is 888 by a former King of Morocco.) In short, promiscuity (if he can get away with it) is a huge reproductive advantage for the male but a disadvantage for the female. It is high-risk for her, even in a time of contraception. And the theory says that is how men were selected for polygamous reproductive instincts. And indeed, most human societies in history have been polygamous either formally (where men are allowed multiple legal wives) or informally (adultery and multiple mating are common today, if not actual multiple marriage). As it happens, we are living in a time of resurgent serial polygamy in the Western world due to the ease of divorce and remarriage. Wealthy men may marry a half-dozen or more (usually younger and fertile) women in their lifetimes if they are so inclined. No – this does not mean *they* want to have a lot of babies. That's what *their genes* want (goes the story). Of course, they may, and usually do, block that normal consequence with contraception as they "go through the motions" for sexual pleasure only. In short, multiple mating has a large sexual and reproductive payoff for men but an equivalent penalty for women. We might expect this evolved difference to deeply affect their emotional lives and instincts. It does.

Sexually, women everywhere (alright, let's forget the few exceptions) are aroused more slowly and with more difficulty than men. Women, as we say, get to sex through love, whereas men get to love through sex. Men are aroused visually far more readily than women, usually instantly on viewing pornography or a woman's private parts. But most women could care less about men's private parts unless they are already aroused (the parts, as well as the women), and for this they usually require some sincere emotional response in advance to create the arousal. Women are accordingly more sexually reserved than men and use their natural reticence to seek out the most genetically fit, dependable, and resourceful (i.e., smart and wealthy or at least very capable) men, who are most likely to stay around to ensure their own offspring survive. When longing to mate, women avoid the slam-bam type like the plague. And even in this postpill period, early sex for most girls is still considered a kind of price they have to pay to keep their man, or rather, his love. Promiscuous girls are still considered "sluts" by both sexes. I know that in many places such as the modern university campus, we may find a minority of girls who "behave like men." They seem to enjoy one-night stands and multiple partners (or both at once). But they are the exception, as university is the exception. Such girls generally hasten to clean up their act in order to attract a husband. They will dress sexy for a trick, so to speak, but will come to the door buttoned up for a fellow they sense may be the marrying type. And they all know instinctively that male sexual jealousy is another powerful adaptive trait that operates to reject sluts so as to avoid male confusion over progeny.

As for the rest, the majority of college girls? Some years ago an interesting research project was set up for which drop-dead beautiful actresses and Marlboro-man actors were hired and asked to roam a number of campuses in different states, attempting to solicit sex. They would approach someone of the opposite sex and proposition them in a variety of ways ranging in boldness from "I've been watching you for some time and find you very attractive, would you have a coffee with me?" or "Would you go out with me tonight?" to "What about coming to my place for some sex?"

The theory predicted accurately what would happen. And it did. When invited to have a coffee with these very attractive strangers, the expected number of girls and boys said, "sure." But when invited to have sex, 0% of the girls but almost 100% of the boys accepted. The very few boys who refused wanted to make it very clear that they only did so because their girlfriend was in town, or they were on their way to see their parents, or had an appointment with a professor, or whatever. In most of these cases, some of them still tried to make dates for a later connection. Of interest, too, is that the "coyness response" (looking to show interest and then averting the eyes modestly) has been observed even in one-year-old girls but hardly ever in boys. It is a universal female psychological trait expressed from earliest life *that is found even in girls born blind who have never seen it displayed.* Some say it is a ritual invitation to a chase. Evolutionists say it is an adaptation to encourage stronger male competition for sexual favours and thus to select the fittest males.[44] Female modesty is in the same way an innate female trait. The social engineers of the Israeli Kibbutzim were flabbergasted to see that young girls who had been raised alongside boys all their lives, using the same washrooms and dormitories since birth, insisted on private rooms and on covering their sexual parts as soon as they hit puberty. The boys complained.

Parental investment theory also predicts differential sex strategies for things like adultery. In general, men are predicted to commit adultery for reasons of sexual novelty, while women do so when they perceive the other guy as superior to or more attentive (or both) than their mate. By the same token, men get universally jealous – agonized, actually – over (even the thought of) sexual penetration of their loved one by another male, while for women the biggest jealousy issue is a loss of love, protection, trust, and … the relationship. Again, men compete aggressively for the attention of the choicest females – these days "with tears, rather than spears," as Donald Symons puts it – the best men getting more of them or more of their attentions, which predicts more sexual perversion and sex crime among males than females due to the higher number of less-favoured males. And this is what we see. Correspondingly, as sex is universally perceived by females as a service to males, rather than to themselves, almost all prostitutes are females servicing males. Countless studies confirm what L.A. Kirkendall wrote in 1961: "The situation, to put it bluntly, is that the girl wants a boy and the boy wants sex. So in order to get the boy the girl provides (or offers) him sex, hoping that this will entice him into a permanent association."[45] When a very wealthy man was asked by a social scientist why he bothered to pay prostitutes for sex when he could easily attract and afford the finest women, he answered that he wasn't paying them for sex. He was paying them to go away after the sex! This was a male answer too subtle for the theory to have predicted but one that fits it exactly.

But perhaps the sharpest sex difference of all – and the one that fairly hollers the evolutionist song – is found between male and female homosexuals. Whereas committed lesbians are restrained in their choice of partners – seldom exceeding three or four in a lifetime – and do not generally practise homosexual promiscuity, male homosexuals live the male heterosexual dream. For them, promiscuity is the rule. On survey after survey, male homosexuals admit to astonishing degrees of promiscuity, about 50% of white males confessing to more than five hundred sexual "partners" in their homosexual careers to date and 28% to more than one thousand partners![46] Even male homosexuals "committed" to each other often admit the word has a unique and much looser meaning for them, such that some fooling around is allowed and mutually expected.[47] To put it bluntly, "eventually, most [homosexual males] seek all sexual activity outside of the relationship with their partner."[48] In short, male homosexual unions are notoriously short-lived even by today's looser heterosexual standards. Symons's work suggests that if male heterosexuals could live the gay type of promiscuous lifestyle but without having to be gay and with the assurance of no detection and no guilt ... almost every red-blooded male would do so. In evolutionary terms, we could say that gay males have figured out how to live the genetically ideal male sex life, gesturally, so to speak, while avoiding the reproductive consequences of diapers and debts. They have found a way to express the heterosexual erotic dreamworld without any of the hetero baggage (although they certainly have baggage of their own!). But face it – few except some troubled females would ever consider such promiscuous behaviour with total strangers, on a regular basis, "just for the fun of it." They do it only for money.

Symons summarizes the main male-female differences attributable to differing sexual investments as follows: (1) intrasexual competition is far more intense among males and also accounts for a lot of male violence; (2) men incline to polygyny (having many sex partners), whereas women are more malleable and may be satisfied in monogamous (one mate), polygynous (multiple wives), or polyandrous (multiple husbands) societies; (3) universally, men experience more sexual jealousy than women; (4) men are much more likely to be instantly aroused by visual sexual stimuli; (5) physical characteristics correlated with youth are the most important determinants of a woman's sexual attractiveness, whereas political and economic prowess are far more sexually attractive in men than is youth; (6) men desire a variety of partners far more intensely than do women; and (7) universally, copulation is considered a service women render to men, not vice versa.

This has been a quick review of the sex differences in human sexual behaviour. Countless studies the world over have supported the theory and the many predictions it makes possible. We may well be wondering: if all this is true of the body, the instincts, and emotions – is it also true of the brain? Is the human brain "a sex organ," as the saying goes?

Sure seems so.

SEX, BRAIN SEX, AND THE POLITICS OF SEX

Boys and girls are as different above the neck as they are below.[49]

    JoAnn Deak, from her speech "Taking the Mean out of Teen" (2003)

[We were taught] that gender differences were socially constructed [but] we now have clinical, reliable evidence that this is simply not the case. There's not a gender gap. There's a gender chasm.

    Dr Leonard Sax, quoted in the *National Post*, 10 May 2003

For sociobiologists, the brain is essentially a reproductive organ.[50]

    John Alcock, *The Triumph of Sociobiology* (2001)

We have been moving from the biologically large to the small, from the widest-ranging biological universals common to all organic life to human biological universals, to social and psychological universals and their possible evolutionary biological foundations ... and right into the human mind/brain itself.

This is dangerous territory. For most of human history, men and women, while obviously of the same species, were nevertheless considered to be different *to the core* – that is, to be psychologically and biologically different "by nature." And this general assumption seemed enough to explain the different aptitudes, skills, and behaviours of men and women, all of which in a traditional society were deemed essential and complementary. Politically and socially speaking, men and women were deeply different but equally valuable to society and part of a natural, created order. Their differences were exalted.

But these assumptions have been challenged periodically in history, usually by radical egalitarians of one sort or another. The record speaks for itself, from Protagoras to Rousseau and Marx, to legions of twentieth-century radicals such as the peacenik theorists of Israeli Kibbutzim,[51] to the murderous Communists of the "Evil Empire," and finally, to their intellectual brethren still ensconced as impatient and weary utopians in the dreary halls of Western academies. Every man and woman among them has believed passionately in the blank-slate ideal of the mind. Not because they were particulary good philosophers. To the contrary. Their work was marked by enthusiasm and self-serving polemic rather than rigorous thinking. Rather, they *needed* to believe in the blank slate and the predominance of nurture over nature because it served their idealistic purposes. Having accepted the convenient theory that human beings are all born with empty brains, they concluded that human differences must all be due to learning. And if this is true, they reasoned, then humans *can be moulded from cradle to grave by right-thinking utopians* – meaning, by themselves. That is why Noam Chomsky said "the blank slate is a dictator's dream."[52] We can think of the blank slate as a fundamental article of faith for anyone seeking to manipulate other human beings in order to bring about a utopian society. And this means that for such people, *biology is always the enemy.*

After all, most people can see that boys and girls and men and women have always behaved differently and not only have but also, when left to themselves, normally desire different kinds of lives. But American social scientists and ideologues resisted this truth. They had been caught up in a historical "anybody can become president" dream. So when the 1960s came, egalitarian feminists *set out to change biology,* mostly by ignoring it entirely, disputing its findings, or attempting to reverse male and female behaviours through social conditioning. As biologist Glenn Wilson emphasizes, they were interested not in what *is* but in what they felt *ought to be.* If boys are too aggressive, let's punish aggression. If girls are not aggressive enough, let's reward aggression. My own high school, formerly a boys-only school, is now co-ed and boasts of teaching boys and girls "against the grain." A school brochure boasts that teachers and parents are urged to make sure that boys and girls "spend time in activities that they may not be 'hardwired' to choose of their own accord." I think that "make sure" means "to force them." The underlying faith of such teachers is – has to be – the idea that boys and girls start the same everywhere and that all human differences are "socially constructed." Many social scientists of this type end up being forced by their own passionate ideals to let the political agenda of the day define the scientific one.

But fact-based natural sciences such as neurology have always said "no" to all this. Boys and girls are different for many reasons. As JoAnn Deak strikingly puts it, cited above: "Boys and girls are as different above the neck as they are below." The reason for the differences is that their chromosomal base (girls' XX, compared to boys' XY) at conception is different, hence their hormonal life from the womb onward is different, hence their entire biology is different, and hence their brains are different. From this perspective, it is true that "the brain is a sex organ," and there are clearly two kinds of human brain: male and female. So very quietly, against this political trend and with a certain apprehensiveness in the face of considerable hostility, a goodly number of social scientists throughout the past century have been compiling pretty clear evidence that men and women have universal biological, and therefore brain-based, differences in their makeup.

Until around the 1970s most of this argument was conducted in words. It was a verbal nature-nurture slugfest. Words and *lots* of statistics. But since then it has been fought – and won, in favour of clear biological differences – with machines, among other things. CAT and PET scanners. MRI machines. Electron microscopes. These and many other combinations of extraordinary technology and biochemistry have revealed irrefutably that various parts of the brains of men and women are structurally different and, even where they are the same, that they often function very differently in fascinating ways when confronted with the same tasks. Such findings soon began causing sex-difference researchers such as professor J.R. Urdry to recant their previous faith in the blank slate. As Urdry has said, "it is no longer tenable to believe that males and females are born into the world with the same behavioural dispositions."[53]

So now let us look as some of the findings, keeping in mind that while many of them are absolute certainties, others, although widely observed, await more certain confirmation. But on the whole, the modern evidence for an impressive number of biological and brain-based sex differences is widely accepted, and no one but a doctrinaire egalitarian (or someone very frightened of professional censure for political incorrectness) denies them any longer. North American radical feminists have been the most vitriolic opponents of biological as well as sex-difference research because they are near-blinded by the egalitarian myth. Their European counterparts are different. They call not for equality for women but for the protection of many of the so obviously innate female differences. By contrast, much of the North American research on sex differences has been conducted by women seeking to disprove these very differences.

This is a lay book for the general reader, so I do not want to burden this chapter with proofs. Those interested are encouraged to find them under topics such as "cognitive sciences," "sex and cognition," the "psychology of sex differences," as well as copiously in the books listed in the notes.[54]

Brain Sex

There is an obvious difference of degree between men and women in many of their shared abilities and cognitive skills, so it helps to think of overlapping circles when imagining such things. In other words, a large number of skills and behaviours are shared between the sexes, but the averages for each sex are distinctly nonaligned. This means we can never say all men or all women do so and so or behave in such and such a way. But we may say that on average, they do. Suffice it to say for now, however, and merely to whet the appetite, that such brain-sex differences – most of them universal and cross-cultural (in all societies studied to date) – are discovered as distinct male-female differences and are presumed to have a biological basis, whether hormonal or brain-based but usually both. Patterns found show clear differences in such things as:

- levels of sense awareness
- verbal abilities
- math abilities
- spatial abilities, both imaginal and actual
- throwing and targeting skills
- fine-motor skills
- rotational and directional skills

- skills in games like chess (spatial emphasis) and scrabble (verbal emphasis)
- problem-solving psychology

There are also all sorts of actual brain structures, functions, and activity patterns that have been revealed by high-tech machinery in the past few decades for all to see. The brains of boys and girls examined by PET scanners produce different images for many of the same tasks, and many different patterns are visible even when the subjects are at rest and there is no task at all!

Examples of results in this field (with more examples and detail in the appendix at the end of the book) include:

- Gendered senses: A great number of studies show that male and female babies behave differently in the womb (movements, heart rates, etc.) and also moments after birth (give different attention and have different intensity of reaction to the same objects, sounds, and tactile sensations).[55]
- Infant girls – but not infant boys – distinguish a baby's cry from other general sounds.
- Boys prefer objects to people.
- Girls and language: Girls develop language, fluency, and verbal memory earlier than boys and process such information faster, a difference observed by all researchers.
- Play differences: Girls are less rule-bound and boys more so. Boys need rules to tell whether they are winning or not. Their pre-adolescent play is often such rank-related play.
- The aggression difference: From birth, boys are more aggressive, competitive, and self-assertive than girls (perhaps the most common finding, worldwide, even by feminist researchers like Eleanor Maccoby and Carol Jacklin).[56] Even when one-year-old babies are separated from their mothers and their toys by a fence-like barrier, the girls tend to stay in the middle and cry for help, while the boys tend to cluster at the ends of the barrier, apparently trying to find a way out.[57]
- Human cognitive patterns: "Human cognitive patterns and their related brain organization are apparently permanently influenced by physiological events that take place by the fourth fetal month."[58]
- Boys' and girls' brains differ.[59] Highly sophisticated atomic brain imaging at Yale University's School of Medicine has shown that cognitive tasks presented to both sexes tend to be localized in the inferior

162 The Book of Absolutes

frontal gyrus of both hemispheres of the female brain but in the same area in only one dominant hemisphere of the male brain.[60]

• Brain metabolism: At the University of Pennsylvania's School of Medicine, a combination of PET scans and high-resolution MRI technology used to study brain metabolism has shown that *even at rest*, doing nothing in particular, there were male-female differences in brain metabolism in seventeen different brain areas.[61]

• Males and violence: Beginning at puberty men are more prone to physical violence (most crime is by males between the ages of 15 and 25), and women are more prone to emotional volatility. In the same period, men show more confidence, concentration, and ambition, whereas women show more social sensitivity and interest in relationships. On the aggression difference: about 85% of all crimes are committed by males, and there are specific, universal sex differences in the styles, types of victim, and postcrime behaviours of male and female perpetrators of violent crimes.[62]

• Spatial skills: Boys are better than girls on a variety of spatial skills. This advantage is cross-cultural and "is practically universal" in males.[63] The spatial-skill sex difference becomes quite marked after puberty and is even observed in animals.[64]

• Location of objects: Women are superior to men at certain tasks requiring memory for the location of objects.[65]

Readers will find many more interesting details on brain-sex differences in the appendix.

The intent of this chapter has been simply to show that there are a great number of universals and absolutes of a biological nature, from the indisputable existence of which we may take comfort. Contrary to the claims of relativists everywhere that nothing of an essential or innate human nature exists, we find that there is indeed a basic universal, biologically rooted human nature, in which we all share. This is so from DNA to the smiling instinct. It is a human nature that runs broad and deep, and nothing about it is socially constructed, or invented. It is the common foundation on which all known gender differences rest. At a minimum, this shared human nature – in which I include the universality of complementary gender universals – ought to serve both as a mirror and a lamp: a mirror in which to see ourselves reflected accurately and a lamp to light our way together through this sometimes darkened life.

8

Universals of Law:
The Natural Law and the Moral Law

THE DEATH OF CICERO

This was the end.

There had been weeks of flight and terror. And so a strange peace came over him when he glimpsed the first of many centurions through the window of his windswept villa at Formiae. Bobbing heads and worn armour weaving between old rocks. They crept like scruffy animals, surrounding him. There would be no escape. His heart was filling with fear and love, his mind with triumphant sound. Everything he cherished gripped him at once. His children's sweet smiles. Graceful gulls carving the air hundreds of feet above a rolling sea. His gardens, wild with dewy roses. He felt suddenly faint, and it bothered him that his lips were sticking together. He had been warned so many times to remain silent, not to speak against Mark Antony, the mightiest of Rome. Even as he saw the door splintering and crashing inward and the glint of blades drawn, he felt the sharp indignity of such an end to a carefully crafted life. And a fleeting, remorseful irony, for silence had always been possible – and now he could not speak. But even if he could, he preferred to die rather than forsake the truth. Could he stand as bravely as he should, for the blade? Most certainly.

After fleeing Rome for Greece, Marcus Tullius Cicero was driven back to shore by violent weather and sought final refuge at his beloved villa on the west coast of Italy, where he was assassinated on 7 December 43 BC for the crime of speaking against tyranny.[1] As he lay in his own blood, the soldier Herrenius swiftly cut off his head and both his hands for delivery to Mark Antony, whose wife, Fulvia, the moment she saw Cicero's pallid face, flew immediately into a rage and pushed one of her long hairpins through his blue tongue. His head and hands were then nailed to the door of the Forum Rostra, where Rome's most famous orators had always spoken. It was a bloody lesson for any who dared follow his example.

Shortly afterward, the masses now silenced, Antony ordered the deaths of some three hundred Roman senators and a couple of thousand of the most influential Roman citizens. Nothing could be more clear. Cicero stood for an unchanging higher natural law, a noble – and ennobling – legal and moral reality grounded in reason, nature, and the common good, a truth higher than any individual or any state, while Antony, like Caesar, stood for mere human law, which could be made and remade – daily, if necessary – by whomever was in power. These opposing principles of law were at war then and are still at war today.

THE NATURAL LAW IN HISTORY

Traditional natural law in the Western world was first articulated morally and philosophically by the Greeks, then made systematic and internationalized by the Romans. It was incorporated into a Christian-Platonic form by Saint Augustine in the fifth century and then into a Christian-Aristotelian form by Saint Thomas Aquinas in the thirteenth century. All forms of traditional natural law point to God as their ultimate source, for the reason that no one until about the twentieth century ever took seriously the strange idea that the universe created itself. Although often presented as a scientific fact, there is still no believable proof of that notion. So for millennia the conclusion was that as natural physical law and moral law seem to manifest everywhere in human experience, there must be a Lawmaker somewhere.

The traditional natural law is therefore based on four assumptions:[2]

1 There are universal and eternally valid criteria and principles on the basis of which ordinary human law can be justified (or criticized).
2 These principles are grounded both in nature (all beings share certain qualities and circumstances) and in human nature.
3 Human beings can discover these criteria and principles by the use of right reason.
4 Human law is morally binding only if it satisfies these criteria and principles.

REASON AND RIGHTS TAKE CENTRE STAGE

By the eighteenth century, however, with mechanistic and secular views taking over, political and legal theorists began flirting with the problem of how to invent a natural law through reason alone, without need of God. They achieved this by making reason itself into a god. During the French Revolution of 1789, a giant *papier-maché* Goddess of Reason was set up in Paris in place of the desecrated Christian altar in Notre Dame Cathedral. Intellectual votaries with candles and flowing robes circled all day, singing her praises. The social and moral devastations of this revolution in the name of reason, in which perhaps a quarter-million French citizens were grotesquely murdered by their own countrymen, are by now well known, as is the failure of mere reason to guide us to the truth – perhaps the only enduring lesson of that disastrous experiment.

Despite this, by the nineteenth century, traditional natural law – central to which is the role of human duties and obligations – had gotten thoroughly derailed into a radical form by political theorists who exerted themselves to separate what they began calling "human rights" from traditional natural law,[3] and hence from duties. For such distinctions, it helps to remind ourselves that *rights* are mostly about getting and *duties* mostly about giving. These newly conceived rights – now sometimes called "revolutionary rights" – were soon to be cited as grounds for revolt against various forms of authority and so, eventually, against any law said to be higher than human law. In the emerging modern democracies, for example, the most popular rights slogan became *Vox Populi, Vox Dei* – "the voice of the people is the voice of God."

Such rights were originally tied to claims about improving the common good (although that phrase was often invoked as a rights justifier even if no common good was readily to be found). Today, rights-talk has become far more extreme. It is now generally concerned not with the rights and freedoms common to all but with *individual* rights and freedoms, even when these are clearly claims *against* the body politic and the common good rather than an expression of it. Morally speaking, modern rights are usually about getting, not giving.

Unfortunately, a lot of the new rights-talk continued to travel under the label "natural rights." But that was – and still is – mostly a rhetorical ploy by advocates eager to claim that whatever rights they have in mind ought to be provided for all people as a natural part of what they believe it means to be human. In an insightful article on such distinctions, however, Professor Stephen Hall observed rather neatly that most modern rights-talk is really "an attempt to load the dice of public discourse heavily in favour of a desired outcome [as part of] a political strategy to reorder society."[4] The same day I read these words I saw a news flash from the Fourth World Toilet Summit in Beijing China, where 400 international delegates agreed unanimously that "a toilet is a basic human right, and this basic human right has been neglected. So the world deserves better toilets."[5] Perhaps there should be a right to eliminate ridiculous rights!

Although often paying lip service to God as an authority, modern rights-talk is almost everywhere deeply secular. Canada's Charter, for example, starts off boasting about how it rests on the "supremacy" of God and the rule of law but never again mentions God in connection with anything. Instead, it stresses a long list of deemed economic and political rights and political arrangements of an egalitarian nature as prior to, or constitutive of, society with nary a mention of responsibilities or duties.

It is now abundantly clear, however, that the weakness of all rights jurisdictions is that rights promised in abstract general terms always require someone – usually a judge – to determine what they mean in particular cases. The result is that even though such charters declare themselves to be proudly democratic – or of the people – the need to supply legal meanings for general terms means that unelected judges, rather than elected representatives of the people, end up assuming responsibility for the moral direction of society. In this fashion, rights jurisdictions often end up as legal oligarchies. At first, many judges, used to the traditional legal injunction to interpret and apply but not to make the law, don't want that responsibility. But it doesn't take long for them to warm up to the idea that through their personal preferences they can "correct" democracy. There has to be *some* meaning to these abstract words, they think, so why not mine?

But this process soon results in a kind of "rights fatigue" and in a corresponding worry that the liberal democracies of the West are becoming too fractious and onerous to govern due to the weight of so many bitterly contested individual claims, especially when they have the effect of destroying former traditional understandings of the common social and moral good. At a certain point – one already reached in countries such as Canada – this causes widespread incredulity, moral alienation, and worrisome citizen disconnection from, or dropping-out of, public discourse.

"NATURAL LAW WITHOUT NATURE"
TRIES TO PLUG THE GAP

Partly in reaction to such worries about social fragmentation, some late twentieth-century forms of legal thinking called *modern* or *contemporary* natural law have emerged. Wearied – and worried – by so many unanchored rights, the new natural lawyers speak instead of bundles of "values" or "goods," such as friendship, play, religion, knowledge, and so on. They say that these goods are so obviously and self-evidently necessary for human flourishing that they are "natural" to all and that all therefore have a right to them. The half-dozen or so goods in the mix (the number depending on who you read) are said to be *incommensurable*, which means they are deemed equally important and cannot be bargained for or traded off, one against the other. The subtext, as they say, is that once we agree on the list, everyone ought to work hard to arrange society so that no one is deprived of any of these goods. Now elegant theories are inexpensive, but putting them into practice is another matter. So this, too, can easily sound like a new plan to reorganize society, but this time in the name of goods.

The main weakness of such modern natural law thinking, however, is that it is not accompanied, as is the traditional type, by a hierarchical moral framework in terms of which to distinguish the priority of one value or good over any other. As its critics say, it claims to be a system of natural law but with no metaphysical object, or higher moral goal, in mind. The result is that "any item, any good we can name, can be part of a means-end chain leading to a corrupt end."[6] Friendship, for example, can be recruited for corrupt or vile ends, as in the case of Mafia friendship. That is because unlike those *acts* that are self-evidently bad in themselves, such as murder, rape, incest, lying, and so on, *abstract goods* such as friendship, play, religion – to pick only a few of those proposed – are not self-evidently good in themselves without good motives or unless converted into good actions. So when it comes to these so-called goods, our judgment of them must depend entirely on what *kinds* they are and on the purposes at which they aim, which may be good or bad. Cruel friendship, or cheating play, or the religious sacrifice of humans, for example, are clearly not good. Defenders of this modern type of natural law may answer that as cruel play offends against friendship, it can easily be ruled out as good play. Fair enough. But many are suspicious of circular moral reasoning according to which nothing is bad in itself but only if it fails with reference to another ostensible good. This is the reason critics of modern natural law say it is really an attempt to create "natural law without nature."[7]

But the real weakness of a goods-based morality is easiest to see when we think of goods like love. All kinds of people get very annoyed when they are told the "love" they passionately feel for something, or someone, may not necessarily be good; that it can be good only if it is in fact good love. A blinding love of self, a love of sex with children, love of money, or love of food and drink – all these are arguably very strong and compelling forms of love. The psychiatric manuals list hundreds of forms of love (usually suffixed by the term *philia*, the Greek word for love) along with their destructive effects. In other words, love is good – but bad love is not good. Under traditional natural law, we can say a certain type of love is not of the right *kind*, which means it is not love according to right reason, neither fulfilling and following human nature nor aiming at a natural or common good. For example, traditional natural law argues that self-love turns us away from others, that love of sex with children is self-evidently evil, that love of money is a destructive love of things, and so on. In short, traditional natural law says no human good (or passion, or emotion) is *necessarily* good unless it is valued within a reasoned and natural moral framework. By definition that cannot be something relative, not simply a personal "perspective," not something that is good merely because it seems self-evidently so (or what is sometimes termed an "intrinsic good") or just because we love it or have chosen it.

However, the most prominent modern legal philosophers, such as John Finnis and Germain Grisez, not only assert that nature is irrelevant to our practical reasoning on moral matters but even deny that nature *ever* played an important part in natural law, even in the natural law theory of such famous natural law thinkers as Aquinas. In his landmark book *Natural Law and Natural Right*, for example, Finnis states that the natural law "does not rely, even implicitly, on the term 'human nature.'"[8] These are confusing claims and simply not credible. Anyone who takes the trouble to read Aquinas will see that in his fascinating sections on law in the *Summa Theologiae* the most commonly repeated statement he makes is that we have a law in our hearts that is "in us by nature." He also speaks repeatedly of the "seeds" of the virtues as an objective foundation for the pursuit of them through right reason.[9] He clearly thought that although we need and have sufficient right reason to discover this natural law, "reason's ultimate standard is the law we have in us by nature,"[10] not the other way around.

But perhaps the terminal weakness of modern natural law is that few experts agree on what exactly ought to be included in their preferred bundle of values, or goods, or why. Readers will see what I mean by glancing at the confusion to which the idea of common goods gives rise, below.*

To pick only one example: when people start talking about things like "absence of pain" as a natural good, we ought to get very anxious, for everyone knows that a certain amount of pain in one's life is a salutary thing. Furthermore, once people begin to think that life is valuable only if it is pain-free (to stick with this example), it is amazing to watch the definition of pain change. It goes from unbearable suffering nobody could stand to ordinary physical pain everyone occasionally suffers, to mental pain, to emotional pain, to daily hassles, to inconveniences, and so on. Soon, we are getting sued for causing someone else's "pain and suffering."

To summarize, the historical sequence examined here went from *traditional* natural law to natural *rights*-talk to *modern* natural law, and the differences between them are laid out schematically below. The key

---

* Here is a sampling, from the *Stanford University Enclyclopedia of Philosophy*, of the different bundles of "goods" offered by some theorists as "natural rights" and an indication of the confusion this approach entails:

> It is clear ... that even if natural law theorists are right that this implicit knowledge is widely distributed, it would be easy for natural law theorists to disagree in their catalogs of basic goods. For the task here is that of formulating propositionally, and in as illuminating a way as possible, what items need be affirmed as intrinsically good in order to make sense out of our inclinations. And there are, unsurprisingly, disagreements in catalogs of basic goods. The goods that Aquinas mentions in his account include life, procreation, social life, knowledge, and rational conduct. Grisez 1983 includes self-integration, practical reasonableness, authenticity, justice and friendship, religion, life and health, knowledge of truth, appreciation of beauty, and playful activities. Finnis 1980 includes life, knowledge, aesthetic appreciation, play, friendship, practical reasonableness, and religion. Chappell 1995 includes friendship, aesthetic value, pleasure and the avoidance of pain, physical and mental health and harmony, reason, rationality, and reasonableness, truth and the knowledge of it, the natural world, people, fairness, and achievements. Finnis 1996 affirms a list much like Grisez 1983, but includes in it "the marital good." Murphy 2001 includes life, knowledge, aesthetic experience, excellence in work and play, excellence in agency, inner peace, friendship and community, religion, and happiness (p. 96). Gomez-Lobo 2002 includes life, the family, friendship, work and play, experience of beauty, theoretical knowledge, and integrity.

thing to remember, however, is that for the two latter types, neither God nor nature (in the sense of supplying a transcendent law or a moral norm of nature or of human nature) is a central feature. And the last type actually speaks of its chosen list of goods as a group of incommensurable and self-evidently and intrinsically good things or activities *in themselves*.

Table 8.1 indicates almost thirty areas of distinction that separate traditional natural law from rights-talk and modern natural law. Readers less interested in such distinctions should skip to the next section for a full discussion of traditional natural law. That is the main focus of this chapter because it strikes me as the only theory of law that provides a universal framework in the form of higher principles serving as a compass for *general* human conduct. Accordingly, it avoids the confusion generated by contested claims to government-guaranteed rights and also the endless debates over "goods" said to be of self-evident value even though their kinds are not specifiable and they aim at nothing higher than themselves.

Table 8.1
Distinctions between natural law, natural rights, and modern natural law

ACCORDING TO	TRADITIONAL NATURAL LAW (since ancient times)	REVOLUTIONARY NATURAL RIGHTS (since 17th and 18th centuries)	MODERN NATURAL LAW (since late 20th century)
Examples	Stoic Greek and Roman law The Bible and English common law Burke US Constitution British North America Act (1867)	Hobbes, Locke, Rousseau All social contract theories French "Rights of Man and the Citizen"(1789) US Bill of Rights Canadian Charter of Rights (1982)	Works by Grisez, Finnis, and Boyle,[a] among others
Authority	God's will and human reason Settled common law Nature and human nature	Human will and reason Contracts	7 basic "goods" (e.g., life, knowledge, play, aesthetics, friendship, religion, reasonableness)
Moral emphasis	Permanent duty and obligation	Rights as subjective claims	Equal "goods" for all
Accessible via	Right reason, nature, human nature	Written charters, codes, claims	Intelligibility, modes of responsibility

Table 8.1
Distinctions between natural law, natural rights, and modern natural law (*continued*)

ACCORDING TO	TRADITIONAL NATURAL LAW (since ancient times)	REVOLUTIONARY NATURAL RIGHTS (since 17th and 18th centuries)	MODERN NATURAL LAW (since late 20th century)
Made evident by	Transcendent natural law	"State of nature" theory	Intelligibility & self-evidence
How we know	"Written on the heart" Intuitive	Written in charters, codes, abstract language	Practical reason Respect for all "goods"
Basis of law	Eternal, natural, universal Exists prior to all states	Created by human reason and changeable	Intrinsic value of "goods" "Natural law without nature"
Relation to us	Independent of human will	Alterable by sovereign body	Flows from definitions and value of "goods"
Main theorists	Plato, Aristotle, Cicero, Aquinas	Hobbes, Locke, Rousseau	Grisez, Finnis, Boyle
Human law	Should conform to natural law	Conforms only to will of people and judges	All "goods" to all
Binding	Obliges all people and governments	Obligations defined and revocable by states/courts	Obligations arise from intrinsic value of "goods"
Happiness	Living according to natural law	Satisfied by rights	Satisfied by "goods"
Priority	Priority to common good	Priority to individual	Priority to all 7 "goods"
Sovereign	Subordinate to higher natural law	Source of highest law	Often unclear; often autonomous individuals
Life, liberty, property, family	Eternal rights inherited and prior to all government	Defined and granted by government and interpreted by courts	Extensions of "goods" necessary to flourishing
Revolution right	If natural law breached	If contract rights breached	If "goods" denied
Knowledge of higher law	Innate, intuitive "Planted in us by nature"	Dictated by state Taught there is no higher law	Deduced from irreducible value of basic "goods"
Dominant passion	The common good	Individual freedom and happiness	Flourishing of all

Table 8.1
Distinctions between natural law, natural rights, and modern natural law (*continued*)

ACCORDING TO	TRADITIONAL NATURAL LAW (since ancient times)	REVOLUTIONARY NATURAL RIGHTS (since 17th and 18th centuries)	MODERN NATURAL LAW (since late 20th century)
Human nature	Corruptible, needs natural law as compass Individual foolish, species wise	Good by nature Corrupted by bad society Species foolish, individual wise	Good or evil depends on available "values"/"goods"
Civil society	A good society fulfils law of nature A civlizing force	Society always in need of "progress" and correction	Healthy if it provides access to 7 basic "goods"
Society and the individual	Good society and customs create good individuals	Autonomous individuals create a good society	Individuals and society defined by degree of flourishing
Liberty	Liberty must be morally regulated for natural ends in a hierarchy of values geared to human nature and common good	Equality primary Morality private, up to individuals	Liberty is flourishing via all 7 "goods" Morality is choosing according to all goods
Equality	All equal in moral nature but differ by merit Individual to correct personal deficiencies	All equal and equally good by original nature We are made unequal by society State corrects inequities	Equality of basic "goods" makes us as equal as necessary
Origin of moral evil	Internal: from wrong reason and avoiding natural law	External: from unequal and therefore imperfect society	Absence of 7 basic "goods" or acting against them
Politics	Must adjust to natural law and human nature	An instrument for social engineering, "progress," and changing human nature	A sytem for ensuring basic "goods"
The good	Defined by natural law Evil is absence of natural good in self and society	Absence of external political and social problems	Good is flourishing via respect for all basic "goods"
Political power and law	Morally binding if it follows natural law	Human law the only power and legitimacy	Power that denies basic "goods" is illegitimate

Table 8.1
Distinctions between natural law, natural rights, and modern natural law (*continued*)

ACCORDING TO	TRADITIONAL NATURAL LAW (since ancient times)	REVOLUTIONARY NATURAL RIGHTS (since 17th and 18th centuries)	MODERN NATURAL LAW (since late 20th century)
One weakness of theory	Easily dismissed if God, human nature, or right reason are dismissed	Rights are always abstract Interpretation gets captured by strongest parties and courts	The 7 basic "goods" have no inherent superiority vis-à-vis each other There is no final ordering principle

[a] For the common view of these three philosophers, see Germain G. Grisez, John Finnis, and Joseph M. Boyle, "Practical Principles, Moral Truth, and Ultimate Ends," *American Journal of Jurisprudence* 32 (1987): 99–151.

TRADITIONAL NATURAL LAW IN THEORY AND PRACTICE

Practically speaking, the general opinion in upscale legal circles is that rights are in and traditional natural law is a dead duck. This opinion dominates despite the fact that the common law of all Western nations – especially those mothered by England – is permeated with traditional natural law concepts and assumptions. Indeed, in the United States "the use of natural law theories for various purposes has been continuous ... from Colonial times to the present day,"[11] and the eminent legal theorist Roscoe Pound noted early in the twentieth century that these same natural law ideas may be found in all practical decisions and legal theories throughout Europe.[12] In effect, there is a hard core of traditional natural law principles (to be reviewed below) that, as historian Peter Stanlis puts it, "are so deeply ingrained in human thought that, however much they may be ignored or obscured, they have successfully resisted every effort to destroy them, and [were] as alive in the twentieth century as they were in the fourth century B.C."[13]

In short, after a century during which radical legal theorists did their best to bury the natural law, it began rising again, and Pound was able to observe as early as 1911 that it was "not an accident that something very like a resurrection of natural law is going on the world over."[14] He sensed an observable return to the solid principles embedded deeply in the Western tradition by such great legal thinkers as Sir Edward Coke, who always spoke of *lex aeterna* and of "the law of nature," and after him Sir William

Blackstone, still widely considered the greatest commentator on the common law, who was convinced that the law of nature "is binding all over the globe, in all countries, and at all times: no human laws are of any validity, if contrary to this," and all valid laws, he was persuaded, "derive all their force and all their authority ... from this original."[15]

So it seems curious that despite the dominance today of legal theories pretending to operate without need of natural law principles, there remains a yawning gap between legal theory and practice, between the theoretical repudiation of natural law in law schools and the widespread, if mostly implicit and unconfessed, reliance on it for many actual court decisions. Indeed, until the end of the nineteenth century, traditional natural law was still taught in most Western law schools. But by the twentieth century, a rising social trend of moral relativism had become deeply rooted, partly in response to the fear that political absolutism could arise from the idea of a higher natural (or moral) law applicable to all. That some strongman's notion of natural law could be used to justify oppression was the not unreasonable fear. So in keeping with the breakdown of public moral conviction that resulted from the bubbling brew of Darwinism, scientism, Freudism, and relativism – all of which produced the bold new conviction that "God is dead" (and therefore that a common morality is dead) – people began to believe it was about time for a more "pluralistic" or "relativist" conception of law and morality. This seemed to make sense. After all, if there is no moral God above, how could there be a legal one? The whole idea of God was by then considered by many cultured people to be a little infantile anyway, even embarrassing. Freud and many other intellectuals were actually saying so. As a result, it was not long before legal thinkers were eagerly elevating mere human law to the highest level on the ground that there is no other kind. And so today, believers in human law (also called "positive" law) claim that the law is whatever gets declared law by duly constituted lawmakers, whether dictators or parliaments, and enforced. Some of these laws might be bad, they agree. But they are laws nonetheless. Moderns infected with relativism and rights fever readily repudiate any form of authority that sits upon them as a silent moral judge. Today's judges do not want to be judged, so they ignore any theory that could make that possible.

In stark contrast to Aquinas and other natural law theorists, who have always claimed that law must serve reason and the common good and thus that it has no meaning without morality, positive-law theorists work hard to separate law from morality, arguing that there is no necessary connection between the two. They say that those who think there is a connection are moralizing, that all legal concepts or principles of law said to be higher than human law are more like "religion," and that all claims to the existence of a universal, transcendent natural law are akin to a belief in magic.[16] But to this day, what distinguishes a natural lawyer from others is this: the natural lawyer insists that law *must* reflect morality in order to be just; indeed, the law is always a teacher, and all good law is but morality institutionalized. Few things are more thoroughly shot through with clear statements about good and evil actions than the criminal codes of nations.

By 1950, however, the German legal scholar Hans Kelsen, styled "the jurist of [the] century," had became famous for his purely utilitarian concept of human law and for his withering scorn for natural law. He proudly espoused a "philosophical relativism" that claimed reality exists only within human knowledge and, as such, is always relative to the knowing subject. To you, the thing is blue, but to me, aquamarine. So what is its real colour? For Kelsen, the absolute – reality in itself – is unknowable and beyond human experience. He therefore rejected and derided outright the claims of "philosophical absolutism," which insist there is a foundational reality that exists independent of human knowledge. As we will see in later chapters, this makes Kelsen an early "postmodernist." He pushed this point of view because he feared that philosophical absolutism would lead to political absolutism, whereas his brand of relativism would lead to ... a pluralistic democracy. But just the opposite has proved to be the case.

His interesting criticism of natural law was that if there really exists an absolute anything, such as an absolute good, then it is meaningless to let people vote, or choose among political options, because tolerance should have no place within a system of absolutes.[17] This chain of reasoning amply illustrates how relativism (and wrong reasoning) led him to declare that if no one can know absolutely what is right or wrong, the resolution of such questions must be left up to the political process. But his entire argument is presumptive because one way to be sure you can never know right from wrong is to reject the possibility of natural law in principle. Kelsen did so, and this attitude quickly became widespread. It was heard loud and clear from the positivist (and relativist) US justice Oliver Wendell Holmes, a man "irrepressibly hostile to natural law theory,"[18] who had notoriously defined *truth* as "the majority vote of the nation that can lick all others." He was directly equating truth with human will and power, as had Mark Antony and so many other tyrants. He was also echoing Kelsen's view that there is no such thing as absolute justice. There are only interests and conflicts of interest. That is why Kelsen argued that justice is "an irrational ideal."[19] Well, I don't think even a diehard relativist would want such a person as a father, teacher, or judge. As for justice? All human beings know it exists as an ideal concept, and they know instinctively what it means in principle (fairness, equity, reasonableness, and so on). With enough time to inform themselves on particular cases, that is enough for most ordinary people to judge the justness or unjustness of a law without need of a law degree.

Kelsen took the wrong road because he mistook the compass of natural law for a map. If it were in fact a map, I would reject it as well because nothing would rob free beings of the profoundly necessary moral challenges of life with more certainty than a perfect formula for all future actions and choices. For we would then live like automatons – no loves, no agonies, no victories or mistakes – like mere moral-dictation machines, rather than free moral agents. Better to shoot yourself! The beauty of the natural law is that it specifically does *not* dictate particular choices or actions. Like a compass, it merely points out what is generally the best direction, leaving the particular route choice up to us. We will never have, and ought not to have, a little manual of dictated solutions; but the morally responsible man or woman ought surely to have at a minimum a firm set of basic principles as to what is generally good and worth choosing. The late Leo Strauss expressed this idea insightfully when he wrote that "natural right must be mutable in order to cope with the inventiveness of wickedness." It is essential that principles be fixed, but with a mutable practical application, he continued, because "There is a universally valid hierarchy of ends, but there are no universally valid rules of action."[20]

Kelsen was also quite wrong about what he then considered the relativism of democracy. That is only true of our very recent form of democracy, which imagines sovereignty as something resident in autonomous individuals rather than in whole communities, as was formerly the case. I have written about that fatal turning elsewhere.[21] Suffice it to say for now that until the very recent turn to such radical autonomy, the Western democracies have always presumed a community of shared values of a classical and Judeo-Christian nature. Almost to a man, all the American and Canadian founders, in addition to their knowledge of so many classical thinkers – especially of natural law thinkers such as Aristotle and Cicero[22] – were believers in the Christian God, the Bible, and the Ten Commandments, which were considered the primary form of natural law shared by all religions and governing all people everywhere, Christian or otherwise.

Ironically, although Kelsen's position in defence of a relativist human law has been dominant for most of the twentieth century, it has been losing its grip somewhat of late. For many have begun to see that it is not relativism that offers a reasonable constraint on human law and totalitarianism but rather the principled standard of a higher law aiming at the common good. (The next chapter examines this truth in the light of international law.) So it turns out – it is inevitable – that the fatal weakness of any relativist legal theory is that it is forced by its own logic to accept even immoral laws as perfectly legal. Kelsen himself declared that the laws of the Nazis and other totalitarian regimes, regardless of their content, were valid simply because they were duly enacted.[23] In his most famous article, so astonishing that I italicize the entire statement, he wrote that "*the legal order of totalitarian states authorizes their governments to confine in concentration camps, persons whose opinions, religion, or race they do not like; to force them to perform any kind of labor, even to kill them ... the law under the Nazi-government was law. We may regret it but we cannot deny that it was law.*"[24]

But we can deny it, and we do. However, this capacity to judge human laws invalid, as we shall see, is only possible by reference to some absolute standard of natural law. The gist of this is that the divorce of human law from the higher law, and the abandonment of the moral compass it provides, allows all sorts of tyrannies to slip in the back door – the exact opposite of what Kelsen presumed! And we might add here that for traditional natural law theorists, the distinction between natural law and human law is specious anyway because rightly understood, all good human laws are – or ought to be – manifestations of natural law. The natural law is meant to help direct, but also to sit in judgment upon, human law. As Heinrich Rommen wrote in his classic work on this subject, "the natural law has to be realized in the positive [human] law since the latter is the application of the universal idea of justice to the motley manifold of life."[25] So, strictly speaking, human law may wander from natural law in many ways, but when it wanders too far it draws down upon itself – usually quite spontaneously from the people suffering under it – the famous judgment of perhaps the greatest natural law theorist of all, Saint Thomas Aquinas, who declared: *lex iniusta non est lex* – "an unjust law is not a law." Today, he might say: okay, I grant you positivist folks that an unjust law may be *called* a law. But because it is unjust, *it is not morally binding* and therefore not a law. He would likely also add that the innate ability of ordinary people, given sufficient information, to tell whether a law is unjust or not is itself part of natural law. All great rulers know that the greatest danger to all government is when the people separate themselves from a felt moral obligation to the laws, no matter how "legal" they may be.

A TURN OF THE LEGAL WHEEL

From about 1900 until 1970 human-law ideas ruled Western law schools. During this period the natural law was considered archaic, a dinosaur, and by many it still is. But all circles are round, as we say, and the natural law has never gone away. It began its quiet comeback after the turn of the twentieth century and has been getting stronger ever since. Readers may go to the notes for a good list of influential studies of the past half-century.[26] Whereas in 1970 a university course on the natural law was a rarity, more schools now offer such courses. The *kinds* of natural law theory offered may differ a lot, but there is definitely a return to some form of natural law thinking. There are several reasons for this return.

(1) Natural Law Trumps Human Law

Most important is the fact that modern jurists have discovered in one international court after another that without some concept of higher law, all sorts of evil people try to defend themselves from their heinous crimes by saluting human law. They say: "look, I was a duly and legally elected or appointed official of my country, ordered under the supreme laws of that country to gas those Jews or Kurds (hang those Somalis, shoot those Poles, whatever). So don't you fancy judges sit up there and tell me I did something illegal! That is just victor's justice. Shame on you!" Such defendants often feel justified and even noble in having carried out their nation's duly constituted "laws" (which they often decreed themselves).

When they hear this standard legal defence from evil people who have committed obvious atrocities, our human-law judges can only hang their heads in silence. Then they ask for a recess, slip away to their quarters for a straight scotch, and ask each other how – in the name of what *principle* – will they be able to convict these murdering rascals? These are often the same judges who throughout their careers took every opportunity to mock the natural law. But as Etienne Gilson – a wonderful mind if there ever was one – put it, "philosophy always buries its undertakers" (and by "philosophy" he meant truth and natural law), so as the day follows the night our former worshippers of human law find they have no recourse than to run as fast as their moral convictions will propel them to resuscitate the natural law. The two most famous modern examples of this legal flip-flop are the post-World War II Nuremberg trials held to convict Nazi criminals and the American civil rights revolution of the 1960s. In the first case, the judges' job was somehow to reclassify the law-abiding citizens of the Nazi Party (all of whom were obeying properly constituted laws and who pleaded endlessly they were "only doing their duty") as murdering criminals. In the case of US racial segregation, they had to insist that slavery and caste systems, even though legally supported by laws passed in a properly constituted democratic system, are not "natural." In order to hang their Nazis, the judges realized immediately they would have to put human legal concepts to the side and bring back transcendent concepts of natural law, for if they relied on German human law alone, all would go free.

Recess over, our defiant defendants were absolutely stunned to hear that it didn't matter that they had dutifully obeyed human law. They were told that the German courts "recognized the necessity of universal higher standards" and that any human law "loses all obligatory power if it violates the generally recognized principles of international law *or the natural law,*" or more simply put: if human law comes into conflict with true justice, which is "self-evident ... it must give way to justice." Why? Because, they said, *natural justice* automatically converts an unjust human law into "a lawless law."[27] Well, that's precisely what Aquinas had said seven centuries earlier! Even long after the war, in their efforts to restore or compensate war victims for confiscated property, the German courts appealed to the *suprapositive principles* of the *natural* equality of all citizens before the law and of *natural* property rights.

As for American racial segregation? There are few better natural law arguments in history than Martin Luther King's famous speech, "I have a dream," and his letter written from Birmingham jail, which held that "an unjust law is a code that is out of harmony with the moral law."[28] A very recent example of this same collision of human with natural law is the case of the tyrant Saddam Hussein, who in September of 2004, two years after his capture, still "insisted his position as Iraq's president gave him legal authority for all he did and that his victims were 'traitors.'"[29] It is true that everything he did was lawful under the laws of Iraq. He gave himself permission to legally slaughter a few hundred thousand citizens under Iraqi law. But not under the natural law. These notorious cases – history is filled with them – make the need for a higher law seem pretty obvious.

(2) *Natural Law Is Discoverable by Reason*

A second reason for the return of natural law is the recently revived understanding that to support the natural law you don't have to be some kind of religious fundamentalist because natural law, although not a *creation* of reason, is accessible to reason. Surprisingly, many of the most influential natural law theorists of the past who believed deeply in God nevertheless argued that there are things even God cannot change. As the Dutchman Hugo Grotius put it in 1625, "Just as even God cannot cause that two plus two should not make four, so He cannot cause that that which is intrinsically evil be not evil." In other words, even God cannot make false what is true, or make 2 + 2 = 5, or make a square a circle, or make good what is bad. God would have to be crazy (without right reason) to do that, and then God would not be God. Aquinas argued persistently that through reason alone man can discover the higher law of man and nature, for right reason directs us to what is objectively good and steers us away from what is objectively bad, just as a compass gives the correct direction for our journey but tells us nothing about the particulars of the route. On this reasoning, a thing is not made good, or transformed into something good, just because God chooses it or points us to it; He points us to it because it is good in itself. In other words, although it is always nice to have God on your side, and although some kind of faith may be required to explain *how* it is possible for a universal law of this or any other kind to exist unless it has an author, *what* the law is may be understood by right reason in its practical manifestations alone.

There are physical parallels we live with every day. For example, anyone can understand and predict with unerring assurance that an apple will always fall down, never fall up (even the phrase is unnatural!), without being able to describe the law of gravity. Indeed, all of us intimately understand the universal *effects* of gravity – that is why normal people do not try to jump off buildings – but very few can cite the exact mathematical *law* expressing it. That is because the law has nothing do with the physical substance of the apple. It governs the fall of the apple, and of us, absolutely but is not *in* the apple or in us. If it were, then we could eat the law as we eat the apple. Rather, the law of gravity, like all other laws of physics and all the principles of the natural law, as we shall soon see, are properly considered *transcendent*. They govern things but are not themselves a part of things. An immediate objection is that a lot of humans do not follow the natural law as I am about to explain it.

True enough. And that is because a basic natural law principle is that there is a difference between humans, who have reason and higher consciousness, and mere things, which do not. Rocks and birds and fish strictly obey the laws of nature and of their own very particular biological natures. But humans, who alone have higher consciousness and free will, are able to decide they would rather resist or follow something else. So we can easily have a universal natural law (such as the command not to steal) that operates for all right-thinking people but does not appear to operate for a thief. I say "appear" because no one knows better than a thief that stealing is wrong, and that is why a thief never steals anything when there may be a police officer watching.

So for this chapter, it is important to grasp that the natural law as I am going to outline it here is considered to exist in itself and is discoverable by human reason whether or not we want to bother determining its ultimate source. In short, for many, the origin of natural law (as well as natural physical law) may remain always a mystery. But that should have no effect on its self-evident universality or reasonableness. It is important to clear this up because the enemies of traditional natural law always try to diminish it by calling it a form of religious belief. And indeed, God is most often claimed as its source. But we can understand, if not fully explain, the natural law in every detail without recourse to a theological source, just as we can understand the effects of gravity without recourse to physics. And we have seen in an earlier chapter that even those who rely on complex gravitational computations for their work and understand perfectly how the law of gravity works nevertheless do not know what gravity actually *is* or *why* it works the way it does rather than some other way. That is a mystery in broad daylight. But the mystery does not prevent an extraordinary precision in gravitational calculations. The existence of the natural law is a similar mystery. But that ought not to stop us from seeking to discover and understand its subtle workings.

(3) The Natural Law and Revolution

Finally, the third reason why natural law is making a gradual comeback also supplies the reason for including such a subject in this book. Namely, more and more people are fed up with relativism in most of its forms and certainly with legal relativism. So in some respects the revival of interest in natural law is an attempt to rectify the legal confusions brought about by so many conflicting standards of human law.

At bottom, then, *all true natural law theories challenge relativism* (whether moral, cultural, or legal) by arriving at some basic notion of a permanent higher Law (with a capital "L") that is *universal, immutable, eternal, and objective.* Such a conception strives to put higher law firmly *beyond the reach of any particular person or government.* For this reason alone, natural law has always been deemed dangerously conservative by social radicals and progressives, even though they also will run to it with alacrity when they want to rebel against some unjust law. The reason is obvious: natural law provides a *transcendent standard* by which not only to judge our own behaviour and that of others but also, and especially, to judge the behaviour of governments and states. If we indeed share a common human nature – and every chapter of this book indicates as much – then somewhere, in some heaven of ideas, there must be common principles that are universally derivable and applicable according to that nature. In the end, what makes human-law theorists and statists of all types shudder is that natural law provides a standard for ordinary citizens to cry bloody murder and revolt if necessary, for as mentioned, it declares that *no human law can be morally binding unless it conforms to the natural law.* As such, natural law is always a "quest for absolute values, justice and truth."[30] That is why the Nuremberg judges embraced it. Little speculation is required to see that a chief reason for the decline of natural law during the rise of the modern state is that just about every law school, every granting institution, every legal journal, and every public court and tribunal is largely funded by the state. And no modern state wants to be told by ordinary citizens that any of its laws are not morally binding. That is why Lord Acton referred to natural law as "a revolution in permanence." He meant a revolution by those who cherish a traditional society and a morality rooted in human nature against all those who attempt to uproot, reorder, and deny or replace these realities. We saw previously that rights-talk supports the idea of revolution in the name of breached individual rights. But the rights relied on may have nothing to do with nature or human nature. They spring only from the inventions of human will and are usually rooted in egalitarian and utopian theories, which is to say, in leftist politics. Natural law supports revolution, too, but not in the name of individual rights or utopias – only in the extreme case of breaches of natural law and morality so grievous that the common good cannot be sustained.

But what truth? Whose values? Whose justice? Whose law? What can we say about the natural law that is convincing, binding, and universal?

TRADITIONAL NATURAL LAW EXPLAINED

I will be arguing here that the label *natural law* ought to be used only for the traditional type because unlike subsequent variations, it is to this day the only kind concerned with discovering the transcendent principles of a higher law that can serve as a compass pointing to the highest and best ends of human existence. The main focus will now be on the arguments by which this law is justified and (in the next chapter) on how it manifests in all cultures of the world, in international law, and in all religions of the world.

So let us return to Cicero, certainly one of the most influential natural law theorists to this day. Cicero lost his head because he insisted on the Stoic principle that there exists a moral law higher than all human law, to which even governments are subservient, which existed before any written law or any state and which will outlast them all. But he also improved upon this insight, for whereas the Greeks saw society and government as a single entity, he insisted *that all government is separate from society* but morally obligated to serve it and to protect the liberty and property of all citizens. No one had ever said such things before and would not again as powerfully until Christ, who also separated the state from morality by counselling us to render unto Caesar that which is Caesar's and unto God that which is God's. For having thus given the eagle of government "two heads" – one political and one moral – Cicero is today considered a hero of human liberty and of anti-statism. That is why he was so disliked by later theorists of the unitary state like Hobbes and Rousseau, who wanted only one head on the eagle of state. He was also a beautiful writer and one of the great orators of history. It is said that when mighty Julius Caesar first came to hear Cicero speak against tyranny, he became so emotionally transfixed by the power of Cicero's words ringing in the hushed hall that he trembled visibly and dropped all his papers on the floor.

In his *Republic* (51 BC), Cicero defined the natural law in a way that is still cited in legal studies: "*true law is right reason in agreement with nature, universal, consistent, everlasting, whose nature is to advocate duty by prescription and to deter wrongdoing by prohibition.*" He further stated that "we do not need to look outside ourselves for an expounder or interpreter of this law." God, he said, is the author and promulgator and enforcer of this law, and whoever tries to escape it "is trying to escape himself and his nature as a human being." Accordingly, no law that contradicts man's nature, reason, or common sense can be a valid law.

For it is right reason that distinguishes us from the animals and all other things of this world and that enables us to perceive or discover the natural law of our own being, as well as the common good, which is the aim of all reasonable men as naturally social beings.

Drawing, as he was, from the wisdom of the Stoic philosophers, Cicero repudiated the relativism, skepticism, and sophistry of his time. The chief guides to the natural law then were the same as today: human *right reason* (not wrong, or deranged, reason), human *conscience* (which all normal men have but not abnormal men, who either deny it or do not feel it in the first place), and the ideal of *the common good* (something increasingly ignored today, with preference given to individual autonomy and personal choice). All the core principles of this natural law are said to be intuitively understood by all men and are "written on the heart," as Saint Paul was later to put it when explaining how it was possible for people to be good before Christ.

The vastness of the Roman Empire obliged Cicero to draw many of his conclusions from the practical Roman effort to apply law to all people. While every tribe and nation had its own customary or civil law, reason showed that "there were universal and eternal principles of equity and justice common to all legal systems ... [which was called] ... *Jus Gentium*, the law of peoples, or world law."[31] This law is based upon reason and the innate sense of right and moral justice that is common to all races. Two important and universal aspects of this law were the *rule of good faith* (for a contract to be legal, there must be a "meeting of the minds," as we say today) and the determination of consequences *by the intentions of the parties* (not merely by the words used). Much later, as we shall see in the next chapter, legal thinkers spelled out the law of nations even more explicitly, so that there is now a very developed law of nations that includes an internationally accepted law of just war. The most striking feature of such law is that even though there has never been a moment in time when a supersovereign power among nations handed down or enforced this law, all nations accept it because it is based on self-evident natural law principles.

THE ARGUMENTS

Many treatments of the traditional natural law, as good as they may be, can be a little confusing for those approaching the subject for the first time. They are often too complex or, after singing the praises of the natural law in abstract theory, simply drop the reader off without saying much about exactly what it is in practice. So in what follows, I will discuss a number of core principles, each of which I think can be defended as a universal of human experience, and then try to show how each flows and follows from those prior. The goal is to show how the whole structure of natural law forms an argument rooted in interlocking and persuasively self-evident principles and truths. Let us begin with a brief definition of the natural law and then follow the ideas that lead to this conclusion:

The natural law is an ordinance of right reason that follows nature and is promulgated for the common good.

The simplicity and beauty of this definition will become clear as we go forward. But suffice it to say for now that it has to do with laws of right reason, not wrong reason, with following nature rather than opposing it, and with doing so in ways that promote the common good rather than only the individual good. So let us begin at the beginning.

A MEANINGFUL UNIVERSE
We find ourselves on an immense, and immensely complex and beautiful, planet in a universe beyond our powers to comprehend that was not created by us. For some reason we will never fathom, there is something, rather than nothing, in the universe. Everything in it appears to function according to strict, universal, and constant physical law, and each of the myriad complex manifestations of law seems aimed at some purpose in its own way. Cells, seeds, and even stars develop or combine to form fully completed higher entities such as organisms, flowers, galaxies, and so on.

MATERIALISM CANNOT EXPLAIN EVERYTHING
"Scientific materialism" is the current orthodox explanation for the existence and development of things. It is a theory stating that only matter exists and that even ideas, for example, are just the result of patterns of physical nerve impulses. But it defeats itself because materialism cannot explain the mystery of existence, its purpose, nor any other purpose, for the plain reason that no strictly material thing can render judgment on, or have a point of view about, another strictly material thing. In other words, things in themselves are dumb and cannot have opinions. Pascal made this point in 1670 when he said, "there is nothing so inconceivable as the idea that matter knows itself. We cannot possibly know how it

could know itself."[32] In the same vein, a trenchant modern critic asks, "if ideas are just patterns of nerve impulses, then how can one say that any idea (including the idea of materialism itself) is superior to any other? One pattern of nerve impulses cannot be truer or less true than another pattern, any more than a toothache can be truer or less true than another toothache."[33] An admirer of this conclusion adds: "in other words, human judgement and evaluation, which are necessary to determine truth and error (including the truth or error of materialism), presuppose a world of moral meaning that transcends the merely material. The very effort to demonstrate the truth of materialism thus refutes materialism."[34] But surely the *coup de grâce* for the theory of materialism in recent times has been the *indeterminism* arising from fundamental work in quantum physics.[35] Scientists cannot explain how nonmaterial things like ideas can arise from matter, but most of them agree that ideas are not themselves matter.

HUMAN CONSCIOUSNESS AND REASON ARE UNIQUE

This brings us to the conclusion that humans have a unique consciousness and a capacity for higher reasoning that permit them to analyze and reflect upon their own nature, on the nature of existence as a whole and all its laws, and on the outcome and meaning of human action and existence. No other form of being has this capacity. Humans are also distinguished universally from all other beings by their capacity for right reason. Cicero summed up this capacity very well when he wrote that by the gift of reason "Man comprehends the chain of consequences, perceives the causes of things, understands the relation of cause to effect, and of effects to cause, draws analogies, and connects and associates the present and the future – easily surveys the course of his whole life and makes the necessary preparations for its conduct."[36]

MIND IS MORE THAN MATTER

As a result of the above capacities, the human mind is different from, and more than, the brain, which as far as we know is made only of matter; neither can it be explained by the physical actions of the brain alone, as it is not reducible to the material action of the brain. It is mind – as some kind of emergent property of the brain, perhaps – not the brain itself, that somehow generates free will and the capacity for reason, value, and judgment. How it does so remains a mystery, just as how we lift a finger is a mystery. It is the firing of neurons in the brain, you say? But a neuron is made of material, and pure material cannot think or will anything.

HUMANS ARE SOCIAL BEINGS

All humans everywhere discover themselves to be free agents who are sociable by nature and flourish only in society. Human mind, reflective reason, and language, among other things, make this possible. As this social nature is common to all people, we all have a duty to care for our fellows and to resist threats to human freedom and to our common social life. Society is not just a collection of people but, as Cicero stated long ago, "an assemblage of people in large numbers associated in an agreement with respect to justice and a partnership for the common good."[37] In short, our individual good can be fully achieved only through the common good, not against it or without it, and that is something toward which we all should aim when we are behaving normally. We answer to the demands of natural law not so much by our theories as by our practices. (It should be noted that until the twentieth century the notion of the common good meant far more than a majority vote. It always had a moral aspect and was very much a part of our original democratic ideal – which is to say that the majority was always expected to seek and to express a moral common good, which is something greater than a mere tally of individual wants or self-interested opinion. That is now considered somewhat of a historical relic, for as we saw above, the public dialogue has now almost wholly shifted from a consensus about natural duties to a fractured dialogue about contested rights, which is to say: from giving (in the sense of doing one's duty) to getting (in the sense of making a claim, insisting on a right, getting what one wants).

ALL BEINGS AIM TO FULFIL THEIR OWN NATURAL GOOD

All normal human beings – indeed, all living beings – strive toward their own final good, or flourishing. The acorn becomes the tree, the seed the flower, the caterpillar the butterfly, the child the adult. This is the movement of all things toward their individual good. As defined by Aquinas, "the good" is the master drive, so to speak, shared by all beings, by which all seek the perfection of their own highest development. A human being belongs to a threefold order of existence, having some inclinations shared with all other creatures, others with some creatures only, and still others with humans only. We saw in chapter 7 how this is also mirrored in the biological world because humans share some things like DNA coding with all organisms, others things with primates only, such as opposable thumbs, and some with humans only, like rational thought. The crucial difference lies in the fact that the rational creature directs the self to its appropriate end and activity – we are not directed toward the good by genes or instincts (contrary to evolution theorists) but, indeed, often must get there by resisting them. All normal human beings feel the desire for the good inwardly as the drive to be happy, completed, and hence fulfilled.

NATURAL UNIVERSAL KNOWLEDGE

There are two fundamental precepts from which all natural law flows, and the first has to do with the *logic* of reality. The natural law assumes that human knowledge (even the idea of doubting or relativizing everything) can proceed only upon the acceptance of certain universal truths such as the law of non-contradiction. Aristotle summed this law up when he said, "it is impossible for the same thing at the same time both to be-in and not be-in the same thing in the same respect."[38] Put more simply, you cannot simultaneously affirm and deny the same thing. That would put us in a logical mess. For example, if we say something is both true and false at the same time, it would be false that the statement is true. Children are aware of this fundamental law of non-contradiction when they argue about, say, a promise made: "You did promise" / "I didn't." They just know implicitly that *if it is true* that you promised something, then it cannot *also* be true that you did not.[39] There are many similar universally known logical truths, such as: "the whole is greater than the part"; "equals taken from equals, leave equals"; and so on.

DOING GOOD AND AVOIDING EVIL

The second fundamental precept guiding rational creatures who naturally seek their own highest good is a *moral* directive that has to do with practical experience. It states that "the good is to be done and pursued, and evil avoided." This maxim is the moral foundation of all other natural laws and is understood instinctively by all normal people everywhere. It does not specify exact objects – which can never be known in advance of a situation – but serves as a guideline for human conduct. It is not a recipe for *particular* good behaviours but a compass pointing us in *general* away from evil and toward the end of our natural good and the common good. It is about the ends of human behaviour, not the means. All other natural laws will be extensions of this overriding moral law, which is expressed by all normal people. The precepts of natural law for rational human creatures are, then, rational directives of logic and morality aimed at the common good for humanity and at avoidance of everything destructive of the good. This means that human rational fulfilment may be found in such things as preserving the existence of ourselves and others by begetting and protecting children, by avoiding dangers to life, by defending ourselves and our loved ones, by hewing to family and friends, and of course, by hewing to reason itself. We know many such standards in religion as commandments. In daily life we know them as natural commands and prohibitions: love others, do unto them as you would have them do unto you, be fair, do not steal, do not lie, uphold justice, respect property, and so on.

THE DESIRE FOR SEXUAL UNITY

Because of the universal drive to exist and to preserve and prolong existence, natural organisms manifest a deep desire to unite sexually, and the vast majority to beget offspring. Human beings can do just about everything alone, but when it comes to creating life they are incomplete creatures: for this, they require someone of the opposite sex. Hence fundamental to human life and the survival of society is the bringing together of biological opposites in unitive sexual love. This is fundamental to the marital and family order of all societies, and as the most important of human relationships, marriage warrants the encouragement and protection of the state. Darwinists and other materialists attribute the procreative drive to some power over us directed by our genes. And that is true for animals. But for humans, it is explained as well by our deep love of existence itself, by the desire felt in our whole being for sexually unitive love that flows from this, and by the desire just as deep for the continuation of life through offspring. The making of another human life is the closest we come to self-continuation through the mystery of creation. So we could say it is our attraction to the mystery of creation that pulls us more than it is genes that push us.

THE HIGHER SELF OF HUMANS AND THE STATE

Just as all normal people develop a higher self (rooted in general understandings about things like reason and justice), which they rely on to control and direct their lower self (their passions, appetites, and unruly urges), so the state as an expression and protector of the common good must strive to create its own higher self in the form of just and reasonable laws by which the people and the state itself are guided. We must not confuse a merely popular government with a just government, for a popular government may not be just, but a just government will always be popular.

NOT A THEORY

Proponents of natural law do not ask us to adopt a moral or legal theory to dictate our behaviour. Rather, they ask us to recognize that all mature human beings *have already made certain judgments and cannot help making them.* That is because in our very nature we know the basic universal precepts of natural law – naturally, so to speak. Aquinas said normal adults know them by intuition, or *synderesis.* All the basic precepts of natural law – seek the good, avoid evil, and the like – are grasped, as he put it, *per se nota*: they are self-evident principles, things known to be true without need of further proof. As one astute natural law writer put it, there are a number of basic things that "we can't not know."[40] These things constitute a common fund of human knowledge of which all of us are already in possession. For example, long before professors of philosophy instruct them to question such things, all normal human beings intuitively comprehend concepts like fairness, justice, equality, love, courage, logic, truth, the idea of good and bad, and so on. Indeed, all normal human relations, and even the study of all philosophy, *presuppose* the existence of such natural understandings before they can even begin.

NATURAL LAW AND THE FOUR CLASSICAL VIRTUES

With free will and reason, all normal people everywhere seek harmony and proportion through what the ancients called the four virtues: all seek and revere *wisdom* (or *prudence*, which is right judgment), demand *justice*, venerate *courage*, and counsel *moderation*. There are no exceptions, save for in sick (unnatural) people or societies, so we may say such virtues are among the universal outcomes of human nature in search of the good. They are convictions of human right reason. And what is morally binding law but right reason expressed as commands and prohibitions?

THE DENIAL OF NATURE PRODUCES BAD CONSEQUENCES

The above universal aspects of human nature produce corresponding evils when they are denied. Cheating and lying, for example, produce a friendless life of distrust. Such things as incest – a universal taboo – produce weakness and mutation. Sexual profligacy produces sexually communicated diseases, high rates of sterility, and a host of moral deformations and alienations (such as arise from treating others as mere sexual objects), broken homes and distressed children, and domestic violence. Homosexual behaviour, unnatural on the face of it, means the rejection by practitioners of all offspring via unitive love with each other and for many a host of deadly diseases combined under the label AIDS.[41] In other words, there are natural bad consequences to denial of what is naturally good. Some will complain that many "natural" human desires and actions are bad. That is true. And that is why we may say that the purpose of right reason *and* the natural law is to guide ourselves (and our governments) in the pursuit of what is natural and good as well as in suppressing what may feel natural but is clearly bad (i.e., all hurtful or damaging actions and behaviours, no matter how natural they feel, that offend right reason and the common good).

MIGHT DOES NOT MAKE RIGHT

It is a universal truth that people everywhere agree might does not make right. The authority of law arises not, as modern human law experts tell us, from the mere fact a law is duly constituted but rather from the compatibility of law with generally understood concepts of natural moral law, reason, and duty. Humans are not bound by natural law itself, as if by force, but rather morally through their sense of the justice of laws that conform to right reason and the common good. This alone procures human moral allegiance. So we can say that humans everywhere actively *participate* in the natural law because in any specific situation or dilemma that may befall us, it is our awareness of natural law alone that elicits a positive or negative response as felt through our innate sense of fairness, equity, love, justice, truth, and so on.

NATURAL LAW IS DISCOVERED, NOT INVENTED OR CHOSEN

Once we have agreed that we have a rational human nature, then it follows that rational principles of practical conduct aimed at flourishing in the context of the common good ought roughly to guide personal choice. This requirement for the priority of the good over personal desire, wilfulness, or inclination is the reason we may say the eternal principles of natural law are to be discovered and are not invented. That is because these laws themselves do not arise from the rawness of desire, or will, or inclination. Rather, they must be recognized as transcendent ideals of conduct. And that is why natural law concepts are seen today as threats to unlimited personal freedom as well as to state power. People don't like them. And that is why, as philosopher Alasdair MacIntyre notes, the natural law predicts even its own rejection.[42]

Let us now try to compress these thoughts into a chain of ideas linking what I think are the most fundamental assumptions underlying natural law, from the most basic propositions forward. Each proposition ought to stand on its own but also lead naturally to the one following. The hope is that those who accept this series of propositions as reasonable, self-evident, or demonstrable by their own experience will likely then embrace the whole concept of natural law.

THE NATURAL LAW IN A NUTSHELL

We exist and discover a universe that is governed by natural physical laws, as are we. But in addition to our physical being, we humans have a unique higher consciousness and reasoning capacity that enable us to reflect on the meaning of existence and to discover the nature of the laws both governing the material world and other forms of life and guiding human action. Consciousness and reason cannot be explained by materialism because a merely material thing cannot pass judgment on or evaluate or choose to affect another material thing. For this reason, the human mind, which is the expression of consciousness, must be more than the material brain and cannot be reduced to it. Because all normal humans have a mind, they also have the capacity to reason rightly or wrongly and hence the moral freedom to choose for good or for evil. With this reason and moral freedom, humans everywhere and at all times have discovered a set of general natural laws or principles upon which they instinctively rely to guide individual and social existence. This is only possible because in contrast to all lower animals, humans can comprehend cause and effect, the consequences of their actions, and many indubitable and universal truths of reason, such as the law of non-contradiction. We see that all forms of being develop according to their natures and move toward their own flourishing, or natural good, or happiness. This is the individual good of each individual being. Humans differ from all other forms of being because although they have the capacity to discover the law of their own nature, they may also freely decide either to follow it or to deny it. Despite this capacity for denial, most humans everywhere strive for their own flourishing. This is self-evidently best accomplished in human society, where we exist as free and yet inescapably social beings. As this social nature is common to all humans, we have a duty to care for our fellow beings and to promote – and resist threats to – the common good. This combination of self-flourishing and the need for a common social existence results in the universal drive of all to preserve, protect, and extend life. Accordingly, we have a natural desire for sexual unity, with the vast majority desiring procreation. This framework of social life, reason, the common good, happiness, and the creation of new life leads to the discovery of the first and greatest of the natural laws: "do good and avoid evil." Arising from the foregoing are many other natural laws that preside as principles over our behaviour, such as truth telling, refusing to steal, respecting moral equality, the centrality of the family, self-defence, treating others fairly, respecting property, the priority of the common good, and so on. These are expressed as commands or prohibitions in all societies of the world. To this end, all societies universally respect certain moral and legal values such as courage, moderation, wisdom, justice, and the notion that might does not make right. All of these values and many more indicate an intuitive grasp of the universal natural law as a standard of justice higher than human law. This law is discovered as a common universal outcome of free human beings participating in a search for the good. All humans are able to understand through right reason (when acting for the common good according to nature rather than against nature or against the common good) the priority of this common good over their own personal wants. This priority of the good, justice, equity, and the like over personal wants is why we can assert that such natural laws exist as transcendent principles, for we must have an idea of the good, of justice, of equity, in general before we ask what these may be in particular situations. That is why we can say such laws are discovered, not invented. The consequence is that all humans must cultivate a higher self (guided by the compass of natural law) that seeks the common good and is based in right reason in order to control or guide their own wayward or unnatural passions and unjust urges. It follows from this that the state, which ought to be more than a collection of autonomous individuals – namely a partnership for the common good – must do the same and be judged by the same standard, for the natural law itself is the higher self of the state. Finally, as a consequence of their common human nature and social existence, we can see that all normal human beings carry the compass of natural law within: an innate sense of the rightness of things like justice, truth telling, fairness, equity, love, courage, wisdom, and so on, which are understood universally as rough standards of moral conduct and right reason by which all human beings attempt to guide themselves.

This is the natural law.

9

The Natural Law and
the Moral Law at Work in the World

A beautiful theory is a fine spectacle. But is it true? And what can such a question mean in the real world? How do we tell the difference between two elegant theories about reality, both of which cannot possibly be true? The only way to know is to see whether the older theory can be falsified by the new and whether the new theory allows more accurate predictions or explains what previously could not be understood. That is what happened with Galileo's so-called heliocentric (sun-centred) theory, proving that the earth travels around the sun, not vice versa, as previously believed, and everyone today believes Galileo's theory to be true, even though the vast majority believe it on faith, as an orthodoxy poured into their heads by teachers and textbooks, and for no other reason. I mean to say that very few human beings have any idea how to prove that the earth, quite contrary to appearances, travels around the sun, not vice versa.

By the time Newton got to thinking and writing about all this, he showed that the behaviour of physical things like planets and falling apples (and people) were obeying universal laws never before perceived or understood. The regular behaviour of all objects with mass was a manifestation of the hidden mathematical laws of gravity, motion, inertia, and so on.

There is an argument that the same must be true of the natural moral law. Although we cannot simply presume that if a belief or behaviour is manifested everywhere it proves the existence of a law, the opposite must also be true: we cannot say that if something is universally manifested there must *not* be a law. So which is it? Alas, when it comes to human behaviour and belief, we cannot weigh, or package, or pin down a thing called a law. But a reasonable assumption is that if all people in the world – including people who have never had contact with each other – believe and behave in a similar way, then something universal and law-like is probably at work. For example, all people practise incest avoidance. But what is the cause of such uniform and universal behaviour? They may all practise this avoidance a little differently. But there is definitely something common to all people: the avoidance. In the same way, we can say that even though all people walk differently, they all walk. So where and what is the law of walking? One answer is that the act of walking is obedient to a universal human biological law. I am certain that is so. And many biologists would say that moral laws also obey some biological mandate. This idea will be examined below – and found wanting.

In asking these questions, I am preparing the reader for the idea that natural law manifests in all human beings as rational law aimed at the common good, not as biology, because it is not *particular* things or behaviours that manifest and are universal – indeed, they differ slightly among all peoples – but *general* things. There are many forms of marriage. But all cultures do it. The natural law is in this sense a transcendent generality of an abstract nature that manifests everywhere in concrete and particular ways. It is only in its abstract or general manifestation, however, that it can serve as a universal reference for particular human-made laws or for particular moral behaviours. Hume and many other philosophers warn us *ad nauseam* that we should never derive an *ought* from an *is* (although Hume did plenty of this himself). This prohibition is also the supposed touchstone of good science. But a strong case can be made that there is an *ought* to be found somewhere in every *is* simply because it is impossible to describe anything without value-laden concepts, first in the form of ideas and then of language. Indeed, we have seen already that a key distinguishing feature of human beings, as distinct from all things material, is their capacity for valuing. This is not to argue against myself by suggesting that nothing can be objective – for indeed, one of our values may be a striving for objectivity.

Nonetheless, it is true to say that the fact of being universally believed, or done, makes something neither a law nor necessarily good. If all people use slavery, for example, this does not make it good or a law in the natural law sense (although everywhere slavery has been officially practised, it was governed by a complex kind of category law).[1] Leaving aside for the moment that most ancient people used slavery as

a form of war reparation and thought it highly moral to make their surrendered enemies slaves rather than to slaughter them, as they deserved, it is easy to agree that being universal does not make something
good or right.

But natural law thinkers will argue – as do I – that any universal human behaviour or belief must be judged according to standards of natural law. It is this evaluation alone that will distinguish a behaviour that
may be universal but very bad – stealing is found universally, for example – from one that is universal but very good – the prohibition on
stealing. What makes the first a universal practice but not a law and the
second a universal practice but also a law is answered by the response to
the question: Is it *an ordinance of right reason that follows nature and is promulgated for the common good?* If the reasonable answer is *yes*, then we
have a ground to say the natural law is evident and at work. If *no*, then
we have a reasonable ground to judge the behaviour as contrary to natural law. Stealing is a particular practice of certain individuals in every
society and is typified by the absence of any moral standard. So although universal, it cannot be a law. The prohibition of stealing, in
contrast, is found universally and is typified by a universal moral justification, not by any particular individual practice. Hence it functions as a
law, not as a practice. It seems, then, that the universals of natural law
aimed at the common good eventually drive out mere universals of human practice aimed only at individual benefit. Transatlantic commercial slavery, for example, although so widespread at one time, is no
longer so. The moral logic that drove it out of existence was derived
from natural law and nowhere else.

The point to be made here is that what is unifying for humanity is what
is universal, accords with right reason, and is aimed at the common
good. In contrast to this, what is often charming, but potentially divisive,
is what is only particular and relative. So when it comes to statements
about the practical universality of law, we can start by asking a simple
question about how the natural law manifests in all *societies* of the world,
how it manifests between these societies in *international law*, and how it
operates in the common moral law of the world's major *religions*.

In chapter 4, on human universals, we saw how modern anthropology has been justifiably accused of contributing to the breakdown of
civilization through its insistence on moral and cultural relativism –
that is, on cultural particularism. We have also seen the self-serving political nature of this "scientific" posture and how, as cultural relativism,
it backfired on its proponents despite their initial good intentions. At

the height and in the heat of the cultural relativist movement, however, others were quite alarmed by the social dissolution it was introducing and set to work to discover whether, to the contrary, something like a universal natural moral law exists in all societies of the world, and if so, why it was being intentionally ignored.

One of the earliest and most lucid critiques of cultural relativism, and one that is also a summary of our universal human moral reality, was presented in an excellent article by the Canadian Richard H. Beis, now Professor Emeritus of Philosophy at St Mary's University in Nova Scotia.[2] He drew together most of the important anti-relativist work in cultural anthropology of his time and presented it in 1964.[*]

It is a shame this article was confined largely to the readers of the natural law journal *The Thomist,* in which it was published. It deserved – still deserves – a far wider audience.

It is important to stress here, however, that although social scientists like to speak mostly of "ethics" rather than of morality, all of the items below constitute a kind of international cultural tablet of shared moral norms, standards, and practices meant to guide human behaviour. The cultures sharing these beliefs hold them to be true and to constitute something very close to what some moral philosophers call "exceptionless moral norms." These are the things all people of the world hold to be absolutely true in principle, not relative in the least, and for which practical exceptions may sometimes be forgiven (such as a mother stealing bread to feed her starving child) but only according to special circumstances unforeseeable in the present and to be judged right or wrong according to these general standards. These moral prohibitions are both self-explanatory and, we might add, self-evidently good,

---

[*] This by no means exhaustive list of ethical/moral universals is found in Richard H. Beis, "Some Contributions of Anthropology to Ethics," *The Thomist* 27, no. 2 (April 1964): 174–223. It is one of the clearest analyses of the conflicts and contradictions arising from the theory of moral and cultural relativism and draws the moral universals listed here from a wide selection of the most influential anthropologists of the time. Among them are Boas, Kroeber, Kluckholn, Benedict, Linton, Macbeath, Bidney, Brandt, Malinowski, Edel, Casserley, Montagu, and many others. All of them were operating in a predominantly relativist environment, so their common findings are all the more surprising and courageous, as they were all swimming against the tide by expressing interest in moral universals. Very little has altered since, except that more and deeper work has been done on all human universals, as outlined in chapter 4 of this book.

by which I mean they aim at the common good. As such they require no
further explanation. But they stand as a rock against the claims of moral
and cultural relativists, and my hope is that in future deliberations about
morality the fact and knowledge of their existence will contribute to human solidarity. I have added some brief comments to Beis's list, in square
brackets, which are to be taken as my own commentary on his universals,
not as his opinion (which he may or may not share):

1 Prohibition of murder or maiming without justification. [Murder
   must be distinguished from killing, which, in self-defence, or war, or
   as capital punishment, is often practised as moral.]
2 Prohibition of lying, at least in certain areas such as oaths, etc. [It is
   interesting that even children far too young to debate philosophically can be observed in high moral outrage if lied to. They sense
   the undermining of all meaning.]
3 Right to own property such as land, clothing, tools, etc. [This universally acknowledged desire and right substantially explains why egalitarian and communistic systems, such as in the former Soviet Union
   and in Kibbutzim, have always failed to follow their own theories.]
4 Economic justice: reciprocity and restitution. [This is at work in all
   individual societies and between them in international law.]
5 Preference of common good over individual good. [The subordination of self and personal will is required for any society to form as other
   than a collection of individuals, and the organic entity constituted by
   this preference emerges as the personality of society as a whole.]
6 Demand for co-operation within the group. [One of the three universal political categories, in addition to the public-private and com-
   mand-obedience distinctions, is the insider-outsider distinction,
   without which, arguably, no social group can form.]
7 Sexual restriction within all societies. [All are required to control
   sexual profligacy, jealousy, and apportionment of partners in some
   way and to control male sexual cruelty and aggression.]
   (a) Incest prohibition within nuclear family. [This is perhaps the
       clearest and best-known universal moral prohibition.]
   (b) Prohibition of rape. [This is the universal expression in sexual
       relations of the equally universal moral understanding that
       might does not make right.]
   (c) Some form of marriage demanded. [This universal is every-
       where required for the more certain rearing and protection of
       children, as well as for an attempted guarantee of paternity.]

(d) Prohibition of adultery (with only a few strictly limited legal exceptions). [As well as an expression of sexual jealousy – another universal – this is likely also an attempt to protect and predict paternity of offspring.]

(e) Opposition to promiscuity in the sense of having a large number of partners. [Although now rather popular in Western societies, true indiscriminate promiscuity is everywhere scorned.]

(f) Lifelong union of the spouses is the ideal. [The ideal survives the wave-like ups and downs in its history.]

(g) Exogamy [marriage outside the family] as a further determination of the incest rule. [Self-explanatory.]

8 Disrespect for illegitimate children. [It is the parents who ought to be disrespected, not the unfortunate children of such liaisons. However, this universal sanction has the effect almost everywhere of enforcing marriage as a haven for children.]

9 Reciprocal duties between children and parents: parents care for and train children – children respect, obey, and care for parents in old age. [Another universal bond of reciprocity everywhere felt, if not everywhere perfect in practice.]

10 Loyalty to one's social unit (family, tribe, country). [This is an illiberal universal and is psychologically essential to all forms of social bonding.]

11 Provision for poor and unfortunate. [Think of the massive welfare states of the Western world.]

12 Prohibition of theft. [Universal – and for obvious reasons.]

13 Prevention of violence within in-groups. [Survival value, again.]

14 Obligation to keep promises. [Based on the universal rational understanding that human practices are not possible without promise keeping.]

15 Obedience to leaders. [An expression of the universal social and psychological need for organization.]

16 Respect for the dead and disposal of human remains in some traditional and ritualistic fashion. [Think of *Antigone* and the universal law of respect for the dead.]

17 Desire for and priority of immaterial goods [such as knowledge, values, etc.]. [From its earliest traditions, Western philosophy has placed the highest value on contemplation, and all religions universally promote spiritual values.]

18 Obligation to be a good mother. [A universal awareness of the necessity for a close mother-child bond.]

19 Distributive justice. [The universally felt sense of "fairness."]
20 Inner rather than external sanctions considered better. [The universal emphasis on self-control.]
21 Courage is a virtue. [The universal reverence for bravery and self-sacrifice.]
22 Justice is an obligation. [This is universally the main concern of all religions and philosophies.]

We must conclude with a feeling of some fascination that each of these ordinances, prohibitions, and standards, without exception, is aimed at the common good and that in all human societies for which we have records, something like a common human moral nature seems to be at work as a practical expression of these as natural law. Otherwise, how is it possible that it is manifested in all people at all times? It is this that needs emphasis, celebration, and wonder, not the myriad differences between us. Having now seen that these moral standards and ideals exist among all peoples of the world, we can ask: Is there some equivalent moral practice between the nations of the world?

THE NATURAL LAW IS PRACTISED BY ALL NATIONS

There has been a long and venerable tradition of natural law in the Western world as manifested in what the Romans called *ius gentium* – the law of peoples, or from medieval times until now, the law of nations, or by some, international law. The positive, or human, law, as I prefer to call it, was an attempt to separate law from morality in order to develop law as a pure science and as a political practice unfettered by any transcendent moral ideal. The law, the positivists said, should take its essential, stripped-down meaning *as law* not from the private morals of judges or legal theorists but as a thing in itself. And what is it as a thing in itself but a pure command from a sovereign power to those commanded by it? From the middle of the nineteenth century forward, this has been a loose working definition of positive law. But no sooner had the human law experts dismissed natural law in all its forms as too concerned with morality and religion to qualify as real law than they bumped into international law. And they didn't know what to say. They still don't.

That is because throughout history nations have agreed to conform to the binding covenants of international law even though *no sovereign nation ever made or imposed that law*; that is, no nation has ever had legal authority or command over all other states. That being so – and if we agree with the human law theorists that a law is defined as a command from a sovereign power – then how, according to this principle, could international law be real law? If it were the result of a treaty, we could at least say it is a contract and thus true law. But what makes it so binding if it has never been a command to those commanded? For almost a century, legal theorists wrestled with this question in very clever ways.[3] One of the solutions they dreamed up was the argument that international law is indeed real law because although you can't see or touch an identifiable sovereign, there is indeed a sovereign giving commands, for *all the nations give the law to themselves and command themselves to obey it*. Hence, they happily concluded, international law is really only another legal invention of human beings. That was considered a clever try, and the history of this sort of legal contortionism is quite fascinating. But it is not convincing, and much clearer legal minds have been forced by the facts to agree that international law indeed rests on a dozen or more permanent principles that are obviously *antecedent to any agreement* among nations and that these international principles form the sort of *suprapositive*, or transcendent, law of which the judges at Nuremberg spoke.[4] In short, they constitute a fact of history and a form of *discovered* natural law that has always existed as what one scholar calls "a persistent spectre" in the collective mind of nations and international relations.[5] Below are thirteen "general principles" that form this international law as summarized by John Finnis, one of the most influential modern natural law theorists, and slightly modified here to read a little more plainly.[6] I have placed the straightforward natural law bases of these understandings are in square brackets:

1 Property right cannot be taken by compulsion without compensation, which is to be according to actual losses, not according to expected profits [natural property rights].
2 There is no liability for unintentional injury, unless there is fault [intent or fault is essential].
3 There is no criminal liability if the perpetrator is not of sound mind (*mens rea*) [we cannot be blamed if it is not possible to form an intent to harm].
4 Estoppel [a legal doctrine that blocks a person from taking a position on any fact that is contrary to a position the same person previously took on the same fact].
5 There is no judicial aid to anyone who pleads his own wrong (which means anyone who seeks equity, must do equity) [natural justice and equity].

6 There is no aid for abuse of rights [wrongs must not to be rewarded].
7 Fraud unravels everything [lying and deception are universally deemed wrong].
8 Profits gained without justification and at the expense of another must be restored [that is, justice must be restored].
9 All treaties and contracts must be performed (*pacta sunt servanda*) ["agreements must be honoured"].
10 There is freedom to change existing legal relationships by agreement [for example, contracts and changes to same require mutual consent].
11 In assessments of the legal effect of purported acts-in-the-law, the weak are to be protected against their weakness [not taken advantage of; that is, charity must prevail].
12 Disputes are not to be resolved without giving both [all] sides an opportunity to be heard [a plea for natural equity and justice].
13 No one is allowed to be a judge in his own cause [fairness is to be objectively determined by third parties].

What needs to be emphasized in the above is that these principles of the law of nations constitute firm understandings held in common between nations with very different histories, peoples, races, languages, traditions, and customs, yet they "bear a striking resemblance to the general principles of law and equity which feature prominently in the work of the International Court of Justice and other tribunals applying international law."[7] The plain fact, then, is that legal theorists attempting to explain human law on strictly positivist grounds "cannot coherently account for the internationally binding force of the general principles [of international law]."[8] The absence of any sovereign power over the nations of the world means that legal theorists are forced to concede *that the principles on which international law rests are prior to all state-to-state agreements.* They are principles that have never been "willed into existence" by anyone, or by any state, nor imposed by force, and neither has their general application to international law ever been consented to by the states of the world. Nevertheless, they exist "quasi-spontaneously in every civilized legal order, including international law, and are deductions from the natural law."[9] Even the ultrapositivist Hans Kelsen, who, as we have seen, spent a lot of energy trying to escape the self-evident implications of natural law, admitted that his own last-ditch effort to defend strictly positive law itself contained a minimum of natural law, "without which," he said, "a cognition of law is impossible."[10]

NATURAL LAW PRINCIPLES OF JUST WAR

We find the same sort of traditional natural law understandings inherent in the law of "just war." The distinction between just and unjust war has been of concern to the Western world since ancient times, and the first attempt to clarify the distinction was by Saint Augustine in the fifth century AD. I include the basic principles of just war as they would be accepted by almost all just-war thinkers, as outlined in Jay Budziszewski's *Written on the Heart*.[11] The first seven criteria have to do with *when* one may justly go to war (*jus ad bellum*), and the next three concern how a just war must be waged (*jus in bello*). When the first seven are satisfied, war is said to be permissible but not mandatory. Thinking about them, we can see that they all spring from deeper natural law principles.

Jus ad bellum
1 Competent authority: war may be declared only by a government, not by private parties.
2 Just cause: war may be waged only to protect innocent life, to ensure that people can live decently, and to secure natural rights.
3 Right intention: not only must there *be* just cause to go to war, but this just cause must be the *reason* for going to war.
4 Comparative justice: we do not require that one side be *wholly* in the right; that never happens. However, war should not be waged unless the evils to be fought, on the one side, are sufficiently greater than those on the other to justify killing.
5 Proportionality: war should not be waged unless the goods that may be reasonably expected from taking up arms are greater than the evils.
6 Probability of success: there must be a reasonable likelihood that the war will achieve its aims.
7 Last resort: war should not be waged unless all peaceful alternatives have been exhausted.

Jus in bello
1 Right intention: because the aim of those who go to war should be the achievement of a just peace, they should avoid any acts or demands that would hinder ultimate reconciliation.
2 Proportionality: no tactic may be employed unless the goods that may be reasonably expected from its employment are greater than the evils.

3 Discrimination: directly intended attacks on noncombatants and nonmilitary targets are impermissible.

Budziszewski comments that these very points were most recently debated in the United States during the first Gulf War, which, he writes, was "the first war in American history in which military and political leaders explicitly committed themselves to following the principles of just war."[12]

THE PERENNIAL PHILOSOPHY
AND THE MORAL LAW OF THE GREAT RELIGIONS

Suffice it to mention that there have been many secular attempts to explain the natural and the moral law. Hundreds of them. And that is the problem with this approach: it is impossible to construct a moral or ethical system without some believable ground of authority on which the system is based and from which it may serve as a guide for human conduct that is beyond distortion by human will. The natural law, as outlined above, is at least grounded in three indisputable goods: it asks us to do what is *humanly natural,* by following *right reason,* and for the *common good.* These three terms constitute a rational and universal boundary, or framework, for the judgment of all human conduct. For no one could successfully argue that humans everywhere ought always to pursue what is unnatural, unreasonable, or against the common good. That much, at least, is self-evident, and anyone to whom it is not will soon be classified as either a fool, demented, or possibly a criminal.

For most natural law theorists, the ultimate answer to the question "Where does this natural law come from?" is God. The Creator. The Divine Ground. Or some such spiritual source. For Kelsen, the ultimate rationalist, the source of authority for all law is the *Grundnorm*: the normative, or customary, ground of hierarchical values for a given state. That is the source for his "ultra-minimalist" notion of natural law. One of his critics opined that this *Grundnorm* is "rather like the idea of the world supported by an elephant, the rules not permitting you to ask what supports the elephant."[13] At any rate, those who regard as unbelievable the near-universal answer of God, or the Creator, or Divine Ground (which is itself the ground of all the great religions, as we shall see) will always tend nevertheless to ground their personal ethical system in some other form of faith. I mean to say that if we dig deeply enough, we discover that all the secular moral systems ever invented also rest on a belief system, or a faith of some kind. And although this faith, like any other, is not demonstrable or provable, it is confidently cited as an authority for moral claims. It is usually found to be a faith in human *reason* alone, for secular humanists; or in *biology* and evolution theory, for social scientists; or in some theory of human *rights*, for egalitarian political thinkers; or in some usually incoherent mixture of these three.

At the bottom of so-called "secular humanism" is a blind faith in human reason, materialism, and evolution theory. The creed of this "religion" (it was declared a secular religion in the US case of *Torcaso v. Watson*) is spelled out in the *Humanist Manifesto I* (1933) and *II* (1973),[14] and illustrious signatories such as John Dewey, Isaac Asimov, Sidney Hook, B.F. Skinner, and a raft of other left-liberals describe themselves in it as "religious humanists" who are the founders of "a vital, frank, and fearless religion" with which they intend "to reform the world." It is humankind they worship, or the human-god, which they call "humanity," and they declare they want this brand of humanism to foster "social and mental hygiene." It is likely that most modern academics and many other self-styled intellectuals subscribe to this depressing faith in whole or in part, mostly because it does not invoke any higher spiritual authority for moral values than a sanctified abstract conception of humanity. For secular humanists, all values are "situational" and "autonomous," which means they can be made up to serve any purpose. Humanists believe this is a good thing even though there is by now sufficient demonstration from actual history that modern secular humanism is a doctrine that has been relied upon to justify all modern totalitarian systems.

As for biology? Is it possible to derive from it a believable moral system? People such as E.O. Wilson, whose *Sociobiology* was discussed in chapter 7, tried this, cheerfully supplying us with some strangely sophomoric thoughts about morality. And then there was Richard Dawkins, who is still the leading high priest and most caustic pontificator on modern evolution theory and morality. His final deflating conclusion was that our genes make us do everything, but if we wish, we can rebel against them. As Frans de Waal (a prominent evolutionist who believes that morality in humans evolved from our ape-like history) complained about this, Dawkins "explained at length that our genes know what is best for us," and then "he waited until the very last sentence of *The Selfish Gene* to reassure us that, in fact, we are welcome to chuck all of those genes out the window" because, as Dawkins wound up his own strange logic, "we alone on earth, can rebel against the tyranny of the selfish replicators."[15] In other words, Dawkins contributed nothing very insightful to this moral discussion. He simply reiterated what moral philosophers have always taught: that we have good and bad instincts and that the highest goal of moral teaching is to help us to understand the difference and then to avoid the bad and pursue the good – that is, to follow the natural law. In a sense, this by now mainstream biological position on genes and morality is, quite fascinatingly, tinged with an ancient religious morality that imagines the spirit repudiating the claims of the flesh. De Waal himself takes the pre-lapsarian position that we are by nature good and that our moral sense and our goodness have evolved from tribal practices of (this is his minimalist definition of morality) "caring for each other" as evidenced by forms of primate empathy. To refute his argument, it suffices to argue that animal emotions are directed only internally to mates, offspring, or tribe (not even to other primates), are incident-specific, are severely limited by momentary emotive contexts, and cannot be universalized into any kind of code of heritable behaviour because, unlike humans, animals are not capable of formal abstract thought.

Perhaps the most infamous attempt to link morality with biology, however, was Robert Wright's *The Moral Animal* (1994). This is an engaging book that spins enough philosophical blarney about morality to hang its author many times over. The title alone is self-defeating, for what distinguishes animals from humans is precisely that the former are not free to rebel against their own instincts. So there cannot be such a thing as a "moral animal." A man who murders an innocent child is universally defined as evil because he could have chosen otherwise. But a lioness who kills an innocent deer is not; she is just hungry, wants to feed her cubs, and is doing what comes naturally. Wright supports modern evolutionary psychology and is excited that the new Darwinian anthropology focuses "less on surface differences among cultures than on deep unities." He thinks biology explains why it is that people everywhere gossip the same way and about the same things, evidence the same sex-difference patterns, feel the same guilt, and share the same sense of justice, and also why moral axioms, like "an eye for an eye" or "one good turn deserves another," shape human life everywhere on the planet.[16] Biology, he believes, is rediscovering a human nature – a moral nature – long dismissed by believers in the now-defunct Standard Social Science Model and in the tired blank-slate theory of the mind. Mind you, he would look less foolish if he stuck to his biology and left moral philosophy to philosophers. But most social scientists make that mistake. Indeed, a great deal of social science is an attempt to justify some researcher's camouflage morality with numbers and measurements. Wright says that morally speaking, we are genetic machines hardwired with "knobs," and with brain mechanisms for "tuning" those knobs, that have been acquired through natural selection and were laid down in the long Pleistocene period of evolutionary adaptation. Understanding our biology in the new way will, he believes, reveal our true selves – *selves previously hidden from us by our own biology.* It is hard to escape the hint of revelation in this. He firmly believes that altruism, compassion, empathy, love, conscience, the sense of justice, all the things that "hold society together" and allow us "to think so highly of ourselves," can now "firmly be said to have a genetic basis." Wright is not a mainstream evolutionary biologist. He is a popularizer of the subject. But all the more reason to spend time on what he says because vulgarizations of any theory are often the most revealing of its underlying errors. His book, which stayed on the *New York Times* bestseller list for two years, was an expression of a newly emerging "genetic essentialism" that departs radically from the idea that moral behaviour is linked to free will while arguing instead that it is "*connected* to the genes responsible for the human essence."[17] For Wright, "*every conceivable kind of behaviour,* both moral and immoral, is attributed to our genes' shrewd strategizing effort."[18] The appearance of his book gave rise to a furor of indignation because he as much as declared that rape, for example, which occurs in all societies, is just an evolutionary adaptation found typically in males who have struck out in the sexual pecking order, so what they cannot get by ordinary means they take by violence. Here, biology came close to excusing rape. He does not see that once we go down the materialist road, biology can justify any behaviour as natural, for it eschews all external moral standards outside biology in terms of which to judge behaviour good or bad.

Yet Wright goes on to say that although humans are a species "splendid in their array of moral equipment" (he makes this sound the same as having a great dishwasher!), they are also "tragic in their propensity to misuse it, and pathetic in their constitutional ignorance of the misuse." Here was the rope with which he hanged himself, and he brought it out only a few pages before informing us that "we're all puppets" and that our best hope for "even partial liberation is to try to decipher the logic of the puppeteer" because, even though "natural selection created us," this "doesn't mean we have to slavishly follow its particular agenda."[19] So about now I give up on Wright (and all his kind) as a serious thinker. For can we really say that a puppet with free will is a puppet? And if so, how would deciphering the evolutionary calculus of the puppet's puppeteer help a puppet to live a better life? Well, spiritual people have always said humans are not puppets. We create ourselves as moral beings only by resisting what is bad in ourselves and encouraging what is good. But this we can do only by knowing the difference according to a moral standard that does not originate from us and that we cannot alter as we please. Wright is proposing that self-correction can emerge from puppets, even though they have no free will and no standard for self-correction, as though the mere knowledge of what makes us do something (but how can a puppet have knowledge of anything?) will also make us stop doing it. But why should it?

No, the entire project to derive morality from biology must fail because knowledge of a solely material reality can be neither good nor bad. If we really are just an extension of the material world, we can behave only like the lioness and do what our biology dictates. To say otherwise, to say we are free to develop as good or bad people according to a moral standard, as all the great moral teachers have said, is to admit that biology may matter but not a great deal. It may dictate quite a bit – our breathing, our longing to eat, to make love, to protect ourselves and our young, and so on – but anything that can be called "moral" in any meaningful philosophical or practical sense implies *absolutely*, and by definition, a capacity to perform and alter our own moral actions.

A more elegant effort to discuss moral behaviour is *The Moral Sense*, by Harvard sociology professor James Q. Wilson.[20] He is considered the dean of American social scientists because of the thoroughness of his research and the sober, gentlemanly balance of his analyses, and we learn a great deal from his mustering of the current social science. He wrote his book because he earnestly wants "to re-establish the possibility and the reasonableness of speaking frankly and convincingly about moral choices." He seeks to show "that mankind has *a moral nature* to which we commonly and inevitably appeal when trying to defend our moral arguments."[21] This moral nature, he writes, "is an intuitive or directly felt belief" about how we ought to act in certain situations. He adds that most of us today try to talk ourselves out of our own moral intuitions, and he justifiably worries that the widely assumed belief that because we cannot "prove" our moral principles they cannot be taken seriously "has amputated our public discourse at the knees."[22] That is a social tragedy because, as he points out, "the teachings of the heart deserve to be taken as seriously as the lessons of the mind."[23] That is what Pascal said in 1670 and, more poetically, in his *Pensées*: "the heart has its reasons, of which reason knows nothing."[24]

Wilson focuses on four moral senses – sympathy, duty, self-control, and fairness – which, by whatever name, are *found universally in all cultures of the world*, as Professor Richard Beis, above, had already demonstrated so well in 1964. What is a little puzzling, as Jay Budziszewski has pointed out, is why Wilson persists in calling them *feelings*. For "they are not feelings at all. Rather, they are capacities and dispositions – states of character. All four deal with feelings, but that does not make them feelings."[25] The reason proposed by Budziszewski for this habit of Wilson's is, I think, correct: Wilson describes almost everything moral as a feeling, or impulse, or sense, or inclination because he wants "to deny that he is talking about universal rules or laws," or – let it be said – moral absolutes. So it seems that for Wilson we do have a universal human nature, but it is made up only of universal feelings or intuitions (much like de Waal's focus on primate "empathy") and nothing more solid. Nevertheless, Wilson defines his moral sense as a directly felt belief about how we ought to act, and he adds, "by *ought*, I mean an obligation binding on all people similarly situated." So despite his timidity about moral rules, Wilson's *ought* is clearly being described here as a rule that is a moral absolute. He adds that what researchers have found to be binding universally are "those rules governing the fundamental conflicts of everyday, intimate life – keeping promises, respecting property, acting fairly, and avoiding unprovoked assaults."[26]

But in the end, and despite the value of his book, its wealth of interesting insights, and its earnest attempts to understand feeling and the moral sense, Wilson is but another materialist whom we sense sometimes wishes he could escape his own scientific training. But as he cannot do so, he takes refuge in Darwinism as the source of human behaviour and feeling, although he does issue caveats. Evolution theory, he says, has told us a lot about the species but not much about individual behaviour. The urge to reproduce our genes, for example, cannot explain why a mother may care for an adopted child as deeply as for her own (and sometimes more so), or why the world is filled with billions of sterile ants that do not procreate, or why some people will fly across the world to ease the suffering of total strangers. Gene replication as a motive for human action is most poignantly vulnerable and deniable when it confronts the case of thousands of barren Western couples streaming to Asia in the hope of adopting a homeless Tsunami child that neither carries their genes nor even looks like them. Although Wilson struggles to explain morality and the human mind in purely material terms, he nevertheless persistently mentions, compares, and admires the nobler moral choices we all make from time to time, knowing full well that scientifically speaking, no feeling can be nobler than another without a standard by which to judge it so. In the end, he is an example of an emerging trend among modern scientists who have seen the moral devastations wrought by unguided naked reason and are trying to find a way out without, as yet, surrendering their materialism.

Until now I have been discussing attempts by materialists to explain universal moral behaviour that is by definition rooted in free will. Materialists are followers of a philosophy sometimes called "realism" according to which nothing exists except matter. This is also sometimes called "scientism," and I dare say it is a limited and erroneous conclusion that is at odds with real science but has nevertheless shaped – perhaps I should say warped – all of Western intellectual perceptions. Why? Because whereas all other civilizations have seen matter as only a part, or aspect, of reality, not the whole of it, our modern Western civilization is the first and only one that has turned this upside down by attempting to explain the whole by the part. We have thus condemned ourselves to believing that all things "real" must emanate from, can be produced only by, other things. Yet this is not really what modern science has been telling us. The counter-evidence and the scientific interface with mystical religion come from exalted thinkers such as Nobel Laureate in physics Paul Dirac, the father of antimatter, whom we met in chapter 5, on the constants of nature. About matter and nothingness, he wrote: "All matter is created out of some imperceptible substratum and ... the creation of matter leaves behind it a 'hole' in this substratum which appears as antimatter. Now, this substratum itself is not accurately described as material, since it uniformly fills all space and is undetectable by any observation. In a sense, it appears as nothingness – immaterial, undetectable, and omnipresent. But it is a peculiarly material form of nothingness, out of which all matter is created."[27]

For anyone alive to the stunting effects of modern scientism (of science as it is misunderstood) on human spiritual insight, this is an astonishing and refreshing truth about the material "reality" that most of us grew up believing was "all that there is."

Their opposites are followers of "idealism," and they disagree with the idea that matter is all that there is (the word "idealism" is meant here to refer to ideas about nonmaterial things – such as ideas themselves). What is most real for such thinkers is the realm of ideas, of consciousness, and of spiritual reality, of which the material world is but a part and, it is often argued, an emanation. They believe that abstract concepts, ideals, laws, and essences are higher and more important than mere sensory things, that we understand reality ideally as a total concept rather than partially via particular physical or sensory experiences. This distinction plays a key role in discussions of moral behaviour because realists such as Wright and Wilson are forbidden by their own assumptions from sourcing morality (or anything else) in an external or nonmaterial standard such as a universal concept of justice or a natural law. For some reason, they don't mind agreeing that there is an extremely mysterious law of gravity that controls all matter but that is not itself a part of matter, but they will not consent to other types of laws that govern or guide human behaviour, such as a natural moral law.

But those who follow traditional natural law do believe this – that the only way we can possibly make judgments of value at all is by reference to something beyond, or other than, the mere material world. The reason for this, we have seen, is that no material thing can judge or evaluate another material thing. Accordingly, as no act or thing can be the judge of itself, no moral judgment can be made about it unless we invoke an absolute standard according to which a particular act succeeds or fails or may be seen as falling somewhere in between.

What is clear by now is that there is some international consensus that there exists a great number of moral universals.[*]

---

[*] In 1993 the United Nations, through UNESCO, met with scholars and representatives of 120 religions to embark on a what it calls its Universal Ethics Project. Here is a statement from its first meeting in Naples, Italy (www. unesco.org/opi2/ philosophyandethics/pronpro.htm):

> The search for universal values has certainly been motivated by the growing urgency of the need to find solutions to the great problems facing humanity today. But it should also be emphasized that such a search was also encouraged by a great shift in the winds of doctrine in philosophy, natural and social sciences. Transcending the once-dominant philosophical abstinence which characterized philosophical reflection on values and norms, philosophers are today questioning the positivistic doctrine of meaningfulness, the doctrines of incommensurability and untranslatability among languages and cultures, and seeking to give the notion of universality a new meaning in the context of cultural diversity. Biologists, neurologists and anthropologists are exploring the universals in the physical and cultural constitution of men and societies. Social and human scientists are emboldened by a global discourse on human rights and by the emergence of an embryonic global civil society as embodied in various movements led by non-governmental organizations. The legitimacy and efficacy of these organizations do not derive from some organized form of coercion; rather they spring from the relevance and persuasiveness of the values and goals which are shared across national and cultural boundaries. This is what gives encouragement to the Universal Ethics Project and what gives substance to the assertion that, if the preceding century has been a century of social sciences, the 21st century is to be a century of ethics.

My comment on such initiatives is only that insofar as governments attempt to ground ethics in a consensus of mere reason, they will always fail. Ethics, as I have argued, is about practical rules of decent behaviour (within organizations and groups) that may be desirable and tolerable but may or not be moral. Morality is quite different and has to do with absolute and universal guidelines. In this sense, ethics must be located within morality, not the other way around.

Where people differ is in the explanation for them – of how this could be so. Their answer, as I say, can be traced to their realist or idealist assumptions. We have examined two prominent types of realist explanation for moral universals, both faulty. So now let us turn to examples of the idealist type, of which there are principally three: the traditional natural law that has been the focus of this chapter, something called the primordial, or perennial, philosophy, and the moral universals of the world's great religions. Having dealt already with the first, let us turn to the second.

The "perennial philosophy" (or, in Latin, *philosophia perennis*), is a term first used in the sixteenth century by the Vatican librarian Agostino Steucho. He was referring to the beliefs held in common about nature, human nature, God, virtue, and so on by all peoples known at the time, and he was especially struck by the common views held by the great Christian writers and by ancient philosophers and writers such as Plato, Aristotle, Cicero, Aeschylus, and Aristophanes, among so many others. The term was made current by Leibniz in the early eighteenth century and more recently has been used to express that all of the world's great religions *share a single universal moral and spiritual truth.* The perennial philosophy, then, describes the world's only universal belief system with respect to the nature of existence and how it is possible to gain direct spiritual knowledge. Its roots go deep into the moral, religious, and life experiences of all humanity, its sources so ancient they are lost in time. In 1976, and although twenty years prior he had published and sold two million copies of *The Religions of Man*, which examines the many *differences* between all religions of the world, Professor Huston Smith, of MIT, published a warm and wonderful, and remarkably clear, little book called *Forgotten Truth*. In it he shows how all the religious traditions of the world converge. Underlying their surface variety, he writes, "is a remarkable unity. It is as if an 'invisible geometry' has everywhere been working to shape them to a truth that in the last resort is single." He also explains that because certain modern cults have latched onto the term "perennial philosophy," he prefers to call it the "Primordial Tradition."[28] I agree with him but will stick with the usual term because it is better known.

Another in-depth examination is Aldous Huxley's *The Perennial Philosophy*, published in 1944, before the end of World War II, when acute minds, appalled by the devastations wrought by the most civilized nations on earth, were keenly in search of some deeper universal truth.[29] Huxley writes engagingly and persuasively, arguing that although nothing in our everyday experience gives us any reason to suppose that water is made up of hydrogen and oxygen, when we subject it to certain rather drastic treatments, its true nature is revealed. Similarly, he goes on, nothing in our everyday experience gives us much reason for supposing "that the mind of the average sensual man" has the potentialities for obtaining direct spiritual knowledge. But through psychological and moral experiments (perhaps here he meant testing moral concepts on experience?), it is possible to discover the intimate nature of mind and its potentialities. This experience has generally arisen not from philosophers but from spiritual thinkers – saints, prophets, sages, or enlightened ones – concerned with "the one, divine Reality substantial to the manifold world of things, and lives, and minds." It is a reality that can be directly and immediately apprehended only by "those who have made themselves loving, pure of heart, and poor in spirit" (i.e., humble). Why should this be so? Huxley answers frankly: "We do not know." It is just one of those facts we have to accept whether we like them or not. As examples of the perennial philosophy, he cites the Indian Shruti writings, the great Catholic mystics of the Middle Ages and the Renaissance, the Persian Sufis of Islam, Hebrew prophecy, the Platonic dialogues, and more. He might also have cited some of the fascinating works on modern quantum physics. At any rate, the perennial philosophy has spoken in all the languages of Asia and Europe while making use of the terminology and traditions of every one of the great religions. Although inspired individuals from different traditions may from time to time impose a certain bias on the core doctrines, whenever words and even personality are transcended in contemplation, the highest common factor of the philosophy in its "chemically pure state" remains. The records left by those who have known the perennial philosophy in this way "make it abundantly clear that all of them, whether Hindu, Bhuddist, Taoist, Christian, or Mohammedan, were attempting to describe the same essentially indescribable fact."[30]

At the core, Huxley tells us, are four fundamental and universal doctrines:

- First, the phenomenal world of matter and of individualized consciousness – the world of things and animals and men and even gods, is the manifestation of a Divine Ground within which all partial realities have their being and apart from which they would be non-existent.
- Second, humans are capable not merely of knowing about the Divine Ground by inference; they can also realize its existence by a direct intuition, superior to discursive reasoning. This immediate knowledge unites the knower with that which is known.

- Third, man possesses a double nature, a phenomenal ego and an eternal Self, which is the inner man, the spirit, the spark of divinity within the soul. It is possible for a man, if he so desires, to identify himself with this spirit and therefore with the Divine Ground, which is of the same, or like nature with the spirit.
- Fourth, man's life on earth has only one end and purpose: to identify himself with his eternal Self and so come to unitive knowledge of the Divine Ground.

Even for Christians, whose God is personal, Huxley says, the knowledge of Him is not discursive but direct, synthetic, timeless, and "of the heart." At any rate, I cite the perennial philosophy here not to convert anyone but to show, in a book about absolutes, that what Huxley called the "Highest Common Factor" and Smith the "Primordial Tradition" is universal and an absolute of all humankind's religious experience from time immemorial. As Huxley stated, "it is perfectly possible for people to remain good Christians, Hindus, Bhuddists, or Moslems and yet to be united in full agreement on the basic doctrines of the Perennial Philosophy." I believe that careful attention will show that there is a pretty direct relationship between this philosophy, the universal natural law as described in this chapter, and the universal moral practices discovered to exist in all the cultures of the world.

As a final example of religious and moral universals, I want to mention another remarkable book, of only sixty-three pages, by C.S. Lewis, entitled *The Abolition of Man,* in which he examines the moral flabbiness of modernity and proposes a return to the Tao, or "the Way" (the root of the word "Tao" is door, or doorway), by which he means the way of the universal moral standards found in all the great religions of the world. He writes that because they are universal, "it is by no means certain that there has ever been more than one civilization in all history."[31] His is a searching indictment of modern materialism, according to which, as there is supposedly no other reality, the truth of things, including morality, is said to be a matter of personal feeling and opinion. All values are therefore said to be subjective, situational, and relative. Lewis's book, which is a defence of natural law that he gave as three brief lectures in 1943, utterly embarrasses this idea. He shows easily that no one can escape making moral judgments except by defining all their own actions as good, and this supposed goodness is justified only because the actions originate in personal will. At this point, however, the question is no longer what is right or wrong but which group of such morally self-inventing persons has the most power to enforce its views on others. And that is the beginning of tyranny.

To avoid this horrific prospect (one savaging Europe at the time he wrote), he proposed that the task of the modern educator – he is debating some British teachers in his book – is not to cut down jungles of false emotion and sentimentality but to irrigate deserts by teaching the Tao. Examples he cites are such as Shelley's *Aeolian Harp*, Saint Augustine's *Ordo Amoris*, Aristotle's dictum that the aim of education is to make the pupil love what he ought, Plato's teachings on the Good, the *Rta* of Hinduism, the Chinese *Tao te ching*, Jewish law, the *Decalogue*, and so on. And he spells out some of the basic universals of this law. Some examples of the Tao found in all religions of the world are:

- The law of general beneficence: first, negative, as in "do not murder." Then positive, as in "do unto others as you would have them do unto you."
- The law of special beneficence: from many religions and traditions having to do with specific duties.
- Duties to parents, elders, and ancestors, such as: "Honour thy father and thy mother," or the equivalent found in all societies.
- Duties to children and posterity: as found in universal commands to love and protect children.
- The law of justice: having to do with universal commands not to commit adultery, lie, cheat, or steal; with commands to be honest, and equitable, especially in courts; and so on.
- The law of good faith and veracity: having to do with universal prohibitions against fraud and insincerity.
- The law of mercy: having to do with universal commands to help the weak and needy.
- The law of magnanimity: having to do with how we are to live nobly and act generously – and to die, if necessary, for the truth.

The general theme is that emotions, which are not necessarily good or bad in themselves, must be trained to accord with right reason, as Saint Thomas Aquinas and so many of the wise have taught. His metaphor for the well-balanced person is threefold. We are made of heads, chests, and bellies. The head, which innately knows objective right and wrong, must rule the belly, which is the seat of our animal appetites. But it can do so only through the chest, or heart, which is the seat of ordered emotions and just affections. Alas, writes Lewis, with our scientism, our dry rationalism, and our subjective and relativistic morality, we are bringing up "men without chests." And an education in such moral subjectivism, he warns, will eventually destroy any society that accepts it. Why? Because comfortable pragmatism is no test of the truth of things, for the truth – as when we resist true evil – is not always comfortable. It may even lead to our own death, as when we try to do the ultimate good. Remember the lines from John 15:13 with which we still salute all fallen heroes: "Greater love hath no man than that he lay down his life for a friend." It is as clear as the first day that no one would do such a thing for a relative value, only for an objective one. In this sense, Lewis argues, any attack on the truth of the Tao presumes itself that the Tao (i.e., that truth) is possible.

Lewis presents us with an either/or that will serve us well as a closing to this chapter: "Either we are rational spirit obliged forever to obey the absolute values of the Tao, or else we are mere nature to be kneaded and cut into new shapes for the pleasures of masters who must, by hypothesis, have no motive but their own 'natural' impulses. Only the Tao [the natural law] provides a common human law of action which can over-arch rulers and ruled alike. A dogmatic belief in objective value is necessary to the very idea of a rule which is not tyranny or an obedience which is not slavery."[32]

10

How Language Theory Changed the (Post)Modern World

Human habit conceals human mystery, and this is especially and deeply true for habits of language. For we do not know by what miracle of history or necessity we are able so effortlessly – should I say unconsciously – and with such unseemly instruments as lips, tongue, and teeth to whisper soft words in a lover's ear that move to tears or bark commands that fill the hearts of fighting men with pride.

There are presently some 5,000 language on the planet, not counting dialects, creoles, and idioms, unknown hundreds that have become extinct, and some that may now be forming. Despite this extraordinary diversity of human speech, careful scholars have discovered a growing number of *universals of human language and literature* common to all people. How this can be so when languages seem so very different and their speakers so widely separated in time and space is still a matter of speculation – sometimes dangerous speculation, for careers are often built or broken and philosophical and political revolutions won or lost in arguments over the meaning of ... words. Indeed, by the end of this chapter we will see that for the past half-century there has been a sustained attack by radical language philosophers on the common-sense idea that language has the capacity to communicate objective meaning. (I leave aside for the moment the obvious fact that we cannot make such an attack successfully without some objective point of reference.) More sinister is the fact that an attack on objective meaning in general is also an attack on the traditional foundations of accepted meaning in particular for any civilization in which this occurs.

This is not so surprising. Language has always been a hot political and philosophical object of study because in addition to everyday language, we have *metalanguage*, or language about language. And if it is true, as I think very likely, that most, if not all, human thought of the rational and conscious kind is impossible without language, then we arrive at the equation "language = thought" – or at least most of the communicable kinds of thought. This means that anyone who wants to attack your ideas can begin by attacking your understanding of language because language about language is also – following the equation – thinking about thinking. In the sense that the pen is often mightier than the sword, a subtle weapon in the battle for the control of ideas, this chapter and much of those that follow is about the modern – especially the so-called "postmodern" – war over language and thought. Mightier than the sword, you say? Well, yes. For example, modern Germany lost both world wars in the twentieth century to the sword. But what might be called the modern "idea-language" of the German people, or at least of their most influential philosophers, has during the past century been adopted as a "true" description of reality that has by now almost completely conquered the conquerors. The Allied forces conquered German armies, but readers may soon agree German philosophers have conquered our minds. It is no small irony that Jacques Derrida, a French-Algerian Jew, and Michel Foucault, both of whom were driving forces of postmodern theory, drank deeply at the cup of German philosophy, and although Derrida disavowed all relativism, he initiated its most popular and corrosive modern form.

But in order to understand "the linguistic turn" of recent times, we first have to stand outside our own language habits to ask: How does language actually work? In what follows I want to convey some of the intricacies of this question and clear up some of the confusion that surrounds it. None of what follows is essential to describing the universals of language or literature. They could be plunked down on the page right now, and that would be the end of it. But a book about constants and universals* is also by implication a repudiation of modern relativism. Ancient relativism, as we saw much earlier, was rather triumphantly disposed of by Plato and Aristotle, and for almost a thousand years talk of relativism was highly suspect, if not a joke. But it has made a comeback in very recent times not through any defeat of the ancient and

---

* To repeat: an absolute such as the law of gravity or the mass of the electron is a constant, true at all times and in all places. But a universal such as the prohibition of incest, while it may be universally true now, may not always have been so. So we can say the incest prohibition is now a universal but may not be a constant. By the same token, some language universals may not be constants.

rather conclusive logical arguments against it but by an interesting attempt (now referred to by the grab-bag term "postmodernism") to say that everything is relative because all thinking is trapped within a circle of linguistic self-reference from which no one can escape. Even logic is said to be such a trap. This is largely due to the modern view that human languages function as *systems of relations*. The sounds, words, and meanings of language are said to be understandable due to their distinctive contrasts with other sounds, words, and meanings. We grasp the meaning of one word in a dictionary by reading a description of it in other words. So whether inside a dictionary or inside our own language universe, we are trapped, as some language cynics put it, in "a prison house of language." This "language = thought = relativism" equation is then extended to all social, moral, and political reality to argue that there is no fixed or essential truth or foundation to be found anywhere. And even more cynically: that because no language can produce truth, all uses of language claiming to do so are a camouflage for political, moral, or economic power.

I have spent many decades both intrigued by and critical of this idea and have long wanted to write about it. For I am one of those who believes that a sentence such as this one could not be understood by anyone except the writer unless language had some direct relation to a firm and shared reality – which is to say, firm enough to result in mutual human comprehension from outside the prison house. In this respect, as mentioned in chapter 1, I agree with Bertrand Russell's assessment of human language as set out in his justly admired little book *The Problems of Philosophy*,[1] where he explains that words such as "cat" or "run" or "cut" all stand for universal concepts and become particular only when we see or imagine an actual cat, run to the store, or cut a loaf of bread, and so on. In this sense, almost every word in any language is already a universal. However, to clarify some of the modern concepts used to discuss language, and especially how they have been misused by certain language philosophers with an agenda, we must start at the beginning.

THE WAY IT WAS BEFORE
LANGUAGE RELATIVISM TOOK OVER

Professor Herbert Merritt, my teacher of Anglo-Saxon language at Stanford University in the mid-1960s, had a love affair with language. His eyes would twinkle as he asked the class for a word – any word at all

– for which he would then proceed to show the derivation. Hands covered in white chalk, his lecture salted with spry stories and insights, he took the greatest pleasure in showing how after layers of historical change from the ancient Sanskrit or Indo-European root a word that sounded nothing like the one we gave him evolved by intricate changes of sound, meaning, translation, mistakes in transcription by some sleepy medieval scribe, laziness in pronunciation, a quirky event of history – or perhaps a combination of such things – into the one we gave him! We soon learned that every word we use has a particular and fascinating – dare I say an absolute and distinctive – history of which most of us have no knowledge. We learned that we all share unconsciously in making our language history with every word we have ever spoken.

"Herbie," as he was affectionately called, was a "philologist" (from the Greek – "a lover of words"), an expert at an esteemed tradition of language analysis many centuries old that reached its high point of erudition in nineteenth-century Europe. Such scholars – there are still many at work in this older way – by the twentieth century had come to be thought of, and were often unfairly derided as, "historical linguists," a kind of academic fossil. But to them all words are like living entities whose enriching meanings and changes over time can be ascertained by careful historical, or "diachronic," study. The opposing term, "synchronic," is used for the study of things as they are at a single point in time, frozen in history, so to speak. A geologist who studies a deep core of rock diachronically looks at the changes in the many layers over geological time. A synchronic study would look only at the features of a single layer.

An example of what Herbie enjoyed is the English word "nickname." Most of us have no idea where such an everyday word came from – although many of us have a nickname. It turns out that in Middle English of the kind Chaucer spoke, the word *eke*, for *also*, could mean an *addition* or *extension* of something. So *eke* was combined with the word *name*, and people began to say that you had an *ekename*, or an additional name. But laziness in pronunciation soon set in, and that is how *an ekename* eventually became *a nickname*.

For putting words together, we used to have teachers of grammar. They knew how words could be linked properly to produce more complex meanings according to certain not very logical historical rules of accepted usage. I was taught this way all through elementary school, where we had to learn a lot of "exceptions to the rule." We learned that all complete sentences have a subject, a verb, and an object and that ones that do not are called "incomplete." A noun was defined as the name of "a person, place, or thing," even though we thought it was confusing to call a word like "love" a thing. At any rate, much of language teaching had to do with getting the "correct" usage into the heads of little boys and girls so they would grow up speaking "properly." One newcomer to our school, when accused of some misdeed, persisted in saying, "I ain't done nothin'," to which our teacher replied, quite logically: "Well, if you ain't done nothin', then you must have done something." "No sir," the perplexed boy kept repeating, having utterly missed the point, "I ain't done nothin'," after which a look of general pity went around the room.

Little did we know that behind the scenes, slowly making its way into the forefront of academic language studies in the Western world, was a new way of speaking about language that by the next generation was to revolutionize – rather, to radicalize – not only all academic subjects that rely on language (they all do in some way) but millions of students as well. In this chapter I want to show how new language concepts that began innocently enough in pursuit of humanistic and scientific truth were adopted and distorted by radical thinkers in order to promote a caustic and nihilistic form of language relativism that denies the possibility of knowing the truth about anything except relativism itself – which is always presented as absolute truth.[2]

STRUCTURALISM:
THE NEW WAY OF SPEAKING ABOUT LANGUAGE

The founding of modern "structural" linguistics began with a Swiss thinker named Ferdinand de Saussure (1857–1913), whose lectures were published after his death by his students as *Course in General Linguistics*,[3] a book that has had a far greater influence on Western life than its modest title would suggest. Indeed, Professor Roy Harris of Oxford University, the translator of the edition used here, states unequivocally that the implications of Saussure's technique for dealing with language analysis extend far beyond the boundaries of language in ways that make the book "without doubt one of the most far-reaching works concerning the study of human cultural activities to have been published at any time since the Renaissance."[4] That is quite a statement. Unfortunately, its truth springs as much from what Saussure said and did as from the many ways his teachings have been misunderstood and irresponsibly used by nonspecialists – mostly by literary theorists – to justify various versions of language relativism. He would not have approved.

As it happened, Saussure was born at a time when the demand for more objective scientific method was being felt in every field. Religion had already been relegated to the status of myth by Darwinian evolution theory. Psychology was bifurcating into a strange medicine of the mind via Freud and into stimulus-response laboratory work via behaviourism. Einstein's theory of relativity was looming on the horizon. But language and literature? My goodness, there seemed to be Herbies everywhere, loving language but mixing their analyses with "subjective" things like philosophy, myth, morality, and manners. Saussure began to worry that with such confusion we would never be able to identify a scientific object called "language." So he set out to create a new science that could describe linguistic objects of study as independent of all other objects. He was not against studying language changes in the old way, as Herbie did. He just felt that all historical changes operate "over such long time spans that ... although the individual unconsciously participates in bringing about such changes, they are not real to him or her."[5]

By now, Saussure had realized two things more clearly than most. First, he understood that for any communication system to work, in whatever medium, there has to be an underlying *system* by which information is initially encoded and then decoded. But how is this possible? He knew as a matter of common sense that whatever the system he was hunting down turned out to be, one that allowed a listener to understand a speaker with full competence would be an abstraction, *not part of the act of speech* (just as the law of gravity is not part of the falling apple, or the written score of a symphony is not part of the actual sound of the symphony). Second, he understood that the hidden system governing the production of sound and meaning in all human languages is not only nonmaterial but also unconscious (although I prefer the term "preconscious"). Here was a daring idea hinting at the existence of an invisible system that in some preconscious sense might be partially controlling human thought! We will return to that notion shortly. For now, it is enough to agree that although the language system we use so freely is "ours" in the sense that it is created and sustained by many millions of users daily, the vast majority of speakers are not at all conscious of the intricate system that makes their daily, and often incredibly subtle and intricate, communication possible. They just do it. They use the system, so to speak. (Or as some cynical thinkers would soon begin to say – *the system uses them.*)

SIGNS: THE METHOD

Saussurean structural linguistics began not as a creed but as a method. It proposed to deal not with the substance of language or its history, as all prior linguists had done, but with the *relations* between the elements of language that enable it to function as a total *system* (Saussure rarely used the word "structure"). The first important concept that Saussure emphasized was the *sign*. To understand it, we can compare and contrast it with the *symbol*. Simply put, a sign is an operative term in a complete system of meaning, whereas a symbol can, and often does, stand alone. Take the colour red. As a symbol, it may mean blood, anger, passion, fire, and many other things. But when we see a red light in a traffic system, it means only "stop" because there it is being recognized (and utilized) only as a sign. Anyone new to the traffic system who approached such a red light for the first time and began thinking about it as a symbol of human passion, for example, might miss the sign-meaning of red (which has a purely relational meaning contrasted with the colours green for "go" and yellow for "caution") and could end up in big trouble for hesitating or by confusing symbol-value with sign-value.

In all communication systems, a *sign* is comprised of two joined elements: a *signifier*, which for human language is typically the sound of a word (or its written letter), and a *signified*, which is the distinctive concept attached to the signifier. So along with the sound "mountain" comes the concept, or idea, of a mountain. A third element that may also but not necessarily be present is a real-world *referent* of the sign – that is, a real mountain. Again, the sound "cat" (the signifier) somehow triggers in the mind the general concept of a cat (the signified), but if at that moment a real cat runs into the room, we will also have a living referent. The sounds and signs of each human language always operate in a specific rule-bound and relational context that *generates* meaning by way of the distinctive contrasts between the terms – the many different sounds and words – of the system.

The science of sign systems is called *semiology* in Europe and s*emiotics* in North America (from the Greek word *seme* for "meaning"). The claim of modern semiotics is that all sign systems, no matter of what their substance is constituted (colours, clothing, words, food, literature), rely to a greater or lesser degree on language for their meaning because that is how meaning must eventually be communicated and, as we saw, words are generally equated with thought. Whereas symbols are deep, historically rich, and have diffuse meanings, or soft edges, so to speak, signs operate on a clear and distinct all-or-nothing basis. In fact, we can easily endanger ourselves or others if we insist on thinking of a sign as a symbol, as when a driver misses the sign-value – "stop" – of a red light or when an enemy soldier mistakes the "I surrender" sign-value of my white flag.

LANGUAGE AND SPEECH

Saussure distinguished between *language* and *speech*, which is to say, between the preconscious general code of the system (language) and the particular utterances of individual users (speech). The *code* of any communication system is always "used" preconsciously (unless it is made conscious by the structural analyst) and is always general rather than particular and abstract rather than concrete. But speech *acts* are always particular and concrete. Most structuralists are interested more in the abstract system that makes saying or doing possible than in particular concrete acts. However, before you can determine the underlying system, you have to accurately define the *substance* by which it is expressed, whether it be sounds, colours, flags, lights, or something else, for it could be almost anything. The substance of human language is the flowing sound of human speech (which may also have a parallel written system that is broken by spaces between words). But I say "flow" because until we know a foreign language, it always strikes us as just a flow of unfamiliar sounds; we can't tell where the words begin or end. A nonspeaker of English, for example, would hear what I just wrote as *anonspeakerofenglish* and would have no idea how to separate the sounds into discrete elements, or words, so that the flow "makes sense." For all the listener knows, the meaningful elements could be *anon spea ker ofeng lish*. So how does this work?

SOUND: THE FIRST LEVEL OF ANALYSIS

For Saussure, the search for the hidden system of language must begin with actual speech, not with writing, which he considered an inferior, parasitical, and often distorting attempt to produce speech effects in the absence of an actual speaker. So he began by breaking the flow of sound into distinctive units of sound called *phonemes* (from the Greek word for *sound*). Each phoneme is a minimally distinctive unit of sound for a particular language. As an example, consider the words "pit" and "pet." The first and last phonemes – /p/ and /t/ – are the same for each word. But the middle one is not. By asking a competent native speaker of English whether the middle sound difference signals a change in meaning, we learn from the affirmative answer that the English sounds /i/ and /e/ are two different phonemes. (By convention, linguists indicate phonemes by placing them in slanted brackets to distinguish them from written letters.) But that may not be true for all languages, in some of which those two sounds may be heard as the same because they do not signal a distinctive difference. In other words – strange as it may seem to us – someone from such a language would hear the English words *pit* and *pet* as the same word. And so it goes as the linguist tries many more sound pairings to determine which sound contrasts signal a difference and thus play a role in meaning. Eventually, the linguist discovers every phoneme in a particular language (and the rules of usage that allow some phonemes to go together but not others). In standard English we have a written alphabet with twenty-six "letters," but we have (on last count) forty-five phonemes. That means some written letters, or combinations of them, have to do double or triple duty. For example, the letter "c" is used for a "k" sound in "cat" and for an "s" sound in "celery," and it also plays a role in the "ch" sound in "chew" because English does not have a single letter to indicate that sound. Discovery of the total inventory of phonemes in any language is the starting point. It is like knowing all the basic materials with which a building can be built.

MEANING: THE SECOND LEVEL OF ANALYSIS

Once we have all the units of sound defined, we can combine them to discover not words but the *minimal units of meaning*, or *morphemes* (from the Greek word for *form*), of which words are constructed. Such units of meaning may be combined to form larger units of meaning according to quite fixed (and unconscious) rules of combination. For example, "worthless" is an English word made of two morphemes: the base {worth} and the ending {less}. Here, the brackets are used to indicate morphemes, the latter of which {less} has the meaning of negating or reducing the meaning of any morpheme to which it is attached. Sometimes, even a single phoneme can have a morphemic status, as when we change *cat* to *cats*, with the phoneme /s/ acting as a unit of meaning to signal a number change from one to more than one. At this stage, Saussure has figured out how to assemble various types of raw material according to fixed rules of what works with what. You can cement brick to brick but not to wood; you can nail wood to wood but not to stone; and so on.

RULES OF COMBINATION:
THIRD LEVEL OF ANALYSIS

Saussure is now working his way up to another level, at which morphemes are not only combined in complex ways to get what we loosely call "words" but also arranged relative to each other in terms of allowable positions and combinations to get what we call "sentences." For example, there is a grammatical rule that allows all English speakers to say "the boy hit the ball" but not "the boy the ball hit" (although that would be normal usage in German and Japanese). We learn (and will see that this is a universal of English and is true of most but not all languages) that English has a subject-verb-object, or svo, structure (unlike German and Japanese, which are sov). So if you try the latter combination of morphemes in English, you will get a worried look if you are an English speaker because others will think something is wrong with you. The same will happen if you betray the rules of ordinary logic in the way language connects with reality. For example, you may say, "the cat ate the mouse," but you will stop the music if you say, "the mouse ate the cat" or "the bridge hit the car," even though each is grammatically correct. These little examples also illustrate (contrary to what language radicals would later argue) that *language cannot make sense without some distinctive connection with a common external reality.* In effect, we do not judge the world via language. It is the reverse. We judge the adequacy of language by the standards of real-world experience (the bridge cannot "hit" the car) and also by reason and by various intuitive and logical tests such as "non-contradiction." This latter rule-based and reason-and-reality-based level of analysis, which has to do with combinations of lower-level elements, is called *syntax* (a Greek word for "a systematic ordering of parts"), and a lot more will be said about it in a later chapter when we get to the universals of language.

At any rate, this is the very brief story about how Saussure went about analyzing language like a scientist instead of like a historian or a literary man. Today, the techniques of structural linguistics have become so sophisticated that a really good linguist does not need to know anything about a new language or its history or to speak even a word of it in order to write a complete grammar of that language. At Stanford I had a dear friend and mentor, Professor Alphonse Juilland, who when he was a young professor wanted to study the Gypsy language. The only Gypsies he could find were four women working in a brothel in Portland, Oregon. So he went up there to interview them. In six weeks of hard work (I didn't ask), he had finished a complete grammar of the Gypsy language without himself ever being able to speak any of it. What? You can understand the complete system of a foreign language but as a matter of scientific pride decline to speak it? All this was unheard of – actually, it was considered impossible – before Saussure. This points to the first radical innovation of modern structural linguistics: its insistence upon seeing language as an objective, preconscious, and synchronic communication *system* that generates meaning. Whereas the previous historical (diachronic) linguistics thought of language as a treasure house of the human spirit, the influence of Saussure was to shift scholarly interest in language "from the private past of words and groups of words and individual languages to the depthless lattice of a system of phonetic, syntactic, and semantic co-ordinates."[6]

It would not be long before certain European, and then copycat North American, intellectuals began to argue that so strong is this systematic production of meaning that we as subjects are like inconsequential operators of a system that drives itself and thus drives us. In short, there are some radical aspects to Saussure's thought that were soon taken to the next level by the generation that followed the brief postwar popularity of structuralism. But why, exactly, were Saussure's teachings to affect the way we view literature, all humanistic studies, and yes, even politics for the next three-quarters of a century?

THE RADICAL — AND RELATIVIST — ASPECTS OF SAUSSURE'S SYSTEM

It was pretty clear from the start that Saussure and many other European and North American structuralists had quietly embarked on a search for the "universal features"[7] of human language(s) and by implication of the human mind. This humanistic search had been going on in various fields for centuries, often locked in a struggle with theories opposed to universalism and even to the very idea of "objectivity." In fact, much of Western intellectual life could be characterized by a to-and-fro alternation between universalism and particularism under one label or another. Universalists are humanists who look for and defend what is common to all in the hope of developing some kind of ethical and political harmony. But particularists (who say they, too, are humanists) stress the differences and hence the relativistic aspects of human life because they fear (sometimes rightly) that ethical and political oppression are too easily justified by universals and absolutes, especially by any hint of biological absolutes based in race. Neither movement ever disappears; each is an opposing version of truth struggling for intellectual dominion in the name of one of two contrary ideals.

So it happened that just prior to the rise of structuralism in a devastated post-World War II Europe for which all universalist dreams of a real humanism had clearly crashed, particularism once again took over, and there was for about a decade a popular enthusiasm for "existentialism." This was a philosophy that attempted to come to grips with the ethical meaning of individual freedom in a world clearly devoid of all credible ethics. It appealed to despairing individuals seeking personal values in a valueless world. Writers like Sartre and Camus in France and actors like Jimmy Dean across the water set the mood of romantic despair. By the late 1950s, however, there was already a general disappointment with the extreme relativism of this new philosophy and its glaring failure to produce its own promised ethics. As the pendulum began to swing back, structuralism was standing in the wings.

Here was what looked like a brand new humanistic possibility – and even a method! Everyone was talking about how the new science of linguistics might finally discover universal features of humanity manifested in a wide range of sociocultural phenomena. So by the 1960s "structuralism" was the new buzzword on everyone's lips amid a flood of daring European and American studies all claiming to have revealed some previously unperceived "deep structure" of human experience. The American Noam Chomsky, working quite independently from Europeans, began what remains a stellar career in language philosophy with the publication of *Syntactic Structures* (1957).[8] He argued that speakers of all human languages are able to generate original and grammatically correct utterances due to the existence of a deep and very complex universal structuring of language that is innate and intuitively grasped and used by all people. We know this because it is relied on by very young untutored children. Of course, just this hint of an innate biological structure meant he was challenging the old, albeit now shaky, blank-slate belief that for many – especially social radicals – is still the basis of the Standard Social Science Model in the Western world. As we saw in earlier chapters, this is the increasingly discredited idea that the mind is empty until experience puts things into it.[9] So this was felt by his numerous enemies as a very loud call to arms, and controversy reigns today accordingly.[10] But Chomsky has always insisted that "there is only one human language," which he and his followers later labelled "UG," or "Universal Grammar."[11] We will return to this intriguing subject in a later chapter.

A decade after Chomsky shocked language philosophers everywhere with this thesis, the French anthropologist Claude Levi-Strauss was busy producing his own monumental book, *The Elementary Structures of Kinship* (1969),[12] which also flew in the face of mainstream cultural relativism by arguing that beneath the surface differences of peoples and tribes of the world there exist certain archetypal, or universal, themes, customs, and social patterns such as the incest taboo, marriage, and other things forming what we have seen are now called "human universals." Accordingly, Saussure, Chomsky, and Levi-Strauss, due to the clear demonstration in their work of innate universal structures, all fell under deep suspicion and have always been considered reactionary threats by the much larger liberal-relativist camp.

So it was to be expected that such a powerful initiative to uncover human universals, one developing almost simultaneously in America and Europe and loosely gathered under the term "structuralism," would soon provoke a powerful retaliation. This arrived swiftly as a very cynical form of linguistic relativism soon called "poststructuralism" (which would shortly spread far and wide and morph into a diffuse sociopolitical and aesthetic movement called "postmodernism." But these two terms, for our purposes, are almost the same). So the pendulum was swinging once again. But we need to ask how and why this happened – and what significance it had for the universals of language and literature. This subject is of such importance that it justifies taking the time to explain what has in retrospect been called "the linguistic turn" in Western intellectual life, which got us all marching, once more, down the road to relativism.

IT BEGAN WITH "ARBITRARINESS"

A key aspect of modern structuralism is so-called *arbitrariness*. When an English person and a Japanese think of a very high snow-capped place on the earth, one calls it "mountain" and the other "yama." Both mean (or signify) the same thing, but each with a different sound (and written) signifier. To say the two signifiers are arbitrary means there is nothing in those sounds that is connected in any way with the signified concept (or reality) of a mountain. It is common knowledge that all languages use different words to refer to similar concepts. Saussure simply elaborated on this to establish the interesting idea that the basic elements of human language are *negative* – which is to say that they get their distinctiveness and hence their usefulness in each language from the *differences* between them, not from anything *positive* they have in common. All his life he pushed the idea that language is a *form*, not a *substance*: it is the contrasts, or oppositions, between sounds and concepts that *produce* meaning in any sign system. Of course, that makes some basic sense because if all sounds and concepts were similar, we could not make distinctions at all, and language would not be possible. And that is about as far as Saussure took the notion of the negative and the arbitrary. He applied these two terms to the function of the signifier and the signified considered as isolated aspects of the form of language. But he made it absolutely clear that just as two minus values make a plus in algebra, it is the union of a negative signifier with a negative signified – of a sound pattern and a concept – that produces a positive term such as a word. In short, *the whole sign* is an *objective* entity referring to a positive and objective world. Saussure was also clear that the word "arbitrary" does not imply an individual choice of signifier and – of utmost importance in this entire discussion – that "*the individual has no power to alter a sign in any respect once it has become established in a linguistic community.*"[13]

The sad truth about what I might as well describe as this instance of intellectual manipulation is that so-called poststructuralist, and then postmodern, theorists badly and I think intentionally misused Saussure's language theory to argue that because the connection between words and things is arbitrary, then so must be all other connections between thought, language, and culture. And they presented Saussure as having said so. And he did. But he soon modified his statements. Let us hear Saussure on this, for his meaning could not be clearer: "To say that in a language everything is negative holds only for signifier and signified considered separately. The moment we consider the sign as a whole, *we encounter something which is positive in its own domain.*" And a little further on he says that although these two aspects of the sign considered in isolation are purely differential and negative, "their combination *is a fact of a positive nature.*"[14] In other words, as Raymond Tallis puts it in *Not Saussure*, where this deception is roundly criticized: although the signifier and signified are purely relational, "the sign as a whole, realized and put to use, is none of these things."[15] Alas, too many literary critics and language theorists untrained in structural linguistics have assumed that because the language system is produced by negative relations, then so too are all its final terms. Not so, says Tallis, for "in speech we deploy not signifiers or signifieds in isolation but signs in which they are fused. Differences are used to establish positive, present meaning."[16]

From this elementary mistake, however, a disastrous conclusion was drawn: intellectuals of a radical temperament began to argue that because all sign systems are made of arbitrary terms, then whole cultures and philosophies (all of which, they insisted, are but sign systems expressed in language) must also have only an arbitrary connection with reality. Through this chain of misunderstandings, structuralism proper – from the beginning it was always a method in search of universals – was co-opted as yet another form of particularism in support of cultural and moral relativism. Thus began the slide toward "poststructuralism."

The basic claim of poststructuralism was that if all signifiers are arbitrary, then so is what they signify, the thing signified. The whole sign, it was now argued, must be negative. It suited – actually, it very much excited – the relativist mentality to say that signs no sooner come into being than they start over as new signifiers creating a labyrinth of meanings. For just as we use words to define words, went the argument, so do we use meanings to define meanings. The false conclusion was now that *underneath all meanings, there are just other meanings.* Try translating any language, and you will see, these new relativists said triumphantly. But they conveniently ignored the counterargument: the amazing fact that people all over the world, although using such different "arbitrary" sign systems, can mean very much the same concept (such as the idea of a mountain) or the same referent (the same real mountain) – from which no one would volunteer to leap to prove there is no positive reality!

A similar campaign promoting language relativism grew out of North America studies of native languages and was eventually called the "Sapir-Whorf hypothesis." It refers (still) to the idea that language shapes reality, and because each language is different, then reality must also be different for each language community. Cultural relativists have cherished this idea for a long time. But it has been lately and rightly criticized on the ground that linguistic terms relate more to practical customs than to relative perceptions – which is to say that unlike a city dweller who may have only one word for "green," a native hunting in the jungle who needs to learn to perceive twenty shades of green will have distinct words for them all, so as to become a successful hunter. He has no use for a nonspecific general word. In the same way, an Inuit, or a fanatical cross-country skier like this writer, has little use for the general term "snow," except that it makes me happy to hear it. I must learn to distinguish twenty different kinds of snow in order to apply the right grip wax, or I will have a bad ski. So whether for an individual or an entire culture, it comes down to the number of purposes and needs for which particular terms are generated. This does not mean that nonskiers cannot perceive many types of snow, say, but rather that they have no practical use for them.[17]

A SYSTEM OF RELATIONS

Imagine describing a soccer game not by the actions of individual players but in terms of the relative motions and rule-bound possibilities of placeholders. In a way, this is what coaches do when they prep their teams with diagrams, and it gives a rough idea of how structural analysis works, whether applied to language, to folk tales, to kinship systems, or to the totality of an author's plays or novels. For anything that sends a message requires some deeply structured and very regular system to do so, and that is always what structuralists look for.

Examples began to appear in 1960s Europe, prolifically so in France, where they were lumped under the rubric of "*la nouvelle critique*" (or "new criticism"). Under this banner there were many exciting new modes of European criticism attempting a deeper understanding of literature and culture through the application of hitherto external methodologies imported from fields such as psychoanalysis, Marxism, linguistics, and phenomenology. One of the most interesting and successful examples was Roland Barthes's *On Racine* (1960).[18] The first part of this small book about one of the most revered of traditional French playwrights is devoted to an examination of spatial and dramatic structures and roles abstracted from all of Racine's plays. These interconnect to form a kind of "grammar" of "Racinian Man," the various terms of which unfold as a kind of theatrical syntax in each play.[19]

At any rate, whether we are speaking of small units of sound and meaning, as in the case of languages, or of actors and characters, as in the case of drama or the novel, they are described not by their essences or substance but by the functional contrasts and relations between them. Just as each phoneme and morpheme depends for its whole identity and function on its fellow phonemes and morphemes, so too do the characters in a literary work function rather like nouns, and their actions like verbs, and the story like a narrative grammar. These ideas were opening a lot of new doors because now the meaning of something could be related to *the sum total of the structural relations of the placeholders*. All this came at a time when literature, the arts, humanities, philosophy, and various social sciences were searching hungrily for new and productive methods to refresh themselves.

STRUCTURALISM TAKES OVER

By the late 1960s there was in the air a fascination with leaving behind older style "surface" analyses (boring, superficial, so much of it around already) and getting at the "deep structure" of things (new, profound, with a hint of revealed truth). Structuralism seemed eminently suitable for this purpose, and soon structuralist talk began invading and transforming almost all intellectual fields. It was certainly an intriguing time. Those in the know were looking for deep structures of literature, poetry, psychoanalysis, the fine arts, history, architecture, folk tales, and even whole cultural systems. At its height the euphoric French author Tsvetan Todorov was dreaming of a boundless "universal grammar" of all reality, something that is "*the source of all universals [and] gives definition even to man himself. Not only all languages but all signifying systems obey the same grammar. It is universal not only because it informs [that is, controls] all the languages of the universe, but because it coincides with the structure of the universe itself.*"[20] This was the extreme, of course, and structuralism was here setting itself up for the poststructuralist counterattack.[21]

At this point, many academics already predisposed to relativist thinking, especially in North America, found themselves slipping easily into the poststructuralist camp, even to the extent that they began worshipping proudly at the shrine of Nietzsche, who had so famously quipped that "there are no facts, only interpretations." This was the point at which the two camps went off in different directions. Practising linguists, however, did not cross over. They simply continued their hunt for deep structures and language universals, while poststructuralists took "the linguistic turn" down the road to a relativism more extreme than any previously known.

Soon, those with a political or ideological axe to grind were arguing that it was precisely "deep structures" that were controlling various groups of people, races, classes, and so on. Many of these poststructuralists were already feeding on Marxist ideology, and now there was a fresh structural version of what many of them had been feeling and arguing in a less systematic way. So we soon got the strange notion of the "disappearance of the subject," the player, the actor, the author, or the agent of human action. All of these were now to be considered place-holders in sign systems. Barthes had anticipated all this with his book *The Death of the Author* (1968),[22] in which he argued for "intertextuality," the notion that the reader is no longer a coherent subject but rather a "site" for the conjunction of codes, conventions, and signifying systems, his or her role limited to the selection of allowable options from systems that were "already written" in one or another established literary, philosophical, or cultural code.

By this time the new relativist equation that gullible literary theorists were creating to justify their craving for a totally malleable reality was this: sign systems result from linguistic differences > meaning is difference > literature and language are closed textual systems > everything is text > there is no external or controlling text > therefore, there is no extra-linguistic reality > therefore, consciousness, reality, and society are the only reality, and they are made of language. So all there is, crowed the literary critic Edward Said, is "wall to wall text"; we are all living in "a prison house of language."[23]

Saussure, as has been pointed out, took great pains to prove that the signifier could not be separated from the signified, so "it is rather surprising that there should be such a prominent strain of thought claiming to be 'post-Saussurean' which begins from the assumption that the linguistic sign is essentially a signifier and one that is so enfeebled that it cannot even reach out to its own signified, never mind to a proper extra-linguistic referent."[24] This is clearly an anti-Saussurean use of his theory to make a case against ordinary (bourgeois) realism by arguing that all texts, and the world itself, are nothing more than "a galaxy of signifiers." Never mind, either, as Tallis trenchantly observes, that if it were true that no signifier could reach its signified, it would not be possible to demonstrate such a claim!

By this time, as a consequence of the effort to eliminate all foundations, or essences, we end up with a kind of "inverted essentialism, where it is language rather than reality that is, as it were, calling the shots."[25] I will leave aside for the moment what ought to have been a mortal blow to the whole linguistic-relativism school, namely that it is impossible to confirm that we live in a prison house of language without coming to this judgment from some firm reality outside the prison house. For how would we know? As Tallis puts it so well, "the very fact that there is evidence for the relativity hypothesis constitutes evidence *against* the hypothesis."[26] And again: "if discourses cannot reach to a reality outside of themselves, if they cannot be truly 'about' anything, then they certainly cannot be used to comment on the relationship be-tween themselves and reality."²⁷ This sort of hanging oneself with the rope of one's own argument Tallis calls "pragmatic self-refutation," a situation "where the very act of asserting something provides the best possible counter-example to what is being asserted."²⁸ Even a minor ex-ample shows that language cannot make sense without a known world with which it connects and that in the most fundamental respect shapes language. If I say "the car hit the bridge," we understand immediately. But if I say "the bridge hit the car," we know from worldly experience alone exactly why it is an impossible reality and therefore a ridiculous statement. Nevertheless, let us follow the course of these ironies, for it was in fact the success of structuralism in discovering and describing so many sign systems of different kinds that made it vulnerable to takeover by much more radical theorists eager, as always, to struggle against one or another "systemic oppression." In short, the early structuralism that spread so fast to so many fields of thought was all the while sowing the political seeds of its own rejection.

So now it is time to ask how and why the poststructuralism that began as a theme based on so many misunderstandings morphed so easily into something eventually called "postmodernism" (or "Po-Mo") and quickly spread to all branches of the humanities and social sciences, where it has now been stalled for a few decades. Most of all: *how did what began as a search for the universal deep structures of language and thought get undermined so easily and dragged into the service of extreme relativism and radical politics?* How was this done, by whom, and for what purpose?

In the next chapter we have to step back a century or so to locate the roots of our troubles in old Europe – in old Germany in particular – from which what is now the postmodern worldview quickly spread to thoroughly infect the whole Western world, especially North America. This runs very deep. But it is impossible to understand what Pope Bene-dict XVI, himself a German, has called so memorably "the dictatorship of relativism," which has taken the West by storm for almost a century now, without digging this up. What was going on in old Germany that was eventually to blend so seamlessly with contemporary French and American assumptions about reality?

German Philosophy and the Relativist Revolt against Western Civilization

While this chapter might seem at first to be a departure from our central theme, it in fact sets the stage for the discussion of radical relativism in the chapters that follow by explaining first how it was rooted in German culture and then how it infected – I think that is the best word – almost all the softer branches of European and Anglo-American academic work in the wake of World War II. Close inspection reveals that at the very deepest level of German history, there can be found an ancient and bitter antipathy to any universalizing forms of foreign thought and culture that threaten to eradicate the uniqueness and particularity of the German *Volk* (people), their way of life, or their "spirit." Author Peter Viereck spoke of a figurative "Roman Wall" that has always run through the centre of German hearts dividing their loyalties between the mixed rational, legal, and Christian inheritance of the Mediterranean world (from Athens, Rome, and Jerusalem, respectively) and their own Germanic heritage.[1] There is a smouldering German tradition of portraying this mixture as standing for alien and "rationalistic" ideals and value systems superimposed by force on native roots that go deep into the paganism of the old Saxons, the tribal cults of war, blood, and soil, and the vital stuff of home-grown heroic legend. There is some practical truth in this. Prior to Napoleon's invasion, German territory was a loose collection of hundreds of independent principalities of the Holy Roman Empire, which he dissolved in 1806, eventually reducing Germany to thirty-nine states supportive of his policies. (Ironically, in so unifying the enemy, he strengthened it and sealed his own eventual fate.) But in the process, Napoleon indeed imposed on Germany a completely "Roman" system of administrative unity, including a metric system, a form of code law, and so on. Most

Germans saw this as an imposition by the universalizing logical temperament on their deeply organic and spontaneous folk life.

The Hitler movement was nourished by some of the same nostalgia, combining Romantic and collectivist themes in what became a frantic attempt to reassert the dominance of German *Kultur* over a homogenizing – and "essentializing" – European "civilization." It was a movement aiming to assert: "life" over what is merely legal and mechanical; Romantic feeling over classical reason; a uniquely national socialism over unfettered capitalism; a happy and deeply rooted peasantry over badly alienated factory workers; a heroic militarism over snivelling pacifism; organic leadership (through a Fuhrer symbolizing all the people) over a people divided by a bickering majoritarian democracy; collective freedom over individual freedom; Wotan over Christ; blood (human feeling) over gold (money relationships); and Nordic over Mediterranean civilization.

Hitler believed "civilization" means the application of reason to life and that the German patriot prefers to seek the "life forces," the irrational impulses, which seemed to him more characteristic of the German mind. It was a matter of deep, brooding, joyous vitality over cold, calculating, rootless logic and planning. This was pure Nietzsche (as we shall see below). Of course, any modern student asked to analyze a vital poem has felt something of what he meant. Too often, the act of analysis kills the emotional spirit of the poem forever. The general idea is that pure reason breaks living things into dead parts. This became a paradigm for the entire German Romantic complaint against the aftereffects of the eighteenth-century "Age of Reason" – that is, against the depressing effect of Mediterranean reason and civilization on the deeply yearning and vital German soul. For Romanticism supports spirit against form, dynamism against law, flow against stasis, the natural against the artificial, the original against the conventional, and above all emotional expression against unfeeling control. Modern psychologists speak of "flow." The vigorous German response to any life-stifling foreign "civilization" was the phrase "*Blut und Boden*" – blood and soil – the powerful appeal of one's own people, only, and of their rootedness in their own land.

Of special interest was the complaint that Judeo-Christian monotheism, in addition to the foreignness of its universal moral absolutes, has led to a *spiritual disenchantment* of the world. Under ancient paganism the multiplicity of gods inhabiting every material thing had filled people's lives with richness, wonder, and awe – most of all with the sense of a sacred immediacy in life. This immediacy of experience is a theme that has returned with its own messianic force under postmodernism, as we shall see. Both Nietzsche and Heidegger, for example, were philosophers of immediacy. But Judeo-Christian monotheism, goes the argument, killed this feeling off by waging a victorious war on paganism that drove all the happy, bold gods from earth and replaced them with a single God and cringing followers convinced of their personal sin. The Christian God was a transcendent and hidden God, a *deus absconditus*, which is actually something worse than hidden because it implies God slipped away in the night and abandoned us. Even worse, Jesus (in a sense, this religion's attempt to compensate for the absence of God) was said to be too abstract and morally demanding and thus destructive of the people's morale. After all, hadn't Christianity, with its emphasis on love and meekness, weakened the warrior resolve and caused the fall of mighty Rome? Just so, Hitler's people wanted to bring back the spirit of paganism through something akin to the spiritism of their fourteenth-century monk Meister Eckhart, who preached a universal divinity through which all could once again feel connected with the Divine.

Romantic poets or thinkers, of any age, always presage revolutions, and they spelled a lot of this out in worldly terms. Richard Wagner (1813–1883), for example, was a kind of utopian socialist who despised private property rights and wrote tirades against "Christianizing" (a code for weakening) the health-exuding warriors of the north. He composed a lot of famous operas, like *Tristan* and *Die Meistersinger,* that celebrated Nordic legend and spirit. Wagner had enormous influence on the creation of German *Volk* psychology, especially on the formation of "the Fuhrer concept." His notion was that the Fuhrer of the future Germany would be a human god in the line of the fabled medieval Kaiser Friedrich Barbarossa. Wagner saw Friedrich as himself a spiritual reincarnation of Siegfried, the first legendary Nordic Superman (after whom Wagner named his own son), and he made very popular the idea that a new Barbarossa-Siegfried would return as a Fuhrer to save the Germans of his day. Siegfried was to awaken from his long historical slumber in ... Berchtesgaden, the place later chosen by the Nazis as the site for Hitler's hideaway and headquarters (it is now a condo development!). This Messiah-Fuhrer would participate in divinity because he personified all the people. After all, why should a people divide itself? Democracies and their parliaments were disdained by Wagner and many others as mere expressions of the people's opposing interests, a crazy-quilt mathematical sum of a small percentage of wills, and in no way a true collectivity. But ah, the *Volk*-King! Here would be the living symbol of the whole people, a true expression of the collective will, a "hero-dictator" from the common ranks who would lead Germans to freedom. The way was being prepared for Hitler.

And there were other echoes of glory. In 1808 the poet Kleist had written *Hermann's Battle*, a play celebrating the Teutonic warrior who, in AD 9, as the story went, saved all Germany by driving the Roman invaders back across the Rhine. Kleist's poem was seen as a symbolic urging to resist the Frenchified civilization of "reason" spilling over from the Revolution. But it was too late. Napoleon invaded and controlled the Germans for a time. Early in 1940 this same play was revived as a symbolic call to arms, this time urging Germans to continue to resist and overthrow the *Völk*-smothering conditions of the Treaty of Versailles – a document widely perceived as having unfairly demanded punitive reparations from Germans following their defeat in World War I. The Nazis said Versailles made slaves of all Germans for life. They bitterly imagined themselves as a people who had nothing to lose but their chains, and they awakened in national memory a long series of revolts against foreign domination. First, Germans had repulsed the Romans, then the French king Charlemagne, then Napoleon, then Luther had pushed back the oppressive Roman Church, and now ... the National Socialists were dreaming of creating a new thousand-year German Reich.

This German Romanticism was a kind of thoroughgoing mysticism far more religious in its tone than the French or English variety. For Viereck, it was really "the nineteenth century's version of the perennial German revolt against the western heritage," which is to say, "against the Roman-French-Mediterranean spirit of clarity, rationalism, form, and universal standards."[2] For those of us who have always held the Germans to be the very symbol of efficiency and logic, this explanation seems rather puzzling. But not a few seasoned observers have held that the Germans have always had an unrest or disorder in the soul, and that they run not away from prison but into it, precisely in order to be free by at last containing their own spiritual confusion. The grandest prisons, of course, are made of ideas and words, "and the cell into which generation after generation of German Romantics have finally fled from liberty's weight, is a word-cell" that provides them with a frantic faith either in some rigid authoritarian dogma, whether of church or state, or simply in a popular philosophy.[3]

At any rate, this Romantic ethos, as it was angrily developed by Nietzsche and then by Heidegger, greatly fuelled Nazism. After all, it was Nietzsche who had famously written that in the German soul "there are caves, hiding places, dungeons ... its disorder possesses much of the fascination of the mysterious; the German is acquainted with the hidden paths to chaos," and then, in a line that touches the very soul of the German influence on Western postmodernism, he writes that "the German himself is not, *he is becoming.*"[4] The underlying tenets of this mood, if they can be formulated once again, were something akin to: nature worship, respect for "life" over ideas, a happy vitalistic pantheism over Christian suffering and sin, a stress on becoming, rather than being, a mystical worship of wholes rather than parts, synthesis over analysis, feeling and expression over reason, and so forth.

Hegel, too, did a lot of contributory damage because before him intelligent people considered the truth something absolute that could be grasped through effort and reason, the opposite of which was untruth. But he ended that confidence by arguing that existence is made not of absolute opposites but of ever-evolving synthetic wholes that arise anew from the natural opposition of things. An idea is proposed as a solution to something. It generates its opposite. Then a compromise or synthesis is reached, which hardens into a new idea, which then generates a new opposite, and so on, forever. This was his famous "dialectical" process, a cosmic form of relativism with which he all but ended the idea of absolute truth for Germans (and a lot of others, too). Of course, all this stress on particularity and feeling played right into the hands of crafty politicians seeking to embody the unfolding of "History" through their favourite ideology, pitching the voice of the "People" as the voice of God, and it made the sound of fast-moving tank treads. It was a perfect philosophy for the exercise of political will. Novalis summed up the politics of this Romantic spirit in scary fashion when he wrote: "from each true state-citizen glows forth the soul of the state, just as in a religious community a single personal God manifests Himself as if in thousands of shapes."[5] It was this same pseudo-Romantic spirit that fed the philosophical yearnings of Nietzsche and Heidegger, certainly the two most influential German philosophers of recent times and both the original postmodern theorists of the Western world.

NIETZSCHE'S REVOLT AGAINST WESTERN CIVILIZATION

Nietzsche was an intellectual and spiritual child of late German Romanticism, and his writings had a profound effect on the development of

German National Socialism as well as on Italian Fascism, especially on the relativism that formed the basis of their similar political and moral values.* People often assume Nietzsche was a racial anti-Semite. But he was not. He was an intellectual anti-Semite who despised Jewish ideas and ethics as they were manifested in Christianity, and he blamed them for the damage he was convinced this religion had wrought on Western civilization. Through his reaction, he became the first Western thinker who "turned romanticism in a fascist direction."[6]

Romantics of any age (the 1960s witnessed another upsurge) feel suffocated and oppressed by moral dictates, especially universalist ones – indeed, by any general philosophical system that threatens to dissolve or control what is personal, particular, local, and emotionally passionate and powerful. In this respect, Nietzsche was like an unhappy flower child before his time. In principle, he was deeply suspicious of all abstract systems of reason and logic, especially of their weak-kneed political manifestations in democracy, socialism, communism, and in all forms of "equality" talk that assume all human beings are exactly the same. In this sense, he was a German "anti-humanist" demanding an end to abstract intellectual and moral systems and a regeneration of the old German spirit expressed as the will of the vital and the strong. He would crush weak – and weak-thinking – people.

Of course, this very much appealed to Hitler and his new socialist party – so much so that in 1933 he made a special trip to the Nietzsche Archive in Weimar to pay his admiring respects. Almost fifty years later, *Der Spiegel* ran a story entitled "Hitler Perpetrator; Nietzsche, Thinker," directly linking philosopher and Nazi dictator. This would have driven Nietzsche even crazier than he already was, for he surely would have hated the Nazi system and machine. But authors have no control over how their work is misconceived. Hitler loved Nietzsche's emphasis on the value-creating vitality of human will because he was out to change Germany and the world for a thousand years and did not want to be held back by anything like the natural law or any transcendent or universal religious or philosophical beliefs. In this frame of mind he appointed Martin Heidegger,[7]

---

* This quotation from Mussolini suffices to establish an ideological connection: "In truth we are relativists *par excellence*, and the moment relativism linked up with Nietzsche, and with his Will to power, was when Italian Fascism became, as it still is, the most magnificent creation of an individual and a national Will to power" (B. Mussolini, "Relativismo e Fascismo," *Opera omnia* 17 (1951–63): 267–9.

the inheritor of Nietzsche's intellectual mantle, as the new rector of Freiburg University and considered him the unofficial philosopher of the Nazi Party (about whom more below).

What I am trying to establish is the chain of influence from a very old German tribal Romanticism, to Nietzsche, to Heidegger and the Nazis, and from there to postwar French Intellectuals and on to North America. It was a trend rooted in the desire first of Nietzsche and then of Heidegger to return Western civilization to what has been described as its ancient "semi-mystical directness"[8] of contact with reality. Both were convinced that mainstream Western philosophy and religion had ruptured the original and mystical human connection with the truth of experience.

The Age of Reason, or so-called "Enlightenment" of the eighteenth century is often considered the high point of European humanism, resting as it did on a handful of interconnected convictions. Among them: the power of *universal rationalism*; the existence of scientific *laws of cause and effect*; the idea that there is an *objective truth* we can access through reason; the *social progress* this truth makes possible; and the belief all this can be realized *without recourse to superstition or organized religion*. This unshakable faith in reason was grounded in a long and venerable Western philosophical tradition that began with Socrates, Plato, Aristotle, and their followers, and it includes all those who have been educated in this tradition – that is, most Westerners. It is a tradition that tends to divide reality into changeable and illusory physical experiences, on the one hand, and into an abstract "real" world of permanent ideas and values, on the other. Such a system was a radical departure from what Nietzsche was convinced was the more authentic, sensual, life-celebrating, and death-defying (and not death-denying) thought of the pre-Socratic tragedians such as Sophocles and Aeschylus, who, as one of Nietzsche's commentators put it, "had the courage to recognize the fundamentally terrible nature of human existence, and yet still to affirm it."[9] Even more – they joyously celebrated it with great art that did not shrink from that truth. Such poets had a powerful aesthetic and heroic grasp of the tragic sense of life and no desire to diminish or betray it by setting up a cozy intellectual or moral refuge for the spineless. Nietzsche all but worshiped this posture and lamented it was so short-lived – for Socrates and then Plato, his student and explicator, were soon to turn Western civilization away from things heroic and set up in their place a universal system of optimistic rationalism claiming to be a higher form of *knowledge as virtue*.

Most outrageous to any decent Romantic, then or now, was the claim that abstract ideas – rather than authentic contact with existence itself – are the highest good.[10] In a concise phrase, Nietzsche described this new system as "the hideous perfection of optimism"[11] because it claimed that things such as "the Good," "the True," and "the Beautiful" – rather than good, true, and beautiful things, experiences, and actions – exist in themselves as pure concepts that may be discovered by successfully detaching ourselves in their name from the impure experiences of this world. He deeply despised the elaborate systems of Plato and Aristotle with their fantastic abstractions, which he saw as the tyranny of the discursive intellect over flesh-and-blood human beings.[12] He rejected cold reason in favour of the "Irrational Will" proposed by Schopenhauer (a discovery that delighted him immensely as a young man) and the Romantic thunderings of Wagnerian music. In postmodern terms, any form of "essentialism" seemed to him a life-despising mass psychosis, an alienating plague on Western civilization that continues unabated. Even more cynically, he persuaded a host of his followers that philosophers who pretend to be the masters of such systems of abstract reasoning are in fact attempting to control others with the force of their personal beliefs camouflaged as higher truth. Gradually, he had come to realize "what every great philosophy up to now has been: the personal confession of its originator, a type of involuntary and unaware memoirs"; and he adds that if we want to know how the metaphysical assertions of a philosopher arose, we just need to ask: "What sort of morality is this (is *he*) aiming at?"[13] It was in this mood of understanding all formal and systematic philosophies as the wily deceptions of rationalizers – as cold, grey "concept-nets" thrown over the motley sense-turmoil of the world, as disguises for "pre-conceived dogma," or even as "a heart's desire" – that he called the coldly logical British philosopher John Stuart Mill "a pig."[14] This was presumably because Nietzsche was appalled by the idea that what is good should be determined by counting heads. For him, only an animal would live in such a way.

Nietzsche had famously declared that "God is dead," as a result of which there is no longer any transcendent ideal or objective truth possible to which we can appeal. But to him this new corrosive reality presented an opportunity to create new values beyond conventional good and evil. What made this difficult, however, was the entire scaffold of Jewish-inspired Christian morality rooted in guilt and self-hatred, which he described as a weak and snivelling "Platonism for 'the people.'" Christianity,

he said, is a "slave religion" appealing to a "herd mentality" that glorifies
the downtrodden and demands that believers demean their own existence and all of earthly life in the name of an imaginary eternal paradise
immune to change, decay, and death – immune, that is, to the heroic and
tragic sense of life.[15] In the same vein, he protested that all religions and
philosophies are but thinly veiled attempts by their inventors to control
others by persuading them of the "facts" produced only by the logic of
their pet theories. As a result, all human thinking and language for Nietzsche – and we will see the relevance of this claim soon – is always a political
and moral power game. Nietzsche is an important precursor of modern
relativism because his philosophy first powerfully revealed the chaos and
human manipulation underlying the concept of "reason." (We may leave
for another time the ironic and nonrelativist fact that all his life, Nietzsche
believed that the unexamined life is not worth living, that knowledge is virtue, and that by facing the truth of chaos it is possible for the strong to create a higher set of values – permanent ones, we must assume – in a
valueless world.)[16] Indeed, he was the first modern *to turn reason against itself.* He saw systematic philosophies such as Kant's as attempts to bring
about the "total legalization of life."[17] As there can be no final truth, he
concluded that we are left with our brute existence to be lived to the highest degree through the exercise of personal will and the creation of new
values expressed through an aesthetic style of life. For his entire life he
seemed unaware that such an ethic of personal will that refuses to place itself under any higher moral standard opens the door to various totalitarian despotisms that get forced upon the many by those with stronger wills
(or with other advantages, such as political influence and wealth). This
was the historical and actual background of value relativism that nourished Martin Heidegger, still considered by many to be the most influential philosopher of the twentieth century.

HEIDEGGER'S REVOLT AGAINST
WESTERN CIVILIZATION

Heidegger was a peasant intellect of a more elegant and genial cast than
Nietzsche, but he was also in many ways more radical and certainly more
systematic.[18] Here was a man deeply rooted in his beloved Bavarian
mountains and as deeply opposed to Western philosophy because from
the beginning it called for a rationalistic distancing from direct physical
experience of this world in order to *evaluate* and *judge* it rather than to
live it. He insisted that all truth must be subjective because no one can

step outside existence in order to judge it: we can live it only from within. In his first important public lecture as the rector of Freiburg University, he said that if Nietzsche was right that God is dead, then we must recognize our "forsakenness." We have obviously been "thrown" into this world, where we discover ourselves, and so must admit we have only two choices: either a brutal nihilism that eliminates all possibility of values or the life of the Superman who reacts to the abyss of nihilism by going beyond conventional good and evil to create a new world of higher values. It was pure Nietzsche, and for Heidegger it meant the focus of true philosophy would have to be on process, becoming, and questioning rather than on the old Greek virtues of reason, harmony, and idealism. He preferred the oriental view of Heraclitus that philosophy is a journey, not a destination, and hence that we cannot step into the same stream twice, to the views of Plato, who sought to fix the world in conceptual and moral formulae. This meant that for him, as for Nietzsche, all claims to absolute truth must be challenged and uncovered as stratagems for moral and political control. Nazi officials loved this speech because they saw National Socialism as a Nietzschean enterprise forging a new moral order, a new Kingdom of Heaven on earth – their thousand-year "Third Reich" – from the purity of collective Nazi will.

But Heidegger was just getting started. He soon made himself unpopular with his own colleagues by insisting on the elimination of all "academic freedom," a custom he saw as a hangover from a false belief that truth is some free-floating objective that academics must be "free" to pursue (as if humans could somehow be free from their own existence – an absurdity). To replace it, he asked for full commitment of all German professors to Nazi ideals because (this was the ghost of Rousseau speaking) "giving oneself the law" is the highest freedom. Under his rule, all faculty would now have the opportunity to commit together to imposing new ideals on an otherwise meaningless world; it was for him an exciting opportunity to revive the spirit of the German *Volk*.

To move this along, he signed all his letters and began and ended each lecture with "Heil Hitler," made his students give the Nazi salute, wore a Swastika pin, and then turned out to be too radical even for Hitler. So after a year he resigned. But he paid party dues until 1945 and died in 1976 without regret or public apology for his support for the Nazi cause. He had always seen himself as the philosopher king who was meant to "lead the leader" and felt mostly a deep regret that the Nazi regime failed him: it was too blind to see what he always insisted was the "inner truth and greatness of National Socialism."[19]

What was he thinking? Well, exactly like his mentor, Nietzsche, as explained earlier, he yearned for "a pre-socratic revelation of being." His famous book *Being and Time* (1933)[20] was his systematic attempt to return humanity to pagan rootedness and shake off the "pernicious rational prejudices" inherited from Plato (and from more recent philosophers whom he considered monsters of universal humanism, such as Descartes), to reverse the Western embrace of "metaphysics" in favour of the "pre-rational habits" he was sure were common to all men before they got "civilized" by abstract reason.[21]

He detested that Plato thought his imaginary realm of abstract Ideas ought to be more real to men than blood and soil. As for Descartes, who said "I think, therefore I am," well, here again was the pernicious idea that humans can divorce themselves from their own existence to float about observing it like some detached balloon – a bemused spectral mind – as though life were an empty concept rather than a fully charged personal reality. All false, he urged, for a people's true spiritual world "is the force of the deepest preservation of its powers of earth and blood."[22] This was the phrase mentioned above from German Romanticism – "Blut und Boden" (blood and soil) – that found echo all through the Nazi era, and Heidegger was its main ideologist. He felt "a fateful mistrust of all universal concepts" because they indicated to him that a "theoretical tyranny" was at work.[23]

Why a tyranny? In addition to the political fact that systems of thought in the hands of our masters can easily oppress us, Heidegger's lifelong worry was about "authentic" existence. For him, abstract thought constitutes a step away from the truth of being and substitutes for it a mere *representation* in which words and concepts replace things and experience, a substitution that falsifies life and alienates us from our own "being-in-the-world." This story was a repeat of Nietzsche's: before Plato, the pre-Socratics (whom Heidegger so admired and who included Heraclitus and a number of famous Greek dramatists) boldly faced the impermanent beauties and tragedies of life head on and in their daily lives, arts, and struggles expressed an authentic "openness to being."[24] By this, he meant that they did not try to invent a substitute intellectual or moral reality to distance and protect themselves from the true fullness and terror of life. Plato was the original enemy because he was the first Greek to create a permanent "metaphysical" world of unchanging "Ideas" (sometimes called Plato's "Forms"), which he argued were more real and true than direct experience. Instead of the disappointment of a dying rose in the garden, he had taught, why not try to grasp "roseness" and understand the form of eternal "beauty" itself, something higher and imperishable?

The ongoing German complaint was that after the Greeks, Western philosophy more or less assumed that a permanent and absolute truth more real and more valuable than ordinary experience is "present" in key concepts and ideals. Heidegger (and his postmodern followers) attacked this as a vicious misconception he labelled the "metaphysics of presence," charging that it has pernicious consequences that dull us to the depth of experience and produce impoverished ways of thinking that put us out of touch with life as it is lived.[25] To the core, he was "an enemy of ahistorical, absolutist concepts of truth," a relativist who believed there is truth (mostly his version of it) but that truth is never final.[26] Through its embrace of an inauthentic form of life, the West, Heidegger was convinced, got into the habit of *reducing* the manifold of direct experience to a handful of abstract *essences*, which thereafter were to serve as filters of perception. Heidegger called this "essentialism," and the postmodern view is that this tendency not only distanced, or "alienated," us from the deepest truth but, worse, led us to believe that the experiential world from which we are thus distanced is inferior and therefore ours to manipulate and organize according to our personal, corporate, or political ambitions.

Hence Heidegger cried out for the radical destruction of almost all prior Western philosophy and its replacement by things like "facticity," "particularism," and "existence philosophy" because no one "can give more truth than his own existence," which is always and necessarily concrete and historical. For him, there can be no transcendent, objective, or universal truth worth speaking about. But following this line of thought exposed him to more criticism and led to more flawed political conclusions because it was not a great leap from defending *personal* facticity to glorifying the facticity of *the whole people* as a single entity. This meant he soon found himself publicly defending the unifying force of German Nazism and Italian Fascism as superior to the fractiousness of Western liberalism and democracy as well as supporting politicians who in the name of his holy *Volk* were eager to eliminate abstract political protections that got in their way, such as: the *rule of law, human rights,* and *constitutionalism.* His reputation suffered ever after from this poor judgment.

In the end, he began speaking mystically about the "*sendings*" of being, as though blood and soil were animated spiritual things calling out to the German people. He even saw his own words as a form of existential *revelation* (a word he used frequently) offered to his students. The "*small and narrow 'we' of the moment of this lecture,*" he intoned, "*has suddenly been transformed into the we of the Volk.*"[27] He was speaking not of a communion wafer but of his own words. By now, almost his entire focus was on strong emotion and the psychology of the great man as leader (Fuhrer) of the *Volk*. Even the labour camps were to share in the community of labour. In the spirit of the Nazi slogan "Arbeit Macht Frei" – Work Makes You Free – many German factories built on-site chapels glorifying Hitler and the German worker. Heidegger saw the slogan that "all work is noble" as spiritually uplifting, in contrast to the Marxist concept of work as exploitation, which was a concept he derided as a materialist vulgarity. The greatest "work" of all was soon to be the German military machine, the *Wehrmacht*, engaged in swift and crushing victories that Heidegger glorified as the perfect blending of technology and the *Volkisch* spirit.

The kindest view of this confused man is Heidegger-as-philosopher attempting to repair our wounded existence by returning us to an imagined original contact with experience. In this respect, he was an orientalist – like his hero Heraclitus, that most un-Greek of all the ancients – who went as far as anyone could to create in Western words and thought the Eastern, or Buddhist, type of experience of *a wordless oneness or presence with all things*. Enraptured by this frankly mystical ideal – one that played a very large role in his work – Heidegger complained frequently that the West had turned its back on the far more profound Eastern connection with "Being."[28] This is perhaps also why we see a persistent emphasis on a kind of *revelation* in Heidegger's work (which he often refers to as "unconcealment").

Now it is time to examine how such a vigorous rejection of Western philosophy by both Nietzsche and Heidegger came to North America via certain French intellectuals, where it immediately became the latest and most fashionable justification for relativism and where it subsequently infected literary criticism, the humanities, the social sciences, and all culture studies. It took only two influential Germans to infect a handful of French academics, who in turn seemed to infect the intellectual and cultural life of much of the English-speaking world.

12

The Sacred Text: The French Nietzsche and the French Heidegger

SETTING THE SCENE

The first shot across the bow announcing "poststructuralism" was fired in 1966 at the Johns Hopkins University in Baltimore by a French philosopher of language named Jacques Derrida during an international conference on language and literature.[1] He was unknown to most Americans at the time, so the speech he came to deliver was more than a surprise – it was a bombshell. At the time, the enterprise of literary criticism occupied a kind of free-fire zone in intellectual circles and was in search of a serious method to rescue it from the bog of ever more precious personal opinion and "interpretation" into which it had been sinking for a generation or more. There was even a kind of subliminal hope afloat that the new structural theories developing from the language science of linguistics would give literary criticism a real boost. I remember that very year hearing a lecture by a young professor from Berkeley on the "deep structure" of something or other – a phrase then on everyone's lips that held the promise of cognitive revelation. Critics everywhere were wondering out loud how many fields of thought would be revolutionized by Ferdinand de Saussure's extremely successful "structuralist" way of thinking. It was an intellectually exciting time. So when Derrida stepped onto the platform at Johns Hopkins for what one admirer called his "quietly subversive appearance," no one in the room grasped "the full potential for havoc" in the social sciences and humanities that was to issue from his words.[2]

Two undisputed successes on the European scene at the time – before Derrida opened his mouth, that is – were the work of Saussure in linguistics and of Claude Levi-Strauss in anthropology. On the American side of the water was Noam Chomsky, whose language theory was causing a different kind of structuralist revolution. To be aware of the important contributions of all three was to be up to date in intellectual life. Then came the Derridean shockwave – his talk at Johns Hopkins is still revered by his supporters as a "sacred text" – felt as soon as he began to argue that even the ostensibly objective work of Saussure and Levi-Strauss (no mention of Chomsky at that point) was dependent on internal hierarchies of arbitrary value and on "a metaphysics of presence" (one of the many philosophical complaints about Western thought he had lifted straight from Heidegger) – a term many in the room were hearing for the first time. Here was social philosophy in the process of scandalously disrupting the status quo.

The sacred text spelled it out: the concept of "structure" is itself just a metaphor in Nietzsche's sense: an idea humans use to impose order on an otherwise fluctuating and intractable reality. So to argue that structure is an original reality beyond analysis is just like arguing for some other kind of metaphysical presence – like "Reason," or "Forms," or "God." The idea of structure as a synchronic reality, a slice of language or culture frozen in time, so to speak, is suspect as just another effort to set up yet another unchanging rational object. The final conclusion of this early work, long before his own surprising – to many supporters his deeply disappointing – late-life "Turn" to absolutes, was that *no discourse has the objective capacity to analyze another discourse* (even Derrida's own).

The second critique implicit in his talk was about the sign itself. Derrida, like so many literary theorists of the time, saw the two terms of the sign (the *signifier* and *signified*, the sound of a word and the mental concept it calls forth) as sharing in a negative reality: they owe their existence and their ability to communicate meanings solely to contrasts within the linguistic system. In this view, neither term has a fixed reality in itself, which is like arguing that neither exists without the other. However, this was a misunderstanding of the most fundamental reality of the linguistic *sign* as a whole because for Saussure and all practising *linguistics scientists* (as distinct from *literary theorists* such as Derrida) the *product* of the union of signifier and signified – the whole *sign* itself – is a distinctly positive term, not a negative one.

Unfortunately, however, many philosophers who use the word "sign" – I am thinking now of the American language philosopher C.S. Peirce, by whom Derrida was strongly influenced – taught that even whole signs, once formed, function immediately as new signifiers. The sound "mountain" calls up the idea of a mountain, but then the mountain serves to indicate yet another concept (like "adventure") and so on, *ad infinitum*. In other words, for Peirce, all signs point to other signs and this process never ends. So in this view, there is no finality to meaning, no positive final state at which meaning can arrive, for the signifying process never "stops" at any particular sign. For anyone in search of a foundational justification for relativism, so to speak, this simple notion of the endless polyvalence of words is a gift of the God of Flow, a sort of licence to reconceive all of reality as an ever-changing river of experience that can never be halted, never falsified by fixed concepts. But Peirce may have mixed up the concepts of sign and symbol too readily. In his Lowell Lectures, he held that "the mode of being of a *representamen* [which others call a 'sign'] is such that it is capable of repetition ... [so] I call a representamen which is determined by another representamen, an interpretant of the latter."[3] This is not a swamp into which I want to wade except to observe that Peirce had a threefold notion of the sign that by his calculation resulted in precisely 59,049 possible elements and relations. It is safe to say that no normal person has ever used ordinary language in a way that includes such a numerological abyss underlying an intended meaning. But perhaps due to his considerable reputation, he was too readily believed.[4] It is incredible – in the sense of hardly believable – that Derrida and so many others just as eager for philosophical supports for relativism took this radical and quite incorrect notion of endless sign generation as gospel and used it to undermine human confidence in language and the existence of the real world to which it refers. Here was an irresponsible interpretation of one of Saussure's central ideas for which almost no one – except serious practising linguists – faulted Derrida at the time or for many years afterward. Actually, serious linguists simply dismissed his case as the misguided rant of a relativist.

One of the reasons he got away with this so easily can perhaps be attributed to the fact that structuralism was then quietly invading all the humanities and softer social sciences as a method determinedly aloof from politics. For academics prone to egalitarian and leftist thought, however, especially for those who saw their life's work as dedicated to social justice, this emphasis on apolitical objectivity and structure was proving increasingly uncomfortable. It suggested in ever more certain terms that reality, controlled by so many things operating at a deep-structure level, must always be just what it is, and this idea was unsettling to the progressive temperament. Further to this point, most scholars in literary and humanistic studies ended up there – I was one myself – largely because they did not find the cold scientific temperament very hospitable. That is why at this juncture an attack on the rigidities of structuralism from what seemed like a much higher moral ground inspired and delighted so many: it promised to restore the vitality of poetic and semantic indeterminacy as well as the infinite subtleties of cultural and moral relativism. In so doing, it provided fresh hope for justice and social perfection. For the above technicalities about linguistic theory aside, what soon became rather clear was that implied in the poststructuralist assault that Derrida was initiating was the promise of a new ground for a radical critique of Western capitalism, technology, science, philosophy – indeed, of an entire civilization – calling it to task for the physical devastations it continued to suffer upon the innocence of nature and especially for the many varieties of oppression that would not have been possible without the supporting illusions of metaphysical presence.

Derrida's central claim was that for more than two millennia prior to Nietzsche, Western philosophy was a very old story of repeated expeditions of the mind to find "a transcendental signified," which is to say, a final theoretical and unchanging answer to the mystery of experience neatly packaged as an idea(l), origin, or centre beyond or above – at any rate, external to, more true, and superior to – immediate experience. These attempts Derrida (again, voicing Nietzsche and Heidegger) thought of as stories, or "narratives," invented by intellectuals and power holders with the intent of persuading and capturing followers. Some of the transcendental signifieds he listed that have been tried with this motive in mind were: Plato's "Ideas," Descartes' "Ego" (or "subject"), Marx's "dialectical materialism," Hegel's "History," the Enlightenment idea of "Reason, Progress, and Man," Freud's notion of the "Unconscious," and most recently ... Saussure's idea that all communications are possible only through binding and unconscious objective "Structures." For Derrida, all these things are but convenient fictions serving intellectual and political power, and over them all there is visible what he rather cheekily derided as "the ultimate fiction of God."[5]

For Derrida, the entire Western quest for a final external authority is illusory and doomed to falsify the truth of human experience, which he insisted can refer to nothing foundational outside itself; everything is in the flowing river of existence. It was all an echo of Nietzsche's ultra-relativist claim (later elaborated by Heidegger) that "there are no facts, only interpretations." Clearly, without these two Germans there would have been no Derrida, either, and a lot less relativism in the modern world. It was an influence Derrida never denied, and some six years after delivering his sacred text, he confessed in a humble understatement that "what I have attempted to do would not have been possible without the opening of Heidegger's questions."[6]

To many other intellectuals hit broadside with the implications of Derrida's message, this began to seem a somewhat inauthentic or borrowed story. In a seminal if overdue critique of European poststructural writings, two French critics, Luc Ferry and Alain Renaut, summed up Derrida's contribution to Western ideas in the derogatory but apt formula: "Derrida = Heidegger + Derrrida's Style." After wondering whether this formula was a little crude, if not rude, they concluded, no: "there is nothing intelligible or sayable in the contents of Derrida's work that is not, purely and simply, a recapitulation of Heidegger's [philosophy]."[7] Derrida's strategy, they wrote, by now presenting him as an intellectual copycat, "consists of attempting to be more Heideggerian than Heidegger himself."[8] To give Derrida his due, however, he did eventually leave behind at least Heidegger's later work, and typical of students who attempt to better their master, accused even him of succumbing to "logocentrism" and the metaphysics of presence. At the same time, there were other revelations about the German sources of this new philosophy, by now settled in the public mind as "deconstruction." In several devastating critiques of Derrida written in the 1970s, Jean-Pierre Faye showed that the word *Dekonstruktion* was first used in a Nazi psychiatric journal edited by the cousin of Hermann Göring and that the word *Logozentrismus* was first coined for denunciatory purposes in the 1920s by the protofascist thinker Ludwig Klages. This led one observer to conclude that "sections of French and, more recently, American academic discourse in the 'human sciences' have been dominated for decades by a terminology originating, not in Heidegger but first of all in the writings of Nazi scribblers, recycled through Latin Quarter Heideggerians."[9]

Yet it is fair to say that Derrida never considered himself a relativist, even though that is the inevitable consequence of his method. He was in fact a meticulous and careful scholar with an admirable tenacity and a colourful and performative turn of mind, who although he never willingly departed from the facts before him, nevertheless often selected and used them in ways so self-serving and so lyrical and imaginative as to leave them behind in practice. The most glaring example of this tendency I have already mentioned: his misuse of Saussure's theory of the sign by which he and his many followers promoted a view of the whole world of human interaction as a gigantic self-referential language cut off from external reality. His deconstructive method consisted of emptying the normal and accepted facticity from facts until there were no ultimate or foundational facts. He was practising an absolutism of the relative.

I have discussed the influence of Jacques Derrida first because it was he and his sacred text that were largely responsible for the rather sudden migration of deconstruction – soon called postmodernism, or "Po-Mo" – to North America. I will return to him to flesh out some of the consequences of that influence. But first let us ask some general questions and attempt to describe the German-French voyage to postmodernism in plainer language. Why did these German Romantic ideas cause such a revolution in Western intellectual circles? Did they, and do they, stand up to scrutiny? Why did so many North American academics – especially literary critics and social scientists, such as some of the anthropologists we saw earlier – become overnight followers of a French intellectual trend that never managed to fully establish itself in France? Why did German Romantic theory, much of it entangled with Nazi ideas about radical relativism, emerge as postmodernism in postwar French intellectuals and then migrate so quickly to the Anglo-American world?

Historically speaking, Nietzsche made his mark on Western intellectual life long before Heidegger. So I propose to digress here to discuss how his influence came to France via Michel Foucault, another prophet of radical relativism, and then return to Derrida and finish the story of what he was trying to achieve with his even more radical anti-foundational approach.

FOUCAULT: FROM NIETZSCHE TO PO-MO

Michel Foucault (the French Nietzsche) came to prominence in the mid-1960s, a few years prior to the Paris student revolts of May 1968. This chaos in the streets (it was a *café-au-lait* student revolution, not a deadly one like Hungary's in 1956) was the culmination of a long-brewing crisis in French intellectual life that began after World War II and by the late 1960s had developed into a general disillusionment with European "humanism" – the belief that there are objective, universal truths accessible to reason, that humankind is the subject of history (not its plaything), and hence that there is always hope for social progress.

A distressing series of historical events that would have negatively affected the public mood of any civilization worth the name set all this up. Among them should be counted: the atomic bomb at Hiroshima; the Cold War; the increasingly grotesque revelations of the Holocaust and France's shameful Nazi collaborations; France's embarrassing military defeat in the Far East at Dien Bien Phu (1954); and, on the heels of this, her bloody war of terror with and embarrassing forced withdrawal from French-Algeria (1954–1962). And everywhere, what were once thought of as the civilizing benefits of the Western world were now being recast as oppressions of colonialism.

The sheer cruelty and irrationalism of these events seemed to signal an undeniable failure of morality and reason that made "humanism" look impossibly naive and – could it be possible? – inhuman. So much was this the case that deep thinkers began to wonder whether European humanism was the *origin* of the West's malaise rather than its *solution*! It was not long before most of the core concepts of Western philosophy, such as rationalism, universalism, essentialism, absolutism, and so on, were being counted as weapons of political "ideology," as sweet-sounding "Eurocentric" tools of oppression at work both within states and between them. The conclusion was that intellectuals and the power holders they served had plucked these concepts out of the river of life and used them to impose their oppressive interests.

So by the mid-1970s, mainstream intellectual fashion in France was rapidly shifting from devotion to the absolutist and deeply materialistic philosophy of one German – Karl Marx, who was the intellectual offspring of Hegel, the Über-absolutist – to the new ultra-relativist, existential philosophy of two more Germans. Foucault and Derrida were just their French messengers, and as Ferry and Renaut put it, what everyone then thought of as the "new" French philosophy of the '60s was in fact not new at all. It was rooted in themes and theses borrowed from German philosophers, which these two French intellectuals took up "in order to *radicalize* them."[10] So it appears that in a more or less fawning, lockstep manner, first the French and then, within a decade, droves of Anglo-Saxon academics took on board "*an alternative philosophy of history acquired from Nietzsche and Heidegger.*"[11]

Foucault called himself a Nietzschean "genealogist" – a person who deconstructs belief systems to show their inherent weaknesses, contradictions, and self-serving motives. Just after his death his last interview was published in *Les nouvelles littéraires* (5 July 1984), in which he explained: "I am simply Nietzschean, and I try as well as I can … to see with the help of Nietzsche's texts."[12] This confession was also a declaration that he was not a historian in the usual sense but a "new historian" whose political-moral duty is not to determine objective facts and truth (for him there can be no such thing) but to expose what others call facts as "social constructions" that generate oppressive modes of power and knowledge. As another and more recent postmodernist (also a former Marxist) Jean-Francois Lyotard put it, this was a new historical activity rooted in a profound "incredulity toward metanarratives."[13] He meant that postmodernism can be characterized by its suspicion of all overarching philosophical, moral, or scientific explanations of reality. It was a sound bite that stuck. The open bias of such new historians and of all postmodern thought is that all forms of power and knowledge oppress somebody, so the new historian's duty (it is not clear exactly why) is to foster "the insurrection of subjugated knowledges"[14] – that is, to find out who is oppressing whom, to reveal this heretofore subtly hidden truth, and to weigh in on the side of human liberation. This dominant motive of unmasking power is an ironic absolute that underlies all postmodern work. I say "ironic" because in a world without absolute values one interpretation can be only an attempt to replace or subjugate another interpretation. In the end, this presents an irresolvable contradiction for Foucault, for if it is true that we are all prisoners of the structures of language, culture, and power, and hence that there can be no "subject" of history, then how can we ever become free even to make such a judgment?

Nietzsche had declared that God is dead. But Foucault went further and declared that "man is dead," too. He also further radicalized Nietzsche's remark about there being no facts, only interpretations, by declaring that "interpretation can never be brought to an end ... because *there is nothing to interpret.*"[15] For him, any interpretation is always itself a new interpretation-creating activity, never a truth-creating one. He believed we can never get at a final truth that stands outside of experience as its *foundation* – hence the fashionable term "anti-foundationalism," which is still used to describe this type of extreme relativism.

But readers who follow this thread will find that even anti-foundationalism relies on a variety of implicit foundations of its own. Mostly progressivist. Mostly political. Mostly leftist in character. Stanley Fish, for example, perhaps the most articulate defender of anti-foundationalism in the Western world, argues literary theorists have been "taking ourselves too seriously as a priesthood of a culture already made, and not seriously enough as professionals whose business it is to make and remake that culture even as we celebrate it."[16] To repeat, he believes his job is not just to explain the art and significance of great literature (which is what taxpayers thought when they hired such people to instruct their children), which he happens to do very well, but also *to make and remake culture*! Make no mistake: this was a call to social revolution by an elegant theorist who denies there are grounds for any values. The late Edward Said, another distinguished wordsmith of even more radical temperament, urged literary intellectuals "to break out of their disciplinary ghettos and insert themselves into the social and political processes of the larger world."[17] In other words, these anti-foundationalists want us to rise above experience in the name of some abstract idealistic foundation they find distinctly valuable and to take action to change this world. That is a peculiar stance for people who make careers of arguing that all foundations are forms of fiction.

Anti-foundationalists try to win their case by restricting discussions to experience alone, by refusing to transcend it by pushing thought to the level of things universal. However, Foucault never satisfactorily explained how in such a relativized world (he misses the irony that his "interpretations" are always presented as foundational) we would ever know he was correct, nor why anyone should lift a finger to resist subjugated knowledge, let alone subjugated people. For without some reference to absolute values of justice, freedom, and truth, there can be no good reason whatsoever to do or not to do anything. This truth has exposed all of his work as a personal politics contradicted by a personal philosophy. It was a position that grew from his overly confident insistence that languages and texts do not *refer* to objects outside themselves but *constitute* them and that because the words of all texts may have multiple meanings, are interrelated, and by their nature resist and defer final meanings, there can be no final truth. This cannot be true, of course, for if it were there would have been no possibility for Foucault to write nor for us to comprehend his work. There would be no Foucault factoid. But facts do exist. And that is why the sound bite from the British anthropologist Richard Dawkins stuck: "Show me a relativist at 30,000 feet and I'll show you a hypocrite." Meaning: no one is so relativist as to deny the fact of the law of gravity by jumping out of the airplane.

We conclude that radical relativism was a story Foucault needed to believe and to promote. This is surely why, after admitting he was "well aware that I have never written anything but fictions," or "novels," Foucault nevertheless tried to salvage for them some semblance of truth by asserting that such fictions can nevertheless induce "effects of truth" and even (now using the word as a verb) that it is legitimate for an author "to

fiction" a history or a politics.[18] In the end, however, it seems clear that
he turned to the ruse that history is always a fiction because so many of
the facts and arguments presented in his own "histories" were shown by
other historians in search of objective truth and fact to be untrue.[19] For
this, Foucault has been taken to task repeatedly, decisively, and most recently in a *Times Literary Supplement* review, "Scholarship of Fools," which
zeroes in on Foucault's first popular book, *Madness and Civilization,*
which presents a poorly substantiated case that the Age of Reason in European civilization was an age of a "Great Confinement" that had made
pariahs of hundreds of thousands of ordinary people, characterizing
them as mad, incarcerating them in droves, bundling them off to float
around from town to town until death on "ships of fools," and so on.[20]
He was making the case that the psychiatry of the period was a looking
glass for the oppressiveness of the entire civilization. In this review of his
historical practices, Andrew Scull explains that Foucault was a poor, if
not fraudulent, historian who relied almost entirely on secondary nineteenth-century sources of dubious provenance, "so outdated and inadequate to the task, and his own reading of them so often singularly
careless and inventive, that he must be taken to task," and this makes
Foucault's "isolation from the world of fact and scholarship" everywhere
evident. The review cites far more exacting facts of scholarship to show
that "Foucault's claims about the confinement of the mad in the classical
age are grossly exaggerated." Faulty thesis, invented numbers, and no
ships of fools ever existed. Scull concludes with one lesson to be learned
from Foucault: "the ease with which history can be distorted, facts ignored, the claims of human reason disparaged and dismissed, by someone sufficiently cynical and shameless, and willing to trust in the
ignorance and the credulity of his customers."[21]

I have introduced Foucault mostly to emphasize the fact that what we
have here is neither a French, nor an English, but rather a long-smoul-
dering German Romanticism from the deepest past that re-emerged
with force during the Nazi episode and that, despite this evil provenance, somehow captured the minds of postwar European intellectuals
as a new kind of relativism that spread rapidly via French radicals to almost all North American campuses, primarily through the field of literary studies. American professors of literature and criticism were the
most susceptible to this new trend because by the 1960s they were already pounding out their own "Made in the USA" theory that the meaning of a literary work is independent of the history and reality outside
it, that your "reading" and mine are but two of an infinite number of

possible meanings, which is to say that it is the reader, not the poet, who creates the meaning of the poem. This eventuated in something later called "reader-response" criticism, but poets themselves have never been persuaded by this approach to their art.

But perhaps the starkest reason for the immediate success of postmodernism was something banal and pragmatic. By 1970 the academic market in the softer social sciences, English literature, and the humanities was being suddenly flooded with new Baby Boomer-generation PhDs faced with applying themselves to a lot of worked-over – dare I say – stale fields of thought. After all, how many original essays can be written about the work of D.H. Lawrence or T.S. Eliot without repetition? There were legions of professors wandering like thirsty men in a desert of ideas who could hardly believe their good fortune: here was a new philosophy, applicable to almost anything, that also carried the imprimatur of Nietzsche and Heidegger! The vast majority were already stridently critical of Western civilization, and they could see that Po-Mo would serve as a powerful solvent of the canons of Western philosophy, literature, and morality by opening the door to infinitely varied readings, each one as valid as the next, and more – buttressed by a new and impressive theory. Here was a new form of thought that promised to convert them into sophisticated theorists whose insights would be valued on par with, or even perhaps as superior to, original works of creative art. In short, they smelled a rare professional opportunity to intellectually recast the canon of Western civilization while buoyed by the feeling they were revealing some deeper relativistic truth. This was simply irresistible.

Yet Foucault and his followers were singing a very old song. The two basic doctrines of postmodernism were *textualism* and *indeterminacy*. Joseph Carroll puts it neatly: *textualism* is the idea "that language or culture constitutes or constructs the world according to its own internal principles, and ... *indeterminacy* reduces knowledge to the spontaneous generation of internal contradictions within this system."[22] Together, these two ideas ruin any hope of truth: textualism because it denies the existence of any correspondence between human propositions and a knowable external and independent world outside them; and indeterminacy because if everything is contradicted by something else, then there can be no possible coherence between propositions themselves or between propositions and the universe.

I belabour these points because through his Nietzschean–style deconstructions, Foucault managed almost single-handedly to radicalize Western humanistic studies, in the process initiating an era of profound

distrust, moral alienation, and intellectual confusion. If he had a single
aim, it was "to repudiate reason and nature and to affirm anarchistic irrationalism as a dominant norm."²³ For this, it was sufficient to amplify Nietzsche's thesis that through language human beings impose "their own
arbitrary constructions of meaning on what would otherwise be nothing
but chaos,"²⁴ and then he radicalized even this for easy consumption by
young students eager to justify their relativist sentiments and their hostility to all forms of power and privilege (although few are quite as privileged and secure in life as the fully tenured university professors who still
lead this offensive).

In the end, however, and by way of throwing his complaints into stark
relief, not even the best of human societies could survive Foucault's withering gaze because his reference point was a childishly impractical utopian dreamland offering drugs, free love, communes, alternative forms
of consciousness, a new language, and a new form of individuality where
he believed none of the institutionalized oppressions he described (and
imagined!) would exist. In Foucault's world, it seems, children would develop good manners and cooperation by themselves, students would
learn without the authority of teachers, workers would produce without
the authority of bosses, soldiers would fight without generals, mentally
sick people would be healed by redefining themselves as normal, and
money would fall from trees equally into the hands of all.

Readers interested in Foucault's bitterly anarchistic life may turn elsewhere for a full treatment.²⁵ There, they will find a persistent defence of
moral relativism and social anarchy often expressed in sadomasochistic
homosexual desires and a public mockery of all traditional morality. Because he believed that all linguistic, social, and moral distinctions and systems are also arbitrary systems of control, he concluded that we are all
political prisoners of our particular societies and that the mad, the sexually perverse, and the anarchistic are actually *transgressive heroes*. He saw
himself as one of them, was a hero on his own stage, personally pursued
what he called "limit-experiences" in drug use, communal living, and
sexual experimentation, and was drawn erotically to extreme violence.²⁶
Politically, the cruelty that is a natural consequence of all moral relativism (because there exists no defensible limit to personal behaviour)
was revealed in his 1971 debate with Noam Chomsky, wherein his social-
revolutionary agenda became clear: "When the proletariat [working
class] takes power," he said, "it may ... exert toward the classes over
which it has triumphed a violent, dictatorial, and even bloody power. I
can't see what objection could possibly be made to this."²⁷

His most unforgivable personal violence? There are allegations that after discovering his own AIDS, he continued cruising the San Francisco gay scene to infect as many young boys as possible in yet another celebratory transgression. He is remembered for his motto, "sex is worth dying for," and he perished miserably from it. But not before defiantly declaring: "to die for the love of boys: what could be more beautiful?"[28] It is not hard to see that relativism is a convenient philosophy for anyone seeking refuge from moral judgment.

DERRIDA: FROM HEIDEGGER TO PO-MO

Derrida is another matter. He began, as mentioned earlier, by announcing not a theory or a method but what he called a "project," which he presented as a neutral term. He rejected "theory" because it implied – actually, it requires – a metaphysics, a set of fixed and enduring principles explaining reality, and the very idea of this he especially rejected. But I prefer to call what he was doing a "program" because it had a distinct purpose, eventually to be exposed as a utopian moral and political dream disguised, at first, by a pretended neutrality and a beguiling and clever façade of naiveté.

For example, during the question period following the delivery of his sacred text, he declared: "I was wondering myself if I know where I am going ... *I am trying, precisely, to put myself at a point so that I do not know any longer where I am going.*"[29] Not long ago such an admission at a major conference might have ensured it was his last. But not so for Derrida. He never liked where the West went – and is still going via the compass of its Greek, or Hellenistic, metaphysics – and he could sense there was a large audience of disaffected intellectuals ready to amplify his message. So he decided to devote his life to undermining that metaphysics, substituting his own (excuse the term) "anti-metaphysical metaphysics," or as some prefer to call it, his "negative" metaphysics. We will see very soon that his search for a mystically present-yet-absent point of reference was deeply rooted in an oriental – specifically, a Hebrew-style – resistance to Hellenistic philosophy that has been around a long time.

At bottom, Derrida's program called for a return to the oriental relativism of early Greek thinkers such as Protagoras and Heraclitus (and also of certain Hebrew mystics), a return to a concept-free human consciousness immersed in and enjoying a direct, but directionless, flux of experience. Derrida imagined this as a proto-reality *prior to all metaphysics.* To do this required an attack on all "truth-claims" to "objectivity" and on all conceptual frameworks promising such. All his life, he took great pleasure in undermining conceptual terms or foundational assumptions that might threaten this preferred proto-reality by showing that such claims undermine (or deconstruct) themselves. As one critic put it, "Following the then-fashionable habit among late 1960s French intellectuals to regard 'universal ideas' such as 'reason, science, progress and liberal democracy' as 'culturally specific weapons fashioned to rob the non-European Other of his difference,' Derrida early on posited that 'man' himself was a cultural construct; there was no essential human nature, no ideal against which to judge human behavior or compare cultures. 'Man' was a product of language, and language in every case could be taken apart to expose its internal contradictions."[30]

There is a certain attractiveness to this program because *it promises an authentic mystical contact with unmediated experience* and therefore a new platform for intellectual and moral freedom. For such reasons, as we shall see, Derrida has often been called "a Jewish mystic." In his interesting study *Deconstruction in a Nutshell*, which is almost fawning in admiration of Derrida and his work, John Caputo writes "anyone with an ear for the Hebrew and Christian scriptures is soon enough led to remark about how very Jewish, or quasi-Jewish, or hyper-Jewish, Derrida and what is called deconstruction is getting to be. Nobody thinks he sounds like a 'Buddhist.'"[31] By giving deconstruction a messianic twist in his latter years, Caputo explains, Derrida bitterly disappointed many of his secularizing followers, who "thought they found in deconstruction the consummating conclusion of the death-of-God." Instead, Caputo says Derrida was engaging in "a reinvention of Judaism as deconstruction."[32] This led to the forging of an intimate connection between ancient Jewish mysticism and modern secular deconstruction as a hand-in-glove attack on Western values.

The attraction of Po-Mo for all sorts of intellectuals in search of private truth is that it promises any feeling person bright enough to learn the program a licence to indulge in complexly layered verbal pyrotechnics guaranteed to produce unchallengeable new meanings for whatever is being studied. This procedure inevitably produces a kind of discursive chaos because it eliminates not only the expectation of objective truth but also the very conditions for its possibility. By tacitly assuming all readings to be possibly true, it makes them all impregnable to attack. In this sense, the thinking – we can't really call it a philosophy – underlying Po-Mo is directly responsible for the disintegration of modern thought into myriad unrelated pools of private

meaning. The powerful ego-appeal of Po-Mo arises from the fact that
it graces all practitioners with an insular oracular status.

In the realm of the political, however, Po-Mo is itself plainly open to
manipulation, if not to outright totalitarian exploitation. This is not
due to any imprecision in high-level postmodern work, which is often
minutely careful. Rather, it is due to its tendency to undermine all hope
of foundations, leaving no foundation for thought itself – even for postmodern thought. Political tyrants delight in this sort of structural weakness. They can smell the advantage it presents for their schemes a mile
away, as history has amply demonstrated with such as Mussolini's arro-
gant relativism, with the eventual Nazification of Nietzsche's philosophy,[33] and with the seductions of real Nazi politics for Heidegger, who
began the most recent trend.

ATTACKING THE WEST: THE POLITICS OF POSTMODERNISM

The influence of German Romanticism on Nietzsche and Heidegger,
and through them on the French Nietzsche (Foucault) and on the
French Heidegger (Derrida), has been traced sufficiently. But it goes
deeper. As mentioned, perhaps the greatest intellectual trauma conceivable for a whole generation of European – especially French – intellectuals after World War II was the fall of Communism. A couple of
generations deeply disturbed by the civilizational chaos of two world
wars had come to see bourgeois capitalist society as a profoundly empty
response to the need for meaning. Communism – as a theory of pure
socialism and not as it was actually practised – had seemed like a great
utopian solution that would bring "true democracy" and equality to all
people. But eastern Europe, with its cruel invasions of Hungary and
Czechoslovakia and with its deadening totalitarian life and poverty, instead brought great disappointment. The approaching and, it began to
seem, the necessary fall of Communism could be felt long before the
Berlin Wall in 1989 brought final disillusion. Of course, this was not
sensed by Western leftist observers, most of whom supported those extraordinary oppressions, but almost all who actually lived under the system could hardly wait for its end. This daily cynicism was symbolized for
Czechoslovakian students by rubbing an index finger vertically up and
down the temple as their Communist teacher taught them Karl Marx.
It meant that between the ear and what they heard and the eye and
what they saw, there was a permanent gap of disbelief.

Deconstruction, we have seen, had its origin in leftist politics, and its "textual leftism" amounted to "a politically-inspired attack on the philosophical underpinnings of bourgeois society,"[34] a society resting on certain common assumptions such as: we live in an objectively knowable world and can communicate its nature rather precisely to each other with language and thought. Perplexed that the beat of bourgeois life just keeps on going, desperate radicals shorn of a credible Marxism leapt to the conclusion that bourgeois society controls its populace and prevents revolution not through force but by perpetuating and preserving its core assumptions through realistic and rationalist modes of writing and by oppressive "systems of thought." Conclusion? To undermine bourgeois society, you first have to undermine bourgeois philosophy. From this posture sprang wholesale attacks on the entire Western canon of great literature and philosophy, now accused of: ethno- as well as Eurocentrism, authoritarianism, hegemony, imperialism, and so on. As Terry Eagleton, a British Marxist writer, observed: unable to break the structures of state power, radicals attempted instead to subvert the structures of language. In this generalized cultural sense, Roland Barthes was correct that the new enemy was "coherent belief systems of any kind."[35]

Soon we would hear no end of the new anti-metaphysical metaphysics of the left and of new oppositions in which pluralism is better than authority and power, criticism is better than obedience, differences are better than identities, self-contradictory, or "transgressive," philosophies are better than philosophical and moral certainties, or absolutes, and so on. One writer nicely summed it all up as follows:

> The original French deconstructionists, openly calling themselves Marxists and radicals, claimed to have discovered the means by which the bourgeoisie had gotten away with its historic crimes of oppression and exploitation – namely, by employing language itself as a method of social control. According to this view, the ruling classes, pretending that language was a fixed, dependable reflection of reality, used it to enforce and to ratify the existing division of society into haves and have-nots. The French deconstructionists were dedicated to unmasking this bourgeois imposture by means of their own countertheory of the indeterminacy of language and meaning, and in that sense they considered themselves to be embarked on a politically revolutionary undertaking.[36]

In short, the aim of "deconstruction," politically speaking, and despite protestations to the contrary, was indeed about destruction: of

Western philosophy, morality, society, science, the lot. Derrida's brand of radical linguistic polyvalence was the tool.

In what follows, we will see some of the darkly interesting corners into which this brand of relativism painted itself.

13

Po-Mo and the Return to Absolutes

At the end of his days, an intellectually embattled and sometimes embarrassed Derrida, a man so often accused of trashing everything and believing in nothing, made an infamous "Turn," or as some former supporters indignantly described it: a betrayal. Before his Turn, everything was deconstructible, and anyone with a little literary and philosophical dexterity who had caught on to the Po-Mo game could easily show how the deep-structure meaning of just about any text undermines its own surface arguments and therefore its foundations. But Derrida's own work was soon subjected to this same procedure. He was accused repeatedly of publicly destroying the foundations of Western philosophy and morality while resting his own arguments on other, unconfessed foundations. So there came a hue and cry from disbelievers: "Fess up, Jacques!" Which he did. For by the last decade of his life, he had perceived that to say, with the mystic Swamis, that the world is held up by a turtle, that this turtle rests on another turtle, and that from there it is "turtles all the way down" does not explain very much. In other words, of what use is deconstruction if it has no basis or foundation in anything? Eventually, Derrida himself began to feel the logical as well as spiritual need for a foundation of some kind. And out it came, as quite a shock to his adamantly relativist followers: "*'I believe in justice.' Justice itself, if there is any, is not deconstructible.*"[1] In one sentence he said he wanted to recognize justice as a metaphysically present, absolute, and transcendent ideal. For Derrida, this was "an infinite justice that can take on a 'mystical' aspect," and it was this aspect (now that he had painted himself into a corner) that led him to his concluding equation: "deconstruction is justice."[2]

This was the beginning of his Turn, the camel's nose under the tent.

And it meant that the last decade of his life would be spent exploring a number of increasingly theological and mystical topics and defending all of them as "undeconstructible." Deconstruction would soon be equated with *equality, love, democracy,* "*the gift,*" "*hospitality,*" what is "*to come*" (*à venir*), and what is "*wholly other*" (*tout autre*). Many of these concepts Derrida himself labelled "universal," and indeed some began to look suspiciously like ancient and resolutely Western historical and metaphysical concepts of an essentialist and foundationalist sort such as we find underpinning natural law and all serious religions.

Before his Turn, most admirers (and critics) had simply assumed that deconstruction is in practice what is sometimes called a "negative philosophy" that must *exclude* in principle anything claiming to be undeconstructible. But we learn otherwise. In 1997 Professor John Caputo, whom we met in the previous chapter, a most energetic and engaged defender of Derrida who applauded him right through his Turn, published *Deconstruction in a Nutshell* and also *The Prayers and Tears of Jacques Derrida: Religion without Religion*.[3] While often adopting Derrida's impassioned voice as his defence attorney, so to speak, Caputo effectively exposes (sometimes unintentionally) the intensely absolutist and theological nature of the whole deconstructionist project. To achieve this he saw that he had to remove the entire enterprise from the purview of its critics by taking it to the next level. He did this by arguing that we have failed to see that what is negative can be so only in terms of *something*. The undeconstructible "something" that is crucial to the very survival of deconstruction, he protests, is (ready for this?) "beyond both foundationalism and anti-foundationalism"; it is "an *ec-centric ec-stasis* toward what is to come."[4] He follows this up with an even more tortured explanation: "Another way to see this and to say this is to say that deconstruction is 'affirmative' of something undeconstructible, but that it is affirmative without being 'positive.' For it is affirmative of something *tout autre*, something to come, without staking out the positive traits of a plannable project or a programmable position, affirmative beyond the distinctions between positive and negative, foundational and anti-foundational, faith and reason."[5]

This gives a good sense of the evasiveness required to sustain a philosophy that seeks to define itself by avoidance of all positive terms. More to the point for Caputo and many critics, however, is that from his Turn forward Derrida increasingly presented his ideas – and the entire deconstruction movement he was so instrumental in sparking – as a form of messianism.[6] In effect, he increasingly yearned to capture and

describe what one of his critics described as the "ancient pagan narrative of *being as sheer brute event.*"[7] This was the inevitable outcome of
Derrida's original complaint against Western philosophy: that it attempts to formulate truth in unchanging abstract concepts. At bottom,
he was rephrasing the ancient complaint of Heraclitus and all those
since who seek not a rational understanding of reality but an intimate
and mystical oneness, or identity, with the timeless flow of experience.
Here was Derrida, at the end of his life, wrestling with two of the most
powerful and enduring notions of "reality" in Western civilization (for
that matter, they are to be found in all civilizations) as typified by the
contrasting visions of Heraclitus (reality as experiential flow) and of
Parmenides (reality as understood by abstract rationalism). At any rate,
near the end of his life Derrida's ideas became increasingly mystical
and messianic in the mode of his old teacher Immanuel Levinas
(whose writings, as one observer put it, could be described as "a prod-
igy of incoherence"),[8] who at a conference in 1986 looked Derrida
square in the eye and asked him to admit, once and for all, what many
had by then concluded: that he, Derrida, was at bottom a mystic in the
tradition of the ancient Jewish Kabbalah,* which is to say: someone in
search of an ineffable truth that is indescribable in traditional concepts.[9] But as always, Derrida resisted, struggling once again to slip out
of all orthodox definitions on the ground that fixed definitions of him
or his work betray the truth and flux of his personal experience.

It is obvious now (although he often denied it) that Derrida was indeed practising and protecting a negative theology, or at least a personal
style that he later admitted was often indistinguishable from it. Negative
theologians believe that God is so absolute, remote, and perfect that we
cannot define Him in positive terms. Only in negative ones. So, for example, it is not possible to say "God is good" because we cannot know that.
We can say for sure only that God cannot be evil. Derrida often mim-
icked this tradition by naming things in negative but absolutist terms,
such as *absence, trace, différence, différance* (a combination of the French
terms for difference, as between meanings, and deferral of meaning) –
and even by describing *justice* as something that is not yet, "*but is to come,*"
and by defining God as *absence/presence,* and the like. Indeed, during a
1968 presentation when Derrida was expounding on his famous paper

---

* Isaac Luria (1534–1572) was the founder of Jewish Kabbalah, and it is this Lurianic
type of mysticism of which Derrida has been suspected by more than one critic.

"Différance," an exasperated listener piped up: "it [*différance*] is the source of everything and one cannot know it: [so] it is the God of negative theology!"[10] But whenever he got pinned down or accused of inventing what seems like just a trickier version of Western metaphysical presence, he invented more new terminology, thus continually changing the context of understanding. This stance he sometimes called a "negative wisdom" because it does not declare any objective, universal, or transcendent truth that may be used to oppress (or understand fully) but instead provides us with "protocols of vigilance" against all oppressive political or intellectual or moral systems.[11] That is why he always protested that even though he passed quite rightly for an atheist with respect to orthodox religions, he had an absolutely private language in which he spoke of God and said "the constancy of God in my life is called by other names."[12] (About this remark, Caputo says: that is quite an admission for "a leftist, secularist, sometimes scandalous, post-Marxist Parisian intellectual.")[13]

DECONSTRUCTING DERRIDA'S RELIGION

Deconstruction proceeds not by knowledge but by faith.[14]

Deconstruction is set in motion by an overarching aspiration, which on a certain analysis can be called a religious or prophetic aspiration, what would have been called, in the plodding language of the tradition ... a movement of 'transcendence' ... It repeats the passion for the messianic promise and messianic expectation.[15]

John D. Caputo, *The Prayers and Tears of Jacques Derrida* (1997)

There is a very important sense, then, in which postmodernism is but the latest expression of an attack on Western civilization that has been subterranean but continuous since ancient times. More precisely, it is an expression of Western civilization's ongoing struggle with its own internal contradictions. If we can agree that this civilization, in its most fundamental aspects, has been shaped by the mixture of Hebrew, Christian, and Greek civilizations – a brew in which the eventually dominant Greek-Christian worldview came to dominate the Hebrew one – then postmodernism may be seen as a counterattack from the Hebrew worldview,[16] an attempt, as it were, to de-Hellenize the Western world by substituting Hebrew values and ways of seeing the world, and language, and God for Greco-Christian ones. Caputo, who is so thoroughly pro-Derridean, is sympathetic to this attack and says that "happily, there has been all along, a counter-tradition of thinkers [he is thinking of Levinas as the main figure here] who have resisted this ... Hellenizing of God, this Hellenistic God." And he confesses that all along, "*I have been situating de-construction within this de-Hellenizing tradition.*"[17]

Another way to put this is to say that Derrida and his followers stand for a counter-tradition that attempts to restore the flow and immediacy of the experience of the sacred by disentangling it from the overly intellectual and highly abstract distortions imposed by Greek-derived ideas (and ideals) concerning mind/body, time/eternity, matter/spirit, universal/particular, and so on. In this respect, it is a tradition extending from Isaac the Blind in the thirteenth century, through Isaac Luria, mentioned above, to contemporary Kabbalists such as Gershom Scholem, and the postmodernism that emerges from this tradition must be recognized as an anti-metaphysical metaphysics emphasizing the mutual interaction between speech and writing as an infinite drama of disclosure and concealment, being and nonbeing, meaning and non-meaning, beyond which there is no other reality – which is to say that like Kabbalah, postmodernism revels in endless interpretation as the fundamental reality. To understand a little better why mainstream Western metaphysics is Christian-Greek and why most of our anti-metaphysics is Hebrew, we need to go to the heart of the differences between the Greek and Hebrew languages as they embody forms of thought.

The first thing that strikes us is that the Hebrew language, unlike Greek or English, has no written vowels. It is not what we call an alphabet. It is an "*abjad*" (an acronym made from the first four consonants of the Hebrew letter system). Experienced speakers of Hebrew do not need written vowels to decipher the intended words. For that matter, you don't necessarily "need" vowels written out in any language. If I use only consonants and write "tk hm th brd," most native speakers could figure out this might mean "take home the bread." But it could also mean "take him the board" or "take home (or him) the bird." Only a background knowledge of original intent and the actual context of events would help us to know which was the intended meaning. The point is that Hebrew is a written form in which much that is missing, or absent, nevertheless must be produced by the reader, and if the document is at all symbolic or philosophical in nature, the-absent-made-present will play a key role in meaning. The form of thinking this activity generates is part of an old Jewish mystical "Alephtavian" tradition.[18] In this system, the Hebrew name of G-d, for example (Yod Hey Vav Hey, or what has come down to us through Latin as "Yahweh"), is not, and cannot be, fully revealed by writing alone. Here is a case where the substance of the full name, like the entity, is forever hidden – an unknowable, ungraspable, mystical presence/absence.[*] This is pretty close to what Derrida called a "Trace."

The Christian alphabetic tradition (especially so influenced and shaped as it has been by Greek rationalism and philosophy throughout the ages) is something quite opposite. God announces Himself as the Logos, or the Word. Christian knowledge of God comes unmediated from the spoken Word, and even the written Bible can only but approach the clarity of this presence. Jesus wrote nothing. He spoke. Western metaphysics can thus be said to be constructed on the basis of a "Christological" relation to language in which Scripture is really a trans-scripture, or transcription, of the original Word, or Logos, the oral source of truth that has always had priority in the logocentric West. It is on this basis that Derrida attacks our entire philosophical tradition (and all totalizing political and moral systems and ideas) as but *a series of attempts to perpetuate this relation.*

From this perspective, the Western world seems a product of intellectual bricolage, something cobbled together from opposing ideas of God and Truth. For the Greek tradition of clear analytical philosophy – which was so deeply integrated within Christianity (first in the neo-Platonic tradition via Philo, Augustine, and Plotinus and then in the Aristotelian tradition via Aquinas in the Middle Ages) – strives always for clarity in revealing certain and absolute truth, the ground for which it presumes in advance to exist. It also assumes the divine Godhead is intimately and personally knowable (especially in the human form of Jesus), as is divinity's creation – the material world. All of Western science and metaphysics have been overwhelmingly shaped by this confidence in the available *presence of truth through a sustained effort of knowing.* Arguably, the entire enterprise and progress of science and technology has failed rather miserably everywhere else it has been tried, such as in the Chinese, Hindu, and Buddhist empires, because

---

[*] In the mystical Hebrew tradition, the letters of the *abjad* "are more than just signs for sounds ... They are themselves holy. They are vessels carrying within the light of the Boundless One ... Aleph is the first letter. It has no sound. Only the sound you make when you begin to make every sound ... it is the letter beginning the first of G-d's mysterious 70 names, Elohim ... it also begins the most important thing about Him: Echad. One." From Rabbi Lawrence Kushner, *Sefer Otiyot: The Book of Letters: A Mystical Alef-bait* (Woodstock, VT: Jewish Lights, 1990), 5.

this confidence in what can be known was, and remains, missing. (The political downside is the accusation that it is precisely this Holy Grail of metaphysical certainty latent in the Greco-Christian tradition that, once secularized, leads straight to totalizing political systems attempting to create the Kingdom of Heaven on earth and hence onward to such atrocities as the Nazi and Communist slaughterhouses.)

Judaism, in contrast, assumes that as God is an ineffable mystery, this can produce only a system of metaphysical truth that revels in continuous, even infinite, interpretation. Neither God nor ultimate Truth can ever be known – nor should be known – although God's laws may be known and followed. Even the four Hebrew letters standing for G-d without attempting to name Him definitively – indeed, refusing this temptation in principle – suggest profoundly the contrast between the sense of becoming and unfolding in the Hebrew worldview as compared to the sense of and need for certainty and perfection that is typical of the Greek-Christian worldview.

Derrida at first claimed he never learned Hebrew but may have been influenced by it. But in his later life he often implied that his writing expressed "a Hebrew grammar" and that Hebrew had perhaps been his true "home." Indeed, Susan Handelman situates Derrida within a "Rabbinic" scriptural tradition – as distinct from the logocentrism of the Christian and patristic tradition – and describes his work as "the latest in the line of Jewish heretic hermeneutics [systems of interpretation]."[19] His many followers – many of them Jewish scholars quite naturally excited about this revival of a tradition they may have felt themselves as much as articulated – have, with their new anti-metaphysics, strived to make present everywhere the presence of absence (so to speak). All of this suggests, rather ironically, that Derrida – and the entire postmodern tradition that flows from his work – is promoting its own sort of essentialism, one mystical in the highest degree. It is for this reason that he lavishes such energy and attention on the polyvalence of words, on the play of differences between words, and on the endless generation of multiple meanings that may flow not only from and between words but even within and between the punned sounds and letters of individual words. And by giving deconstruction a messianic twist, Caputo writes, Derrida "is engaging in a certain reinvention of Judaism, let us say, a reinvention of Judaism as deconstruction."[20]

From a literary point of view, Derrida stands squarely in the lyrical-metaphorical tradition of Rabelais, Celine, Sterne, Joyce, and the symbolists, even of Dadaism and the conceit of "automatic writing." In all of this, both language and the language arts are seen as mystical, as taps into the unconscious springs of Being, intensely and uncontrollably generative of multiple meanings – a burning lamp, so to speak. This is quite distinct from the clear, rationalist literary tradition of such as Racine, Pope, Flaubert, and Hemingway, for whom language is seen more as a mirror in which, or a glass through which, we see a crisp and firm reality in the world outside of language.

PREDICTABLE DISAPPOINTMENTS

Justice in itself, if such a thing exists, outside or beyond law, is not deconstructible. No more than deconstruction, if such a thing exists. Deconstruction is justice.[21]

> Jacques Derrida, quoted in John D. Caputo,
> *Deconstruction in a Nutshell,* 1997

For this writer, at least, the entire deconstruction movement, while it had moments of true insight and a literary panache that emerged from a few gifted writers such as Roland Barthes and Derrida himself, turns out to have been a predictable disappointment. I will mention just two reasons. To the lasting embarrassment of his reputation, through the 1980s and 1990s Derrida published a number of tracts attempting to defend his brand of Marxism (he was never a card-carrying, vulgar communist) as a lofty embodiment of human "justice." Indeed, he confessed many times that "there is a certain spirit of Marxism which I will never be ready to renounce ... a certain emancipatory and *messianic* affirmation."[22] His critics joked that his idea of justice was "something we all simply need to sit back and await, like a Messiah on a deconstructed donkey, although we can hurry it along by joining the far left."[23] In addition to his highly abstract notion of justice, however, he increasingly promoted something he called "democracy" as a political standard for all human beings. Let us deal with both terms.

Caputo says that while it is true (in the view of deconstructionists) that there is no end purpose or goal for deconstruction (otherwise, it would be just another essentialist program), "this does not mean there is no point to it." In what seems a moment of obfuscation, he then adds that "every *thing* is deconstructible, but justice, if such a 'thing' 'exists,' is not a *thing*." Okay, so what is it? In a breathtaking and I think patently pseudo-mystical summary worthy of Derrida himself, he explains that "justice is the absolutely unforeseeable prospect (a paralyzing paradox) in virtue in which the things that get deconstructed are deconstructed."[24]

Derrida's defence of this abstract nonthing is based on what would appear to be an amateurish distinction between practical "law" on the street (statutes, codes, legal structures and institutions, or just plain old "positive law") and something most experts have always called *natural law.* The latter is indeed eternal, universal, and undeconstructible, or it is nothing, and it is also, as we have seen, the practical abstract standard, both historical and international, against which all mere positive law everywhere is judged as good or bad. This is where, for this writer at least, modern deconstruction theory grinds to a halt: the original sacred text Derrida read at Johns Hopkins in 1966, which for so many had the effect of demolishing belief in universal and transcendent concepts of any kind, clearly did not satisfy. But more to the point, after a few decades of banishing the presence of all traditional concepts, there was simply nothing left as a reference for thought or judgment of any kind. This left Derrida with a lot of contradictions in his own thinking and with a personal yearning for something sacred – something more than a text. With respect to these contradictions, the early Derrida

> is wholly irreconcilable with the Derrida of recent years, who has turned to lengthy disquisitions on the necessity for, and universality of, justice. Such irreconcilability would be fine if Derrida had renounced the premises of his earlier work. He hasn't. But of course Derrida's response would be that pointing out his own contradictions amounts to a *logical* critique, and the thrust of his thought has always been to subvert logic itself. Thus, his inconsistency is perfectly consistent. It's an invincible position. And it is the antithesis of a rational enterprise. If contradicting yourself does not undermine what you're arguing, you're not arguing anything.[25]

As for his use of the term "democracy"? Here, there is only more embarrassment (and for Caputo also, who fulminates like an angry sophomore about the practical injustices of this world as though he, too, believes that some kind of true democracy would improve things). It never dawns on such intellectuals that more democracy could make things a lot worse. It was populist democracy, after all, that brought us the Nazis and that most recently has brought us the terrorist reality of Hamas. And nowhere do we see the slightest awareness of the historical difference between the constitutional liberalism of the Western world, which preceded the advent of democracy by a few centuries, and modern democratic method. Indeed, in *The Future of Freedom: Illiberal Democracy at*

Home and Abroad, an excellent treatment of this distinction, Fareed Zakaria writes that these two things "are coming apart across the globe: Democracy is flourishing; liberty is not."[26]

Derrida tells us (without telling us, of course) what he means by the term "democracy," about how (in Caputo's words) "deconstruction is justice" and "deconstruction is love"; it is "the expectation of an everlasting justice" and also "the messian*ism* of the democracy to come."[27] For Derrida, democracy is "a radically pluralistic polity" that resists all normal forms of identity that produce a "we" and that in doing so, violently oppose one group against another. This is a bit of a mystery for those who have always thought democracy has at least something to do with majority rule, which by definition opposes the larger group against the smaller. At any rate, a little trip through history tells us why this talk about democracy, which we are confidently informed has "a determinate historical genealogy," is both naive and problematic.[28]

What sort of actual democracy does Derrida want? Surely not the participatory democracy of ancient Greece, which survived as long as it did only because somewhere around one-third of all the residents of Athens were slaves. And surely not the Roman sort, with it triumvirates, assassinations, and public slaughters-of-the-week. Well, then, did he mean direct democracy of the Swiss sort? Or American representative democracy (so keen to avoid the Swiss kind, which it characterized as mob rule)? Or the first French "democracy," which, during the French Revolution of 1789–94 was used to justify the slaughter of thousands of innocent French citizens? And surely, even though he was someone who wrote in "the spirit of Karl Marx," he did not want the collectivist arrangement that the communists call "true democracy" but that those of us from the tradition of British liberal democracy call "totalitarian democracy"? Was it perhaps, then, a Canadian-style constitutional monarchy/democracy (one that in 1982 plopped a French-style charter of abstract code law on its English common-law-based tradition)?

He didn't say because he didn't know.

He especially seemed not to know that perhaps the only modern sociopolitical fact of significance on which all theorists, left and right, are agreed – and this makes his dreamland plea for "a pluralist democracy" seem particularly naive – is *the profoundly disturbing and well-documented ignorance that characterize the publics of all modern "democracies"* (so different, each of them, that it is simply inappropriate to use this term without a precise definition).[29] If this is what he wanted more fully expressed, then he ought to have said so. If not, then he might better have avoided setting up his "democracy to come" as yet another mystical ideal. At the outer limit, he craved a "new international" that he hoped might replace the old Marxist one, a community of sorts of all the dispossessed of the earth, of those marginalized, "secretly aligned in their suffering," who are "de-posed" and "de-capitated" by their race, income, gender, nationality, language, religion, or even species (animal rights) – in a nutshell, by their "difference."[30] So, through a philosophy that *relies* wholly on differences, he wanted to end differences? All his tiresome victimology aside, he ought to have been pressed a little harder on such contradictions.

To conclude: the deconstructionist movement that began in the 1960s has run its course. On the way, however – and even though Derrida always denied he was in any way a relativist – it sowed countless seeds of a relativism so extreme as to undermine even itself, if only because the ancient urge for spiritual authenticity, for knowing a primordial reality that precedes all division into concepts of the mind, is a mystical one: it can be satisfied only by the effort to merge our own consciousness with things and events as they happen, prior to all reflection, which is to say, prior to all fixed thought, all fixed moral judgment, and all politics.

In the end, modern deconstruction is a revival of the ancient Heracleitean initiative combined (most obviously in Derrida) with his personal adaptation of a Jewish Kabbalism that strives to overturn all permanent categories of thought, and "insofar as it tends to subsume so many narratives under a single history of metaphysics, and insofar as it attempts to preface every story with a story of undecidability, [such] radical hermeneutics remains a metanarrative, a discourse of power, however much it dissembles itself as a kind of principled powerlessness ... It declares an end to the war of truths by resolving (or dissolving) every disagreement into its own truth."[31]

This and the preceding chapters have been an unexpected – and unexpectedly detailed – foray into language relativism, the most extreme form of all relativisms for the reason that insofar as language and thought are one, it is also an attack on the foundations of all thought and therefore of all civilization.

It is easy to see now that the main political motive of this post-1960s deconstructionism was the undermining of Western philosophical and moral confidence, beginning with the referential capacities of language itself. In this, it has been rather successful, not least for the reason that it came at a time when unprecedented numbers of educated citizens of the Western democracies, swaggering with the sort of cosmic confidence that seems to accompany unprecedented material prosperity, yearned to escape the absolutist moral yoke of Judeo-Christian values. More personal material freedom called for more personal moral freedom, and the relativism buried in deconstruction theory provided a sophisticated intellectual justification for this deliverance.

So much for the short term.

What surprises us for the long term is the consequence. In relativizing reality so successfully by arguing that it cannot be confined by words or concepts, deconstruction returned us to the confusion of our mystical roots. Whatever his faults, it was to Derrida's credit that he saw this coming and did not avoid it. Despite his denials, he was always a mystic who wanted to grasp and relate to the truth of experience, and he fought for deconstruction as his truth-finding technique because he wanted at all costs to avoid sitting in judgment on the purity of that experience (or to have others sitting in judgment on him). But to fuse the self with experience is to lose the self at the moment of fusion for the plain reason that we cannot *relate* to something unless there is more than one term, or *relata*. As Raymond Tallis put it so well when discussing the work of all such philosophers of pure existence: "behind the more technical arguments of these philosophers' writings is a disappointed longing for the union of absolute lucidity and undeniable substantiality, of thing-like thereness with thought-like transparency, for an absolute coincidence of knowing and being."[32]

That is why what we see at the end of Derrida's life is a return to judgment via concepts such as *justice, democracy, hospitality, the gift,* and so many other special terms he used in an attempt to provide the missing *relata* – that is, to provide a foundation for his own very personal thought. He struggled to make these terms ineffable even while coming to the realization that only if they were universal and absolute – or undeconstructible – could they be useful in the first place.

Having now successfully passed through this shadowy labyrinth of language relativism and arrived at the conclusion that it is impossible to use language without general and universal concepts and objective, shared understandings (otherwise, how could anyone read these words?), we will move in the next chapter to a survey of the interesting science of language universals.

14

The Universals of Language

To see these deep parallels in the languages of the French and the Germans, the Arabs and the Israelis, the East and the West, people living in the age of the Internet, and people living in the Stone Age, is to catch a glimpse of the psychic unity of humankind.[1]

Steven Pinker, *Words and Rules* (2000)

Almost daily he could be seen – a dark figure apparently talking to himself as he walked slowly from library to office under the shadows of palm trees on the beautiful sun-drenched campus of California's Stanford University. Professor Joseph Greenberg was a man obsessed in a happy way with words; more specifically, he was intrigued by the many ways human beings all over the world use words in the same fashion. Absolutely and universally.

Prior to the 1960s, however, interest in language universals was still in its infancy and distinctly out of step with the times. Indeed, American anthropology, so formed as it had been by the traditions of "cultural relativism" stemming from Franz Boas and his most influential students, had infected almost everyone with what then seemed a permanent and irrefutable orthodoxy. In 1957, after a review of three decades worth of linguistic research, this mood was summed up as a creed for all students by anthropology professor Martin Joos, who proclaimed that *"languages could differ from each other without limit and in unpredictable ways."*[2] This was also hippie time in America, and everywhere there was happy talk about the idea that human beings everywhere are different without limit and in every imaginable way. Everyone very badly *wanted* them to be different because there was a somewhat paranoid belief – a contemporary conceit that was perhaps a postwar reaction to the evils of uniformity – that sameness in anything must represent some kind of authority by stealth.

But Greenberg, who was more interested in the truth, suspected otherwise and on any given day was likely to be talking to himself excitedly about some of the forty-five "Universals of Language" that he was the first to describe and publish under that title with his colleagues in 1963.[3] They were the few universalists still toughing it out against the relativism crowd, and they were operating from an older, alternative tradition. They were bucking the tide because, as one of them put it succinctly, it seemed "simply to be not true that languages differ from each other in unconstrained ways. In fact ... data points in exactly the opposite direction ... that *languages resemble each other much more than they differ from each other [and] ... are actually very limited in the extent to which they may differ.*"[4]

Greenberg's own shot across the bow was pretty clear, too, for "Underlying the endless and fascinating idiosyncrasies of the world's languages *there are regularities of universal scope.* Amid infinite diversity, *all languages are, as it were, cut from the same pattern.*"[5] For all those fascinated by what unites human beings, the very existence of human language and the possibility of translation from one to the other stood as a challenge to search out the hidden truth about language universals.

There were also in the air at the time a few other motives driving what has since become a widespread search for such universals. Everyone agrees that the eyes are the mirror of the soul. But for many linguists and other researchers in a growing variety of fields, *language is the mirror of the mind.* It may be true that many kinds of human "thinking" such as are necessary for ordinary body movement, reflexes, or wordless intuitions do not require language. But language seems inseparable from most kinds of complex thinking, much of which may be a kind of language without sound, and that is why all the so-called "cognitive sciences" – new fields dedicated to studying brain-mind functions – that are currently ascendant are so language-dependent. In short, people like Joseph Greenberg were certain that to discover the universal patterns of human language was to reveal something deeply significant about the unity of human experience and the operations of mind. There are millions of different apples that fall to the ground, but Newton was hunting for the law that caused them to do so. In the same fashion, language universalists are hunting for the set of universal realities and laws that make human language possible.

In this respect, universalists have been mining a very different aspect of language from the one that concerned the postmodernists examined in the last few chapters. For me at least, it helps to lay out this difference in a simple way so that the two connected but extreme poles of human language can be seen visually (fig. 14.1).

Figure 14.1
Schematic of Language Polarities

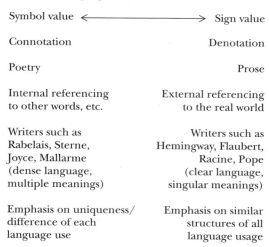

Symbol value ⟵⟶	Sign value
Connotation	Denotation
Poetry	Prose
Internal referencing to other words, etc.	External referencing to the real world
Writers such as Rabelais, Sterne, Joyce, Mallarme (dense language, multiple meanings)	Writers such as Hemingway, Flaubert, Racine, Pope (clear language, singular meanings)
Emphasis on uniqueness/difference of each language use	Emphasis on similar structures of all language usage

This is obviously a rough and ready contrast, but it should be easy to see that Jacque Derrida, for example, spent most of his life concentrating on the left side of this pole and people like Greenberg (and Noam Chomsky, as we shall see) on the right. At both ends there are constraints. Emphasis on the left extremity leads postmodernists to claim we are all trapped in the prison house of language. For them, reality is a consequence of the infinitely self-referential web of words we spin with layered meanings that are fluid and without foundation or clear borders. At the right end we get the claim that there is a definable, clear, and law-like universal grammar common to all human language users and that once differences are put aside, we see a foundation that is innate, or hardwired, in all of us. That is why we are all able to read this sentence or translate it from one language into another. The rest of this chapter will examine the facts and claims of language universals.

WHAT ARE LANGUAGE UNIVERSALS?

They can be gathered under a few headings, as follows:

1 Absolute universals: these are linguistic features found in all known human languages, without exception.

2 Statistical universals: these are common features found in human languages with a greater than chance frequency.

3 Implicational universals: these are features that are implicated by other features and that do not occur alone. For example, if whenever A is found in a language, B is also found, but not the reverse, then B is an implicational universal.

4 Substantive universals: these are concrete, surface universals having to do with things like the physical sounds of human languages and with their common word-order patterns, as discovered by Greenberg. Such universals are observable, are located "in the data" of language, and are verified or disproved according to data from as many languages of the world as can be examined. To be considered an absolute, such universals must be shown to be exceptionless.

5 Formal universals: these are universals that take the form of unobservable underlying abstract laws of universal grammar (UG) such as detailed by Chomsky. Such rules or laws are not "in the data" any more than the law of gravity is in the falling apple, and it is assumed that such laws are due to biological innateness, or neuron patterns, in the brain – or if you are a Platonist on this matter, like Bertrand Russell, that most words are themselves universals that have a timeless Being that is "nowhere" and "nowhen." To specify formal universals, a hypothesis about language structure is usually formed in the abstract and tested against a small number of languages to see whether it holds on the grounds that if the structure in question is truly innate, then there is no need to examine all 5,000 of the world's languages to prove it.

Now let us look at a few of the settled universals of human languages, beginning with sounds, then moving to the level of words, and finally arriving at some rules of universal grammar. Needless to say, no one has come even close to surveying all of the world's languages, the majority of which have never been documented, so some of these claims are open to possible refutation. But insofar as we have data, they stand.

UNIVERSALS OF HUMAN LANGUAGE SOUNDS

In the previous few chapters we saw how Ferdinand de Saussure conceived of human language as "a totally self-contained system of elements that functioned purely through their differences from one another"[6] without regard to the substance of sounds, words, or anything else. Saussure himself was no relativist, as we have seen, and insisted that once the differential system of "arbitrary" connections (we may say "mountain," while a Japanese says "Yama," although we are each referring to the same real-world thing) between signs and their referents in the real world is established, an individual user is more or less powerless to alter it: the language system as a whole is a pervasive social reality, not an individual one.

We have seen how the idea that a language arises from a system rooted in arbitrary differences or relations was enough to send some language theorists into the intellectual ether, claiming that because connections between signs and their referents are arbitrary, then everything is arbitrary. But others, also very influential theorists, became firm doubters. One of these was the Russian émigré Roman Jakobson, an intense and brilliant student of language, literature, folklore, and culture who ended up in the Prague Linguistic Circle after the Russian Revolution of 1917. Jakobson was at first a Saussurean, like everyone else at the time. But he had a great interest in poetry and in the sound systems that make speech possible, and by 1930 he realized he could no longer support the idea that languages resulted purely from systems of arbitrary difference. Something else, something deeper, was going on. For one thing, he had noticed that children from all over the world seem to develop their first language sounds in nonarbitrary, fixed, and regular – dare I say, universal – ways. This suggested to him not only that there must be *universal laws of human sound acquisition* at work, that the acquisition of meaningful sounds is regular rather than arbitrary, but also that there are levels, or deeper relationships, between certain sound features within languages that are dictated by their actual physical shape, or substance. In 1939 Jakobson published an important paper on "the sound laws of child language," which inaugurated a new "hierarchical structuralism." Contrary to Saussure, for whom arbitrariness meant that any sounds that could be distinguished from each other would suffice to create a language, Jakobson proposed that "a universal hierarchy of sounds was valid across all languages of the world," which for him explained the universal existence of words like "mama" and "papa." His critics said: nonsense – all children say these words first because they are easiest. But Jakobson was able to show that in the babbling stage prior to the formation of actual words, children manage to produce all possible language sounds and hence that what makes certain words "easier" must be due to the brain, not the tongue. As with the child, so with all the world's languages: children learn to produce sounds according to a universal order. Those sounds with maximal contrast are learned first, those with weakest contrast last. Accordingly, all languages include sounds of the former type but not all include the latter, weaker type. Interestingly, aphasic individuals who lose their ability to form sounds do so in reverse order to that by which they were acquired.[7] This was radical stuff, for Jakobson was demonstrating that language cannot be conceived either as pure form (Saussure) or pure substance (as historical linguists had been saying). It is indelibly both. For Jakobson, there were hidden principles structuring language, and just as musical form cannot be abstracted from the musical matter – the sounds it organizes – so form in spoken language cannot be abstracted from the sound matter of speaking. The two poles of form and substance are not disconnected entities that just happen to bump into each other; they are not "arbitrarily" related.[8]

Having fled the Nazi regime,* Jakobson ended up teaching in America in 1941, where he later met Claude Levi-Strauss and also the young Noam Chomsky. Levi-Strauss was immediately influenced by Jakobson's brand of structuralism, and he rejigged his own work on cultures of the world accordingly. And it was Jakobson's influence on Chomsky that was to lay the groundwork for the latter's lifelong belief in the existence of a universal grammar common to all languages. Jakobson's new substantive structuralism was gradually leading him away from Saussure's arbitrariness in a hunt for the permanent underlying universals in all things human. This was the direction taken by Levi-Strauss, Chomsky, and many others. It is an

---

* It is interesting that the anthropologist Franz Boas, who was Jewish and whose work we reviewed in chapter 4, fled the totalitarianism menacing Europe for America. He was properly frightened of absolutism for fear that whenever and wherever it becomes political, we find pogroms of one kind or another, so he spent much of his life promoting cultural and moral differences between all people as equally valid norms within each society. He was trying to construct a kind of cultural firewall against political absolutism.

Jakobson was also Jewish and fled the Nazi regime for America. But his response to the realities of civilizational chaos that drove him there was to seek universals that could unite human beings, whether found in art, language, or culture. In other words, his very different firewall against arbitrary political and intellectual absolutism would be the ground of human universals. For this writer, Jakobson's strategy works best for the reason that once we ascertain the true scope of human universals, we can encourage social forms that express and protect desirable ones (such as the fact of and need for social bonding) and discourage the worst (such as certain universal instincts of hostility). As for the cultural and moral relativism option? It is, as Chomsky put it, "a dictator's dream."

approach that appeals to those "who want to believe that they are unlocking the secret architecture of the human mind, which perhaps mirrors that of the universe, while repelling those who regard unobservables as repellent to science."9

SOME PHONOLOGICAL UNIVERSALS

Jakobson was among the first to lay out what he discovered as the "twelve basic oppositions" that are found universally as "distinctive features" in the *sound system* of all human languages. A particular language may not manifest all the sounds derivable from these oppositions, but the sounds it does use will be derived in those terms. Readers may wish to go to Jakobson's original work for more details.[10] Here, I will give only a few examples, as these are easily grasped by common sense once we are made aware of them. Here are just two of the twelve oppositions that may be found operating in most languages, as they do in English:

- The distinction between *voiced* and *voiceless* sounds. For example, the sound /m/ is "voiced" but /t/ is not. You can feel the difference by holding your throat as you say the word "mat," for example. Your throat will vibrate on the /m/ but not on the /t/.
- The distinction between *nasal* and *oral* sounds. For example, between sounds that are shaped either in the oral or the nasal cavity. The French language, for example, will "nasalize" a lot of /r/ sounds that in English are simply oral.

There are a great many other specific phonological universals in addition to the underlying "system" of formal sound universals that Jakobson was elucidating. Greenberg and his colleagues chased down many phonological universals of a surface, or "typological," variety – indeed, so many that one volume of the famous four-volume collection *The Universals of Human Language*, published by Stanford University in 1978, is devoted to these.[11]

If we resist the temptation to take the amazing complexity of human language for granted – I mean the human language faculty, an ability with teeth, tongue, lips, vocal chords, and so on to utter sounds that are *intricately and systematically organized* at all levels to produce the most delicately nuanced communications – then we can stay close to the true mystery of language. The mystery is due to the universal "recursive" capacity of human language systems, *which makes possible the generation of an infinite number of utterances and meanings from finite materials.* In the case of English, forty-five phonemes are all that is required to produce an infinite number of new utterances. As Steven Pinker puts it, "a person might know 60,000 words, but a person's mouth cannot make 60,000 different noises (at least, not ones that the ear can easily discriminate)." Human language, at the level of sound, and also at the level of words and sentences, "has exploited the principle of the discrete combinatorial system again. Sentences and phrases are built out of words, words are built out of morphemes [minimally distinctive units of meaning], and morphemes, in turn, are built out of phonemes [minimally distinctive units of sound]."[12]

Here are just a few observations on the sound system of the world's languages:

- A historical tendency toward sound (phonological) symmetry is universal.
- Every phonological system contrasts phonemes that are typically stops (such as the /p/ sound at the end of the word "stop," which ends the sound altogether) with phonemes that are never stops (they are "continuous" sounds, like the /a/ in "bag," where the /a/ does not stop by itself but is stopped only by merging into or ending with the sound that follows it).
- Sound change is universal (and there are also regularities of sound change that obey their own universal laws).[13]
- All languages have consonants and vowels.
- Half of all languages have seven vowels, others fewer. Most languages have /i/ /a/ and /u/ as part of their vowel system.
- All languages have "plosives" (sounds that explode with breath, like the first /p/ in "pop." The last /p/ is called a "stop" because it does not explode. Hold your hand in front of your mouth as you say "pop" and you will feel the difference in these "p" sounds on your hand).
- Almost all languages have /p/ /t/ and /k/, and those that don't have all of these sounds, have at least two of them.
- Almost all languages have nasals; for the few that have only one, it is usually /n/, and for those that have only two, it is usually /m/ and /n/.
- 95% of all languages have "fricatives" (like the /f/ in "fast"); 90% of all languages have a sibilant (like the /s/ in "soap"); 64% have /h/; the rarest fricatives are pharyngeals, which are formed in the throat (about 7% have these).

- 95% of all languages have a liquid, or flowing, sound (like /l/ in "liquid"), 80% have an L-sound, and 77% have an R-sound.
- 97% of all languages that have /p/ also have /t/.

SOME UNIVERSALS OF LANGUAGE ACQUISITION

The Fundamental Problem of linguistic theory is to explain the possibility of language acquisition.[14]

> Neil Smith, *Chomsky: Ideas and Ideals* (1999).

There are myriad studies of language acquisition in children that seem pretty good evidence for innateness. First, language learning tends to follow the same developmental path in all normal children, and thus many researchers believe that "all infants come into the world with linguistic skills ... [and] do not learn them from their parents' speech."[15] The initial sounds they make at about 7 or 8 months "are the same in all languages and consist of the phonemes and syllable patterns that are the most common across languages."[16] The vast majority of kids say their first words at between 9 and 12 months and, for the next half-year or so, acquire about fifty words, after which there is a vocabulary explosion of sorts. At about 18 months, language "Takes off. Vocabulary growth jumps to the new-word-every-two-hours minimum rate that the child will maintain through adolescence ... [and] children's two-word combinations are so similar in meaning the world over that they read as translations of one another."[17] At about a year and a half to two years, they start to combine words to form two-word phrases, and from there they develop short and then longer sentences. Between the late twos and the mid-threes, "children's language blooms into fluent grammatical conversation so rapidly that it overwhelms the researchers who study it, and no one has yet worked out the exact sequence. Sentence length increases steadily, and because grammar is a discrete combinatorial system, the number of syntactic types increases exponentially, doubling every month, reaching the thousands before the third birthday."[18] By the age of four almost all children, everywhere, are speaking in grammatically correct sentences. The order in which children build up words from their base forms is also fairly uniform, and so is the order in which they all start to use more complicated constructions, including questions, negative statements, passive statements, complex intonations, and so on. Indeed, whether we are speaking of a slow or fast learner, the stages of language acquisition through which all children pass are the same and universal. What is even more interesting is the case of deaf children born to hearing parents who do not use or teach their children to use sign language. These children grow up with lots of normal love and affection but no language input at all! Nevertheless, right on schedule, such children begin to make "babbling" hand motions and invent their first signs, gestures, and gesticular "phrases" at the same age as other children produce their first words and verbal phrases.[19]

THE DIFFERENCE BETWEEN THE WHAT AND THE WHY

The study of language universals that began in earnest in the late 1950s was characterized by two radically different approaches from the start. The first approach, made famous by the extraordinarily industrious Professor Joseph Greenberg of Stanford University, is called the *typological* approach. It is mostly interested in discovering and classifying the "what" of language universals. What are the empirical facts as proved or disproved by the examination of actual languages?

The second approach, made as famous by the equally industrious Professor Noam Chomsky of MIT, is mostly interested in the "why" of human language. Why are the facts the way they are? What underlying laws are producing or "generating" the surface realities? The first approach focuses on establishing a typology, or classification, of the facts. The second approach focuses on discovering the laws that generate the facts and the typology.

We may understand this difference by analogy. Suppose two visitors from outer space come to earth. One of them observes that wherever on earth there is a certain temperature, water changes into ice. He makes an exhaustive classification of all places on earth for which this is true before pronouncing it to be a universal truth. He is a typologist. He is able to make a rule connecting temperature to the appearance of ice, and he is aware that if anyone can show him a case where high temperature and ice are found, his rule will be disproved.

The other fellow looks at the evidence of the first observer and says that is very interesting, but why is it so? He wants to know what law of nature could possibly make water turn into ice. While the first observer is travelling all over the earth to make sure this is true in all cases, the second is formulating a law that says in all cases where we find still air and still fresh water at sea level and at temperatures of zero degrees

Centigrade or less, the water will always turn into ice. He may even develop a molecular explanation for this. But he does not need to examine every case since he feels he has found the universal cause.

Greenberg was an anthropologist, and his typological approach to the discovery of language universals in many respects represented "a reaction against anthropological relativism," while Chomsky's generative approach was "a reaction against behavioristic psychology."[20] In short, they were both reacting, each in his different way, *against theories that said we are shaped as human beings by random events from outside us*: by cultural relativism in Greenberg's field or by language "learning" in Chomksy's field.

The anthropological view of language at the time "was that the languages of the world can vary arbitrarily," or as Martin Joos, quoted above, had put it in 1957, that "languages could differ from each other without limit and in unpredictable ways." Greenberg and others set out to disprove this relativism by classifying the many universal facts of the world's language that operate everywhere as constraints on variation, even in cultures forever divided in space and time from any possible influence on each other.

Meanwhile, Chomsky was striking out at the simplistic stimulus-response, or reward-and-punishment, learning theory then fashionable in psychology by writing a devastating critique in 1959 of B.F. Skinner's book *Verbal Behavior*. His review of that book, "perhaps the most devastating review [of any book] ever written, not only sounded the death knell for behaviorism, but also laid the foundation for current mentalist linguistics [built-in language structures] and cognitive sciences more generally."[21] As a behavioural psychologist, Skinner was also by definition an anti-universalist for whom the mind is a blank slate with no innate mental tendencies or faculties. For him, what ends up in the mind gets there through a process of "conditioning" based on reward and punishment. In contrast, Chomsky's generative approach proposes "that certain general abstract principles governing the grammatical structure of all languages are genetically encoded in the brain" and that "children come into the world already primed to acquire a particular species of the genus 'human language.'" In this respect, Chomsky's linguistic theory "is a branch of biology … he aims to uncover the nature of our biological endowment, and the extent to which that endowment determines certain universal features of language."[22]

These two methods overlap but are at opposite poles and often in disagreement in terms of method. The typologist argues that analysis of a single language or of only a small number will not suffice to reveal true universals. However, both methods are abstract. The typologist abstracts *across* as many languages as possible, using empirical evidence and no prior theory. The generativist abstracts *within* a single language or within only a few and considers a theory that explains the facts to be sufficient evidence. But both approaches ultimately come to rest in biology. For Chomsky, the source is ultimately genetic, while for Greenberg, the source is indirectly biological and evolutionary. [23] Let us now see just a few of Greenberg's language universals before looking at Chomsky's generative approach to universal grammar.

Only specialists will be interested in the wide range of work in the field of language universals to be found in such as *Universals of Human Language* (1978), by Professor Greenberg and his colleagues, and a glance at these books will give a sense of the richness of discoveries in language universals since the 1960s. Another source for ongoing work is the database of language universals at the University of Konstanz in Germany.[24] The Konstanz website logs over 1,200 universals of human language (while specifying that some of these may be disproved as research continues). Universals are ranked on this site as "absolute" (which means they are so far exceptionless), or as "implicational" (which means they occur in all cases where some other language feature is present), or as "statistical" (which means they occur with greater frequency than chance). I will show the box-method of classification of the Konstanz inventory following some of Greenberg's original forty-five universals.

What the reader needs to keep in mind through all this is that *most of these are descriptions of absolute or implicational language universals to which there are no exceptions, unless noted.* The wonder of it all, of course, is why this is the case, when so many of these language groups have never had contact historically or geographically? At the least, the mere existence of so many language universals suggests that the more than seventy-five years of flirtation with linguistic relativism – typified by Joos's statement, above, and by the work of so many cultural anthropologists charged with the enlightenment of so many hundreds of thousands of students – was the wilful result of pedagogical ideology or blindness, not of value-free inquiry.

Here are two "word-order" universals:

- Universal 1. In declarative sentences with nominal subject and object, the dominant order is almost always one in which the subject precedes the object.

- Universal 3. Languages with dominant VSO [verb-subject-object] order are always prepositional.

Here are two universals of sentence making, or "syntax":

- Universal 14. In conditional statements, the conditional clause precedes the conclusion as the normal order in all languages.
- Universal 20. When any or all of the items (demonstrative, numeral, and descriptive adjective) precede the noun, they are always found in that order. If they follow, the order is either the same or its exact opposite.

Here are two universals of word formation, or "morphology":

- Universal 31. If either the subject or object noun agrees with the verb in gender, then the adjective always agrees with the noun in gender.
- Universal 44. If a language has gender distinctions in the first person, it always has gender distinctions in the second or third person, or in both.

Readers can review the rest of Greenberg's forty-five language universals in the appendix.

Table 14.1 shows how the University of Konstanz logs the language universals it receives from researchers all over the world.

THE UNIVERSALITY OF ORDINARY WORDS

In his lucid and popular book *The Problems of Philosophy*, Bertrand Russell laid out a straightforward proof of his case that "when we examine common words, we find that, broadly speaking, proper names stand for particulars, while other substantives, adjectives, prepositions, and verbs stand for universals." And when "we hear the sentence, 'Charles I's head was cut off,' we may naturally enough think of Charles I, of Charles I's head, and of the operation of cutting of *his* head, which are all particulars; but we do not naturally dwell upon what is meant by the word 'head' or the word 'cut'"[25] – and such words (without qualification as to whose head, or what sort of cut, or what sort of instrument was used and by whom) are universals. Universal words without any particular context, he adds, are felt to be incomplete and insubstantial, demanding a context to make them particular, and hence most people

Table 14.1
Example of inventory of language universals catalogued

Number	*4*
Original	If the exponent of vocative is a prefix, then this prefix has arisen from a 1st person possessor or a 2nd person subject.
Standardized	IF the exponent of vocative is a prefix, THEN this marker has been reanalysed from a 1st person possessor marker on nouns or a 2nd person subject marker on verbs.
Formula	
Keywords	case, vocative, prefix, possessor, person, 1st, 2nd
Domain	Inflection
Type	target < source
Status	Diachronic
Quality[a]	Absolute
Basis	mainly based on a survey of Nootkan languages (Almosan), but also on a sampling of vocative forms in other langugaes, and is assumed to be valid generally
Source[b]	Jacobsen 1994: 34
Counterexamples	
Comments	To rephrase it without If-Then: The only source of vocative prefixes are 1st person possessor or 2nd person subject markers, while vocative suffixes presumably have other sources, perhaps including 1st/2nd person markers.
Number	*20*
Original	In all languages, if a nominal possessor carries external case, so does the pronominal one.
Standardized	IF a nominal possessor carries external case, THEN so does the pronominal one.
Formula	
Keywords	case, attribution, agreement, Suffixaufnahme, noun, pronoun
Domain	inflection, syntax
Type	Implication
Status	Achronic
Quality[a]	Absolute
Basis	Suffixaufnahme-languages surveyed in Plank (ed.) 1995
Source[b]	Moravcsik 1995: 470, G4'
Counterexamples	
Comments	This universal is about all instances where possessor has external case (i.e. that marking the whole NP) regardless of whether it also shows internal case (as in Suffixaufnahme), hence is a generalization of #19.

[a] tells us which type of universal
[b] the scholar who submitted this universal to the inventory

Source: University of Konstanz, Germany, database, http://ling.uni-konstanz.de:591/Universals/Introduction.html.

"succeed in avoiding all notice of universals as such, until the study of philosophy forces them upon our attention."[26] He concludes that no sentence can be made up without at least one word that denotes a universal and that nearly all the words to be found in the dictionary stand for universals.

THE CHOMSKY REVOLUTION

In his excellent book *The Language Instinct* Steven Pinker describes the universals discovered by Joseph Greenberg as "Greenbergisms" and as "a laundry list of facts." That is somewhat uncharitable given that prior to this work no one had much of an idea as to the existence of specific language universals. Greenberg was a real pioneer. Furthermore, it is the facts that should be used to prove or disprove more abstract claims. So facts have their place. Greenberg and company established a lot of the *what* that is visible at the surface in language usage all over the world. But what was underneath, in the "deep structure," as it was at first called, that might answer the question *why* remained to be discovered.

That was a role that Noam Chomsky, a young professor at MIT, embraced with relish. His first book to really make an impact was *Syntactic Structures* (1957),[27] published the same year that Joos made his famous declaration about the infinite variability of human languages. As Pinker put it, it was as though Joos had just confirmed the fact of human linguistic chaos that followed the Tower of Babel, and then Chomsky took us right back to Genesis 11:1–9, when "the whole earth was of one language, and of one speech."[28]

In earlier chapters we saw how Saussure had successfully argued – in a view that held for the first half of the twentieth century and more – that language is *a social object* of which individual speakers have only a partial grasp. Then Chomsky arrived on the scene with talk of "deep structure" and "generative grammar" and the underlying idea that all human beings possess an innate language acquisition device (LAD for short), "a species-specific capacity to master and use a natural language. In this perspective, language is a natural object, a component of the human mind, physically represented in the brain and part of the biological endowment of the species."[29] Although there have been modifications along the way, the basic idea underlying what Chomsky, in referring to his own ideas, called the "second cognitive revolution" (after the Cartesian one) has not changed. It remains the case that every natural language is expressed via the generative functions of grammar, which is to say that it has "a finite number of phonemes (or letters in its alphabet), and each sentence is representable as a finite sequence of these phonemes (or letters), though there are infinitely many sentences."[30] This is to say, in turn, that the basic rules of general language acquisition and formation are due to a *universal grammar* that is like a biologically set general language device in the brains of all normal human beings and that is also characterized by a small set of basic rules, change rules, and subsets of rules that are invoked by every natural speaker to learn natural languages – that is, to learn his or her *particular grammar*. Language is not first and foremost a *social object*, as Saussure had taught, although society is essential to its emergence. Chomsky gives an example to illustrate that a grammar conceived as an innate device or "mental organ" for generating grammatically correct utterances can, and must be, separated from semantics, or meaning. For example, any speaker of English could attest immediately that although both sentences below are nonsensical, only the first one is grammatically correct:

- Colorless green ideas sleep furiously.
- Furiously sleep ideas green colourless.

And thus he states – and this was quite a shock for traditionalists – "we are forced to conclude that grammar is autonomous and independent of meaning."[31]

Due to the Chomskyan revolution, linguistics as a study of language soon became also a study of the mind, or of cognitive function, and its methods began branching into many different fields. Language came to be seen as a mirror of the internal workings of the mind rather than as a mirror of the external workings of culture or society. To go further, and because (as one of his followers puts it) "we now have evidence from around the world that exactly the same constraints are operative in every language, wherever it is spoken,"[32] we can now speak of a *universal mind* common to all human beings.

This is surely a vast change of emphasis. Instead of thinking about language as a *passively learned* cultural or social artefact somehow written on a blank-slate mind, language was now to be understood as an innate, genetically based, general and universal human code by means of which, and only by means of which, particular languages could be *actively produced*. The arguments for universal grammar can be summarized as follows:

- The innateness hypothesis: That children all over the world acquire a language at the same rate, in the same sequence, and with full competence despite their ignorance of the complicated rules underlying their particular languages must be due to a capacity with which they are born. Children, Chomsky insists, do not learn a language. They "grow" it during a specific window of time, prior to puberty, just as they grow teeth at a specific time and at a specific rate.
- The logical argument: All human languages have the capacity to generate an infinite number of possible utterances. But infinities are in principle unlearnable. A generation module or organ is therefore required.
- The poverty of data argument (sometimes called "poverty of stimulus"): There is an enormous gap between the complexity of the generative grammar a child uses unconsciously and the minimal learning data supplied by adult speakers.
- The argument from universals and typology: All the languages of the world share hundreds of common properties known as universals of language. These properties are both concrete and abstract – or structure-dependent.
- The biological argument: All normal human beings learn to speak their language competently and in the same series of interdependent steps, which points to language as a species-specific genetic endowment that can be lost by brain injury and studied by PET scans in the brain.
- The system argument: Human language is clearly not produced by memorization or learning, as all humans are able to produce unique utterances they have never heard before. So this must be due to an innate rule-based system that guides them in which finite elements and rules enable the production of such infinite utterances. The point is that to learn a *particular* language you need already to have a general, or *universal*, grammar in your head. All children come equipped with this, *which is why they can learn any language to which they are first exposed.*
- Speed of acquisition: All children begin to speak at more or less the same age and are able to converse using complex verbal structures in a remarkably short period of time.
- Age dependence: Language acquisition is fastest during a critical period prior to puberty, when children learn their native language much more easily than an adult can learn a new language.
- Convergence: Although children have very different speaking environments and the levels of input they receive differ radically, they all end up competently speaking the language their elders speak.

- Empty categories: It is evident that children learn to speak with an innate acknowledgement of "empty categories," or words/thoughts without sounds, and of absent concepts, or "traces." For example, if we overhear A ask: "Is John going to the movie?" and then hear B answer: "Yes, and I'm also going []," both we and B supply the missing words "to the movie." Empty categories are real with respect both to words and phrases and to the role they may play in altering meanings.

There are objections from other linguists to each of these points, some of which are telling. But when the whole picture is considered (in addition to the experience of any parent watching a child's language ability emerge), the argument for innateness is overwhelming. Readers who wish to follow the attacks on universal grammar and generative theory will find it all aggressively argued in Geoffrey Sampson, *The Language Instinct Debate*. I have read this book carefully twice and marvel at the extent to which "beliefs" control arguments on both sides. Sampson *believes* that language is wholly learned from our culture, like dancing, or driving, or riding a bicycle, and that "there is actually no such thing as a language instinct." What Chomsky and Pinker are telling us about innate language instincts, he pleads, "just ain't so. Believe me, it's not."[33] But Chomsky counters by insisting that such things as driving and riding a bicycle are physical skills, whereas the tacit knowledge of language we all have is not an acquired skill; it is something we "grow" at the right time. But, Sampson protests, "I do not believe in Chomsky's distinction." For Sampson – and here he follows the teachings of Sir Karl Popper – all human learning is achieved through a process of "guessing-and-testing."[34]

I am not a practising language theorist, but I would say the interested lay reader must here draw a personal conclusion. Mine is that although Chomsky may in many places make more claims for innateness than he should or may sometimes dismiss learning too readily, and although the universal generative structures of language he has spent a lifetime seeking to define are still rather elusive and open to redefinition (usually by him!), this does not mean he is wrong. They are elusive and open to redefinition and will always be so because we cannot excise the language sectors of the brain and study their biological structures directly. And finally, I have a problem with pure learning theory and the blank-slate model of the mind that underlies it. It seems obvious to me – I *believe*, if you wish – that there is something innate and universal in our brains that enables us to produce a particular language or skill naturally at a particular time in our lives. As one commentator put it, "We can't just have memorized a huge list of words and sentences that we dredge up from our memory on the appropriate occasion."[35] Rather, language is much like walking. Sometimes we say that children "learn" to walk. But any parent knows that you can try to make them walk all day long, but unless they are ready they will just slump back down on the floor and probably cry. But there are always a few lucky and very surprised parents who will never forget returning to a room where they momentarily left a crawling child to see (with astonishment!) the child suddenly stand up and walk on its own!

Pinker does a great job of explaining Chomsky's basic language theory, so I want to proceed by drawing chiefly from chapter 4 of his book *The Language Instinct*, without bothering to note the source of every quotation. In this new language-as-a-code view, a part of speech, such as a noun, has nothing to do with the meaning of a thing in the real world, as we were taught (as in the definition "a noun is the name of a person, place, or thing"). Rather, "it is a kind of token that obeys certain formal rules, like a chess piece, or a poker chip." The various placeholders of a grammar can then be grouped into phrases, and "one of the most intriguing discoveries of modern linguistics is that there appears to be a common anatomy in all phrases in all the world's languages." A noun phrase (NP) in English, for example, always has a noun as its "head," and the phrase tells us something about the head. Verb phrases (VP) are the same: a verb is always at the head, and the rest of the phrase says something about it. Then there are special terms and rules to describe the relations between various entities (role players in the overall grammar) and the so-called "adjuncts" (what we used to call "modifiers"), which, well, modify something, such as an action, a thought, or a thing. In all of the world's grammars, there is a very special place for the "subjects" of phrases: they are always the causal agents of an action.

The resulting "geometry" of phrase-structure analysis got so complicated by 1960 that even though it was satisfying for linguists trying to figure it out, they produced so many hundreds of "rules," "trees," and "transformations" that a "nagging problem came to dominate discussion: *how could children acquire this complex edifice of rules?*"[36] Chomsky himself amusingly complained of his own theories that "we cannot seriously propose that a child learns the values of 10^9 parameters in a childhood lasting only 10^8 seconds."[37] He realized at once that his central argument about an innate "mental organ" could not be sustained in the face of such a complexity of rules. So, he concluded, there must

be some set of "Super Rules." Language acquisition of such complicated grammatical rules must be possible because of nested hierarchies, so to speak, that drop down when called upon.

So with the job in mind of ever greater simplification, Chomsky and
company invented a streamlined version of phrase structure called "X-
bar theory" to explain how a super rule for a grammar can behave like a
drop-down menu of the mind and supply a child with grammatically acceptable speaking rules. One such super rule, for example, can be found
operating throughout English, such as the subject-verb-object (svo) order, which is simply flipped in Japanese to sov. I speak a little Japanese
myself, so this example felt immediately recognizable. And in turn, once
flipped, other things fall into place, such as the rule that "if a language
has the verb before the object, it will also have prepositions; [but] if it has
the verb after the object [as for Japanese] it will have postpositions." In
this fashion, a speaker just needs to grasp that a grammar requires only
the knowledge of certain "principles," which entail specific "parameters," and we get Chomsky's "Principles and Parameters" theory – the
first major revision of his original ideas. According to Chomsky, "the un-
ordered super-rules (principles) are universal and innate," so "when children learn a particular language, they do not have to have a long list of
rules, because they were born knowing the super-rules."

When Pinker gets to the longest possible type of grammatical construction, the sentence, he defines it as "the smallest utterance that can
be either true or false" (and it is interesting that this is a semantic and
logical definition, not a structural one). He then explains the differences and relations between the *surface* structure and *deep* structure of
all grammars. At this point he is pretty much elated because "science
has begun to crack the beautifully designed code that our brains use to
convey complex thoughts as words and their orderings," and all this, he
insists, amounts to a clear refutation of the old doctrine "that there is
nothing in the mind that was not first in the senses." Rather, he argues
persuasively, the details of grammar, the various rules and paraphernal-
ia of syntax, demonstrate that "complexity in the mind is not caused by
learning; learning is caused by complexity in the mind."

Since Pinker wrote *The Language Instinct* in 1994 a great deal more
has happened in the field of language theory, and much of it continues
to be led by Chomsky's restless and innovative mind. Theory development has moved on from principles and parameters, to locality theory,
to case theory, to theta theory, to licensing theory (which has to do with
the idea that words need a kind of licence from the grammar to appear

in a particular position),[38] and on to the most recent development, called minimalism, which is "probably the most radical of the periodic upheavals in Chomsky's thinking"[39] in a fifty-year career of revising his own groundbreaking work. With minimalism he has once again rejected many of his own past innovations as being too complicated – even such standard distinctions as deep and surface structures – in favour of a newer idealized computational system based on simpler rules, such as merge, agree, and move. All these developments have been variations and simplifications of Chomsky's original idea of "generative" grammar – that is, *an innate mental organ that has the rule-based capacity to generate an infinite number of acceptable linguistic utterances from a finite number of sounds and words.*

And so it is with minimalism: *merge* is an option to build larger structures from smaller items; *agree* establishes relations between items and domains; *move* identifies part of a grammatical tree that has already been formed by merge, makes a copy of it, and then merges it with another part of the tree, thus enabling the construction of larger and larger utterances.[40] All this is quite fascinating because it is an intricate display of the human mind trying to figure out, via language, the universal operations of … the human mind – a quest governed all along by the requirement for a credible theoretical simplicity sufficient to explain how any normal child, from anywhere in the world and from any period in the history of human language, is able to master such a complex system so effortlessly.

In conclusion, if we restrict our curiosity about human language to an interest in the infinite – yes, infinite! – variety of utterances, writings, statements, poems, and so on of which humans are capable, it does look like language is some kind of fluid reality that suggests all the features of relativism. Words and their combinations seem to be polyvalent and susceptible to multilevelled variations in meaning, and more to the point, any even minimally complex verbalization, such as a short poem, a personal letter, or a diary entry, may stand as an absolute verbalization: it may well be the first and last time in all eternity that anyone has ever put such words together in this precise way. There is a good chance of it. Consider the following short poem:

The Hummingbird

It's embarrassing to write a poem
at first, until it takes you by the arm;

to think of words as sparks of sound
that leap from heart to heart alone,
a conflagration set in stone.

As for subjects,
they just appear,
like the startled hummingbird,
burning red and gold
with a high octane panic
rising boldly from our darkest garden,
to query, in hung isolation at my window.

I think he comes just to stare,
at a poet he heard
fluttering somewhere.

I am quite certain that no one since the Big Bang has ever written or seen this exact arrangement of words before this author wrote them, and the thought gives a strange feeling of the absoluteness that is a constituent reality of almost every human utterance. Combinations of words come into existence and most of them, unless they are preserved for posterity in some way, go out as soon like sparks that flash and then die in the night. This is the marvellous reality of speech in its existential absoluteness. But equally astonishing is the systematic universality at the very origin of, and in the continuous operation of, all human languages that makes this absoluteness possible. We have seen evidence in this chapter for the universality of ordered language acquisition in very young children, for universal patterns of human language sounds, for universal word-order patterns, and finally, for the universal generative patterns of syntax, or sentence building. We can only marvel at the fact that each of us has a capacity for an absolute and unique linguistic creativity, made possible by a universal and generative linguistic capacity common to all.

15

A Postscript, with a Word about the Universals of Literature, Myth, and Symbol

The ongoing discovery of the universals we share in common through activities such as the production of literary and of mythic, symbolic, and other aesthetic works is interesting for its own sake, of course, but mostly because universals of all kinds point to a common humanity. From anthropology, we have learned that all human societies have "literature" in the most general sense of some kind of continuous tradition of storytelling, either in an oral form as stories said or sung or in sophisticated written forms, as seen in all the more technologically advanced societies. This is a human universal.

What is less known, however, is that many of the forms, structures, and types of literature, myth, and symbol thought to be particular to each society are also common to all of them at some level and that a great deal of work is underway at present to discover and more fully comprehend these universal realities of human life. Such work is now being produced in a broad range of fields as disparate as cultural anthropology (myths have been considered cultural telltales for a long time); psychology and psychoanalysis (there is much prospecting among universal psychic symbols, archetypes, and dreams); and biology and such new fields as "biopoetics" (exploring causal connections between literary productions and biological universals); and finally, there are a great many branches extending from the "cognitive sciences," from various evolution theories,[1] and from other newly emerging fields of thought too numerous to mention. It is beyond the scope of this book to attempt even a basic treatment of such broad topics, but as a service to the reader, some general comments and suggestions will be made and some direction indicated for those who wish to explore further.[*]

---

[*] I should add, however, that I do not believe that any of these new fields, despite the considerable interest they hold, add much of value to the grand

One of the first and greatest essays on literature is Aristotle's *The Poetics*. Not surprisingly, this short piece of work is another brilliant display of the clear analytical thinking for which Aristotle is known, and in it he speaks of a great number of things literary that he assumes to be universal. On this theme, he differs from his teacher Plato, who argued in his *Republic* that poetry is an inferior activity because it depends for its effects on illusion, fiction, and untruth: poets succeed by lying.

On the contrary, Aristotle says: poetry is "a more philosophical and a higher thing than history: for poetry tends to express the universal … and it is this universality at which poetry aims."[2] Aristotle throughout assumes a common human nature in all people, which manifests through art in a *universal desire to imitate* and *to repeat* the great and gripping human actions and events in imaginative works. It also manifests in *the general structure of human stories* (all good tragedies, for example, have a formal and natural beginning, middle, and end, thus forming a structural and aesthetic whole). Further, the emotional work is accomplished by great stories through catharsis and *the purgation of universal human emotions* – all this by means of a few *central and universal literary devices,* such as *reversal of the situation* (where the action swings to its opposite, as when good fortune turns to disaster) and *recognition* scenes (such as a sudden change from ignorance to knowledge, which often occasions a corresponding change in emotion in the key figures, from love to hate or the reverse). The *Oedipus* cycle by Sophocles, for example, illustrates – indeed, hangs upon – all these devices. And not to be overlooked are the universally powerful and moving effects of *lyric* and *song,* among other aesthetic and emotional devices. For Aristotle, literature in its very existence as a human art form stands as something general, permanent, and universal that is expressed locally through particular experience but is not contained by it.

Beginning in the Renaissance and lasting until roughly the end of the eighteenth century, there was a revival of Aristotle's classical, or generalist, view of literature, called the neoclassical movement in letters and the arts. During these many centuries it was simply assumed and taught as orthodoxy that the purpose of literature and all the other

---

question of whether a particular work of literature or art is any good. And to me this is and ought to be the central concern of all serious literary studies. That is the best way I know to protect literature as high art from marauding social science types prospecting for new material, who couldn't tell a bad poem from a great one.

arts was to embody the universals of human experience. Anyone who
argued against this to say that the important thing is uniquely personal,
as we do today, would have been considered self-interested, if not perverse, and would certainly have been faced with the question: Why
should we be concerned in the least with idiosyncratic experiences
since they are yours alone? Accordingly, such classical teaching urged
and even developed rules for the *imitation* of the great masters of all the
arts and discouraged any deviation from these standards – that is, it
frowned on personal forms of imagination that failed to capture things
universal and general. The great works of classical Greek and Roman
drama, the plays of Shakespeare, and so much else of value in the Western canon (as it used to be known) were, and were expected to be, ancient stories retold. The people often knew the stories already. What
excited them was how well, and with what contemporary flourish, they
were told anew. Examples of this literary ethic – for it was like an artistic
and ethical imperative to reproduce the greatness of humanity in general – can readily be found in works such as Alexander Pope's poem *Essay on Man*, in anything by Samuel Johnson (who famously argued that
we should not be interested in the streaks of the tulip), and in the gen-
eralizing works of a large variety of other British and European writers
of this epoch.

But by the end of the eighteenth century, and for reasons too numerous to describe here, this classical imperative began to weaken because
it became formulaic and rule-bound, and thus stifling and dull, and
increasingly suppressive of original artistic spirits. So it fell away rather
suddenly and was replaced for a time by an energetic embrace of
the alternative – that is, by a particularist (rather than generalist) ambition that was later called "Romantic." This new, contrary ambition was
emerging around the 1750s and lasted until about 1830 (and it was reviewed in its German form in an earlier chapter). This was a reactionary movement striking out against classicism and striving for expression
of things deeply personal and intensely emotional and particular in all
high art. In England the poetry of Wordsworth, Shelley, and especially I
would say John Keats embodied this sense of the personal embodied in
the particular. It is true that Romantic poets – I am thinking of Keats
again, especially of his lovely *Ode to a Nightingale* – were also seeking the
universal in their own way. But for them, the universal was to be found
and felt not in any general experience or abstract aesthetic and rule-
bound ideal, or standard, or formula, but in very personal and emotional (and often spiritual) experiences. The hauntingly pure sound of

the distant and invisible nightingale in Keats's beautiful poem is clearly *his* experience alone – he is utterly alone at that moment – but he is quite certain it is a deeply passionate moment anyone in the same circumstances could experience.

I describe all this only to say that the shift in Western civilization from the long classical period to the Romantic revolution against all things general and standardized may be thought of as the most important watershed in the aesthetic and moral experience of Western civilization. In a sense, most movements since that time have been repetitions, or to and fro variations, of these two alternatives, which emerge because human beings have always had an underlying yearning for things universal and general, but at the same time they value deeply the uniqueness of personal experience. So it seems that whenever we grow tired of being controlled by general rules or standards, the reaction often takes the form of a repudiation through a passionate embrace of things emotional and particular.

The entire 1960s postwar, or "hippie," reaction began this way as a kind of "new romanticism." Among other things, it was a deep-seated reaction against the failed integrity and public moral standards of the immediately preceding war generation. From the viewpoint of youth, Western civilization considered as an example of moral integrity had blown itself up with the atom bomb. In a matter of a decade or so, this reaction found its most extreme expression in the now-waning "postmodernist" movement, discussed in earlier chapters of this book. Po-Mo was a repudiation not only of all standards, foundations, and concepts of the general and universal but even of the very *idea* of such things.

But we are tired of that now. For life without some foundation in reason and morality is in the end unbearable. So once again we sense in the air a rebirth of the human desire to locate and discover universals of all kinds. This recurring hunger for universals seems to be itself a universal! As it happened, in the same late-1960s period, one of the most prominent and fascinating efforts to elevate literary standards to the universal level was attempted by the late Canadian scholar Northrop Frye in his *Anatomy of Criticism*. This engaging book quickly became standard reading for PhD candidates, who were generally impressed by such a bold attempt to gather all of Western literature under a single, if esoteric, universal scheme involving seasonal cycles (spring for romance, fall for tragedy, etc.), universal character types – especially the changing type of the hero – and universal literary genres. But Frye was unfortunately before his time. His intriguing and sophisticated effort was soon displaced –

perhaps smothered is a better word – by the abrupt advent of the post-modern era of roughly 1970 to 2000, during which the argument that all forms of universalism are intellectually oppressive held its own oppressive sway.

My point is that there is a continuous tension present between the human yearning for things general and the opposed yearning for things particular. What starts the pendulum swinging from one pole to the other is the impetus it receives from the rejection of authority and impersonality during its generalist phase or alternately from the rejection of idiosyncratic self-indulgence in the particularist phase. As it happens, curious Western intellectuals are just now looking for a way out of the quagmire of critical gobbledygook produced by the postmodern generation and once again hunting for things general and universal. So there is new activity.

In addition to the many articles and books presently emerging on the topic of literary universals, for example, a website has been mounted by the Faculty of Letters at the University of Palermo entitled the Literary Universals Project – and contributions are presently being solicited.[3] The driving force at this point seems to be Professor Patrick Colm Hogan of the University of Connecticut, and I will now give just a taste of his work, extracted from his brief article "Literary Universals," published in *Poetics Today* in 1997.[4]

Hogan begins with an obligatory apology for his interests by observing that "today there is little enthusiasm among humanists for the study of universals" because the main focus continues to be on "difference" and on "cultural and historical specificity." When universalism is mentioned at all in humanistic writing, he goes on, "it is most often denounced as a tool of oppression" – some of its critics labelling even the notion of universalism "a hegemonic European critical tool." But Hogan defends universalist studies by insisting that a distinction (borrowed from a colleague) be made between "hegemonic" and "empathic" universals. The former implies the imposition of one set of merely local beliefs on all others (thus such beliefs are not truly universals), while the latter "is based on the assumption that all people share ethical and experiential subjectivity." His own interest is to establish a program "that succeeds in uncovering genuinely universal principles of human thought and human society." This, he feels, is interesting for its own sake, but in establishing a common underlying humanity, it also happens to be the best way to resist oppressive moral and political regimes.

This out of the way, Hogan sets out his objectives, which are rather like Chomsky's objectives in language studies. He wants to develop "The structure of a theory of universals," and he begins by defining what he means by these terms. He mentions that distinctions must be made between *absolute* literary universals (found in all traditions), *statistical* universals (which occur with a frequency greater than chance in genetically and geographically unrelated cultures), *implicational* ones (where universal A is found, B will also be found, but not the reverse), and so on. Then he gets into it, as they say, with a discussion of literary art and technique.

First, we learn the obvious: all societies, whether small nomadic tribes or highly organized urban societies, have verbal arts. This may seem a banal statement, he continues, but it is not, for "there is no logical necessity in the production of verbal art, and in our own society very few people actually produce it." Why, then, should we expect it to appear in every society? The fact that it does underlines the general truth that human universals of any kind ought to surprise us, for it is only habit – we get used to them – that camouflages what ought to produce amazement.

With respect to the basic techniques of verbal arts, he explains that "the ones used in English literature appear to be universal," and he gives a partial list that includes such things as the use of *symbolism, imagery, assonance, rhyme, alliteration, parallelism, foreshadowing, plot circularity,* and other "possibly universal organizational devices." Continuing, we read that the three major genres of European literature – poetry, prose fiction, and drama – appear to be universal categories. Such genres are relied upon to convey universal stories about human conflicts usually centred on love, politics, or money and status and usually expressed in common forms of comedy and tragedy. There are entire literary trees to be constructed giving the equally common variations of such themes, conflicts, and "prototypical" stories (about lovers, lovers and parents, lovers and society, broken love relations, reunited lovers, heroes and heroines, the hero's confidantes, companions, and so on).

There are also interesting relations between universal story types and numerous universal symbols, forms of seasonal imagery (such as birds and springtime or winter and death), and so on. There is enough of this research into universals going on that at some future time there will be the question of discovering a possible hierarchy of literary laws, universals, and relations between them. Hogan is alluding here to what linguists used to call the "deep-structure" relations of the field. In this sense, we could say that someday we may have a grip on the way literary universals in themselves form a kind of language, or metalanguage, or grammar, giving deeper insight into human nature.

Finally, when it comes to the universality of myth, we may begin by stating the obvious: that almost the whole of Jungian psychoanalysis and much of the Freudian type are devoted to the universality of archetypal myths in human conscious and so-called unconscious, or subconscious, life.* Freud's four-part mechanism of id, ego, superego, libido, for example, is presented as a universal structure of human consciousness, and Jung's "archetypes," or "primordial images," are assumed to haunt all subconscious life and remain the material for so-called depth psychology. Such images are considered the pictorial forms of the instincts by means of which the unconscious mind reveals itself to the conscious mind in dreams and fantasies. As Jungian interpreter Erich Neumann puts it in *The Origins of Human Consciousness*, these universal images or archetypes interact in a specific way with each other in a series of crucial and successive stages through which both the individual and humanity itself must evolve, the individual having "to pass through the same archetypal stages which determined the evolution of consciousness in the life of humanity."[5] Well, let us not quibble with such statements, for this is a massive topic, best pursued elsewhere. I mention it to show only that there has always been a great deal of interest in universally shared human archetypal or primordial imagery. Neumann's work takes the reader as clearly as can be imagined through the various universal stages of this development, linking archetype to universal myth and symbol as he goes along. This progression runs through a series of cycles, such as the "creation myth" (with its phases of birth, suffering, and emancipation) and "the hero myth" (in which the ego, consciousness, and the human world become conscious of themselves – here, we encounter universal images of light, the circle, the snake, and the like). When speaking of the mythic perfect state of being in which all opposites are contained, Neumann insists (concerning the important stages and symbols of human – and of humanity's – development) that "all these symbols with which men have sought to

---

* I say "so-called" because while it is no secret human beings think and do many things while being unaware of the origin of (or motive for) them, the term "unconscious" or "subconscious" is for this author far too particular and implies a God-in-the-Machine, which is to say, a kind of force or agent, or a not-me, that determines me. I prefer the term "preconscious," as it implies something of which I may be vaguely but not wholly aware but that is nevertheless part of me.

grasp the beginning in mythological terms are as alive today as they ever were; they have their place not only in art and religion, but in the living processes of the individual psyche, in dreams and in fantasies."[6] His entire book draws from a universal inventory of myth, symbol, and archetype to explain how such things are true for all humankind.

Other works that give useful insight into the universality of human symbols as found in myth and literature (and that are too much relied upon by students eager to impress teachers with the breadth of their learning but too lazy to read original material) are such as Hans Beidermann's *Dictionary of Symbolism*. A quiet hour spent here will soon draw readers into a kind of imaginative underworld where the author discusses "the universality of many of these images and their meanings,"[7] connecting the universal realities of human psychological and mythic experience.

I close this postscript by encouraging interested readers to consult a few more of the classic works, such as James G. Frazer's *The Golden Bough*,[8] an examination of myth worldwide, and Joseph Campbell's *The Hero with a Thousand Faces*,[9] in which he argues that the universal role of the hero is always the same, although told differently in a thousand ways.[*]

Of great interest, too, is the work of the Romanian scholar Mircea Eliade, *The Myth of the Eternal Return*, and also his *Myth and Reality*. Finally, not to be overlooked is another classic in this field (the title tells all): Carl Jung's *Man and His Symbols*.[10]

By way of signing off, I am pleased to say that this book has given a lot of pleasure in the research and the writing, for although many of these topics had beckoned with hints of what might be found, much of the territory entered was previously unknown to me. The book has had a double objective: to expose the intellectual weakness of the relativism that pervades modern – especially postmodern – thought and also to

---

[*] Of interest is that such universal folktale and myth patterns may emerge even in unrelated fields of thought that are shaped by them. For example, in her 1991 study *Narratives of Human Evolution*, Misia Landau of Yale University maintained that the arguments of many classic texts of paleo-anthropology were determined as much by traditional narrative frameworks as by material evidence. In other words, even in "scientific" fields, which attempt rigorously to explain the evidence for human evolution, "the typical framework was that of a folktale in which a hero [such as our ape ancestors] leaves a relatively safe haven in the trees, sets out on a dangerous journey, acquires various gifts, survives a series of tests, and is finally transformed into a true human being."[10]

offer a basic overview of the absolutes, constants, and universals that
constitute the substance of the many fields explored here. We have
seen them at work in culture through human universals, in physics via
the constants of nature, in moral and legal thought via the natural law,
and in the human body via our hardwired biology. And not least, of
course, in view of its close approximation to human thought itself, we
have looked at the constants and universals of human language.

If there has been one overriding objective of this book from first
page to last, it is to satisfy the reader that whether speaking of things
physical, moral, legal, cultural, biological, or linguistic, we do not live
in a foundationless or relativistic world in which reality and meaning,
or what is true and false, are simply made up as we go along and according to personal perceptions. On the contrary, we live in a world in
which every serious field of human thought and activity is permeated
by fundamentals of one kind or another, by absolutes, constants, and
universals, as the case may be, of nature and of human nature.

Some Universals and Constants
of Nature and Human Nature

These are by no means complete lists. Support for all these items may be found here or in references cited in the relevant chapters of this book.

HUMAN UNIVERSALS

This is a small selection from a list of 311 human universals compiled by Donald E. Brown, author of *Human Universals* (1991) and a professor of anthropology (now retired) at the University of California at Santa Barbara.[1] They describe the behaviours, traits, concepts, and tendencies commonly expressed or practised by human beings in every culture on earth. Interested parties may find a great deal more about human universals at Yale University's website, www.yale.edu/hraf, where hundreds of studies on human universals are catalogued.

Table A.1

actions under self-control distinguished from those not under control
aesthetic standards
affection expressed and felt
age statuses
anthropomorphization
antonyms

belief in supernatural/religion
beliefs about death
beliefs about fortune and misfortune
binary cognitive distinctions
biological mother and social mother normally the same person
body adornment

childbirth customs

choice making (choosing alternatives)
classification of behavioural propensities
classification of inner states
classification of kin
classification of sex
classification of space
coalitions
collective identities
conflict, mediation of
conjectural reasoning
continua (ordering as cognitive pattern)
cooperative labour
copulation normally conducted in privacy
corporate (perpetual) statuses
coyness display
culture/nature distinction

Table A.1 (*continued*)

dance
death rituals
distinguishing right and wrong
division of labour
dream interpretation

economic inequalities, consciousness of
envy, symbolic means of coping with
ethnocentrism
etiquette

facial expressions, masking/modifying of
family (or household)
father and mother, separate kin terms for
females do more direct childcare
figurative speech
folklore
future, attempts to predict

generosity admired
government
grammar
group living
groups that are not based on family

inheritance rules

kin terms translatable by basic relations of
  procreation

language is translatable
language not a simple reflection of reality
law (rights and obligations)
leaders
linguistic redundancy
logical notions
logical notion of general/particular

male and female and adult and child seen
  as having different natures
males dominate public/political realm
males more aggressive
males more prone to lethal violence
marriage
materialism
murder proscribed
music

narrative
normal distinguished from abnormal states

Oedipus complex
oligarchy (de facto)

phonemic system
planning
play
poetry/rhetoric
preference for own children and close kin
  (nepotism)
prestige inequalities
private inner life
promise
property

rape proscribed
reciprocity, positive
redress of wrongs
rites of passage

sanctions for crimes against the collectivity
sanctions include removal from the social unit
self as neither wholly passive nor wholly
  autonomous
self distinguished from other
self is responsible
sex (gender) terminology is fundamentally
  binary
sexual modesty
sexual regulation
sexual regulation includes incest prevention
socialization
symbolism

territoriality
time
trade

units of time

worldview

PHYSICS:
THE FUNDAMENTAL CONSTANTS OF NATURE

Table A.2

Name	Symbol	Numerical Value (SI units)
Charge on proton	e	1.60×10^{-19}
Planck's Constant	h	6.63×10^{-34}
Speed of light	c	3.00×10^{8}
Newton's gravitational constant	G	6.67×10^{-11}
Rest mass of proton	m_p	1.67×10^{-27}
Rest mass of electron	m_e	9.11×10^{-31}
Weak force constant	g_w	1.43×10^{-62}
Strong force constant	g_s	15
Hubble Constant	H	2×10^{-18}
Cosmological constant	Lambda	$< 10^{-53}$
Cosmic photon/proton ratio	S	10^{9}
Permittivity of free space	E	8.85×10^{-12}
Boltzmann Constant	K	1.38×10^{-23}
Planck Length	l_P	1.62×10^{-35}
Planck Time	t_P	5.39×10^{-44}
Planck Mass	m_P	2.18×10^{-8}
Proton Compton Wavelength	l_p	1.32×10^{-15}
Proton (nuclear) Compton Time	t_N	4.41×10^{-24}
Hubble Time	t_H	5.00×10^{17}
Hubble Radius	r_H	1.5×10^{26}
Bohr Radius	a_o	5.29×10^{-11}
Radiation constant	a	7.56×10^{-16}
Electromagnetic fine-structure constant	Alpha	7.30×10^{-3}
Weak fine-structure constant	$Alpha_w$	3.05×10^{-12}
Gravitational fine-structure constant	$Alpha_G$	5.90×10^{-39}

Source: Paul Davies, *The Accidental Universe* (Cambridge, UK: Cambridge University Press, 1982), table 3, 39. Although the essential formulations of physics are supplied for the specialist, this book is a wonder of clarity for the nonspecialist.

Davies's note to this table reads: "The fundamental constants of nature listed here largely determine the essential features of most known physical structures. Many of these features are remarkably sensitive to the values of the constants, and to certain apparently numerical relations between them."

Readers will find many more physical constants at the website for the US National Institute of Standards and Technology (NIST), where internationally recommended values are listed for hundreds of fundamental physical constants: http://www.physics.nist.gov/cuu/Constants/index.html.

Here is a small sample of what is to be found there, and this runs only through the letter "B"!

alpha particle mass
alpha particle mass energy equivalent
alpha particle mass energy equivalent in MeV
alpha particle mass in u
alpha particle molar mass
alpha particle-electron mass ratio
alpha particle-proton mass ratio
Angstrom star
atomic mass constant
atomic mass constant energy equivalent
atomic mass constant energy equivalent in MeV
atomic mass unit-electron volt relationship
atomic mass unit-hartree relationship
atomic mass unit-hertz relationship
atomic mass unit-inverse meter relationship
atomic mass unit-joule relationship
atomic mass unit-kelvin relationship
atomic mass unit-kilogram relationship
atomic unit of 1st hyperpolarizablity
atomic unit of 2nd hyperpolarizablity
atomic unit of action
atomic unit of charge
atomic unit of charge density
atomic unit of current
atomic unit of electric dipole moment
atomic unit of electric field
atomic unit of electric field gradient
atomic unit of electric polarizablity
atomic unit of electric potential
atomic unit of electric quadrupole moment
atomic unit of energy
atomic unit of force
atomic unit of length
atomic unit of magnetic dipole moment
atomic unit of magnetic flux density
atomic unit of magnetizability
atomic unit of mass
atomic unit of momentum
atomic unit of permittivity
atomic unit of time

atomic unit of velocity
Avogadro constant
Bohr magneton
Bohr magneton in eV/T
Bohr magneton in Hz/T
Bohr magneton in inverse meters per tesla
Bohr magneton in K/T
Bohr radius
Boltzmann constant
Boltzmann constant in eV/K
Boltzmann constant in Hz/K
Boltzmann constant in inverse meters per kelvin

BIOLOGICAL UNIVERSALS AND CONSTANTS

Also included here are some biologically dependent universal behaviours and traits.

Constants of Organic Life

Below are some biological "laws," which are easy to dispute in some of their details because they operate to describe general universal trends in biology. Nonetheless, they are remarkably constant. Such laws are considered "ceteris paribus" laws because, "everything else being equal," they are reliable predictors. I present them in plain language, not as formal statements:

• Von Baer's Law: says that characteristics of larger groups of species are likely to be more ancestral, and are likely to appear earlier in embryos, than characteristics common only to subgroups of that group.
• Wallace's Law: says that every species has come into existence coincident in time and space with a pre-existing closely allied species.
• Marsh's Law: says that mammals (warm-blooded animals) increase relative brain size within a lineage over geologic time.
• Cope's Law: says that size increases in a lineage over geologic time.
• Dollo's Law: says that evolutionary change in tetrapod lineages is generally irreversible. In other words, the dinosaurs are gone forever. There do not seem to be any good examples of species-reversal.
• Hardy-Weinberg Law: this is a statistical law relating gene frequency to genotype frequency. It predicts how gene frequency will be transmitted from generation to generation given a specific set of assumptions.
• Wilson's Law: says the number of body parts decreases over geologic time within a lineage. For example, the number of bones in the forelimb decreases over time within the theropod class.

- Fisher's Theorem: says the rate of evolution – improvement in adaptation – is proportional to the amount of genetic variability.
- Williston's Law: says earlier members of a lineage will tend to have many appendages that are more or less alike, whereas later members will tend to have fewer appendages but of more different kinds.
- Universal Scaling Laws of Biology: Working with biologists James Brown of the University of New Mexico and Brian Enquist of the Santa Fe Institute, Los Alamos researcher Geoffrey West has developed some theoretical principles that form the basis for a set of universal scaling laws of biology.[2]

Some Specific Universal Biological Constants, or Standards,
Applying to All Organic Life

These are drawn from a paper by Professor Stephen Freeland, University of Maryland, entitled "Evaluating Biological Constants and Standards at the Root of Life." He writes that "although in a few cases these universal constants have subsequently weakened into standards ... they form the platform upon which all subsequent evolution has built and their significance to biocentric chemistry is as fundamental as physical constants are to evaluating the biocentric universe."[3]

- All organisms have come to use lipid membranes.
- All organisms have come to use nucleic acid, which carries information in the form of a linear sequence of chemical letters.
- All organisms have come to use an alphabet of exactly four such chemical letters to spell out their genetic messages.
- All organisms have come to use DNA for genetic information storage and proteins for metabolically active molecules.
- All organisms have come to construct proteins from an alphabet of twenty amino acids.
- In order to transform genes into living organisms, all organisms have come to use an identical genetic code (the system of rules by which "letters" of every nucleic acid gene are translated into corresponding "letters" of a protein).

Some Distinctive Biological Features Humans Share
with Other Mammals and Primates[4]

- Shared with other mammals: warm-bloodedness, body hair, lungs, four limbs, an elaborate brain, ability to learn and communicate, female mammary-gland milk production.

- Shared only with primates, in varying degrees: upright posture, flexible arms and hands, separated fingers and opposable thumbs, prolonged immaturity of offspring, greater reliance on stereoscopic vision than on smell, a high order of intelligence.
- E.O. Wilson, in *On Human Nature*,[5] adds that humans also share with most other primates the fact that intimate social groupings number in general from 10 to 100 adults, never just two as in some species, or thousands, as with fish and insects. Also, social play is a strongly developed activity featuring role practice, mock aggression, sex practice, and exploration.
- John Alcock, in *The Triumph of Sociobiology*, adds another human-chimp trait: "Humans and chimps are ... the only species among the 4,000 species of mammals in which male relatives form groups to raid other groups while living in and defending the area of their birth."[6]
- John Allman, in *Evolving Brains*,[7] writes that the *ventral premotor area* is a cortical site of the brain having to do with visual-motor coordination that is present only in primates.

Some Physiological, Biological, and Biochemical Universals of Human Beings

- All humans have a species-specific at-rest normal body-temperature range between 36 and 37 degrees Celsius (around 98.6°F), which may fluctuate with sickness, stress, or exercise. Convulsions leading to death will occur at about 106°F. (Horses have a body temperature of 100.4°F, the whale 95.9°F, the sheep and rabbit 102.2°F, the goat 103.1°F).
- Humans also have a species-specific respiration rate and heart rate and alone are nearly hairless (the so-called "naked ape") among the anthropoids. No one knows why.
- Humans have from two to five million sweat glands, far more than any other primate species.

Some Human Physiological and Biochemical Reference Ranges

- blood pH (a measure of the ratio of acidity to alkalinity): 7.35 to 7.45; if the human body falls below a pH of 6.8 (acidosis) or above a pH of 8.0 (alkalosis), death follows in a few seconds
- glucose (nonfasting blood sugar): 60-120 mg/dL*
- sodium (salt level): 137-147 mmol/L

---

* mg = milligram; L = litre; dL = decilitre; mmol = millimole

- oxygen (in arterial blood): 15-23%
- creatinine: male, 0.6-1.3 mg/dL; female, 0.5-1.1 mg/dL
- potassium: 3.4-5.3 mmol/dL
- calcium: 8.7-10.7 mg/dL
- total cholesterol: healthy is less than 200 mg/dL

These are just a few of *several hundred standard and universal clinical reference ranges* for human biochemistry and physiology verifiable by any good biomedical laboratory. Others refer to universal standards for such physiological factors as albumin, ammonia, bilirubin, copper, free fatty acid, immunoglobulin, lactate, lead, lithium, magnesium, potassium, testosterone, total protein, uric acid, leukocytes, and on and on. There are minor laboratory differences according to type of instrumentation, calibration, and so on, but *these ranges are remarkably stable over all healthy human populations.*

Some Distinctive Human Biological Universals

- A species-specific heritage: humans have a species-specific genetic heritage, unlike that of any other species.
- A complex consciousness: all human beings have a brain-mind consciousness, self-awareness, knowledge of death, confrontation with the meaning of life, and so on, which manifests at a level of depth and complexity not approached by any other life form.
- A mind-body dualism: humans are the only life form to experience a mind-body dualism that produces a brain-mind "freedom" of action in the context of its own biological constraints, to the extent that humans can even rebel against their own biology (as they do in using contraception).
- Symbolic calculation: all normal humans have a brain-mind ability to reason and calculate with symbols at a level of difficulty and abstraction not remotely approached by any other life form. As a result, humans alone are able to learn about and solve immensely complicated matters solely by insight, foresight, and imagination.
- Language and metalanguage: all humans have a brain-mind language and symbolic ability not approached by any other life form. Human communication even without sound by way of paralinguistic signals is the richest known. Other species can communicate in very sophisticated and intricate ways beyond human abilities (sight, hearing, sonar, navigation, etc.). And other animals can use rudimentary signs. But only humans possess the powers of rule-based syntactic language constructions and a profound symbol-using capacity of infinite scope. Perhaps most distinctive of all, humans have a brain-mind

capacity to form and use metalanguages. A grammar, for example, is a language about language, or a metalanguage.

- Capacity for mathematical abstraction: humans alone have the brain-mind capacity for mathematical and physical abstract conceptions and can describe all physical phenomena in the universe in mathematical terms.
- All-pervasive cultural systems: alone among the species, humans have the capacity to create all-pervasive cultures in the form of created and shared symbols and traditions that are learned and passed from generation to generation. Other creatures can be prompted to learn symbols, and even have some "traditions," but none have ever invented true symbols, or systems of symbols, or true transgenerational inherited cultures on their own.
- Brain to body-mass ratio and brain size: humans have the largest brains relative to their body size among living creatures. The growth of the brain and human intelligence are so great – about a tablespoon of brain matter every thousand years – that no scale has been invented that can objectively compare man with chimpanzees and other living primates. No biological organ in the history of life on earth has grown faster.
- Human mind and human nature: "The human mind is not a tabula rasa, a clean slate on which experience draws intricate pictures with lines and dots. It is more accurately described as an autonomous decision-making instrument ... but the rules followed are tight enough to produce a broad overlap in the decisions taken by all individuals and hence a convergence powerful enough to be labelled human nature."[8]
- Distinctive human sense traits: humans have a biologically distinctive hearing, seeing, taste, and tactile sensitivity range that is like a biological fingerprint different from that of other animals. It is also sex-differentiated.
- Human sexual dimorphism: there is a distinctive human sexual dimorphism. Human males are on average about 7% taller than women in all races and about 23% heavier. Women on average have lighter skeletons, a higher body-fat percentage, lower lung and oxygen uptake capacity, wider pelvis/hip area, and a different hormone-based aggression profile than males.
- Human infant dependency: alone among the species, human babies everywhere are unable to feed themselves when weaned, and human children have by far the longest infant dependency.
- Female lifespan beyond fertility: alone among the species, human females live for decades after their fertile reproductive years have ended. Evolutionists explain this as an adaptation to protect the human newborn during its extended dependency.

- Ratio of female to male births: more male humans than female are born every year – about 105 to 100 – but more male than female children are sick in their first year and die in their first years.
- Female lifespan: female humans everywhere outlive males. Evolutionists explain this as an adaptation of the caretaker parent, a phenomenon that holds true for all species.
- Concealment of ovulation: unlike all other mammals, human females conceal, rather than advertise, ovulation.
- Privacy for sex: unlike other mammals, humans universally seek privacy for sexual activity.

Some Human Behavioural Universals Attributed to Natural Selection

- Contracts and reciprocal altruism: unlike other species, humans engage in long-remembered contracts and acts of reciprocal altruism that may be spaced over generations. (Reciprocal altruism is adaptive because it reinforces social bonding and hence mutual protection and survival. It is a selfish altruism, as all altruism may be from an evolutionary perspective.)
- Complex kinship ties: humans are preoccupied with kinship ties to a degree inconceivable even in other extremely social species, such as the bees, ants, apes, and so on (for the same adaptive reason as above).
- Humans anatomically unique: their erect posture and wholly bipedal locomotion are not even approached in other primates that occasionally walk on their hind legs. (Lots of reasons have been given for why bipedalism, as it is called, is adaptive, especially the freeing of the hands and fingers for finer work and tool making.)
- Year-round sexual activity: human beings have a year-round sexual activity not specifically linked to estrus (the female being periodically "in heat") as for other mammals. But neither is human sexual activity linked solely to procreation as in other mammals. Wilson stresses that man is not like other animals in this way, so to make a religious protest that human sex ought not to be separated from procreation is to wish we were more animal-like.
- Male domination: there is universal male dominance. In no human society have women ever dominated the political and economic life.
- Barter and money: as a result of a unique sharing capacity, only human beings have formed true barter economies, the latter made possible by another human universal – the symbolic capacity (money, market values, etc).
- Biology of the incest taboo: all human societies have an incest taboo, likely for the reason that inbreeding results in children who are abnormal and may also carry a deadly genetic risk. So advantageous is outbreeding that it

spread throughout human populations long ago and simply carried cultural evolution along with it.

- Hypergamy: this is the universal female practice of marrying men of equal or superior wealth and status. Large and healthy high-status vertebrates mate and reproduce at a higher frequency than smaller unhealthy members.

- Some universal human sexual traits: men universally prefer virgins for wives and wives younger than themselves, and they are more powerfully attracted to females who exhibit a universal range of physical features that indicate fertility. Evolutionary psychologists argue that there exist hormone-based (and therefore genetically based) biological cues of youthfulness that men find powerfully and universally attractive, such as: small chin, large eyes, full lips, small nose, a more hour-glass hip-to-waist ratio, smooth unblemished skin, large and symmetrical breasts, and a body-mass index of 20–24 kilograms per metre of height.

- The friend-enemy distinction: The friend-enemy distinction is universal. "We seem to be fully comfortable only when the remainder of humanity can be labelled as members versus non-members, kin versus non-kin, friend versus foe."[9] Humans everywhere practice "pseudo-speciation" – the tendency to define outsiders as less than human, who can then be degraded without conscience. In human history, genocides large and small have occurred on every continent, except Antarctica (where there are no people!). For the performance of such genocides, human beings are universally adept not only at invoking the friend-enemy distinction but also at acting upon it in the cause of human liquidations in good conscience.

- Human aggression is species-specific: "The human forms of aggression are species-specific ... they contain features that distinguish them from aggression in all other species ... Human beings are strongly predisposed to respond with unreasoning hatred to external threats and to escalate their hostility sufficiently to overwhelm the source of the threat by a respectably wide margin of safety."[10]

- Male-female sex differences: The male "investment" in reproduction is infinitesimal compared to that of the female (a single human egg is 85,000 times larger than the sperm that fertilizes it, itself one of millions). Hence it pays males to be aggressive, hasty, fickle, and undiscriminating, and females to be coy and to hold back until they can identify the males with the best genes/prospects in life.

- The family is universal: there is near-universality of the pair bond and the prevalence of extended families with men and their wives forming the nucleus.

- Religion and self-sacrifice: religions are universal and unique to the human species, even when secular, as with political religions or with so-called

secular humanism. Religious practice is the ultimate case in defence of reciprocal altruism, of surrendering self to a powerful and benevolent force,
whereby individuals will often gladly give their lives for the believer group
and its god(s).

- Human males unique in provisioning females: the human species apparently departed from the usual mammalian feeding mode (females provisioning for their own young) about 2 million years ago when males started
provisioning for their young. Humans are the only mammalian species
where males do this, and it is a universal of human behaviour.

Some Universals of Human Psychological Life and Behaviour

Below is a summary of some findings by evolutionary psychologists, all
of which rest on assumptions about, and get their predictive power
from, the theory of Darwinian evolutionary adaptation. Some of them
seem rather self-evident. But that is because they are part of us now.[11]

- Altruism toward kin: people universally favour kin over strangers, which increases "inclusive fitness" by reproducing our genes, or fractions of them,
through marriage, blood relatives, and so on.
- Prestige seeking and imitating high-prestige individuals: essential for material success and for identifying the most useful skills, values, and beliefs.
- Preference for present risk to avoid future loss: helps to preserve material
resources in uncertain circumstances and environments.
- Preference for foods rich in sugars and fats: increased caloric intake at levels
beyond daily minimums required for good health is an example of a Pleistocene adaptive trait that is maladaptive for modern times. (Consuming and
burning high levels of fat and sugar for warmth and hunting was once adaptive, but today it leads to high cholesterol, obesity, and other lifestyle diseases.)
- Preference for salty flavours: to maintain sufficient sodium chloride in the
body – perhaps an example of an unconscious adaptation related to exer-
tion and primal fears of sodium imbalance.
- Fear of snakes: obviously, to avoid poisons and death. City dwellers who may
never have seen a snake persist in naming snakes as one of their automatic
fears. This fear reaction is automatic in most humans and in many animals.
Horses who have never seen a snake will recoil in panic at the sudden sight
of a tangled garden hose – until they realize it is not a snake. Calming them
afterward takes a long time.
- Landscape preferences: universally, people prefer savannah-like environments. Open spaces with trees and shelter, water, hills, or view of same. In

the Pleistocene period these environments provided food, survival, and protection from enemies. Real estate agents sense this preference in clients.

- Females choose good-provider mates: to provision for their children – hence the universal tendency for women to marry men older than themselves and to favour successful providers over weak providers.
- Males choose mates for youthfulness, attractiveness, and favourable hip-to-waist ratio: men universally, if unconsciously, choose potentially high-fertility mates. Women without the above traits have fewer children.
- Superior female spatial-location memory: said to have evolved as an adaptation for successful foraging/gathering (tests show women easily outscore men on this variable for remembering where things are – if not where they are themselves!).
- Male sexual jealousy: an evolved adaptation to better ensure paternity certainty. Such jealousy is often felt to be "irrational" even by the jealous person but nevertheless something he "cannot help feeling."
- Natural language: communication and manipulation through the language instinct.
- Keen detection of cheaters: prevents exploitation in social contracts. Devices such as the Wason test illustrate dramatically that humans who cannot solve even simple logical problems very well can suddenly do so with a very high success rate if the problems are re-presented as schemes for cheating them.
- Male desire for sexual variety: said to increase the likelihood of more sexual partners. This follows from "parental investment" theory. Males make a low-cost investment in the effort to replicate their genes. But pregnancy is a very high-cost event for the mother. So on average women evolved with the opposite trait: they are very choosy about who is going to complicate their lives with children and saddle them with a lifetime of caring.

Sex, Brain Sex, and the Politics of Sex

All sex-difference researchers seem to agree there are a certain number of genuine biologically based sex differences, the cause of which is due either to hormonal differences, to brain mechanisms, to actual brain structure or function, or to some combination of these. But as yet there is no consensus as to how many differences there are. As background commentary on what follows, consider the attitude of Professor Doreen Kimura, a well-known and highly respected Canadian sex and cognition researcher, who attempts to put the many facts and findings in perspective by writing that "some people" are worried that knowledge of sex differences in abilities will put women at a disadvantage because "it is true that the largest established differences we know about favour men."[12] She says radical feminists are prone to the view that the knowledge of sex differences should be suppressed. That is putting it mildly. But as everywhere else in her excellent work, Kimura is gentle and careful to avoid political criticism, and overall her interest in the value of scientific truth shines through.

General Human Sex Differences

The following selection of findings on human sex differences (related to brain and hormonal causes) is presented in my own words, paraphrased from studies, or quoted from the works of a number of authors. Once again, in a book that is an attack on relativism and a defence of absolutes and universals, these findings are most arresting.

- Hormones rule: the release of gender-specific hormones begins to influence human personality and behaviour even before birth. All babies begin development as females, but the male testes produce testosterone, which is the telltale hormone that fundamentally alters a baby's physical development, including the brain, as it redirects development as a male.[13] The same hormone at puberty produces a different biological "set" for boys and girls. Brains are affected respectively. Obviously, there is some overlap. For example, some girls are "tomboys," and some boys are "sissies." But in each case studies show a hormonal and behavioural correlative.[14]
- Brain patterns: "Human cognitive patterns and their related brain organization are apparently permanently influenced by physiological events that take place by the fourth fetal month."[15]
- Male and female differences in the womb: a great number of studies show that male and female babies behave differently in the womb (movement, heart rates, etc.) and moments after birth (give attention to different objects, sounds, and tactile sensations).
- Girls' sensitive to baby's cry: baby girls – but not baby boys – distinguish a baby's cry from other general sounds.
- Boys prefer objects: although baby boys get more affection and physical contact from their mothers than girls, they nevertheless prefer objects to people.
- Gendered senses: girls are more sensitive to sounds, smells, tastes, touch, voice, and musical nuances than boys. A girl's sense of smell is anywhere from 200 to 1,000 times better than a boy's; touch is twice as sensitive; and hearing two to four times better than a boy's. Women can detect much lower concentrations of sweet, sour, bitter, and salty tastes and have different preferences from men. The eyes of baby girls are more sensitive to the long

light-wave spectrum than the eyes of boys. Girls give highest ratings to foods at a sucrose level of 10%, while boys do so when the level reaches 20%. Men tolerate seven or eight more decibels of sound (twice as loud) at every frequency than do women.[16]

- Girls and language: girls develop language, fluency, and verbal memory earlier than boys and process such information faster (as confirmed by all researchers).

- Play differences: girls are less rule-bound, boys more so. Boys need rules to tell whether they are winning. Their preadolescent play is usually rank-related (as per most researchers). I would go further and say that the lifelong work, as well as play, of males is rank-related. This is especially visible in materialist societies – hence quips like: "the man who wins in life is the one who dies with the most toys."

- Aggression: from birth, boys are more aggressive, competitive, and self-assertive than girls (perhaps the most common finding, worldwide, even by feminist researchers like Eleanor Maccoby and Carol Jacklin).[17] When one-year-old babies are separated from their mothers and their toys by a fence-like barrier, the girls tend to stay in the middle and cry for help, while the boys tend to cluster at the ends of the barrier, apparently trying to find a way out.[18]

- Boys' and girls' brains differ: the physical brains of boys and girls are different, and this shows mostly from puberty. Females have more connections (commissures) between the left and right hemispheres than males and hence more intrahemispherical sharing of information and sensation. The splenium, a subregion of the corpus callosum, is significantly larger in women than in men and more bulbous in shape.[19] Highly sophisticated atomic brain imaging at Yale University's School of Medicine has shown that cognitive tasks presented to both sexes tend to be localized in the inferior frontal gyrus of both hemispheres of the female brain but in the same area of only one dominant hemisphere of the male brain.[20]

- Brain metabolism: at the University of Pennsylvania's School of Medicine, a combination of PET scans and high resolution MRI technology used to study brain metabolism has shown that even at rest, doing nothing in particular, there were male-female differences in brain metabolism in seventeen different brain areas.[21]

- Males and violence: at puberty men are more prone to physical violence (most crime is male, between the ages of 15 and 25), and women are more prone to emotional volatility. In the same period, men show more confidence, concentration, and ambition, whereas women show more social sensitivities and relationship interests. With age, men tend to become less aggressive (due to their steady estrogen level and falling testosterone) and women to become more aggressive (due to a steady testosterone level in relation to their falling estrogen). On the aggression difference: about 85% of all crimes are committed by males, and there are specific, universal sex differences in the styles, types of victim, and postcrime behaviours of male and female perpetrators of violent crimes.[22] From one-half to four-fifths of all female crime, hospital admissions, and suicide occurs just prior to or during menstruation.[23]

• Spatial skills: boys are better than girls on a variety of spatial skills, such as mentally rotating a drawing of an object (called "imaginal rotation"), including 3-D rotation. This skill is cross-cultural and "is practically universal" in males.[24] The spatial-skill sex difference becomes quite marked after puberty and is even observed in animals.[25] "In normal young men and women, spatial ability is systematically related to testosterone (T) levels."[26] T levels in men vary with season and time of day. They are higher in autumn than during any other season and also higher later in the day than earlier.

• Locating objects: women are superior to men at certain tasks requiring memory for the location of objects. This is seen dramatically during self-location in space: women tend to do poorly at map reading compared to men and tend to locate their position by memory of objects and landmarks ("turn left at the coffee shop"). Men, in contrast, tend to think in terms of compass directions ("turn north when you get to the corner"). Removing landmarks handicaps women, while changing the dimensions handicaps men.[27]

• Abstract reasoning: men tend to be better at tests of abstract mathematical reasoning and problem solving, whereas women tend to be better at tests of mathematical calculation. This difference increases with age. Although males and females tend to get the same math scores in school, men tend to outscore women consistently on math aptitude tests. Such sex differences in math ability appear to a greater or lesser degree in all countries and in all ethnic groups within countries.

• Verbal memory: adult women excel at memory for verbal material and also do very well (generally better than men) at tasks of verbal fluency and at "speed-calling" tests for rapid matching of visual items.

• Targeting: boys, from an early age, outdo girls by a wide margin on targeting tasks (throwing an object at a target accurately), and this difference is due not to experience or to differences in strength or size. Kimura states that it is "one of the largest, most reliable sex differences in ability that we know about" and that it is seen "across all human societies."[28] The evolutionist explanation for this innate ability difference is that over millennia it was naturally selected: good targeters, spear throwers, and the like got to eat and survive, while poor ones got eaten, died of starvation, or were killed first in war.

- Fine-motor skills: universally, girls tend to outperform boys at more detailed, fine-motor skills.
- Rough-and-tumble play: boys universally engage in a lot more rough-and-tumble play than girls in all societies where this has been studied. Prenatal exposure to hormones and the existence of the Y chromosome in males is the key factor. Such gender-specific behaviour has often been dramatically modified in boys and girls when mothers have had to undergo hormone treatment while pregnant.[29]
- Empathy: in all cultures women "emerge as more caring, religious, traditional and opposed to hedonism than men."[30]
- Sense differences: "Women appear to be more sensitive to external stimuli than men in all modalities except vision." As Kimura puts it, this means "they can detect lower [weaker] levels of stimulation in all areas except vision." They also surpass men in "perceptual speed," in which rapid identity comparisons must be made, and they tend to be "consistently better than men at reading facial and body expressions."[31] Men, in contrast, "have better daylight vision and depth perception, and faster reaction times."[32]
- Verbal recall: women are consistently better than men on "the recall of words or of material that can readily be mediated verbally." The difference between men and women in verbal memory may be stronger "when recall of a meaningful text or paragraph is required, and this sex difference emerges across cultures."[33]
- Sex hormone receptors: "Concentrations of sex hormone receptors are found in the hypothalamus, the hippocampus, and parts of the cerebral cortex. These areas are structurally different in males and females, and the structural differences are known to be determined by the action of sex hormones early in life."[34]
- Engineering sex differences: transplants of hypothalamic tissue (in animals) from male to female brains "cause recipient females to behave in male ways."[35]
- Brain size: "The biggest structural brain difference between men and women is size. Men's brains are larger and heavier than women's by 10 to 15 percent." When men and women of the same body size are compared, men's brains are about 100 grams heavier than women's. Danish investigators have found that men have about four billion more cortical neurons than women and that "there are many other structural features of the brain that appear sexually differentiated."[36]
- Intelligence differences: although overall intelligence differences between men and women are minimal, this is because testers arrange to cancel out

the obvious, repeated, and worldwide superiorities of each gender. That is, tests are arranged so that the higher verbal scores of women cancel the higher math and spatial scores of men. But the differences in each realm, after taking overlap into account, are consistent and universal. One indicator of this difference in verbal and spatial ability is that the best female chess players in the world rank around 2,000th among the best men and cannot gain entry to the men's world championship. Chess matches are normally sex-segregated for this reason. But world-championship scrabble matches and contests in games such as Mastermind are not sex-segregated because there is no detectable difference for those skills.[37]

• Defensive and offensive aggression: female aggression is mostly defensive (protective of oneself and one's family), whereas male aggression is mostly offensive (having to do with various competitions for dominance).[38] Unlike female crime, much male crime, especially among those aged 15 to 25, is gang-related, and this seems to stem from the powerful bonding force of a primitive insider-outsider distinction combined with territorial instinct. Both the gang aggression of the male and the defensive aggression of the female are predicted by standard neo-Darwinian theory, and both are universal.

UNIVERSAL ASPECTS OF HUMAN MORALITY AND NATURAL LAW[39]

1 Prohibition of murder or maiming without justification.
2 Prohibition of lying, at least in certain areas such as oaths, etc.
3 Right to own property such as land, clothing, tools, etc.
4 Economic justice: reciprocity and restitution.
5 Preference of common good over individual good.
6 Demand for co-operation within the group.
7 Sexual restriction within all societies:
   (a) Incest prohibition within nuclear family.
   (b) Prohibition of rape.
   (c) Some form of marriage demanded.
   (d) Prohibition of adultery (with only a few strictly limited legal exceptions).
   (e) Opposition to promiscuity in the sense of having a large number of partners.
   (f) Lifelong union of the spouses is the ideal.
   (g) Exogamy [marriage outside the family] as a further determination of the incest rule.

8 Disrespect for illegitimate children.
9 Reciprocal duties between children and parents: parents care for and train children – children respect, obey, and care for parents in old age.
10 Loyalty to one's social unit (family, tribe, country).
11 Provision for poor and unfortunate.
12 Prohibition of theft.
13 Prevention of violence within in-groups.
14 Obligation to keep promises.
15 Obedience to leaders.
16 Respect for the dead and disposal of human remains in some traditional and ritualistic fashion.
17 Desire for and priority of immaterial goods [such as knowledge, values, etc.].
18 Obligation to be a good mother.
19 Distributive justice.
20 Inner rather than internal sanctions considered better.
21 Courage is a virtue.
22 Justice is an obligation.

Universal Moral Grammar

Of great interest for the future, but not covered in this book, is the rapidly developing field of *universal moral grammar,* a new area of social science research seeking ways to apply a methodology such as that developed by Noam Chomsky in his research on the universal grammar of human languages to the field of human morality. Similar to universal grammar, the assumptions of a universal moral grammar are that all human beings have an innate, or hardwired, capacity to behave as "moral lawyers," so to speak, and can accurately and impressively weigh and evaluate the right and wrong of complex moral situations without prior training or education. An important recent book that has started the controversy certain to follow any view that morality is hardwired is Marc Hauser's *Moral Minds: How Nature Designed Our Universal Sense of Right and Wrong.*[40] In an e-mail interview with Hauser in July 2006 by the journal *American Scientist,* he explains:

I argue that we are endowed with a moral faculty that delivers judgments of right and wrong based on unconsciously operative and inaccessible principles of action. The theory posits a universal moral grammar, built into the brains of all humans. The grammar is a set of principles that operate on the basis of the causes and consequences of action. Thus, in the same way that we are endowed with a language faculty that consists of a universal toolkit for building possible languages, we are also endowed with a moral faculty that consists of a universal toolkit for building possible moral systems ... By grammar I simply mean a set of principles or computations for generating judgments of right and wrong. These principles are unconscious and inaccessible. What I mean by unconscious is different from the Freudian unconscious. It is not only that we make moral judgments intuitively, and without consciously reflecting upon the principles, but that even if we tried to uncover those principles we wouldn't be able to, as they are tucked away in the mind's library of knowledge. Access comes from deep, scholarly investigation.[41]

THE LAW OF NATIONS AND INTERNATIONAL LAW

1 Property right cannot be taken by compulsion without compensation, which is to be according to actual losses, and not according to expected profits [natural property rights]
2 There is no liability for unintentional injury, unless there is fault [intent or fault is essential]
3 There is no criminal liability if the perpetrator is not of sound mind (*mens rea*) [we cannot be blamed if there is no intent to harm possible]
4 Estoppel [a rule of law that precludes a person from denying certain facts because of that person's previous inconsistent conduct or statements]
5 There is no judicial aid to anyone who pleads his own wrong (which means anyone who seeks equity, must do equity) [natural justice and equity]
6 There is no aid for abuse of rights [wrongs not to be rewarded]
7 Fraud unravels everything [lying and deception are universally deemed wrong]
8 Profits gained without justification and at the expense of another must be restored [that is, justice must be restored]
9 All treaties and contracts must be performed (*pacta sunt servanda*) [agreements must be honoured]
10 There is freedom to change existing legal relationships by agreement [for example, contracts and changes in same require mutual consent]
11 In assessments of the legal effect of purported acts-in-the-law, the weak are to be protected against their weakness [not taken advantage of; that is, charity must prevail]
12 Disputes are not to be resolved without giving both [all] sides an opportunity to be heard [a plea for natural equity and justice]
13 No one is allowed to be a judge in his own cause [fairness is to be objectively determined by third parties]

The Law of Just War[42]

Jus ad bello

1 Competent authority: war may be declared only by a government, not by private parties.
2 Just cause: war may be waged only to protect innocent life, to ensure that people can live decently, and to secure natural rights.
3 Right intention: not only must there *be* just cause to go to war, but this just cause must also be the *reason* for going to war.
4 Comparative justice: we do not require that one side be *wholly* in the right; that never happens. However, war should not be waged unless the evils to be fought, on the one side, are sufficiently greater than those on the other to justify killing.
5 Proportionality: war should not be waged unless the goods that may be reasonably expected from taking up arms are greater than the evils.
6 Probability of success: there must be a reasonable likelihood that the war will achieve its aims.
7 Last resort: war should not be waged unless all peaceful alternatives have been exhausted.

Jus in bello

1 Right intention: because the aim of those who go to war should be the achievement of a just peace, they should avoid any acts or demands that would hinder ultimate reconciliation.
2 Proportionality: no tactic may be employed unless the goods that may be reasonably expected from its employment are greater than the evils.
3 Discrimination: directly intended attacks on noncombatants and nonmilitary targets are impermissible.

First Four Elements of The Perennial Philosophy

First is the (idealist) claim that all matter and all consciousness, the world of things and animals and men and even gods, are the manifestation of a Divine Ground within which all partial realities have their being and apart from which they would not exist.

Second is that humans are capable of knowing about the Divine Ground and, further, may realize its existence by a direct intuition that is superior to discursive reasoning. This immediate knowledge unites the knower with the known.

Third, human beings possess a dual nature: an ordinary ego and an eternal Self, which is the inner self, or spirit, the spark of divinity within the soul. It is possible for a person to identify the self with this spirit and Divine Ground.

Fourth, human life on earth has only one end and purpose: for a person to identify with the eternal Self and so come to unitive knowledge of the Divine Ground.

Examples of the Tao, or "the Way"⁴³

Found in all religions of the world are:

- The law of general beneficence: first, negative, as in "do not murder"; then positive, as in "do unto others as you would have them do unto you."
- The law of special beneficence, from many religions and traditions having to do with specific duties. Duties to parents, elders, and ancestors, such as "honour thy father and thy mother," or the equivalent, found in all societies. Duties to children and posterity, as found in universal commands to love and protect children.
- The law of justice, having to do with universal commands not to commit adultery, lie, cheat, or steal and with commands to be honest and equitable, especially in courts, and so forth.
- The law of good faith and veracity, having to do with universal prohibitions against fraud and insincerity.
- The law of mercy, having to do with universal commands to help the weak and needy.
- The law of magnanimity, having to do with how we are to live nobly and act generously and to die, if necessary, for the truth.

HUMAN WORD-ORDER UNIVERSALS⁴⁴

1 In declarative sentences with nominal subject and object, the dominant order is almost always one in which the subject precedes the object.
2 In languages with prepositions, the genitive almost always follows the governing noun, whereas in languages with postpositions it almost always precedes.
3 Languages with dominant verb-subject-object (VSO) order are always prepositional.
4 With overwhelmingly greater than chance frequency, languages with normal subject-verb-object (SOV) order are postpositional.
5 If a language has dominant SOV order and the genitive follows the governing noun, then the adjective likewise follows the noun.
6 All languages with dominant VSO order have SVO as an alternative or as the only alternative basic order.

7 If in a language with dominant SOV order, there is no alternative basic order, or only OSV as the alternative, then all adverbial modifiers of the verb likewise precede the verb.

8 When a yes-no question is differentiated from the corresponding assertion by an intonational pattern, the distinctive intonational features of each of these patterns are reckoned from the end of the sentence rather than from the beginning.

9 With well more than chance frequency, when question particles or affixes are specified in position by reference to the sentence as a whole, if initial, such elements are found in prepositional languages, and, if final, in postpositional.

10 Question particles or affixes, when specified in position by reference to a particular word in the sentence, almost always follow that word. Such particles do not occur in languages with dominant order VSO.

11 Inversion of statement order so that verb precedes subject occurs only in languages where the question word or phrase is normally initial. This same inversion occurs in yes-no questions only if it also occurs in interrogative word questions.

12 If a language has dominant order VSO in declarative sentences, it always puts interrogative words or phrases first in interrogative word questions; if it has dominant order SOV in declarative sentences, there is never such an invariant rule.

13 If the nominal object always precedes the verb, then verb forms subordinate to the main verb also precede it.

14 In conditional statements, the conditional clause precedes the conclusion as the normal order in all languages.

15 In expressions of volition and purpose, a subordinate verbal form always follows the main verb as the normal order except in those languages in which the nominal object always precedes the verb.

16 In languages with dominant order VSO, an inflected auxiliary always precedes the main verb. In languages with dominant order SOV, an inflected auxiliary always follows the main verb.

17 With overwhelmingly more than chance frequency, languages with dominant order VSO have the adjective after the noun.

18 When the descriptive adjective precedes the noun, the demonstrative and the numeral, with overwhelmingly more than chance frequency, do likewise.

19 When the general rule is that the descriptive adjective follows, there may be a minority of adjectives that usually precede, but when the general rule is that descriptive adjectives precede, there are no exceptions.

20 When any or all of the items (demonstrative, numeral, and descriptive adjective) precede the noun, they are always found in that order. If they follow, the order is either the same or its exact opposite.

21 If some or all adverbs follow the adjective they modify, then the language is one in which the qualifying adjective follows the noun and the verb precedes its nominal object as the dominant order.

22 If in comparisons of superiority the only order, or one of the alternative orders, is standard-marker-adjective, then the language is postpositional. With overwhelmingly more than chance frequency, if the only order is adjective-marker-standard, the language is prepositional.

23 If in apposition the proper noun usually precedes the common noun, then the language is one in which the governing noun precedes its dependent genitive. With much better than chance frequency, if the common noun usually precedes the proper noun, the dependent genitive precedes its governing noun.

24 If the relative expression precedes the noun either as the only construction or as an alternate construction, either the language is postpositional, or the adjective precedes the noun, or both.

25 If the pronominal object follows the verb, so does the nominal object.

26 If a language has discontinuous affixes, it always has either prefixing, or suffixing, or both.

27 if a language is exclusively suffixing, it is postpositional; if it is exclusively prefixing, it is prepositional.

28 If the derivation and inflection either both follow or both precede the root, the derivation is always between the root and the inflection.

29 If a language has inflection, it always has derivation.

30 If the verb has categories of person-number or if it has categories of gender, it always has tense-mode categories.

31 If either the subject or object noun agrees with the verb in gender, then the adjective always agrees with the noun in gender.

32 Whenever the verb agrees with a nominal subject or nominal object in gender, it also agrees in number.

33 When number agreement between the noun and verb is suspended and the rule is based on order, the case is always one in which the verb precedes and the verb is in the singular.

34 No language has a trial number unless it has a dual. No language has a dual unless it has a plural.

35 There is no language in which the plural does not have some nonzero allomorphs, whereas there are languages in which the singular is expressed only by zero. The dual and the trial are almost never expressed only by zero.

36 If a language has the category of gender, it always has the category of number.

37 A language never has more gender categories in the nonsingular numbers than in the singular.

38 Where there is a case system, the only case that ever has only zero allomorphs is the one that includes among its meanings that of the subject of the intransitive verb.

39 Where morphemes of both number and case are present and both follow or both precede the noun base, the expression of number almost always comes between the noun base and the expression of case.

40 When the adjective follows the noun, the adjective expresses all the inflectional categories of the noun. In such cases the noun may lack overt expression of one or all of these categories.

41 If in a language the verb follows both the nominal subject and nominal object as the dominant order, the language almost always has a case system.

42 All languages have pronominal categories involving at least three persons and two numbers.

43 If a language has gender categories in the noun, it has gender categories in the pronoun.

44 If a language has gender distinctions in the first person, it always has gender distinctions in the second or third person, or in both.

45 If there are any gender distinctions in the plural of the pronoun, there are some gender distinctions in the singular also.

There are more than 1,200 *language universals* posted on the University of Konstanz website: http://ling.uni-konstanz.de:591/Universals/Introduction.html.

Some Phonological Universals

- A historical tendency toward sound (phonological) symmetry is universal.
- Every phonological system contrasts phonemes that are typically stops [such as the /p/ sound at the end of the word "stop," which ends the sound altogether] with phonemes that are never stops [they are "continuous" sounds, like the /a/ in "bag," where the /a/ does not stop by itself but is stopped only by merging into or ending with the sound that follows it].
- Sound change is universal [and there are also regularities of sound change that obey their own universal laws].[45]
- All languages have consonants and vowels.
- Half of all languages have seven vowels, others fewer. Most languages have /i / /a/ and /u/ as part of their vowel system.

- All languages have "plosives" (sounds that explode with breath, like the first /p/ in "pop"; the last /p/ is called a "stop" because it does not explode. Hold your hand in front of your mouth as you say "pop" and you will feel the difference in these "p" sounds on your hand).
- Almost all languages have /p/ /t/ and /k/, and those that don't have all of these sounds, have at least two of them.
- Almost all languages have nasals; for the few that have only one, it is usually /n/, and for those that have only two, it is usually /m/ and /n/.
- 95% of all languages have "fricatives" (like the /f/ in "fast"); 90% of all languages have a sibilant (like the /s/ in "soap"); 64% have /h/; the rarest fricatives are pharyngeals, which are formed in the throat (about 7% have these).
- 95% of all languages have a liquid, or flowing, sound (like /l/ in "liquid"), 80% have an L-sound, and 77% have an R-sound.
- 97% of all languages that have /p/ also have /t/.

Of interest is a new text published after this book went to press: Mark Hale and Charles Reiss's *The Phonological Enterprise* (Oxford: Oxford University Press, 2008). Hale and Reiss scrutinize recent work in phonological theory from the perspective of Chomskyan generative linguistics and take seriously the idea that phonology is best studied as a mental computational system derived from an innate phonological universal grammar.

Notes

INTRODUCTION

1 In Steven Pinker, *The Blank Slate: The Modern Denial of Human Nature* (New York: Viking Penguin, 2002), there is a thorough examination of these self-serving modern concepts. Pinker draws various conclusions I would not about the origins of mind, but nevertheless, it is refreshing after a century of assumptions about blank-slate psychology to see such a thorough examination of the idea.

CHAPTER ONE

1 There is, however, a continuing and fascinating debate today between so-called "substantivalists" and "relationists" on the matter of space and time. The former say that space and time exist in their own right without regard to the existence or non-existence of things. The latter deny this. They say that we can know space and time only because of the existence of things and that it is in terms of their relations that we are able to describe both. That is the point I have made here also, primarily because I cannot imagine what space or time could be without things. For example, without things, how could we possibly know there was space since there would be nothing in that space to perceive? How could complete emptiness be a thing? In AD 379 Saint Augustine addressed this interesting question in his *Confessions*, where he made the argument that before God created matter there was no time, only eternity, which is timeless. It exists as an eternal present. But once things came into existence, time began as something measurable. Even though there is still an eternal present, things now ceaselessly flow from it both into the past and into the anticipated future.

2 Bertrand Russell, *The Problems of Philosophy* (Oxford: Oxford University Press,
   Home University Library, 1959 and 1972).
3 Plato, *Theaetetus*, in John M. Cooper and D.S. Hutchinson, eds, *Plato: Complete Works* (Indianapolis, IN: Hackett, 1997), 169.
4 Some historians have said that Protagoras did not mean that all things are
   relative. Rather, he meant that Man (humankind), not nature, is the primary object of human study. And so his was a doctrine of humanism, not of
   relativism. On this point, see the entry for "Relativity of Knowledge" in *The
   Enclyclopaedia Britannica*, 11th ed., vol. 23. However, Plato cites the full argument by Protagoras, which is clearly relativist.

   But there is a historical pattern here of some interest. Protagoras (485–
   410 BC) lived under Greek paganism, which, with its many warring and fickle gods, had diluted ancient Greek belief in absolutes. For along with many
   other Sophists of his time (Sophists were the first Greek philosophers to accept payment for teaching, and they took relish in winning logical debates
   without regard to truth or the good), Protagoras had become enamoured of
   Heraclitus's view that all things are in flux. But once having accepted the
   idea that nothing is fixed, he was then forced to argue that all sensations
   must therefore be subjective and that reality can thus never be known for
   certain. This ancient form of relativism led to a swift breakdown of Greek
   philosophy that was not reversed until the time of Plato and Aristotle, who,
   each in his own way, restored concepts of the absolute to philosophy in a
   manner that has framed Western civilization for almost two thousand years.
   Indeed, modern relativism is really a kind of counterattack on the absolutist
   and "essentialist" ideas of Plato and Aristotle as they have come down to
   us in European thought. (In later chapters we will come to grips with
   Nietzsche, Heidegger, and their French acolytes Michel Foucault and
   Jacques Derrida, all of whom were anti-Platonists.)

   From thence forward, the Greek preoccupation with philosophical absolutes and universals was so influential that it was eventually merged with the
   Judeo-Christian teachings about revelation, the existence of a single absolute God, and a single moral authority. It was Saint Augustine's *City of God*
   (early fifth century AD) that first successfully incorporated Platonic philosophy within Christianity in a synthesis that was to last over 600 years. By the
   thirteenth century, however, Aristotle's teachings were replacing those of
   Plato, and another great thinker, Saint Thomas Aquinas, set to work incor-
   porating them into Christian theology via his magisterial *Summa Theologiae*.
   This second synthesis remains in force today as the official theology of the
   Roman Catholic Church, despite the fact that we are clearly living in another
   age of public skepticism and relativism. My point is that once any civilization

abandons belief in some absolute principle of reality that has provided it with the conviction that the cosmos has a purpose, relativism soon fills the vacuum, regardless of the historical period. We await our modern equivalent of Plato and Aristotle.

5 A recent version of this notion was bleakly articulated by Professor William Provine, of Cornell University, in a small circulation Canadian newsletter (*U-Turn*, no. 4, Winter 1997). He was confident enough about the insignificance of the universe to say: "let me summarize my views loud and clear. There are no gods, no purposes, and no goal-directed forces of any kind. There is no life after death ... no foundation for ethics, no ultimate meaning in life." Provine doesn't seem to realize that if he were to take himself at his own word, he could not give a convincing reason why he gets out of bed in the morning, why he is motivated to learn or teach anything, or why he should be upset if someone steals his car, for in a truly meaningless world there can be no ultimate defence of our actions nor any objection to the actions of others.

6 Indeed, the word "science" is rooted in the Latin word for knowledge, and there is no small irony in the fact that just as men such as Galileo and Newton believed their "objective" and "scientific" discoveries were unveiling the natural laws of God, so did their religious accusers and detractors consider themselves to be "scientists" of the highest order. This was so because theology, which was the only discipline that strived to integrate all other forms of knowledge within a higher truth, was widely considered the "Queen of Sciences." In the minds of most serious thinkers, The Book of Nature and the Book of God were considered to be different manifestations of the same truth, and this was the generally accepted view from the Middle Ages until about the middle of the nineteenth century. Indeed, there are still many excellent scientists who feel this way. But it is certainly not the general view any longer.

7 If we start from a faith in materialism and doubt, we indeed may say "I think, therefore I am." However, if we start from a faith in God, we may reverse this and say, "I am, therefore I think." Neither of these faiths can be indubitably proven by science or logic.

8 In his opening words of his *Discourse on Method* (1637), we see the hint of three emerging modern themes: *objective science* (of which mathematics was the new queen), *individualism,* and modern *egalitarianism.* Before Descartes, it was a common assumption that people differed so strongly in their opinions because some were clearly better thinkers or simply far better people than others. But to the astonishment of all, Descartes starts out by claiming that "Good sense is the most evenly shared thing in the world," so much so

that we never hear anyone say they need more of it! As everyone feels this way, he goes on, it is therefore unlikely we are all mistaken, *and so it must be true*, and therefore – just look where this "objective" thinker takes his conclusion: "the capacity to judge correctly and to distinguish the true from the false, which is properly what one calls common sense or reason, is naturally equal in all men." See Rene Descartes, *Discourse on Method and the Meditations*, trans. F.E. Sutcliffe (New York: Penguin, 1968), 27ff. I am indebted to Etienne Gilson, *The Unity of Philosophical Experience* (New York: Charles Scribner, 1937), for his penetrating critique of Descartes and his philosophy.

9 On the question of pandemic public ignorance, see, for example, the journal *Critical Review* 14, nos 2–3 (Summer 2000). This same journal published yet another collection of papers on the same topic, vol. 18, nos 1–3 (Winter-Summer 2006).

10 David Berlinski, *Newton's Gift: How Sir Isaac Newton Unlocked the System of the World* (New York: Simon and Schuster, 2000), xiv. This is an intriguing and accessible account of Newton's life, work, and significance.

11 Ibid., 172.

12 For that matter, the religious beliefs of all three of our greatest scientists, Galileo, Newton, and Einstein, have simply been ignored. Although in their minds science and theology were indelibly connected, in the public mind they became increasingly disconnected, despite the fact that the mysteries they revealed were no less mysterious for having been formulated as laws and universals. Newton, for example, was fully aware that although his law explained for the first time in history how gravity works, and although he formulated it as an absolute, or constant, of nature, the law does not tell us what gravity is. No one has ever told us what gravity is, simply because no one knows. (Newton's law specifies that the attraction between physical bodies is proportional to their mass and inversely proportional to the square of the distance between them.)

13 Margaret Geller, via Jeffrey Satinover, *The Quantum Brain* (New York: John Wiley and Sons, 2001), 4, quoted in S. Weinberg, *Dreams of a Final Theory* (New York: Pantheon Books, 1992), 225.

14 Hobbes was a close friend and supporter of Sir Francis Bacon (1561–1626) and was deeply influenced by Bacon's "objective" methods of scientific observation. Bacon vehemently disliked all religious authority and sought to cleanse the observing mind of all contaminating bias in order to observe The Book of Nature as he was sure it must be in its objectively pure state. He was the first of many Western scientists to replace the omnipotence of God with the omnipotence of Nature (a continuing and only lightly veiled theme in the natural sciences ever since).

15 Thomas Hobbes, *Leviathan* (London: Penguin, 1985), 120.

16 I have argued elsewhere, especially in *Constitutional Crack-Up* (Toronto: Stoddart, 1994), that the French-style, top-down, code-law format of constitutional democracy has everywhere in the West been in conflict with a British-style, bottom-up, common-law parliamentary or congressional style. The former has everywhere imposed itself on the latter. Canada is an acute example of a country that existed for 115 years as a parliamentary democracy in the British fashion, in which members of the House responsible to the people made sovereign law (keeping in mind that until quite recently most parliamentarians believed in fixed and eternal laws of human nature that not even Parliament can alter). This was suddenly overturned by the more French constitutional method introduced by former prime minister Pierre Trudeau, in the form of a Charter of Rights and Freedoms, in 1982, which is now part of the Canadian Constitution and the "supreme" law (sec. 52) to which the Canadian Parliament and its statutes are subordinate. The effect of this is that elected parliamentarians are now subservient to the opinions (which are not only legal but unavoidably also political, economic, and social) of unelected judges who must be asked to interpret the abstract words of the Charter. In a real sense, this has returned Canadians to the condition they were in prior to Confederation, at which time they won "responsible" government from British colonial rule. Prior to that, the governors of Canada were responsible to the British Parliament, not to the colonists they governed. In the same sense, Canadian parliamentarians may now be said to be more responsible to their judges than to their electors.

17 See especially Steven Pinker, *The Blank Slate: The Modern Denial of Human Nature* (New York: Viking Penguin, 2002).

18 Examples are Set Theory in mathematics, Field Theory in psychology, sociology, and physics, the attempt of Western philosophers to escape the particle problem of analytical thinking through phenomenology, and in general the modern interest in organic part-whole relationships, chaos theory, spontaneous organization, and "emergent properties" both in the natural world and in human fields such as economics.

19 J.L. Talmon, *Romanticism and Revolt* (New York: Norton, 1967), 100, my emphasis.

20 Michael Krausz and Jack M. Meiland, eds, *Relativism, Cognitive and Moral* (Notre Dame, IL: University of Notre Dame Press, 1982), 7.

21 Roger Sandall, *The Culture Cult: Designer Tribalism and Other Essays* (New York: Westview Press, 2001), 107–8.

22 Paul Johnson, *Modern Times: The World from the Twenties to the Eighties* (New York: Harper and Row, 1983), 4, my emphasis.

23 Ibid., 5.

24 Renato Rosaldo, "Of Headhunters and Soldiers: Separating Cultural and Ethical Relativism," conference paper, www.scu.edu/ethics/publications/iie/v11n1/relativism.html.

CHAPTER TWO

1 William Turner, *The History of Philosophy* (New York: Ginn and Company, 1903), 600.
2 See the entry for "Relativity of Knowledge" in *The Encylopaedia Britannica*, 11th ed., vol. 23.

CHAPTER THREE

1 Maurice Mandelbaum, "Subjective, Objective, and Conceptual Relativism," in Michael Kraus and Jack M. Meiland, eds, *Relativism, Cognitive and Moral* (Notre Dame, IL: University of Notre Dame Press, 1982), 31.
2 Plato, *Theaetetus*, in John M. Cooper and D.S. Hutchinson, eds, *Plato: Complete Works* (Indianapolis, IN: Hackett, 1997), 190.
3 Aristotle, *The Metaphysics* (London: Penguin Classics, 1998), see especially books 3 through 7.
4 Ibid., bk 5, 98.
5 Ibid., bk 3, 88, my emphasis.
6 I thank Professor Allen Wood for his carefully argued paper "Relativism," which lays out many of the points adapted in these objections to relativism; see www.people.cornell.edu/pagesrcc2/relativism.
7 Ernest Gellner, *Anthropology and Politics: Revolutions in the Sacred Grove* (London: Blackwell, 1995), 4.
8 W.T. Stace, *Religion and the Modern Mind* (New York: J.P. Lippincott, 1952), 118–19.
9 See William D. Gairdner, "Freedom, Democracy, Slavery," chapter 2 in *The Trouble with Democracy*, 41–86 (Toronto: Stoddart, 2001), for an extensive examination of the moral conundrums presented by ancient as well as modern slavery.
10 The ancients, who were often obliged to defend themselves against the slaughter of their young men and rape of their women, were faced with a moral dilemma concerning their prisoners. Once the war was over, should prisoners of war be executed or not? Ancient moralists argued that the killing and rape could not be forgiven but that execution after surrender was too harsh. Slavery as a form of reparation was the preferred solution and was deemed the morally preferable option. In the ancient battle of Aquia

Sextae, Julius Caesar was said to have sold 60,000 of the captured enemy into slavery in one day.

11 David Berlinski, *Newton's Gift: How Sir Isaac Newton Unlocked the System of the World* (New York Simon and Schuster, 2000), xv, my emphasis.

12 Robert B. Edgerton, *Sick Societies: Challenging the Myth of Primitive Harmony* (New York: Free Press, 1992), offers an interesting review of cultural relativism by a former relativist as well as a wealth of historical and contemporary insight into the health and sickness of a wide range of societies, past and present. The evidence offered here is sufficient in itself to make a mockery of cultural relativism.

13 Wood, "Relativism."

14 Stanton Evans, *The Theme Is Freedom: Religion, Politics, and the American Tradition* (Washington, DC: Regnery, 1994), 43.

15 Mussolini, quoted in ibid., 49, my emphasis.

16 Oliver Wendell Holmes, "Natural Law," *Harvard Law Review*, no. 40 (1918): 252.

17 Margaret Mead, *Coming of Age in Samoa* (1928; reprint, New York: Penguin, 1966).

18 These and a number of other questions are neatly put by Kelley L. Ross, PhD, at www.friesian.com/relativie.

19 These objections by Ernest Gellner are reviewed in one of the most thoroughgoing critiques of relativism in the fields of history and anthropology I have seen: Keith Windschuttle, *The Killing of History* (San Francisco: Encounter Books, 1996), 30ff.

CHAPTER FOUR

1 Sir Edmund Leach, quoted in Robert B. Edgerton, *Sick Societies: Challenging the Myth of Primitive Harmony* (New York: Free Press, 1992), 23, my emphasis.

2 This general discussion of the nature and rise of cultural relativism in the West is indebted to the works of Donald E. Brown, *Human Universals* (New York: McGraw-Hill, 1991); Carl N. Degler, *In Search of Human Nature* (Oxford: Oxford University Press, 1991); Elvin Hatch, *Culture and Morality: The Relativity of Values in Anthropology* (New York: Columbia University Press, 1983); Edgerton, *Sick Societies*; Roger Sandall, *The Culture Cult: Designer Tribalism and Other Essays* (Boulder, CO: Westview Press, 2001); Adam Kuper, *Culture: The Anthropologists' Account* (Cambridge, MA: Harvard Unversity Press, 1999); Ernest Gellner, *Anthropology and Politics: Revolutions in the Sacred Grove* (London: Blackwell, 1995); and Ernest Gellner, *Postmodernism, Reason and Religion* (London: Routledge, 1992).

3 A lot of intelligent and informed people still feel this way. One example is the distinguished British historian Paul Johnson, who recently shocked the

liberal world by calling for a "recolonization" of almost all of Africa. Another British scholar, Lord Peter Bauer, has been arguing rather unassailably for years that most liberated former colonies thrived better under their former colonialism than after liberation. See especially his still classic *Equality, the Third World, and Economic Delusion* (Cambridge, MA: Harvard University Press, 1981).

4 For a rigorous and memorable exposition on this concept, and one that has impressed itself on the whole study of "the history of ideas" in the West, see Arthur Lovejoy, *The Great Chain of Being* (1936; reprint, New York: Harper and Row, 1960). Lovejoy explains that from the Middle Ages until the late eighteenth century, "most educated men were to accept without question – the conception of the universe as a 'Great Chain of Being,' composed of an immense ... number of links ranging in hierarchical order from the meagerest kind of existents, which barely escaped non-existence, through 'every possible' grade" (59) up to the most perfect of all, God Himself. And each of these beings in the hierarchy was said to differ from the one above and the one below by the least possible degree of difference. It was Aristotle, we learn, who created the first arguments for such a chain of being, or *scala naturae*. He proposed three different scales. First, he argued for ranking forms of life according to degree of "perfection," from human beings at the top down to zoophytes. Next, in his *De Anima*, he proposed a ranking according to "Powers of Soul," from basic metabolic or "nutritive" forms at the bottom to rational humans at the top (and on through infinite degrees to Supreme Reason, or God). His last grading system was based on the degree of "privation" in things, a measure that tells of the degree to which things are "infected with potentiality." The end result was a complex argument for an unbroken chain of existents from the invisible up to God, comprising a "full" universe without gaps. This was considered logically and morally crucial, as a perfect Being would only create a universe that was rational, continuous, and full, not one that had senseless gaps.

5 Henry Commager, quoted in Hatch, *Culture and Morality*, 30.

6 Ibid., 32, my emphasis.

7 Sandall, *Culture Cult*, 53–4.

8 See especially Edwin Black, *War against the Weak: Eugenics and America's Campaign to Create a Master Race* (New York: Four Walls Eight Windows, 2003).

9 Brown, *Human Universals*, 55.

10 On the matter of the creed of scientific neutrality popular among the original Boasians, see in particular Hatch, *Culture and Morality*, 46, 47, 80.

11 These thoughts, from Stanford University professor Renato Rosaldo, one of the newer breed of "committed anthropologists," are presented in "Of

Headhunters and Soldiers: Separating Cultural and Ethical Relativism," a conference paper available at www.scu.edu/ethics/publications/iie/v11n1/relativism.html.

12 See especially the treatment of Boas as the architect of radical culture theory in American social sciences in Degler, *In Search of Human Nature*, 82n1.

13 Brown, *Human Universals*, 56.

14 Degler, *In Search of Human Nature*, 82–3.

15 Edgerton, *Sick Societies*, 37.

16 Margaret Mead, quoted in Carolyn Warner, ed., *The Last Word: A Treasury of Women's Quotes* (New York: Prentice Hall, 1992).

17 See Ruth Benedict, *Patterns of Culture* (New York: Houghton Mifflin, 1934); and Margaret Mead, *Coming of Age in Samoa* (1928; reprint, New York: Penguin, 1966).

18 Brown, *Human Universals*, 2.

19 See ibid., ch. 1; Keith Windschuttle, *The Killing of History* (San Francisco: Encounter Books, 1996); Sandall, *Culture Cult*; and Derek Freeman, *The Fateful Hoaxing of Margaret Mead* (Boulder, CO: Westview Press, 1999).

20 Sandall, *Culture Cult*, 60.

21 Ibid., 64.

22 Quoted in Brown, *Human Universals*, 84.

23 E.B. Tylor, *Primitive Culture* (New York: Harper, 1958), 539.

24 See especially Gellner, *Anthropology and Politics*.

25 Degler, *In Search of Human Nature*, 134.

26 My emphasis. See www.panam.edu/faculty/mglazer/theory/cultural_relativism.htm.

27 A compressed explanation of the ethical division and confusion among anthropologists is Murray L. Wax, "Some Issues and Sources on Ethics in Anthroplogy," written for the American Anthropological Association's website, at www.aaanet.org/committees/ethics/ch1.htm.

28 Kurt von Fritz, quoted in Hatch, *Culture and Morality*, 98.

29 See Wax, "Some Issues."

30 Richard Dawkins, *River out of Eden* (New York: Harper Collins, 1995).

31 John Tooby and Leda Cosmides, "The Psychological Foundations of Culture," in Jerome H. Barkow, Leda Cosmides, and John Tooby, eds, *The Adpated Mind: Evolutionary Psychology and the Generation of Culture* (New York: Oxford University Press, 1992), 92.

32 Edgerton, *Sick Societies*, 2.

33 Ibid., 36.

34 Walter Goldschmidt, cited in Brown, *Human Universals*, 76.

35 Physicist Charles Nissam-Sabat, quoted in Edgerton, *Sick Societies*, 27.

36 The phrase is Dan Sperber's, quoted in ibid., 28.

37 B.F. Skinner, *Verbal Behavior* (New York: Methuen, 1957). Chomsky published *Syntactic Structures* (The Hague: Mouton) in 1957 and there explored concepts of underlying deep structures of human language, of "transformational grammar," and of "universal grammar." The latter theme is more developed in his *Language and Problems of Knowledge* (Cambridge, MA: MIT Press, 1988).

38 Lionel Tiger and Robin Fox, *The Imperial Animal* (New York: Holt, Rinehart and Winston, 1971).

39 E.O. Wilson, *On Human Nature* (Cambridge, MA: Harvard University Press, 1978).

40 E.O. Wilson, *Sociobiology: The Abridged Edition* (Cambridge, MA: Harvard University Press, 1980).

41 See Degler, *In Search of Human Nature*, ch. 9, for a thorough rendering of this trend.

42 With relativism as the focal point, it is possible in a broad way to speak of an "anthropology of anthropologists" from the 1960s forward, as follows:

   1   The Neutral Scientists/Functionalists. There are still some serious, scientific, and objective-minded people who study cultures the old way, in clear objective language we can all understand. Sometimes they are called "functionalists." They prefer a hands-off, ostensibly neutral, and scientific approach to the study of cultures on the grounds that all cultural practices (whether we happen to approve of them or not) must have some positive social function for the culture in which they occur, or they would not have survived. Although there is no scholarly consensus to support their position, they argue that all human and animal behaviours are "adaptive" for survival. Many have latched onto a renewed interest in Darwinian evolution theory to explain the reason for adaptation (competition for females, reproductive success, etc.). However, adaptationism can lead to circular arguments justifying anything, rather like saying that worms come out in the morning so that robins can eat them or that the human nose exists to support eyeglasses. At any rate, such functionalists are "uncommitted" in the political sense – that is, uncommitted to any political or moral point of view. They do not believe the pure scientist should ever interfere with or try to improve another culture – should not confuse an "is" with an "ought," as the English philosopher David Hume put it. But many of them are really just relativists with a more scientific-sounding name, for they maintain not only that all cultures are different, and all practices adaptive, but also that cultures are so utterly incommensurable they can never be compared in any meaningful way. They have been criticized as the conservatives of anthropology for this position by their more radical brethren. At any rate, one might justly conclude that on the self-defeating ground of incommensurability, there can be no purpose for doing or teaching anthropology in the first place.

2   *The Interventionists.* In contrast to the functionalists, there are interventionists, who believe it is the social scientist's human responsibility first to scientifically study a culture but then to intervene if necessary and assist in any required way for the greater "health, happiness, or survival" of the people studied (Edgerton, *Sick Societies*, 24). They are the "committed" anthropologists, such as Renato Rosaldo of Stanford. In a way they continue a radical trend critical of relativism that began in the 1960s. The view was growing then that relativism contained "an insidious bias toward the status quo and in favour of the preservation of foreign or exotic cultures, as human zoos, or as anthropological specimens" (Hatch, *Culture and Morality*, 116). They have broken almost entirely with relativism. But not quite. Many believe it is possible to be a *cultural* relativist without having to be an *ethical* one. You can be ethical *within* a culture without having to impose that view on all cultures. Some of these people will go so far as to admit (this is where they break with relativism) that many past and present societies – the easiest examples being Aztec human sacrifice/cannibal society, Nazi society, even modern capitalist-exploited cultures – were (or are) malfunctioning and even "sick." The result of this anti-relativism is that some committed anthropologists are now often in sympathy with angry Third World critics of the West who say that relativism is just another form of colonialism, a kind of "romantic humanism" that has failed to see that the exotic cultures to which they grant equal validity are in fact poverty-stricken, powerless, and oppressed (Hatch, *Culture and Morality*, 128ff.). Radical anthropologists such as these believe they have an ethical duty to act on behalf of the exploited (and usually, against the West).

3   *The Interpreters.* Some of the new thinkers of the 1970s began to reason that if it is true we cannot escape the confines of our own minds and language conceptions, as the language theorists and philosophers are insisting, then we should confess to simply writing fictions about other people and their cultures. Older forms of anthropology described other cultures with a confident and clear language of dominion, of empire, and of colonialism. But "interpretive" anthropology can do better. Led by such as Clifford Geertz and David Schneider, it sees human nature in its variousness, not in universals common to all. Geertz dispensed with what he considered the ruse of objectivity in favour of a more sensitive, subjective, literary probing of other cultures where the writer's personality and his or her relation to informants becomes an integral part of the result. Cultures are made of symbols, so they are like texts. They can be interpreted in their own terms but

not explained away. The clear analytical writing of the past, or of any time, is to him and his ilk a sign of the will to dominate rather than to interpret and empathize by fleshing out the true complexities of meaning. In other words, lucidity is a Western positivist tool of cultural domination. Better for the cultural investigator to atone for the sins of the West by baring his complex and tormented soul, "externalizing it in correspondingly tortured prose" (Gellner, *Anthropology and Politics*, 236). Although, as Gellner complained of this new fashion, "It is not obvious to me that, because the world is a diverse, complex and tortured place, which it is, that only cumbersome and ambiguous sentences can do it justice, and that clarity is some kind of intellectual treason" (ibid., 25).

4   *Cloudcuckooland: The Postmodern Folks.* Following this – and still with us in a confused way – came "postmodern" anthropology. It became critical even of the Geertzian school because Geertz still believed there is a truth (however subjective and literary) to be obtained. For postmodernists, however, there is no truth, only fictions, or fabricated "narratives," about other cultures. There can be no unequivocal interpretations because all cultures are contested from within, and there are no privileged readers. People of every culture (culture is now a suspect, "hegemonic" word) live in a world of symbols. Every culture is its own system of symbols. So by and large, these folks "have switched their allegiance from the social sciences to the humanities, and they are likely to practice interpretation, even deconstruction," rather than science (Kuper, *Culture*, x; see also 18–20). As the title of a book announcing postmodern anthropology has it, they are "Writing Culture." And in the words of George Marcus, one of their leaders, the task of this group "was to introduce a literary consciousness to ethnographic practice by showing various ways in which ethnographies can be read and written" (quoted in ibid., 207). Scientific objectivity was an illusion, so let us expose the rhetorical and controlling tricks of authorship and the fictional nature of all ethnography. This "hermeneutic" style "respects the subjectivity both of the object of the inquiry [a native informant, for example], and of the inquirer [the inquiring anthropologist], and even of the reader or listener" (Gellner, *Postmodernism*, 35). If we want to be fully honest, we must portray even the anguished self-aware entrapment of ourselves as actors in the written rather than portray ourselves as camera or scientist. The postmodernists must "indulge their subjectivism ... their repudiation of formal discipline, their expression of deep inner turbulence ... performed in academese prose, intended for publication in learned journals, a means of securing promotion by impressing the appropriate committees" (ibid., 27). Postmodernists must undermine even their own assumptions and avoid "essentializing" a people, must show the hopeless circularity of truth, and (for many) also give

voice to the downtrodden. There is a strong anti-Western and leftist trend in all postmodern work, and many postmodernists insist that the role of the anthropologist is to offer a "cultural critique" of the West (Kuper, *Culture*, 218). But the one thing all these recent fashions insist upon is that *there are no absolutes or universals*. Science itself is just another cultural discourse. For this reason, this brand of anthropology has been quickly absorbed into the nothing-is-ever-certain world of literary criticism and the humanities. That is where things sit on the extreme relativist side of this quixotic and despairing science.

43 See www.yale.edu/hraf.

44 Interestingly, Margaret Mead, Clyde Kluckholn, and Alfred Kroeber, three of Boas's most influential student relativists, and all central figures in the establishment of "culture" as the sole explanation of human behaviour to the radical exclusion of biology and all other conceptions of innate "human nature," had all revised their earlier views by the 1950s, by then accepting that biology, or nature, plays an important role in human behaviour.

45 Brown, *Human Universals*, ch. 6, 130–41.

46 Ibid., 154, my emphasis.

47 Ibid., 154–5.

48 Ibid., 88.

CHAPTER FIVE

1 See, for example, Michael R. Matthews, ed., *The Scientific Background to Modern Philosophy* (Indianapolis, IN: Hackett, 1989).

2 Why is water the only substance in the universe that in its frozen state will float in a pot of liquid water, whereas a frozen bit of any other substance will rapidly sink in a bowl of the same liquid substance? We know how this happens but not why. One reason to care about this unique fact is that if frozen water didn't float in itself, all the fresh water in cold countries would be forever frozen (except for a thin watery layer on lakes in summer. Try to imagine a guilty teenager explaining to his dad how he broke the boat's propeller in 90°F August weather on a piece of submerged ice!). But long before that strange possibility, winters would have filled every hollow in the temperate climes with permanent ice, and life as we know it, for lack of water, would likely never have arisen. For a fascinating chapter on the quixotic nature of water, see Michael J. Denton, *Nature's Destiny* (New York: Free Press, 1998), ch. 2.

3 See Bertrand Russell, *The Problems of Philosophy* (1959; reprint, Oxford: Oxford University Press, 1972), esp. chs 9 and 10, which deal specifically with a logical defence of universals.

4 Roger Penrose, *The Emperor's New Mind* (Oxford: Oxford University Press, 1999), 151.

5 A sobering lesson in rigorous thinking about the question of where, exactly, a form, or essence, or general idea exists may be obtained from Etienne Gilson, *The Unity of Philosophical Experience* (San Francisco: Ignatius Press, 1937).

6 W.T. Stace, *A Critical History of Greek Philosophy* (London: Macmillan, 1965), 281–8.

7 Galileo made himself very unpopular at the time and got a sentence of house arrest for exposing another common illusion. He published a confirmation of Copernicus's earlier view that the earth goes around the sun, not the reverse. There were in fact already some very ancient arguments that the earth travelled around the sun. But they did not survive the overarching Christian dogma that the world created for humankind is the centre of all creation. The circumference of the earth was also calculated with great precision in ancient times. The experiment involved digging two well-holes 100 miles apart and at precisely noon, with the sun directly over one hole, calculating the angle of the shadow in the other hole and then performing the geometry to get the circumference of the sphere. It remains a sobering fact that although everyone today believes that what Galileo said is true – that the earth goes around the sun – few of us have any direct or personal proof that this is true. We believe it by deference to authority.

8 David Berlinski, *Newton's Gift: How Sir Isaac Newton Unlocked the System of the World* (New York: Simon and Schuster, 2000), 35. This is an excellent and very readable survey of Newton's contributions to physical science and our understanding of the constants of nature. My remarks on Newton are all drawn from this book.

9 David Bodanis, *E=mc²: A Biography of the World's Most Famous Equation* (New York: Walker and Company, 2000), 262n84, disputes the vaunted greatness (mostly vaunted by Newton, he suggests) of Newton's work at the farm, a view he says is plagued with inaccuracies and some confusion.

10 Berlinski, *Newton's Gift*, 133.

11 Ibid., xv.

12 Corey S. Powell, *God in the Equation* (New York: Free Press, 2002), 28.

13 Berlinski, *Newton's Gift*, 75, my emphasis.

14 Ibid., 142.

15 See Henry Margenau and Roy Abraham Varghese, eds, *Cosmos, Bios, Theos: Scientists Reflect on Science, God, and the Origins of the Universe, Life and Homo Sapiens* (LaSalle, IL: Open Court, 1992).

16 Hubble's Constant states that the speed of recession of galaxies (from us and from each other) increases proportionately with distance at 15 kilometres per second per million light years.

17 See Newton's *Scholium on Absolute Space and Time*, in Matthews, ed., *Scientific Background*, in which Newton distinguished absolute from relative space and time. Relative time is "common" time, measured by means of some motion, as relative space is measured by relations of bodies. At any rate, a careful reader will notice how Newton struggles to make his distinctions work.

18 Here is a list, in no particular order, of most of the books consulted for this chapter: W.H. McCrea et al., *The Constants of Physics* (London: Royal Society, 1983); Stephen Hawking, *A Brief History of Time* (New York: Bantam books, 1988); Russell McCormmach, *Night Thoughts of a Classical Physicist* (New York: Avon Books, 1982); Stephen Kellert, *In the Wake of Chaos* (Chicago: University of Chicago Press, 1993); Keith Ward, *God, Chance, and Necessity* (Oxford: Oneworld, 1993); Richard Morris, *The Nature of Reality: The Universe after Einstein* (New York: Noonday Press, 1987); James Gleick, *Chaos: Making a New Science* (New York: Penguin, 1987); Alan Lightman and Roberta Brawer, *Origins: The Lives and Worlds of Modern Cosmologists* (Cambridge MA: Harvard University Press, 1990); Rudy Rucker, *Infinity and the Mind* (Princeton, NJ: Princeton University Press, 1995); David Bohm, *Wholeness and the Implicate Order* (New York: Routledge, 1980); Stanley L. Jaki, *The Absolute Beneath the Relative* (Lanham, MD: ISI Books, 1988); Stanley L. Jaki, *Chance or Reality and Other Essays* (Lanham, MD: ISI Books, 1986); Richard Feynman, *The Character of Physical Law* (1965; reprint, Cambridge, MA: MIT Press, 1995); Richard Feynman, *Six Easy Pieces* (1963; reprint, Cambridge, MA: Perseus Books, 1995); John D. Barrow and Frank J. Tipler, *The Anthropic Cosmological Principle* (Oxford: Oxford University Press, 1986); Albert Einstein, *Ideas and Opinions* (1954; reprint, New York: Crown, 1982); Albert Einstein and Leopold Infeld, *The Evolution of Physics* (New York: Simon and Schuster, 1938); Albert Einstein, *Relativity: The Special and the General Theory* (New York: Three Rivers Press, 1961); John Gribbin, *Schrödinger's Kittens and the Search for Reality* (New York: Little Brown, 1995); Dennis Overbye, *Lonely Hearts of the Cosmos* (New York: Harper Collins, 1991); Nick Herbert, *Quantum Reality: Beyond the New Physics* (New York: Doubleday, 1985); Paul Davies, *The Accidental Universe* (Cambridge, UK: Cambridge University Press, 1982); and Jonathan Powers, *Philosophy and the New Physics* (London: Methuen, 1982).

19 Powell, *God*, 18, 29.

20 John D. Barrow, *The Constants of Nature: From Alpha to Omega – The Numbers That Encode the Deepest Secrets of the Universe* (New York: Pantheon, 2002), 51–2.

21 For a fascinating discussion of the mass to energy conversion, see Bodanis, *E=mc²*, ch. 7.

22 Tony Rothman, *Everything's Relative, and Other Fables from Science and Technology* (New Jersey: John Wiley and Sons, 2003), 68.

23 See Powers, *Philosophy*, 86–100. In his Louisiana speech, Poincaré used the term "principle of relativity" and also spoke of "synchronizing clocks," of "mass increasing with velocity," and of the velocity of light as "an unsurpassable limit." This seems a remarkable prefiguring of Einstein's theory. However, Poincaré's principle of relativity still rested on the notion of the *aether* supported by Hendrik Lorentz, whereas Einstein showed how the concept of the aether was no longer necessary. Lorentz later agreed that Eintein's theory was superior to his own.

24 Rothman, *Everything's Relative*, 68.

25 Ibid., 69.

26 Powers, *Philosophy*, 92.

27 Rothman, *Everything's Relative*, 69.

28 Albert Einstein, quoted in Bodanis, *E=mc²*, 261. Einstein complained to an art historian eager to show the parallel between modern Cubist art and the new physics that "the theory of relativity has been incorrectly understood" and that modern artistic language has "nothing in common with the theory of relativity."

29 Einstein, *Ideas and Opinions*, 282.

30 On this topic, see Christopher Herbert, *Victorian Relativity: Radical Thought and Scientific Discovery* (Chicago: University of Chicago Press, 2001). Herbert's book is a useful reminder that many variations of relativism came to fruition in the Victorian period. But the book is marred by a persistent and sometimes strident dismissal of things constant and absolute, and especially by the author's tendency to equate moral absolutism with totalitarian practices and violence in general, almost as though a belief in the Ten Commandments were a recipe for homicide. In contrast, I argue that what has distinguished all forms of totalitarian ideology is their reliance on moral relativism. This was true of Marxism, which dismissed all bourgeois values as class-motivated; of Hitlerism, which was grounded in the relativism of Nietszche and Heidegger; and of Fascism. Mussolini, a very clear writer, bragged about his moral relativism as something that freed fascists to self-create morally. Nonetheless, Herbert has done useful spadework in unearthing so many previously buried relativist thinkers.

31 Cited in Stanley L. Jaki, "The Absolute Beneath the Relative: Reflections on Einstein's Theories," in *Absolute Beneath the Relative*, 4. This essay is a tidy summary of misunderstandings on relativity.

32 Ibid., 2.

33 Bodanis, *E=mc²*, 261, original emphasis.

34 Jaki, *Absolute Beneath the Relative*, 8.

35 Penrose, *Emperor's New Mind*, 361. This is perhaps the most famous of Einstein's sayings. And he must have said it in a variety of ways. Bill Bryson, *A Short History of Nearly Everything* (Toronto: Doubleday, 2003), writes (without a source) that the actual quote was: "It seems hard to sneak a look at God's cards. But that He plays dice and uses 'telepathic' methods ... is something that I cannot believe for a single moment" (139).

36 Powell, *God*, 44.

37 Ibid., 3.

38 Davies, *Accidental Universe*, 9.

39 Paul Davies, *God and the New Physics* (New York: Simon and Schuster, 1983), 221.

40 Feynman, *Character of Physical Law*, 58. This famous series of lectures was first published in 1965 and has gone through twenty-two printings.

41 Davies, *Accidental Universe*, 1.

42 Bryson, *Short History*, 104. Bryson's book is a good layman's read, for he has a knack for the sort of telling vignette such as used here.

43 Feynman, *Character of Physical Law*, 30–1.

44 Ibid., 32.

45 Feynman, *Six Easy Pieces*, 110, my emphasis.

46 Bryson, *Short History*, 125.

47 Barrow, *Constants of Nature*, 49.

48 Ibid., 235.

49 Ibid., 240.

50 Davies, *Accidental Universe*, 77.

51 Ibid., 77–8.

52 Overbye, *Lonely Hearts*, 212.

53 Davies, *Accidental Universe*, 10.

54 Paul Dirac, quoted in Barrow, *Constants of Nature*, 101, 102.

55 Fred Hoyle, quoted in Paul Davies, *The Mind of God: The Scientific Basis for a Rational World* (New York: Simon and Schuster, 1992), 199.

56 These comments about the old and new stories of science are adapted from Robert M. Augros and George N. Stanciu, *The New Story of Science* (Lake Bluff, IL: Regnery Gateway, 1984).

57 Max Born, quoted in ibid., 4–5.

58 Ibid., 7.

59 John Eccles, quoted in ibid., 171.

60 Three such ambitious books are Penrose, *Emperor's New Mind*, wherein he discusses the role of quantum mechanics in brain activity; Jeffrey Satinover, *The Quantum Brain* (New York: John Wiley and Sons, 2001); and Nick

Herbert, *Elemental Mind: Human Consciousness and the New Physics* (New York: Penguin, 1994). Satinover goes further than Penrose toward showing, or at least strongly suggesting, that the mechanical view of the mind as a machine or computer is outdated. The mind operates – indeed, thrives – on the multilevel and original organization of its own essential chaos, and this is what gives us the sense of the mental freedom we enjoy. Herbert explores many angles and theories concerning the possible nonmateriality of mind.

61 Bryson, *Short History*, 134.

62 John Caiazza, "Natural Right and the Re-discovery of Design in Contemporary Cosmology," *The Political Science Reviewer* 25 (1996): 291.

63 Freeman Dyson, quoted in Augros and Stanciu, *New Story*, 69, my emphasis.

64 Barrow and Tipler, *Anthropic*, 4, my emphasis.

65 Augros and Stanciu, *New Story*, 70.

66 Barrow and Tipler, *Anthropic*, 5, my emphasis.

67 Feynman, *Six Easy Pieces*, 20.

68 Francis S. Collins, *The Language of God* (New York: Free Press, 2006), 73. Collins, speaking from his perspective as a brilliant and prestigious scientist who is also a theist, has upset a lot of materialist colleagues.

69 I have drawn a number of these examples from Walter Bradley, "The Just So Universe," in William Dembski and James Kushiner, eds, *Signs of Intelligence* (Grand Rapids, MI: Brazos Press, 2001), 157–70.

70 Augros and Stanciu, *New Story*, 156–7.

71 Erwin Schrödinger, quoted in ibid., 157.

72 Fred Hoyle, quoted in Davies, *Accidental Universe*, 118, my emphasis. Readers interested in the rather extraordinary number of physical phenomena that are exactly favourable to biological life on earth are encouraged to read John D. Barrow and Frank J. Tipler, "The Anthropic Principle and Biochemistry," in *Anthropic*. A book that gathers together a plethora of such favourable circumstances and "coincidences" is Denton, *Nature's Destiny*. He writes with a religious bent, and this makes some of his arguments circular, but the raw science he pulls together to illustrate the "fitness" and fine-tuning of our environment is impressive.

CHAPTER SIX

1 At 1:15 PM EST 5 March 2008, the World Population Clock showed the actual figure to be 6,649,718,695. However, a close inspection would show that the majority of nations on earth have no clear idea what their population actually is because they lack the manpower and methodology to track it.

2 The most extreme practitioners of ancient religions such as Gnosticism specifically constructed elaborate dualistic belief systems in which the spirit

of human beings, conceived as originally free and beautiful, is said to have been abandoned by a remote, but true, God to the physical darkness, corruption, and filth of this material world. To them, our creator God was a fake god, a trickster who trapped us all here on earth. So all true Gnostics (then and now) yearn for a return from their earthly slavery to the pure spiritual freedom they imagine once existed. Readers may wish to study the connection between ancient Gnosticism and modern thinking about liberation and democracy in William D. Gairdner, *The Trouble with Democracy* (Toronto: Stoddart, 2001), esp. chapter 3, "Democracy, the Gnostic Impulse, and the State of Nature," 87–120. For a straightforward examination of the way modern political ideologies are forms of religion secularized, see George Steiner, *Nostalgia for the Absolute* (Toronto: CBC Enterprises, Massey Lectures, 1974). For a more in-depth, less accessible, but deeper account, see Eric Voegelin, *The New Science of Politics* (Chicago: University of Chicago Press, 1952).

3 Ullica Segerstråle, in *Defenders of the Truth: The Sociobiology Debate* (Oxford: Oxford University Press, 2000), 392, writes that Stephen Chorover, a member of the Sociobiology Study Group, a collection of liberals who ganged up for an attack on E.O. Wilson after his publication of *Sociobiology*, thought of the war over biology this engendered as "part of the great struggle between free will and determinism." According to him, she goes on, "the social mythology underlying sociobiological theorizing could be traced all the way back to *Genesis* and the doctrine of original sin, and precedents to the sociobiological debate could be found throughout Church history."

4 Andrew Brown, The *Darwin Wars: The Scientific Battle for the Soul of Man* (London: Simon and Schuster: 1999), 4, my emphasis.

5 William Hamilton, quoted in ibid., 11.

6 Ibid., 13.

7 See, especially, Edwin Black, *War against the Weak: Eugenics and America's Campaign to Create a Master Race* (New York: Four Walls Eight Windows, 2003).

8 John B. Watson, *Behaviorism* (New York: Norton, 1925), 25.

9 From "Found the 'secret of life,'" Sir Francis Crick's obituary in Canada's *National Post*, 30 July 2004.

10 Rudi Rummel, *Death by Government* (New Jersey: Transaction, 1994).

11 Renato Rosaldo, "Of Headhunters and Soldiers: Separating Ethical and Cultural Relativism," at www.scu.edu/ethics/publications/iie/v1 1n1/relativism.html.

12 Konrad Lorenz, *On Aggression* (London: Methuen, 1960); Robert Ardrey, *The Territorial Imperative* (New York: Atheneum, 1966); Desmond Morris, *The Naked Ape* (New York: McGraw-Hill, 1967); Lionel Tiger and Robin Fox, *The Imperial Animal* (New York: Holt, Rinehart and Winston, 1971).

CHAPTER SEVEN

1 See especially chapter 9, "Biology Redivivus," in Carl N. Degler, *In Search of Human Nature: The Decline and Revival of Darwinism in American Social Thought* (New York: Oxford University Press, 1991).

2 Edward O. Wilson, *Sociobiology: The Abridged Edition* (Cambridge MA: Harvard University Press, 1980), 4.

3 Ullica Segerstråle, *Defenders of the Truth: The Sociology Debate* (Oxford: Oxford University Press, 2000).

4 Wilson, *Sociobiology*, 4.

5 Ibid., 3.

6 E.O. Wilson, *On Human Nature* (Cambridge, MA: Harvard University Press, 1978), 1.

7 Richard Lewontin, quoted in a fascinating article by Tom Bethell, "Agnostic Evolutionists: The Taxonomic Case against Darwin," in *Harper's* magazine, February 1985.

8 A fascinating read by a pretty rigorous thinker, from whose book I have drawn these examples of the overly sophisticated human brain, is Stephen M. Barr, *Modern Physics and Ancient Faith* (Notre Dame, IN: University of Notre Dame Press, 2003), 197.

9 The following books provide a starter kit on the evolution debate: William A. Demski, ed., *Uncommon Dissent: Intellectuals Who Find Darwinism Unconvincing* (Wilmington, DE: ISI Books, 2004); Phillip E. Johnson, *Darwin on Trial* (Washington, DC: Regnery Gateway, 1991); Michael J. Behe, *Darwin's Black Box: The Biochemical Challenge to Evolution* (New York: Free Press, 1996); Percival Davis, Dean H. Kenyon, and Charles B. Thaxton, *Of Pandas and People: The Central Questions of Biological Origins* (1989; reprint, Dallas: Haughton, 1993); Lee Spetner, *Not by Chance: Shattering the Modern Theory of Evolution* (New York: Judaica Press, 1997); Michael Denton, *Evolution: A Theory in Crisis* (Bethesda, MD: Adler and Adler, 1985); and finally, Jonathan Wells, *Icons of Evolution* (Washington, DC: Regnery, 2000). These books are full of further references. Readers may also go to Discovery Institute at www.discovery.org/csc for more information on the Darwin Wars.

10 Wilson, *On Human Nature*, 1, my emphasis.

11 Ibid., 1–5.

12 Ibid., 2.

13 Ibid., 201.

14 Ibid., 5.

15 Wilson, *Sociobiology*, 300.

16 Richard Dawkins, *The Selfish Gene* (Oxford: Oxford University Press, 1976).

17 Richard Dawkins, "Why I Am a Secular Humanist," in *Free Inquiry* 18, no. 18
   (1997), quoted in John Alcock, *The Triumph of Sociobiology* (New York:
   Oxford University Press, 2001), 215.
18 "Religion, group affiliation at root of conflicts," www.purify,ind.com/
   IV9.htm, interview with Richard Dawkins at his home in Oxford after
   11 September 2001, by Shiochi Habu, chief of General European Bureau
   for the Japanese newspaper *Yomiuri Shimbun*.
   Q: You define the human brain as rebelling against dictation by genes.
   D: Through most of evolutionary history it has been possible to look at ani-
      mals, their brains and their behavior, and say in a fairly simple sense:
      "This helps the animal to survive. This helps the genes to survive." The
      same is true of brains and the same was originally true of human brains.
      The human brain, like the human eye or the human foot, is an adapta-
      tion to (help the organism) survive and to reproduce. But the human
      brain became so large that it became possible for it to take things into its
      own hands. It could do things that might not actually benefit survival and
      reproduction.
   Q: For instance?
   D: An obvious example is contraception. What contraception does is pro-
      foundly anti-Darwinian. Darwinian selection has built into our brains an
      enjoyment of sex. If it had built into our brains a desire to have children
      – which maybe it has to some extent, maybe especially in women – then
      that would be fine. But it seems that a very strong desire for sex was built
      into males. As long as there is no contraception, this will produce chil-
      dren – so it works.
         When there is contraception, it doesn't work. But nevertheless, the
      rule that has been built into the brain, which is to enjoy sex, still works
      and still plays out. So this is a kind of rebellion. That is a very simple kind
      of rebellion. You can make the same argument for much more compli-
      cated kinds of rebellion.
   Q: What other rebellious actions can the brain take?
   D: By the same token, our brain is powerful enough for us to consciously
      rebel, to say something like, "I actually think that a Darwinian world is a
      very bad world in which to live." It is the world which led to us in the first
      place. It is Darwinian selection which gave rise to us in the first place. We
      can explicitly rebel and say, "The Darwinian world, the world of natural
      selection, the world of dog eat dog, a sort of Margaret Thatcher type of
      world, is not a pleasant world in which to live." We can consciously and
      deliberately rebel and we can even set up organizations, which are called
      things like a socialist party, which are kind of rebellious parties. You

could think of a welfare state as an anti-Darwinian social system, and it is a system that I support.

Dawkins's responses are an example of the pervasive political naiveté to be found in such fields, for hardly anything in political history can rival the oppressive control of egalitarian welfare states, whose regulatory and taxation powers over citizens are vastly superior to those even of the largest corporations. If we see totalitarian states as a kind of nonliberal extension of this sort of social control, we get a sense of the far greater "Darwinian" cruelty possible from Dawkins's political preferences.

19 Wilson, *Sociobiology,* 127.

20 Edward O. Wilson, "Can Biology Do Better than Faith," *New Scientist,* 2 November 2005.

21 The theory developed by Geoffrey B. West and his colleagues looks at such things as the structural and functional properties of vertebrate cardiovascular and respiratory systems, plant vascular systems, insect tracheal tubes, and other distribution networks. In particular, the theory seeks to explain the origins and ubiquity of a set of mathematical laws known as the quarter-power scaling laws as they apply to plants and animals. According to West, "life is the most complex physical system in the universe. Beyond natural selection, genetic codes and the like there are hardly any general principles or laws that we know that it obeys. Scaling laws are the exception. These are quantitative laws and, remarkably, they are absurdly simple given you are dealing with the most complex of systems." See the Los Alamos Laboratory website: www.lanl.gov/orgs/ sr/biology.shtml. Also, see James H. Brown and Geoffrey B. West, *Scaling in Biology* (Oxford: Oxford University Press, 2000). An elegantly written and influential precursor to this approach is D'Arcy Wentworth Thompson, *On Growth and Form* (Cambridge, UK: Cambridge University Press, 1961).

22 Wilson, *On Human Nature,* 20–1.

23 Alcock, *Triumph of Sociobiology,* 76.

24 Of assistance for this section has been Lauralee Sherwood, *Fundamentals of Physiology: A Human Perspective* (New York: West Publishing, 1995). Her first chapter, which is indicative of the focus of this textbook, is entitled "Homeostasis: The Foundation of Physiology."

25 Wilson, *Sociobiology,* 284, my emphasis.

26 Wilson, *On Human Nature,* 34–5.

27 Alcock, *Triumph of Sociobiology,* 201.

28 See William D. Gairdner, "Democracy against Community," in *The Trouble with Democracy* (Toronto: Stodart, 2001), 345–87.

29 Leda Cosmides, John Tooby, and Jerome H. Barkow, "Introduction: Evolutionary Psychology and Conceptual Integration," in Jerome H. Barkow,

Leda Cosmides, and Tooby, eds, *The Adapted Mind: Evolutionary Psychology and the Generation of Culture* (New York: Oxford University Press, 1992), 5.

30 David Buss, "Evolutionary Psychology: A New Paradigm for Psychological Science," *Psychological Inquiry* 6, no. 1 (1995): 85.

31 Leda Cosmides and John Tooby, "Evolutionary Psychology: A Primer" (2004), 12, www.psych.ucsb.edu/researchcep/primer.html.

32 The Standard Social Science Model is flawed in three ways: (1) It overlooks developmental change. We are not born with teeth or breast milk. But the capacity for them is there from the beginning. It is the same for many psychological mechanisms that are triggered by development, hormonal change, and the like. (2) It assumes a strict division between nature and nurture, whereas in fact environmentalist claims require "a rich, evolved cognitive architecture." (3) It operates on the basis of "an impossible psychology," namely the idea that the mind/brain is based on a general, content-free cognitive architecture. Evolutionary psychology, in contrast, operates on the understanding that all cognitive function is both evolved and content-specific.

33 The central manifesto of evolutionary psychology is John Tooby and Leda Cosmides, "The Psychological Foundations of Culture," which is the first chapter of the seminal collection of essays *The Adapted Mind*, cited above at note 29.

34 A useful essay, from which this material is drawn and paraphrased, is Leda Cosmides and John Tooby, "Evolutionary Psychology: A Primer" (2004), which can be downloaded, along with much other useful material, from the website for the Center for Evolutionary Psychology, University of California at Santa Barbara: www.psych.ucsb.edu/research/cep/primer.html.

35 Ibid.

36 Cosmides, Tooby, and Barkow, "Introduction," 115.

37 David Buss, *Evolutionary Psychology: The New Science of the Mind* (New York: Pearson Education, 2004).

38 Stephen M. Colarelli and Joseph R. Dettmann, "Intuitive Evolutionary Perspectives in Marketing Practices," available at www.chsbs.edu/stephen_colarelli.

39 See William D. Gairdner, *The War against the Family* (Toronto: Stoddart, 1992), esp. ch. 9, "Looking after Their Bodies."

40 Donald Symons, *The Evolution of Human Sexuality* (New York: Oxford University Press, 1979), 301.

41 Reported in Canada's *National Post*, 6 May 2004.

42 See an analysis of both magazines in Symons, *Evolution*, 174ff.

43 See ibid. and also Glenn Wilson, *The Great Sex Divide: A Study of Male-Female Differences* (Washington, DC: Scott-Townsend, 1992), which offers a clear

and concise summary of Symons's foundational ideas. Some work has been saved in this chapter by drawing from Wilson's clear summary of the basics of the evolutionist "parental investment" theory from Symons's book. For something more recent that surveys the whole field, see David C. Geary, *Male, Female: The Evolution of Human Sex Differences* (Washington, DC: American Psychological Association, 1998).

44 Symons, *Evolution*, 24.

45 L.A. Kirkendall, quoted in ibid., 218.

46 Two of the earliest books to blow the whistle on the homosexual lifestyle are Alan Bell and Martin Weinberg, *Homosexualities* (New York: Simon and Schuster, 1978), from which the percentages given are taken, and also Karla Jay and Allen Young, *The Gay Report* (New York: Summit Books, 1977).

47 You can't say things like this these days without some evidence. It is easily found in most studies of the so-called gay lifestyle, and many of the studies are by gay researchers who themselves deplore the hit-and-run gay lifestyle.

48 Symons, *Evolution*, 297.

49 JoAnn Deak, from her speech "Taking the Mean out of Teen," cited in Anne Marie Owens, "Boys Brains Are from Mars" (The Catholic Education Resource Center, 2003).

50 Alcock, *Triumph of Sociobiology*, 150.

51 The by now widely acknowledged and resounding failure of the egalitarian kibbutzim is treated roundly in Wilson, *Great Sex Divide*; Anne Moir and David Jessel, *Brain Sex: The Real Difference between Men and Women* (London: Mandarin, 1991); and Melvin Konner, *The Tangled Wing: Biological Constraints on the Human Spirit* (New York: Henry Holt, 2002).

52 In Noam Chomsky, *Reflections on Language* (New York: Pantheon, 1975), 132, we also read: "The principle that human nature, in its psychological aspects, is nothing more than a product of history and given social relations removes all barriers to coercion and manipulation by the powerful."

53 J.R. Urdry, quoted in Wilson, *Great Sex Divide*, 37.

54 References to universal (insofar as these have been cross-culturally examined) human sex differences abound in several books. Eleanor Maccoby and Carol Jacklin, *The Psychology of Sex Differences* (Stanford, CA: Stanford University Press, 1974), is by two avowed feminist scholars who reached their conclusions gingerly but found themselves forced by the copious evidence to admit a number of innate sex differences. Moir and Jessel, *Brain Sex*, is an early display of this reality. Wilson, *Great Sex Divide*, is a very readable treatment of the biochemical and experimental evidence for innate sex differences. Robert L. Nadeau, *S/He Brain* (Westport, CT: Praeger, 1996), is a review of the underlying biochemical and neuro-scientific findings about

sex differences, nested in some appropriately targeted political objections to feminist ideology. Kimura, *Sex and Cognition*, is a careful review of the findings to date, somewhat apprehensively expressed. Geary, *Male, Female*, is a detailed survey of studies on sex differences thought to be rooted in evolutionary theory. Steven Pinker, *The Blank Slate: The Modern Denial of Human Nature* (New York: Viking Penguin, 2002), is another of Pinker's long, cheerfully confident, and informative books. Pinker, like so many evolutionists today, is a Darwinian fundamentalist whose arguments and evidence exclude even the suggestion that Darwinism is a faith more than a fact. See also his *How the Mind Works* (New York: Norton, 1997), a resolutely Darwinian argument for what the title claims. Finally, I suggest Konner, *Tangled Wing*, a nicely written and wide-ranging classic in the field, marred only by occasional heartfelt if naive political innuendo of the egalitarian type.

55 Nadeau, *S/He Brain*, 59.
56 Maccoby and Jacklin, *Psychology of Sex Differences*, 142.
57 Wilson, *Great Sex Divide*, 110.
58 Kimura, *Sex and Cognition*, 177.
59 Nadeau, *S/He Brain*, 50. See also Pinker, *Blank Slate*, 347.
60 Nadeau, *S/He Brain*, 52.
61 Ibid.
62 Wilson, *Great Sex Divide*, 115ff. For a general discussion of the differential effects of hormones on men and women, see Pinker, *Blank Slate*, 347ff. For an in-depth study of sex differences (and many other matters) in crime, see James Q. Wilson and Richard Herrnstein, *Crime and Human Nature* (New York: Simon and Schuster, 1985).
63 Kimura, *Sex and Cognition*, 62.
64 Wilson, *Great Sex Divide*, 100.
65 Nadeau, *S/He Brain*, 56.

CHAPTER EIGHT

1 Jim Powell, Senior Fellow of the Cato Institute, has written a helpful, brief article, from which I have drawn: "Marcus Tullius Cicero, Who Gave Natural Law to the Modern World," in *The Freeman*, January 1997.
2 These assumptions are more fleshed out in a fine study by Pauline Westerman, *The Disintegration of Natural Law Theory: Aquinas to Finnis* (Leiden and New York: Koninklijke Brill, 1998), 12.
3 On this point, see the lucid article by Lloyd Weinreb, "Natural Law and Rights," ch. 10 in Robert P. George, ed., *Natural Law Theory* (Oxford: Clarendon, 1995).

4 See an excellent article by Stephen Hall, "The Persistent Spectre: Natural Law, International Order and the Limits of Legal Positivism," *European Journal of International Law* 12, no. 2 (2001): 269–307. The quotations here are from pages 303–4.

5 "World toilet summit declares clean facilities a basic human right," *National Post,* 18 November 2004.

6 Hadley Arkes, "Reflections on Cicero's Naturalism," in George, ed., *Natural Law Theory,* 263.

7 See a brief and unsympathetic, but accurate, overview of the criticisms of modern natural law theory in Robert P. George, "Natural Law and Human Nature," in George, ed, *Natural Law Theory,* 31.

8 For example, John Finnis, in his influential book *Natural Law and Natural Right* (Oxford: Clarendon, 1980), states proudly that "the argument of this book does not rely, even implicitly, on the term 'human nature'" (50). On the matter of the modern natural law theorists denying that Aquinas ever believed in human nature, see Westerman, *Disintegration,* 247.

9 See the section on objective natural law, pages 232ff, in E.B.F. Midgley, *The Natural Law Tradition and the Theory of International Relations* (London: Elek Books, 1975). This point about the innate seeds of the virtues that exist in us prior to the work of reason that makes them acquired virtues is found on page 238, where on the evidence, Midgley dismisses Grisez's argument that Aquinas would have agreed with Hume's argument concerning the lack of any necessary connection between *is* and *ought.*

10 Saint Thomas Aquinas, *Summa Theologiae: A Concise Translation,* ed. Timothy Mcdermott (Chicago: Christian Classics, 1989), sec. 94.6.

11 Charles Grove Haines, *The Revival of Natural Law Concepts* (Cambridge, MA: Harvard University Press, 1930), 220, quoted in Peter J. Stanlis, *Edmund Burke and the Natural Law* (Lafayette, LA: Huntington House, 1986), 260n5.

12 Roscoe Pound, "The Theory of Judicial Decision," *Harvard Law Review* 36 (May 1923): 802.

13 Stanlis, *Edmund Burke,* 6.

14 Roscoe Pound, "The Scope and Purpose of Sociological Jurisprudence," *Harvard Law Review* 25 (November 1911): 162, quoted in Stanlis, *Edmund Burke,* 4.

15 Sir William Blackstone, *Commentaries on the Laws of England* (New York, 1832), quoted in Stanlis, *Edmund Burke,* 253.

16 Some telling criticisms of natural law are: it is not really universal but presupposes Roman Catholic values; it is inherently ambiguous; it is too abstract and general to be of practical help; it is too malleable and has been used to support conservative, revolutionary, and liberal causes; because there is no rational way

to decide right from wrong, natural law ends up as a subjective form of legal relativism; finally, critics say that law and morality should not be mixed, or as Hume put it, we cannot derive *ought* from *is*. About this I am not so certain. In every *is*, an *ought* may be found. In any case, moral talk makes no sense without an *ought*, as there is no such thing as moral behaviour except in a plural context. That is, individual actions can be moral only with respect to others, and this acknowledgment always invokes either a shall or a shall-not judgment, according to some final end considered morally right. The totality of the body of law in all nations of the world constitutes myriad moral *oughts* derived from what *is*.

17 Hans Kelsen, "Absolutism and Relativism in Philosophy and Politics," *American Political Science Review*, no. 42 (1948): 906, cited in Charles E. Rice, *50 Questions on the Natural Law* (San Francisco: Ignatius Press, 1993), 75–9.
18 Russell Hittinger, "Natural Law and Virtue," in George, ed., *Natural Law Theory*, 67n19.
19 Charles E. Rice, "Natural Law in the Twenty-First Century," in Edward B. Mclean, ed., *Common Truths: New Perspectives on Natural Law* (Wilmington, DE: ISI Books, 2000), 298.
20 Leo Strauss, *Natural Right and History* (Chicago: University of Chicago Press, 1965), 161–2.
21 William D. Gairdner, *The Trouble with Democracy* (Toronto: Stoddart, 2001).
22 For the broad knowledge held by the American founders, see *The Federalist Paper*; on the Canadian founders, see Janet Ajzenstat, Paul Romney, Ian Gentles, and William D. Gairdner, *Canada's Founding Debates* (Toronto: University of Toronto Press, 2003).
23 Rice, *50 Questions*, 78.
24 Hans Kelsen, quoted in ibid., 78–9; see also note 127 therein.
25 Henrich Rommen, *The Natural Law: A Study in Legal and Social History and Philosophy* (Indianapolis, IN: Liberty Fund, 1998), 16.
26 Here are some recent seminal works on natural law: Yves Simon, *The Tradition of Natural Law: A Philosopher's Reflections* (New York: Fordham University Press, 1965); Finnis, *Natural Law*; Rommen, *Natural Law*; Javier Hervada, *Natural Right and Natural Law: A Critical Introduction* (Pamplona: University of Navarra, 1987); Michael Bertram Crowe, *The Changing Profile of the Natural Law* (The Hague: Matrinus Nijhoff, 1977); Henry Veatch, *Human Rights: Fact or Fancy?* (Baton Rouge: Louisiana State University Press, 1985); Russell Hittinger, *A Critique of the New Natural Law Theory* (Notre Dame, IN: University of Notre Dame Press, 1987); Ernest Bloch, *Natural Law and Human Dignity*, trans. Dennis J. Schmidt (Cambridge, MA: MIT Press, 1986); Ernest Bloch, *Natural Law and Modern Society* (Cleveland, OH: World, 1963); Paul Sigmund, *Natural Law in Political Thought* (Cambridge, MA:

Winthrop, 1971); Ernest Bloch, *Light on Natural Law*, ed. Illud Evans (Balti-more: Helicon, 1965); E.B.F. Midgley, *Natural Law and International Relations* (London: Elek, 1975); Jacques Maritain, *The Rights of Man and Natural Law* (San Francisco: Ignatius Press, 1986); Stanlis, *Edmund Burke*; and finally, Westerman, *Disintegration*. The journals *The American Journal of Jurisprudence* and *Vera Lex* are both concerned with natural law questions.

27 Rice, *50 Questions*, 24, my emphasis. Among others, Rice cites Heinrich Rommen, "Natural Law in Decisions of the Federal Supreme Court and of the Constitutional Courts in Germany," *Natural Law Forum* 4, no. 26 (1959).

28 Martin Luther King Jr, "Letter from Birmingham Jail," quoted in Rice, *50 Questions*, 25.

29 "Saddam awaits trial by tending his garden," *National Post*, 21 September 2004.

30 Richard F. Devlin, "Mapping Legal Theory," in *Alberta Law Review* 32, no. 3 (1994): 605. Devlin provides an excellent brief review of the varieties of le-gal theory practised in North America – with an emphasis on the Canadian legal landscape.

31 Robert N. Wilkin, "Cicero and the Law of Nature," in Arthur L. Harding, ed., *Origins of the Natural Law Tradition* (Dallas: Southern Methodist Univer-sity, 1954), 15.

32 Blaise Pascal, *Pensées* (London: Penguin Books, 1966), sec. 15, no. 199, 94.

33 Stephen M. Barr, *Modern Physics and Ancient Faith* (Notre Dame, IN: Univer-sity of Notre Dame Press, 2003), 197.

34 Robin Collins, "Religion and Science Revisited," an excellent review of Barr, *Modern Physics*, in *First Things*, November 2003, 54.

35 This is discussed in chapter 5 of this book, "The Constants of Nature," and far more extensively in Barr, *Modern Physics*.

36 Cicero, *On Moral Duties*, 1.4.11, quoted in J. Rufus Fears, "Natural Law: The Legacy of Greece and Rome," in Harding, ed., *Origins*, 35.

37 Cicero, quoted in Mclean, ed., *Common Truths*, 34.

38 Aristotle, *Metaphysics*, trans. and intro. Hugh Lawson-Tancred (London: Penguin, 1998), bk 3, 88.

39 I am indebted to an essay by Ralph McInerny, "Are There Moral Truths That Everyone Knows?" and to several others in the collection by Edward B. Mclean, ed., *Common Truths: New Perspectives on Natural Law* (Wilmington, DE: ISI Books, 2000).

40 See especially Jay Budziszewski, *What We Can't Not Know* (Dallas: Spence, 2003), and also his *Written on the Heart: The Case for Natural Law* (Downers Grove, IL: InterVarsity Press, 1997).

41 What is now called the Public Health Agency of Canada has produced annu-al reports on HIV and AIDS for some twenty-five years. The most recent

reports can be seen at www.phac-aspc.gc.ca/pphb-dgspsp/hast-vsmt/
public_e. html. From the beginning, these have shown that about 80 per
cent of all AIDS cases and deaths in Canada are homosexual males. A summary of the situation can be seen in the "Archive" of my website at www.wil-
liamgairdner.com in my article "There Can Be No 'Sex' in Homosexual."

42 Alasdair MacIntyre, "Natural Law in Advanced Modernity," in Harding ed.,
Origins, 91ff.

CHAPTER NINE

1 On many aspects of slavery, ancient and modern, see William D. Gairdner,
"Freedom, Democracy, Slavery," ch. 2 in *The Trouble with Democracy* (Toronto: Stoddart, 2001), 41–86.

2 I am grateful to Professor William Ryan, of Bridgewater Nova Scotia, who,
after I mentioned in 1994 that I was interested in the natural law, respond-
ed by sending me a box full of books and articles on that subject, accompanied by an extensive hand-written summary and bibliography. It was
among his papers that I found a reference to this list of moral universals
originally published by Professor Richard Beis in *The Thomist* in 1964. By
way of an Internet search, I located Professor Beis, now retired in Nova
Scotia, and between his trips to help at the food bank and what he calls his
addiction to golf, he has been kind enough to send me a few more of his
engaging articles.

3 Stephen Hall, "The Persistent Spectre: Natural Law, International Order
and the Limits of Legal Positivism," *European Journal of International Law* 12,
no. 2 (2001): 269–307.

4 Summary of international law enunciated at Nuremberg (see http://
deoxy.org/wc/wc-nurem.htm and elsewhere on the Internet):

Principles of International Law Recognized in the Charter of the Nuremberg Tribunal and in the Judgment of the Tribunal (1950)

Principle I
Any person who commits an act which constitutes a crime under international law is responsible therefor and liable to punishment.

Principle II
The fact that internal law does not impose a penalty for an act which constitutes a crime under international law does not relieve the person who
committed the act from responsibility under international law.

Principle III

The fact that a person who committed an act which constitutes a crime under international law acted as Head of State or responsible Government official does not relieve him from responsibility under international law.

Principle IV

The fact that a person acted pursuant to order of his Government or of a superior does not relieve him from responsibility under international law, provided a moral choice was in fact possible to him.

Principle V

Any person charged with a crime under international law has the right to a fair trial on the facts and law.

Principle VI

The crimes hereinafter set out are punishable as crimes under international law:

(a) *Crimes against peace:*

(i) Planning, preparation, initiation or waging of a war of aggression or a war in violation of international treaties, agreements or assurances;

(ii) Participation in a common plan or conspiracy for the accomplishment of any of the acts mentioned under (i).

(b) *War crimes:*

Violations of the laws or customs of war which include, but are not limited to, murder, ill-treatment or deportation to slave-labour or for any other purpose of civilian population of or in occupied territory; murder or ill-treatment of prisoners of war, of persons on the Seas, killing of hostages, plunder of public or private property, wanton destruction of cities, towns, or villages, or devastation not justified by military necessity.

(c) *Crimes against humanity:*

Murder, extermination, enslavement, deportation and other inhuman acts done against any civilian population, or persecutions on political, racial or religious grounds, when such acts are done or such persecutions are carried on in execution of or in connection with any crime against peace or any war crime.

Principle VII

Complicity in the commission of a crime against peace, a war crime, or a crime against humanity as set forth in Principle VI is a crime under international law.

5 Hall, "Persistent Spectre," 269–307.
6 John Finnis, *Natural Law and Natural Right* (Oxford: Clarendon, 1980), 288.
7 Hall, "Persistent Spectre," 296.
8 Ibid.
9 Ibid., 298.
10 This important concession to what Hans Kelsen called the *Grundnorm*, or normative ground, or again, his conception of "an ultra-minimalist natural law," is found in his *General Theory of Law and State*, trans. Anders Wedberg (Cambridge, MA: Harvard University Press, 1945), quoted here in Hall, "Persistent Spectre," 300n133.
11 Jay Budziszewski, *Written on the Heart: The Case for Natural Law* (Downers Grove, IL: InterVarsity Press, 1997), 120.
12 Ibid.
13 From Dennis Lloyd, *The Idea of Law* (Middlesex: Penguin, 1964), quoted in Hall, "Persistent Spectre," 300.
14 Roy Wood Sellars and Raymond Bragg, along with thirty-four signatories, *Humanist Manifesto I* (1933); Paul Kurtz and Edwin H. Wilson, *Humanist Manifesto II* (1973). Readers will find an analysis of both manifestos in William D. Gairdner, *The War against the Family* (Toronto: Stoddart, 1992), 250–4.
15 Frans de Waal, *Primates and Philosophers: How Morality Evolved* (Princeton: Princeton University Press, 2006), 9.
16 Robert Wright, *The Moral Animal* (New York: Random House, 1994), 7–8.
17 Ullica Segerstråle, *Defenders of the Truth: The Sociology Debate* (Oxford: Oxford University Press, 2000), 396, original emphasis.
18 Ibid., original emphasis.
19 Wright, *Moral Animal*, 37.
20 James Q. Wilson, *The Moral Sense* (New York: Simon and Schuster, 1993).
21 Ibid., vii-viii, my emphasis.
22 Ibid., xi.
23 Ibid., 238.
24 Blaise Pascal, *Pensées* (London: Penguin Books, 1966), ser. 2, no. 423, 154.
25 Budziszewski, *Written on the Heart*, 214.
26 Ibid. I am indebted to this author for pointing by way of the selected quotations to the salient features of Wilson's arguments and their weaknesses.

27 Paul Dirac, quoted in Huston Smith, *Forgotten Truth: The Primordial Tradition* (New York: Harper and Row, 1976), 115.
28 Ibid., x.
29 Aldous Huxley, *The Perennial Philosophy* (New York: Harper Collins, 2004). The quotations from Huxley in this paragraph, except the last, are from pages vii-xi.
30 Aldous Huxley, "Introduction to the Bhagavad-Gita, as translated by Swami Prabhavananda and Christopher Isherwood." This text, in which the four principles that follow also appear, is posted at http://members.tripod.com/~parvati/perennial.html.
31 C.S. Lewis, *The Abolition of Man* (Glasgow: Collins, 1978), 49.
32 Ibid., 44.

CHAPTER TEN

1 Bertrand Russell, *The Problems of Philosophy* (1912; reprint, Oxford: Oxford University Press, 1959, 1972).
2 After many years away from this general topic I was refreshed by Keith Windschuttle's *The Killing of History* (San Francisco: Encounter Books, 1996), in which he gives a hefty critique of the whole unfolding from structuralism to postmodernism to "cultural studies," as well as detailed exposes of the intellectual and moral faults – and frauds – of many of the seminal thinkers in these movements.
3 The edition relied on here is Ferdinand de Saussure, *Course in General Linguistics*, trans. Roy Harris, ed. Charles Bally and Albert Sechehaye, with Albert Riedlinger (Chicago: Open Court, 1986).
4 Roy Harris, "Translator's Introduction," in ibid., x.
5 John E. Jospeh, Nigel Love, and Talbot J. Taylor, *Landmarks in Linguistic Thought* (London: Routledge, 2001), 216.
6 Raymond Tallis, *Not Saussure: A Critique of Post-Saussurean Literary Theory* (London: Macmillan, 1988), 7. This book provides one of the best general critiques of the irresponsible uses made of Saussure's ideas.
7 De Saussure, *Course*, 24.
8 Noam Chomsky, *Syntactic Structures* (The Hague: Mouton, 1957).
9 See Steven Pinker, *The Blank Slate: The Modern Denial of Human Nature* (New York: Viking, 2002), for the best general presentation of this older metaphor for mind.
10 See especially Neil Smith, *Chomsky: Ideas and Ideals* (1999; reprint, Cambridge, UK: Cambridge University Press, 2004), for the best overview of these debates.

11 Currently, the most reader-friendly survey of the language theory debates is Steven Pinker, *The Language Instinct* (New York: Harper Collins, 1994). I have difficulties with Pinker's evolutionary biologism, but the book is a useful survey of the debates nonetheless.

12 Claude Levi-Strauss, *Les structures élémentaires de la parenté* (Paris: Presses Universitaires de France, 1949), translated by J.H. Bell and J.R. von Sturmer as *The Elementary Structures of Kinship*, ed. R. Needham (Boston: Beacon Press, 1969).

13 De Saussure, *Course*, 68, my emphasis.

14 Ibid., 118–19, my emphasis. There is no replacement for reading original texts, and this classic work clearly renders Saussure's main ideas on language and, for those coming to it for the first time, also the many ways he has been misunderstood and misused.

15 Tallis, *Not Saussure*, 69.

16 Ibid.

17 The classic text that led the field for a half-century, although it is now much critiqued, is Benjamin Lee Whorf, *Language, Thought, and Reality* (Cambridge, MA: MIT Press, 1956).

18 Roland Barthes, *Sur Racine* (Paris: Club francais du livre, 1960; Editions du Seuil, 1963); and in English, Roland Barthes, *On Racine*, trans. Richard Howard (New York: Hill and Wang, 1964).

19 In the foreword to *On Racine*, Barthes explains his method: "the analysis presented here is not concerned with Racine at all, but only with the Racinian hero: it avoids inferring from the work to the author and from the author to the work; it is a deliberately closed analysis: I have put myself in Racine's tragic world and tried to describe its population (which may readily be abstracted under the concept *Homo racinianus*), without reference to any source in this world (not to be found, for instance, in history or biography). What I have attempted to reconstruct is a kind of Racinian anthropology, both structural and psychoanalytic: structural in content, because tragedy is here treated as a system of units ("figures") and functions; ... [and] psychoanalytic in form." The first essay, Barthes goes on: "is divided into two parts. One might say, in structural terms that the first is systematic (it analyzes figures and functions) and the second syntagmatic (it considers in extension the systematic elements at the level of each work."

20 Frank Lentricchia, *After the New Criticism* (Chicago: University of Chicago Press, 1980), 116, my emphasis.

21 See William D. Gairdner, "The Structure of the Unknown," in *The Critical Wager* (Toronto: ECW Press, 1982), 132–55. Looking back, I would say that structuralism as a method has made enduring contributions to the study of actual languages, kin systems, folk tales, and many other *already-formulaic* systems of communication. With respect to more complicated and nuanced

"languages," however, such as complex literary forms, poetry, the novel, and most intricate artefacts of higher culture, it has been as unproductive as it has been imaginative.

22 Roland Barthes, "The Death of the Author," in *Image, Music, Text*, trans. Stephen Heath (New York: Hill and Wang, 1977), 142–8.

23 Tallis, *Not* Saussure, 48, lays this out in a similar way.

24 Ibid., 88.

25 Ibid., 51.

26 Ibid., 53, original emphasis.

27 Ibid., 126.

28 Ibid., 59.

CHAPTER ELEVEN

1 Peter Viereck, *Metapolitics: From the Romantics to Hitler* (New York: Knopf, 1941), 5.

2 Ibid., 19.

3 Ibid., 27.

4 Friedrich Nietzsche, entry #244, "People and Fatherlands," in *Beyond Good and Evil*, trans. Michael Tanner, ed. R.J. Hollingdale (London: Penguin Classic, 1973), 175, my emphasis.

5 Viereck, *Metapolitics*, 33.

6 Gene Edward Veith Jr, *Modern Fascism: Liquidating the Judeo-Christian Worldview* (St Louis: Concordia, 1993), 81. See also his *Postmodern Times* (Wheaton, IL: Crossways Books, 1993). Both books provide handy overviews of their subjects.

7 I am indebted to Richard Wolin for his two books: *Heidegger's Children* (Princeton: Princeton University Press, 2001) and *The Seduction of Unreason: The Intellectual Romance with Fascism from Nietzsche to Postmodernism* (Princeton: Princeton University Press, 2004). Both are a feast of detail and argument. My remarks are drawn mostly from the latter and are somewhat of a partial summary of his excellent writing on Heidegger's thought and politics.

8 This phrase is from Geoffrey Clive, ed., *The Philosophy of Nietzsche* (New York: Mentor Books, New American Library, 1965), xxiv.

9 Michael Tanner, "Introduction," in Nietzsche, *Beyond Good and Evil*, trans. Tanner, ed. Hollingdale, 9.

10 I have been helped by ibid., 7–26.

11 Tanner, "Introduction," 10.

12 Clive, ed., *Philosophy of Nietzsche*, xxiv.

13 Friedrich Nietzsche, *Beyond Good and Evil*, trans. Marianne Cowan (Henry Regnery: Chicago, 1955), secs 4 to 6.

14 Geoffrey Clive, "Introduction," in Geoffrey Clive, ed., *The Philosophy of Nietzsche* (New York: Mentor, 1965), xix.

15 Friedrich Nietzsche, "Preface," in Nietzsche, *Beyond Good and Evil*, trans. Tanner, ed. Hollingdale, 31–2.

16 Wolin, *Seduction of Unreason*, 48ff.

17 Tanner, "Introduction," 25.

18 This segment on Heidegger is heavily indebted to Wolin, *Heidegger's Children*, a book that carefully links Heidegger's philosophy and politics.

19 Wolin, *Heidegger's Children*, 32.

20 Friedrich Nietzsche, *Being and Time* (1933), trans. John Macquarrie and Edward Robinson (San Francisco: Harper Collins, 1962).

21 Richard Wolin, "Being and Time: A Failed Masterpiece?" in *Heidegger's Children*, 203–32.

22 Veith Jr, *Modern Fascism*, 89.

23 Wolin, *Heidegger's Children*, 175.

24 Richard Polt explains such concepts clearly in *Heidegger: An Introduction* (Ithica, NY: Cornell University Press, 1999), ch. 2, 8–22.

25 On such themes well articulated, see ibid., 5ff.

26 Ibid., 5.

27 Wolin, *Heidegger's Children*, 186, original emphasis.

28 Most who have a speaking knowledge of Heidegger's work consider him to be a product, or at least a continuation, of Western philosophy, for they regard his existential roots as thoroughly "Western." There is, however, a great deal of fascinating material discussing Heidegger's debt to Eastern thinkers. Readers may wish to begin with such as Reinhard May, *Heidegger's Hidden Sources* (New York: Routledge, 1996); Fred Dallmayr, *The Other Heidegger* (Ithica, NY: Cornell University Press, 1993); and Michael E. Zimmerman, "Heidegger, Buddhism, and Deep Ecology," *The Cambridge Companion to Heidegger* (Cambridge, UK: Cambridge University Press, 1993). Heidegger's love of the Eastern ideal of achieving a selfless coincidence with Being is everywhere evident, and this must surely strike us as peculiar for a philosopher who claimed all his life that our salvation can arise only from our own personal (and ethnic-national) existential and historical tradition.

CHAPTER TWELVE

1 The lectures given there were subsequently published and are still available in all their earnest obscurity in Richard Macksey and Eugenio Donato, eds,

The Structuralist Controversy (Baltimore: Johns Hopkins University Press, 1970). Jacques Derrida's unnecessarily obtuse but seminal essay "Structure, Sign, and Play in the Discourse of the Human Sciences," in which the arrival of poststructuralism was announced, is at pages 247–65.

2 See Frank Lentricchia, *After the New Criticism* (Chicago: University of Chicago Press, 1980), for a general overview of deconstruction and postmodern thought, although not one that itself escapes criticism. His rendering of Derrida's subversive appearance, among other matters, is detailed in ch. 5, "History or the Abyss: Poststructuralism," 156–209. In a work of luminous rationality, John M. Ellis, *Against Deconstruction* (New Jersey: Princeton University Press, 1989), mortally exposes the weaknesses of postmodern thought in general and of some of its explicators, including Lentricchia.

3 See www.cspeirce.com, 21–1903 – C.P.5–138, Lowell Lectures V.

4 For an inventory of Peirce's definitions (and twelve further definitions!), readers may go to http://members.net/arisbe/menu/library/sources/76defs.htm.

5 Lentricchia, *After the New Criticism*, 164.

6 Luc Ferry and Alain Renaut, *French Philosophy of the Sixties: An Essay on Anti-humanism* (Amherst, MA: University of Massachusetts Press, 1990), 122.

7 Ibid., 126.

8 Ibid., 130.

9 Quoted in Loren Goldner, "The Nazis and Deconstruction: Jean-Pierre Faye's Demolition of Derrida," http://home.earthlink.net/~lrgoldner/faye.html.

10 Ferry and Renaut, *After the New Criticism*, 19–20.

11 Keith Windschuttle, *The Killing of History: How Literary Critics and Social Theorists Are Murdering Our Past* (San Francisco: Encounter Books, 1996), 202, my emphasis.

12 Ferry and Renaut, *After the New Criticism*, 69.

13 Jean-Francois Lyotard, *The Postmodern Condition* (Minneapolis: University of Minnesota Press, 1984), xxiv.

14 Michel Foucault, *Power/Knowledge: Selected Interviews and Other Writings, 1972–1977* (New York: Pantheon, 1980), 81.

15 Foucault, quoted in Joseph Carroll, *Evolution and Literary Theory* (Columbia, MS: University of Missouri Press, 1995), 3, my emphasis.

16 Stanley Fish, *Doing What Comes Naturally* (Durham, NC: Duke University Press, 1989), 214. Fish is by far the most lucid defender of anti-foundationalism, especially in this book's essay "Anti-Foundationalism, Theory Hope, and the Teaching of Composition," 342–55. It would not take a lot to deconstruct Fish's deconstructions, for he paints himself into a corner in terms of arriving

at any credible justification for human action. He is an archpractitioner of an "anti-metaphysical" metaphysics, and it is all floating along on an erudite egalitarian leftism, the aim of which is not an overtly radical political program (too "foundational") but to propose "remedies and changes that will improve the situation" (243). We learn that even though there can be no foundation for morality or justice, Fish thinks that literary theorists do not take themselves seriously enough as cultural critics, "*whose business it is to make and remake that culture, even as we celebrate it*" (215, my emphasis). This is the softly spoken political program, foundational to its very core, of all deconstructionist theory and practice.

17 Edward Said, quoted in ibid., 212.

18 Windschuttle, *Killing of History*, 151ff.

19 See ibid., 160ff, where various historians cite facts damning to Foucault's theses.

20 Michel Foucault, *Madness and Civilization: A History of Insanity in the Age of Reason*, trans. Richard Howard (New York: Vintage, 1973).

21 Andrew Scull, "Scholarship of Fools," *Times Literary Supplement*, 23 March 2007.

22 Carroll, *Evolution*, 3. This book, which offers a sustained attack on postmodernism and all its variations, is an unlikely place to find enlightenment on literary theory, as Carroll stakes his book's and I'm sure his own reputation on a specific syllogism: namely the idea "that knowledge is a biological phenomenon, that literature is a form of knowledge, and that literature is thus itself a biological phenomenon" (1). In some respects, of course, he is correct. But biology in the sense that Carroll intends is a material phenomenon, and we simply have no idea whatsoever how something material could produce "knowledge," or abstract concepts or ideas, which are immaterial. As far as we know, it is impossible for a material thing to render judgment upon another material thing, like a rock telling another rock to buzz off, for if it could do so, it would not be a rock. At any rate, logic and the syllogism have their uses, but as Ambrose Bierce points out in his *Devil's Dictionary* (New York: Hill and Wang, 1957), 108, the fact that it takes one man sixty seconds to dig a post hole does not mean that sixty men can dig a post hole in one second. However, all of this detracts only in minor ways from Carroll's energetic send-up of postmodernism.

23 Carroll, *Evolution*, 413.

24 Windschuttle, *Killing of History*, 135.

25 For a taste of the bitterly antinomian life of Michel Foucault, see Mark Lilla, *The Reckless Mind: Intellectuals in Politics* (New York: New York Review of Books, 2004); and for insight into Foucault's shoddy scholarship, see Windschuttle,

Killing of History, esp, ch. 5, "The Discourses of Michel Foucault: Poststructuralism and Anti-Humanism," 131–71.

26 Mark Goldblatt, "Dangerous Thinkers: 20th Century Philosophers' Love Affair with Totalitarianism," a review of Mark Lilla's *The Reckless Minds*, at www.reasononline.com, October 2002.

27 Michel Foucault, quoted in ibid., n39.

28 Michel Foucault, quoted in a humourously written trashing of Derrida and postmodernism by Steven Plaut, "The Deconstruction of Jacques Derrida," *FrontPageMagazine*, 11 October 2004.

29 Jacques Derrida, in Macksey and Donato, eds, *Structuralist Controversy*, 267, my emphasis.

30 Goldblatt, "Dangerous Thinkers," 2.

31 John Caputo, *Deconstruction in a Nutshell* (New York: Fordham University Press, 1997), 176.

32 Ibid., 171.

33 Stanton Evans, *The Theme Is Freedom: Religion, Politics, and the American Tradition* (Washington, DC: Regnery, 1994), 49, notes that while Mussolini was imprisoned in 1943, Hitler sent him an inscribed twenty-four-volume set of Nietzsche's works.

34 Peter Shaw, "The Politics of Deconstruction," in *The War against the Intellect* (Iowa City: University of Iowa Press, 1989), 59. This chapter of Shaw's text offers a general overview of the theme.

35 Terry Eagleton, quoted in ibid., 59.

36 Peter Shaw, "The Rise and Fall of Deconstruction," *Commentary*, December 1991.

CHAPTER THIRTEEN

1 There are large sections on the question of Derrida's deconstruction and his concept of justice in both books by John Caputo, cited at note 3 below.

2 For these quotations and a thorough review of the whole disturbing trend, see Mark Lilla, "The Politics of Jacques Derrida," *The New York Review of Books*, 25 June 1998, my emphasis.

3 John D. Caputo, *The Prayers and Tears of Jacques Derrida: Religion without Religion* (Bloomington: Indiana University Press, 1997); and *Deconstruction in a Nutshell: A Conversation with Jacques Derrida* (New York: Fordham University Press, 1997). These two books deal extensively with Derrida's "Turn" and with the entire underlying theology of deconstruction. Caputo writes as an insider and admirer of Derrida's lifelong deconstructionist "passion" and, in doing so, reveals its great weaknesses.

4 Caputo, *Deconstruction*, 128, my emphasis.

5 Ibid., 129.

6 Early in his life, Derrida was deeply influenced by the Jewish theological/philosophical thinker Emmanuel Levinas, and as with so many others who influenced him deeply, he submitted Levinas's core ideas to deconstructive analysis, accusing him (as he had Plato, Husserl, and Heidegger) of succumbing to the sin of "metaphysical presence" and thus betraying the truth of experience.

7 John Millbank, as paraphrased in David Bentley Hart, *The Beauty of the Infinite* (Grand Rapids, MI: Eerdmans, 2003), 36, my emphasis.

8 Ibid., 75. A sample of this feeling of incoherence may be gotten from Emmanuel Levinas, *Basic Philosophical Writings* (Bloomington: Indiana University Press, 1996).

9 Readers may be interested in Inge Birgitte Siegumfeldt, "Bloom, Derrida, and the Kabbalah," *Orbis Litterarum* 49 (1994): 307–14. It is not a very clear article but covers relevant ground.

10 Quoted in Caputo, *Prayers and Tears*, 2.

11 A difficult but useful book for those who wish to follow the theological turn of deconstruction is Hent de Vries, *Philosophy and the Turn to Religion* (Baltimore: Johns Hopkins University Press, 1999); these remarks about "protocols of vigilance" and the like are at pages 429–30.

12 Jacques Derrida, quoted in Caputo, *Prayers and Tears*, 288.

13 Ibid., xviii.

14 Ibid., xxvi.

15 Ibid., xix.

16 A lucid and seminal treatment of the different emphases and tensions of the Hebrew and Greek worldviews, as seen in Western literary tradition and exemplified by the Bible and the *Odyssey*, is Eric Auerbach, "Odysseus' Scar," in *Mimesis: The Representation of Reality in Western Literature*, trans. Willard Trask (Princeton, NJ: Princeton University Press, 1953). This essay has had iconic status among literature students and those who enjoy the history of ideas. It is the orthodox view on the differences between the Greek and Hebraic worldviews of ancient times. In his excellent study Thorleif Boman, *Hebrew Thought Compared with Greek* (New York: Norton, 1970), 23, writes that "Auerbach's comparison between the Old Testament art of narration and the Greek coincides with the viewpoint of the present work so well that it could have been included as a chapter in this book almost without alteration." Boman notes, however, that there have been serious objections to Auerbach's now-famous essay, and he gives the example of one raised by Otto Regenborg, who complains that Auerbach was comparing and contrasting a

Homeric *epic* to an Old Testament *story* that is more akin to the prehistoric *saga*, or *tale*, constructed "in a metaphysical context." In other words, he objects that Auerbach was contrasting different literary genres. Regenborg also found in Homer's work "numerous parallels to almost all the peculiarities of style ... which Auerbach had found in the Old Testament account" (23n1).

17 Caputo, *Prayers and Tears*, 334–5, my emphasis.

18 Two articles on the Internet are instructive in this respect. See "Derrida: Latest Jewish Prophet and Alephtavian Midrashist," at http://home.nycap.rr.com/porush; and also a brief summary of this argument, "Name of G-d," at www.arts.uwa.edu.au/MotsPluriels/MP1901dpName.html.

19 Susan Handelman, quoted in Caputo, *Prayers and Tears*, 232.

20 Ibid., 171.

21 Jacques Derrida, quoted in Caputo, *Deconstruction*, 131.

22 Derrida, quoted in Caputo, *Prayers and Tears*, 131, original emphasis.

23 Stephen Plaut, "The Deconstruction of Jacques Derrida," www.FrontPageMagazine.com, 11 October 2004.

24 Caputo, *Deconstruction*, 132, original emphasis.

25 Mark Goldblatt, "Dangerous Thinkers: 20th Century Philosophers' Love Affair with Totalitarianism," a review of Mark Lilla's *The Reckless Minds*, at www.reasononline.com, October 2002, my emphasis.

26 Fareed Zakaria, *The Future of Freedom: Illiberal Democracy at Home and Abroad* (New york: Norton, 2003), 17.

27 Caputo's *Deconstruction in a Nutshell* (these terms are from his ch. 6, "The Messianic: Waiting for the Future") has to be read to be believed. It is a very personal praise of Derrida and his entire deconstruction project, an effusive, lyrical, even gushing admiration of this style – it is a style more than a philosophy – and one that cannot be read or understood with any concern for logic, which must be suspended.

28 Caputo, *Deconstruction*, 174.

29 See especially the series of publications on public ignorance in modern democracies in *Critical Review* 18, nos 1–3 (Winter-Summer 2006), which begins with a discussion of the enduring validity of the first and most famous critique of public ignorance in democratic systems, namely Philip E. Converse's "The Nature of Belief Systems in Mass Publics," originally published in David E. Apter, ed., *Ideology and Its Discontents* (New York: Free Press of Glencoe, 1964), and republished in this edition of *Critical Review* at pages 1–74.

30 Caputo, *Deconstruction*, 121.

31 Hart, *Beauty of the Infinite*, 424.

32 Raymond Tallis, *Not Saussure* (London: Macmillan, 1988), 226.

CHAPTER FOURTEEN

1 Steven Pinker, *Words and Rules* (New York: Harper Collins, 2000), 239.
2 Martin Joos, *Readings in Linguistics* (Chicago: University of Chicago Press, 1957), 96, my emphasis, and cited as an example of linguistic and cultural relativism in Donald Burquest et al., *Language Universals: Research Papers of the Texas SIL* (Dallas, TX: Summer Institute of Linguistics, 1982), 2.
3 Joseph Greenberg, ed., *Universals of Language* (Cambridge, MA: MIT Press, 1963).
4 Burquest et al., *Language Universals*, 2, my emphasis.
5 Greenberg, ed., *Universals of Language*, xv, my emphasis.
6 John E. Joseph, Nigel Love, and Talbot J. Taylor, "Jakobson and Structuralism," in *Landmarks in Linguistic Thought II* (London: Routledge, 2001), 18. My section on Jakobson relies heavily on this excellent chapter.
7 See Roman Jakobson and Morris Halle, *Fundamentals of Language* (1956; reprint, Berlin: Mouton de Gruyter, 1971), 38.
8 See ibid., 28. I have simplified the description somewhat, but all his important early work on a path diverging from Saussure's purely formal thought began with Jakobson and Halle's seminal text *Fundamentals of Language*.
9 Joseph, Love, and Taylor, "Jakobson and Structuralism," 27.
10 Jakobson and Halle, *Fundamentals of Language*.
11 See Joseph H. Greenberg, Charles A. Ferguson, and Edith A. Moravcsik, *Universals of Human Language*, vol. 2, *Phonology* (Stanford: Stanford University Press, 1978).
12 Steven Pinker, *The Language Instinct: How the Mind Creates Language* (New York: Harper Collins, 1994), 158.
13 This and the prior two universal statements are from Charles Hockett, "Phonological Universals," sec. 5 of "The Problem of Universals in Language," in Greenberg, ed., *Universals of Language*, 24ff.
14 Neil Smith, *Chomsky: Ideas and Ideals* (Cambridge, UK: Cambridge University Press, 1999), 78.
15 Pinker, *Language Instinct*, 267.
16 Ibid., 269.
17 Ibid., 269–70.
18 Ibid., 275.
19 See these and other points in Jennifer Ganger and Karen Stromswold, "Innateness, Evolution, and Genetics of Language," in *Human Biology*, April 1998.
20 The comments here are drawn from William Croft, *Typology and Universals* (1990; reprint, Cambridge, UK: Cambridge University Press, 2003), 4.

21 Smith, *Chomsky*, 101. This is by far the clearest explanation of the Chomskyan revolution in language theory.

22 Joseph, Love, and Taylor, *Landmarks*, 132–7.

23 Croft, *Typology and Universals*, 4.

24 See http://ling.uni-konstanz.de:591/Universals/Introduction.html.

25 Bertrand Russell, *The Problems of Philosophy* (Oxford: Oxford University Press, 1959), 71–2, original emphasis.

26 Ibid., 72.

27 My well-worn copy is in my hand. I remember purchasing it in 1965 when awareness of the linguistic revolution it announced was still tenuous. Noam Chomsky, *Syntactic Structures* (1957; reprint, The Hague: Mouton, 1965), was actually a distillation of a much longer prior book, *Logical Structures of Linguistic Theory* (New York: Plenum Press, 1955, 1975), which was the foundation for almost all of Chomsky's subsequent work and which remained unpublished for twenty years.

28 Pinker, *Language Instinct*, ch. 8, "The Tower of Babel."

29 Adriana Belletti and Luigi Rizzi, "Editors' Introduction: Some Concepts and Issues in Linguistic Theory," in Noam Chomsky, *On Nature and Language* (Cambridge, UK: Cambridge University Press, 2002), 1.

30 Chomsky, *Syntactic Structures*, 13.

31 Ibid., 17.

32 Smith, *Chomsky*, 41.

33 Geoffrey Sampson, *The Language Instinct Debate* (London: Continuum, 2005), 14.

34 Ibid., 38.

35 Smith, *Chomsky*, 27.

36 Ibid., 58, my emphasis.

37 Noam Chomsky, quoted in ibid., 59.

38 Ibid., ch. 2, summarizes these developments, with lots of clear examples.

39 Ibid., 83.

40 Ibid., 88ff. This segment is drawn straight from Smith.

CHAPTER FIFTEEN

1 An interesting instance by an energetic scholar is Joseph Carroll, *Evolution and Literary Theory* (Columbia, MS: University of Missouri Press, 1995). Carroll covers a great deal of ground and gives many insights from his high ground of evolution theory. He also provides a caustic and well-deserved critique of most of the key postmodernist theorists, such as Derrida and Foucault, and as one observer put it, "reduces them to a pile of shreds" (this

latter comment is from a long, intense, and excellent article by Harold
Fromm, "The New Darwinism in the Humanities," *Hudson Review,*
www.hudsonreview.com/frommSpSuo3.html.

 Leaving aside that in the opinion of many scientists the basic theory of evolution is currently in crisis, we are left at the end of Carroll's prodigious effort with no better basis for distinguishing a good novel from a poor one
because no science, no matter how thorough, can provide that.

2 Aristotle, "The Poetics," in Charles Kaplan, ed., *Criticism: The Major Statements* (New York: St Martin's Press, 1975), 30.

3 For the Literary Universals Project, see www.litup.unipa.it/docs/index.htm.

4 Patrick Colm Hogan, "Literary Universals," in *Poetics Today* 18, no. 2 (Summer 1997): 223–49.

5 Erich Neumann, *The Origins and History of Consciousness* (Princeton, NJ:
Princeton University Press, 1949), xvi.

6 Ibid., 16.

7 Hans Beidermann, *Dictionary of Symbolism: Cultural Icons and the Meanings
behind Them,* trans. James Hulbert (New York: Facts on File, 1992), vii.

8 James G. Frazer, *The Golden Bough* (London: Macmillan, 1890).

9 Joseph Campbell, *The Hero with a Thousand Faces* (Princeton, NJ: Princeton
University Press, 1968).

10 Misia Landau, *Narratives of Human Evolution,* quoted in Jonathan Wells, *Icons
of Evolution* (Washington, DC: Regnery, 2000), 222.

11 Mircea Eliade, *The Myth of the Eternal Return,* trans. W.R. Trask (Princeton,
NJ: Princeton University Press, 1954); Mircea Eliade, *Myth and Reality,* trans.
W.R. Trask (New York: Harper and Row, 1963); Carl Jung, *Man and His Sym-
bols* (New York: Dell, 1964).

APPENDIX

1 Brown's list of universals, compiled in 1989, consists primarily of manifest, or "surface," universals and omits a great many innate universals that
may be revealed by psychological experiments but that have not been verified by cross-cultural research. The list also omits *near universals* and *conditional universals,* as well as features of anatomy and physiology. For
definitions, qualifications, and references for most of the items, readers
are encouraged to see his book *Human Universals* (New York: McGraw-
Hill, 1991). Basic conceptual and definitional issues are presented
more briefly in entries under "Human Universals" in *The Encyclopedia of
Cultural Anthropology* (1996) and also in the MIT *Encyclopedia of Cognitive
Sciences* (1999).

378 Notes to pages 314–24

2 The theory developed by West and his colleagues looks at such things as the structural and functional properties of vertebrate cardiovascular and respiratory systems, plant vascular systems, insect tracheal tubes, and other distribution networks. In particular, the theory seeks to explain the origins and ubiquity of a set of mathematical laws known as the quarter-power scaling laws as they apply to plants and animals.

3 Stephen Freeland, "Evaluating Biological Constants and Standards at the Root of Life," a paper presented at the conference *Fitness of the Cosmos for Life: Biochemistry and Fine Tuning*, Harvard University, Cambridge, MA, 11–12 October 2003, 3.

4 From Patrick Nolan and Gerhard Lenski, *Human Societies* (New York: McGraw Hill, 1999), 12.

5 E.O. Wilson, *On Human Nature* (Cambridge, MA: Harvard University Press, 1978).

6 John Alcock, *The Triumph of Sociobiology* (New York: Oxford University Press, 2001), 76.

7 John Morgan Allman, *Evolving Brains* (New York: Scientific American Library, 2000), 152.

8 Wilson, *On Human Nature*, 67.

9 Ibid., 70.

10 Ibid., 99, 119.

11 The list is adapted from David Buss, *Evolutionary Psychology: The New Science of the Mind* (New York: Pearson Education, 2004), chs 3–9.

12 Doreen Kimura, *Sex and Cognition* (Cambridge, MA: MIT Press, 2000), 184.

13 See Wilson, *On Human Nature*, 130–2; and Doreen Kimura, "How Males and Females Become Different," ch. 4 in *Sex and Cognition*, 17–29.

14 For a summary of the differences, see Anne Moir and David Jessel, *Brain Sex: The Real Difference between Men and Women* (London: Mandarin, 1991), ch. 1.

15 Kimura, *Sex and Cognition*, 177.

16 See Robert L. Nadeau, *S/He Brain* (Westport, CT: Praeger, 1996), 58.

17 See Eleanor Maccoby and Carol Jacklin, "Power Relationships," ch. 7 in *The Psychology of Sex Differences* (Stanford, CA: Stanford University Press, 1974), 227–74.

18 Ibid.

19 See Nadeau, *S/He Brain*, 50.

20 See ibid., 51.

21 See ibid., 52.

22 See James Q. Wilson and Richard Herrnstein, "Gender," ch. 4 in *Crime and Human Nature* (New York: Simon and Schuster, 1985), 104–25. See also Glenn Wilson, "Aggression and Crime," ch. 7 in *The Great Sex Divide: A Study of Male-Female Differences* (Washington: Scott-Townsend, 1992) 115–31.

23　See Wilson and Herrnstein, *Crime and Human Nature*, 121; and Wilson, *Great Sex Divide*, 123.

24　See Kimura, *Sex and Cognition*, 62.

25　See Wilson, *Great Sex Divide*, 100.

26　Kimura, *Sex and Cognition*, 122.

27　See Nadeau, *S/He Brain*, 56.

28　Kimura, *Sex and Cognition*, 31.

29　See ibid., 26–7.

30　Wilson, *Great Sex Divide*, 54.

31　Kimura, *Sex and Cognition*, 81–9.

32　Wilson, *Great Sex Divide*, 100.

33　Kimura, *Sex and Cognition*, 95.

34　Ibid., 107.

35　Wilson, *Great Sex Divide*, 35.

36　Kimura, *Sex and Cognition*, 127–8.

37　See Wilson, *Great Sex Divide*, 102.

38　See ibid., 116.

39　This list of ethical/moral universals, by no means exhaustive, is found in Richard H. Beis, "Some Contributions of Anthropology to Ethics," *The Thomist* 27, no. 2 (April 1964): 174–223. Beis's text is one of the clearest analyses of the conflicts and contradictions arising from the theory of moral and cultural relativism, and he draws these universals from a wide range of influential anthropologists of the time.

40　Marc Hauser, *Moral Minds: How Nature Designed Our Universal Sense of Right and Wrong* (New York: Harper Collins, 2006).

41　"The Bookshelf Talks With Marc Hauser," an interview of Marc Hauser by the managing editor of *American Scientist Online* (July 2006), www.American-scientist.org/template/InterviewTypeDetail/assetid/52880.

42　From Jay Budziszewski, *Written on the Heart: The Case for Natural Law* (Downers Grove, IL: InterVarsity Press, 1997), 120.

43　From C.S. Lewis, "Appendix: Illustrations of the Tao," in *The Abolition of Man* (Glasgow: Collins, 1978), 49–59.

44　Drawn and summarized from Joseph H. Greenberg, "Some Universals of Grammar with Particular Reference to the Order of Meaningful Elements," in Joseph H. Greenberg, ed., *Universals of Language* (London: MIT Press, 1963), 110–13.

45　This and the prior two universal statements are just two of a number described by Charles Hockett, sec. 5, "Phonological Universals," in "The Problem of Universals in Language," in Greenberg, ed., *Universals of Language*, 1–28. With respect to phonological changes, see especially 24–8.

Index

107–9; scientific findings re human universals, 57, 118–19; vs "nurture" as moulder of humanity, 48–9, 57–9, 60. *See also* evolutionary psychology; human universals; language universals; sociobiology

human (positive) law: good law manifestation of natural law, 177–8, 182, 183–4, 193; natural law as recourse for unjust human laws, 178–9, 193; relativism of, 175–7; validity of totalitarian laws, 177, 179; vs natural law, 174–7, 200

Human Relations Area File (HRAF), 63

human universals: behaviour attributed to natural selection, 119, 137–41, 318–19; biochemical and physiological universals/constants, 134–7, 315–16; biological and physiological universals distinctive to humans, 136–7, 316–18; biological constants of organic life, 132–3, 313–14; biological features (shared with other mammals and primates), 133–4, 314–15; Chomsky on linguistic universals, 59–60; classical virtues, 190, 193; definition, 62; denial by anthropologists, 44, 56–7, 65; dualism of mind and body, 105–7, 136, 316; "Everyman," 64; Gairdner's Law of social bonding, 141; importance of recognizing, 67–8; knowledge of natural law, 184, 190, 192, 193; literature as expression of universals, 300–2; male-female brain-based differences, 149–51, 160–2, 322–6; male-female sexual reproduction differences, 149–50, 152–7, 319; meaning of universals for

human life, 68; moral sense, 208–9; necessary for scientific study of humankind, 55; "nurture" vs "nature" adherents, 57–9, 60; Platonists' beliefs, 34–5; proper object of anthropology, 66; psychological universals, 145–6, 146–51, 320–1; questioning the purpose of existence, 106; reasoning and learning circuits, 144–5; rebellion against excessive authority, 110; refutation of cultural relativism, 66; scientific findings re human universals, 57, 118–19; sociobiological universals, 138–41; "Universal People," 64–5; universal practice vs universal natural law, 194–6; vs Boas's relativism, 56–7. *See also* evolutionary psychology; human nature as "hardwired"; sociobiology

Human Universals (Brown), 61–2, 309–10

Hume, David, 13–14, 195

Hussein, Saddam, 179

Huxley, Aldous, 212–14

idealism, 210–11

Imperial Animal, The (Tiger and Fox), 60, 118

indeterminacy (in postmodernism), 259

In Search of Human Nature (Degler), 121

international law principles, 200–2, 328

Iraq and cultural relativism, 54

Islam and relativism, 38, 43

Jacklin, Carol, 161

Jakobson, Roman, 282–3

explanations for, 205–11; universal aspects of human morality, 197–200, 326–7; of world's religions, 212–16

morphemes (units of meaning), 225–6

Morris, Desmond, 118

motion: Aristotle's view of motion, 73–4; theory of relativity, 17–18, 20, 70, 79, 83–6

Murdock, George, 63

Mussolini, Benito, 41, 263

Myth and Reality (Eliade), 307

Myth of the Eternal Return, The (Eliade), 307

myths, xv–xvi, 300, 305–7, 335n1

Naked Ape, The (Morris), 118

Napoleon, 239

National Socialism, 240–1, 245

natural law: abridgement, 192–3; assumptions, 164; challenge to relativism, 181–2; classical virtues, 190, 193; in common law tradition of West, 173–4; consequences for denying nature, 190–1; core principles and truths, 176, 183, 184–92; death of Cicero, 163–4; definitions, 164, 183, 185; deposed by secular rights-talk, 165–6; evolution into rights-talk and modern natural law, 165–70, 170(t)–173(t); form of moral absolutism, 18; God as source of, 164, 183, 204; good human law a manifestation of natural law, 177–8, 182, 193; history of, 164; human conscience as basis, 184, 204; in human nature, 184, 190, 192, 193; indisputable goods, 184, 204;

international law principles, 200–2, 328; Judeo-Christian values, 176; law of just war, 184, 203–4, 329; law of non-contradiction, 188, 192; modern natural law, 167–8, 169–70, 170(t)–173(t); moral foundation, 188–9, 193; moral framework necessary, 167–9, 170, 175; moral universals, 197–200, 211–12; at Nuremberg Trials, 18, 179, 182, 201, 363n4; recourse against unjust human laws, 178–9, 193; relativist human law positions, 174–7; return (post-1970) to natural law, 178–82; right reason as basis, 164, 165, 180–1, 184, 192, 204; transcendence of, 180–1, 182, 183, 191, 193, 201–2; universal practice vs universal natural law, 194–6; against US racial segregation laws, 179. *See also* moral law or systems

Natural Law and Natural Right (Finnis), 168

natural scientists, 120

nature: different views of reality, 69; discovery of earthly constants, 74–5; explanations for the working of the world, 70–3; hierarchy of structure, 90–1; inherent one-way design, 73; Newton's scientific achievements, 75–9. *See also* constants of nature; human biology; physics

"nature vs nurture." *See* human mind as "blank slate"; human nature as "hardwired"

Nazism: combination of Superman and Darwinism, 114; deconstructionism and, 253; experiments